Q 12⁵⁰

ESSAYS ON HISPANIC
LITERATURE IN HONOR
OF EDMUND L. KING

ESSAYS ON HISPANIC LITERATURE IN HONOR OF EDMUND L. KING

Edited by Sylvia Molloy and Luis Fernández Cifuentes

TAMESIS BOOKS LIMITED
LONDON

Colección Támesis
SERIE A - MONOGRAFIAS, XCVIII

Depósito legal: M. 20608-1983

Printed in Spain by Talleres Gráficos de SELECCIONES GRÁFICAS
Carretera de Irún, km. 11,500 - Madrid-34

for
TAMESIS BOOKS LIMITED
LONDON

TABLE OF CONTENTS

TABLE OF CONTENTS

EDMUND L. KING

Edmund Ludwig King was born in St. Louis, Missouri, on January 10, 1914. He began the study of Spanish in school in Austin, Texas, as he says, «entirely by accident»:

> I was supposed to study, rather, either French or German — or, had it been possible, Russian —, languages spoken in my family, who knew nothing of Spanish. But neither French nor German could be fitted into my schedule if I was to have the math my parents thought I should have, so I took Spanish. Little by little, in school and college, I developed a serious interest in it, but an interest that had no focus, no direction, it came from a misty, Romantic, sentimental attachment to Mexico. Sometime during my college years at the University of Texas in Austin, I became more or less self-supporting (through tutoring, choir-singing, and the like), and, when college came to an end with no real jobs in sight, I decided to go on living at home free-of-charge and studying in the graduate school of the University on the other side of town.

By 1936, Edmund King had completed all the graduate courses in Peninsular Spanish literature at the University of Texas and had begun his teaching career, as an instructor, at Mississippi State College, where, after «the initial shock of a town and school that made Austin seem to me like Athens,» he stayed for five years. It was there that he first started work on his dissertation which was interrupted by the war in 1941. He was drafted into the Army and served with Military Intelligence till 1945, when he returned to Austin and resumed teaching, this time as an instructor in the English Department. «Then, in the spring of 1946, with no warning, came an invitation from Américo Castro through a friend of his in Austin to come to Princeton as an instructor of Spanish.» He also resumed work for the PhD degree and defended his dissertation at the University of Texas in Austin in 1949. It was subsequently published as a book: *Gustavo Adolfo Bécquer: From Painter to Poet. Together with a Concordance of the Rimas* (Mexico: Porrúa, 1953). On January 29, 1951, he married Willard Fahrenkamp, who herself became a distinguished hispanist.

1

The encounter with Américo Castro was to prove decisive not only in Edmund King's career but in his understanding of *hispanidad:*

> It was only through the deepening association — companionship would be a better word if not too presumptuous — with Professor Castro that I began to have a strong sense of what I was doing, or at least supposed to be doing, as a student and teacher of the Spanish language and of Spanish literature. And yet there is no specific vein of influence that I could point to; in fact, in matters of literary taste our inclinations have often diverged. The influence is more general and all-pervasive. From Castro I have gotten an idea of what Hispanic life and culture are all about, and more through his example and doctrine than anyone else's, I early came to realize the enormous complexity of literary problems and the need for bringing as much knowledge and hard thinking to bear on them as one can possibly manage.

As a result of that relationship, Edmund King was to translate two of Castro's books — *The Structure of Spanish History* (Princeton: Princeton University Press, 1954) and *An Idea of History,* in collaboration with Stephen Gilman (Columbus: Ohio State University Press, 1976) — and three of his major articles: «The Presence of the Sultan Saladin in the Romance Literatures,» *Diogenes* 8 (1954); «Empire: The Golden Years,» *Atlantic,* January 1961; «The Spanish People,» *The Texas Quarterly (Image of Spain* issue), Spring 1961. He also paid tribute to his friend with «Américo Castro and the Theory and Practice of History,» a contribution to the *Collected Studies in Honour of Américo Castro's Eightieth Year* (Oxford, 1965).

Also at Princeton, Edmund King discovered another figure to whom he would become greatly attached, both on an intellectual and on a personal level:

> Gabriel Miró was a writer I had never read, had quite literally never heard of, until I stumbled onto two of his stories in an anthology being used as a textbook in an intermediate Spanish class at Princeton in 1948. There he was, surrounded by all the well-known figures of the Generation of '98, and it struck me at once that he was the best of the lot. I resolved to study him. A Bicentennial Preceptorship allowed me to spend the year 1953-54 in Spain examining the material in the Miró family archives, collecting Miró's correspondence from his friends, interviewing those still living who had known him, and otherwise immersing myself in the *matière de Miró.*

The effects of that passionate immersion have been most beneficial to readers of Gabriel Miró. Edmund King has published two outstanding annotated editions of Miró — *El humo dormido* (New York: Dell, 1967) and *Sigüenza y el Mirador Azul y Prosas de «El Ibero»* (Madrid: Ediciones de La Torre, 1982) — both with comprehensive and thoughtful introductions. He has also published many influential articles that have contributed to the rediscovery of Gabriel Miró: «Páginas inéditas de Gabriel Miró», *Clavileño*, March-April, 1954; «Gabriel Miró y "el mundo según es"», *Papeles de Son Armadans*, LXII, May 1961; «Gabriel Miró y los "Ejercicios Espirituales"», *Boletín Informativo del Seminario de Derecho Político*, March 1962; «Gabriel Miró Introduced to the French,» *Hispanic Review*, 29 (1961); «Gabriel Miró: su pasado familiar», *Papeles de Son Armadans*, October 1962; «Miró, Gabriel,» *Encyclopaedia Britannica*, 1967; «Azorín y Miró: Historia de una amistad», *Boletín de la Asociación Europea de Profesores de Español*, October 1973; «Life and Death, Space and Time: "El sepulturero",» in *Critical Essays on Gabriel Miró*, Lincoln (Neb.): Society of Spanish and Spanish-American Studies, 1979.

Edmund King's contributions in other areas of Peninsular Spanish literature are no less significant. His seminal article «What is Spanish Romanticism?» published in *Studies in Romanticism*, 2 (1962), as well as his activity as a member of the editorial board of that publication, have established him as an authority on that particular period. Edmund King is also a stimulating critic of modern Spanish poetry, as his articles and translations have repeatedly shown. He has written on «Blas de Otero: The Past and the Present of "The Eternal",» *Spanish Writers of 1936: Crisis and Commitment in the Poetry of the Thirties and Forties* (London: Tamesis Books, 1973); «Jorge Guillén: An Appreciation,» *The New Republic*, 9 April 1977; «Lorca, Guillén, Salinas, and Aleixandre,» *The Hudson Review*, 31 (1978).

Edmund King has been on the faculty of Princeton University since September 1946, was chairman of the Department of Romance Languages and Literatures from 1966 till 1972, and, for the past six years, he has occupied the Walter S. Carpenter Jr. Chair as Professor of the Language, Literature, and Civilization of Spain. He claims that his time has been spent «studying, teaching, occasionally publishing a piece of work, and climbing the academic ladder at a rather deliberate pace, contrary to the hopes and wishes of my mentors, who would have me make it all in one great dash.» Contrary to his opinion, Edmund King's activities have been far from lackadaisical. For years, he has been a lively member of the International Institute in Spain, and since 1975 he has been president of the Institute's corporation. «In a modest way, the Instituto has been able discreetly to maintain an atmosphere of cultural freedom in those periods when official Spain has considered cultural freedom a vice to be stamped out.» He has held appointments as visiting professor at Bryn Mawr College and at the Centro de Estudios Hispánicos in Madrid, and he has given many public lectures. He has also served as a member of various advisory committees to Spanish Departments and doctoral programs in Spanish throughout the country.

Through his research, writing and scholarship, Edmund King as contributed a body of work that enriches the field of Hispanic studies. Equally important, however, is his dedication to teaching and the great warmth he has brought to his students. He has served as mentor — and friend — to many at Princeton for thirty six years. It is this rare combination — fine teacher, fine scholar — that best describes him.

Edmund King has retired from teaching but not from the world of himself has written on the subject of his retirement and we believe he scholarship. This volume is an attempt to mark that passage and to show our friendship and our gratitude to him. Nor has Edmund King retired from wit, for which he continues to be exceptionally gifted. He should have the last word:

> He's published little; still, he hasn't perished,
> And now he's asked, while looking straight at dotage,
> To reprint pages here and there, so cherished
> He can only feel he's reached at last his quotage.

PROFILE OF A TEACHER

by

JAMES E. MARANISS

Most people who really know Gabriel Miró know him through Edmund King. At an academic dinner in 1979, I heard Rodolfo Cardona say that yes, it was bad that Miró's centenary was going by uncelebrated, and worse, he had lent irretrievably his copy of Edmund's edition of *El humo dormido*. There was no way of getting another. I remembered a walk I had taken with Edmund between Pyne Hall and the library ten years before. He was telling me about some earlier graduate students, who in answering an exam question about «El sepulturero» had all failed to mention the story's broken-up time sequence, even though he had told them about it ahead of time. I was about to speak some banality about how it was important that he not think his teaching in vain, but instead I blurted: «Gabriel el bien nombrado...» It was a line of Manuel Machado's, from a poem Edmund had reprinted without unnecessary gloss in the edition that R. Cardona had loved and lost.

«I was thinking that exactly,» Edmund said. Then I thought I understood about teaching: it was telepathy. Here was Manuel Machado, a poet you weren't supposed to like and who wasn't read. Edmund can draw him or his brother, or any other Spanish writer, aptly, dogmatically, modestly, in a few phrases or an anecdote. There are times, though, when transmission alone is called for, and at this one, as in his Miró edition, Edmund put Manuel to use. Say what you want about how his brother is better. Certainly Edmund would agree. Once, after I had written something uninteresting about «A José María Palacio» in my generals, Edmund told me what I should have known, that its subject was Leonor's grave. Then he told me what he liked about the poem: its reticence, the way it never mentions what it's about.

I had a bad start at Princeton. I was assigned to be a TA in Edmund's course and my stomach told me I couldn't do it. I went to his office at class time and told him his friends had misled him. I couldn't teach; I couldn't even sleep or eat. He took out a couple of milk of magnesia tablets from a box he carried in his pocket, gave them to me, and told me to chew on them. He said that sometime when I wasn't in such a hurry he'd tell me about his first day in Princeton when he met Américo Castro. He said he had an ulcer. I stayed in his thrall long enough to be led down the hall to the classroom. He opened the door, nudged me in, and disappeared. Later I asked him about his ulcer; he was in-

5

JAMES E. MARANISS

formative. He talked it down, as I was later to hear him speak of his
other *achaques* — his gout, his bad joint, his bad retina, the motes that
float in his eye. These can be themes of some of the verses Edmund
writes and sticks into letters to his friends. Letters from Edmund are
the only ones I save for posterity. Sometimes, when they treat a literary
subject, I give up imitation and just read them aloud to my students.
Then I stand in the reflection of his prose style, the image of his thought.

Américo Castro in Edmund's version is better. The great man must
have known this, else why stay dependent on Edmund the editor, Edmund
the translator and explicator. Don Américo wasn't the only one. A lot
of the rest of us have done it too.

To me, the reason to try to become a hispanist in America in the
1960's was Spain's gift to us of her Republican exiles. I have studied or
taught with them and their relatives for most of my adult life, but always
at a little distance. Edmund brought them to me over that distance. He
knows, or knew, most of them. They all seemed to love him. I'm sure
it's hard to be Enrique Tierno-Galván — mayor, scholar, teacher, party
leader. When Tierno taught at Princeton I admired him wholly but I
never envied his devotion to work. It has paid off, though. Now he can
lift a phone at the *alcaldía* in Madrid and say: «Send out a limo to pick
up my friend Edmund King. Take him wherever he wants to go.»

Amherst College.

6

UNTITLED MANUSCRIPT FRAGMENT

by

GABRIEL MIRO

(Published with the kind permission of D.ª Olympia Luengo Miró
and Dr. Emilio Luengo Miró.)

No sabiendo qué decirle a un niño, le preguntamos: ¿Qué quisieras tú ser? —A mí también me lo preguntaban. Pero nunca supe responder. Yo nunca quise ser concretamente nada. Ni escritor. Ni escritor cuando ya escribía. De modo que es vieja mi desgana de todo profesionalismo. Me ha faltado siempre afición y aptitud para el ejercicio externo, social, itinerarista de mi arte. Casi equivale a decir que no tengo entusiasmo. Es verdad; no lo tengo. No me entusiasma el oficio, el oficio de nada. Es un daño que me pesa. Soy andariego, pero no excursionista; cuando camino, sin querer, voy por los bordes, parándome y mirando. Y si contemplo, si escucho las cosas recordando que soy escritor y que ha de valerme lo que veo o lo que me dicen, es más difícil y escaso el provecho que atendí con goce desinteresado, con curiosidad «únicamente» humana. Quizá por eso no anoto ni apunto. Si alguna vez quise enmendarme, las notas me acercaban en frío las realidades y las ideas concretas, limitándome hasta el valor de la palabra, sintiendo al dictado; y yo veo mejor a distancia de tiempo. ¿Podrá parecer, entonces, que me fío de la improvisación y de la facilidad? Me sonrojan hasta las ajenas. No improvisé nunca. iSempre me parece que es la primera vez que escribo. Sin ese interior balbuceo no sentiría la predisposición para el trabajo. No tengo, lo repito, oficio. Tampoco he cultivado la autobiografía. Era vivir en anecdotario más o menos apócrifo a costa de mí mismo. Las anécdotas auténticas son las que me han probado que yo había de ser irremediablemente lo que soy, que había de ir conformándome según he quedado. ¿Viví, gocé como yo me había prometido en el principio de mi juventud literaria? En seguida, me pregunto: Pero ¿si hubiese vivido y gozado como yo me veía en los primeros horizontes, sería actualmente yo según yo? No me complazco en la imagen de mi actualidad, pero ya es la hora de ser y de afirmarme en lo que sea; y ya recogido en mí mismo, esperar lo inesperado y seguir caminando.

Amo mi arte con el amor de mí mismo. Me he creado, me voy creando siempre como artista, con esfuerzo, acechándome, con ansiedad y con ocios. No tengo antecedentes; no soy de linaje de escritor; no soy heredero. Dirán que mejor. Pero yo soy un tradicionalista desde chico. Recuerdo muebles, tacto de ropas, sabores y olores no por ellos y por mi infancia, sino porque ya entonces me quedaba pensando que eran los mismo[s] de sangre mía. Casi todos los días me imagino una heredad perdida, que yo nunca he visto, porque era de mi abuelo, del que llevo su nombre, y me dicen que en unos viejos manises estaba nuestro nombre y el santo. Allí querría yo escribir. Amo el paisaje de mi comarca porque lo han visto unos niños que fueron abuelos de mis abuelos. Todo el pasado familiar quedó y se deshizo en mi tierra. No creo que se trate de una fácil sentimentalidad, sino de una capacidad de recuerdos, de botánica, de piedras, de idioma, y de una incapacidad para la adquisición; incapaz de adquirir bienes, paisaje, idioma. El arte mismo es para mí un estado de felicidad por el ensanchamiento, por la multiplicación de mi vida, de llegar en mi tierra a posesiones espirituales.

1

No sabiendo

~~Cuando no sabíamos~~ qué decirle a un niño, le preguntamos: ¿Qué quisieras tú ser? — A mí también me lo preguntaban; ~~xxxxxxxxxxxxxxxxxxxxxxxxxxx~~ Pero ~~yo~~ nunca supe responder. ~~xxxxxxx~~ Yo nunca quise ser concretamente nada. Ni escritor. Ni escritor cuando ya escribía. De modo que ~~ya~~ es vieja mi desgana ~~por implícito por~~ todo profesionalismo. Me ha faltado siempre afición y aptitud ~~xxxx~~ el ejercicio externo, social, itinerarista de mi arte. ~~esto~~ casi equivale a decir que no tengo entusiasmo. Es verdad; no lo tengo. No me entusiasma el oficio, el oficio de nada. Soy andariego, pero no excursionista; cuando camino, sin querer, voy por los bordes, parándome y mirando. Y si contemplo, si escucho las cosas recordando que soy escritor y que ~~xxxx~~ ha de valerme ~~y aprovecharme~~ lo que veo ó lo que me dicen, es más difícil y escaso el provecho que si atendí con goce desinteresado, con curiosidad "únicamente" humana. Quizá por eso ~~nunca~~ anoto ni apunto. ~~nada~~ Si alguna vez quise enmendarme, ~~y xxx alguna~~ las notas me acercaban en frío las realidades ~~concretas~~ y las ideas concretos, limitándome hasta el calor de la palabra, sintiendo al dictado; ~~a no dictado xxxxx~~ y ~~Yo~~ ¿Podrá verlo mejor ~~los xxx~~ a distancias de tiempo, pero parecer entonces que me fío de la improvisación y de la facilidad? ~~sabría xxx posición xxx improvisar nada~~ Me surgían hasta las ajenas, no improvisé nunca.

9

en la orden y la esperanza a lo inesperado. La facilidad ~~del arte hacia la agitas, me arroja siempre~~
Siempre me parece que es la primera vez ~~que~~
~~he escrito, sin~~ balbuceo no sentiría la predisposición para el trabajo. No tengo, lo repito, oficio.
Tampoco he cultivado la biografía. Era vivir en
mi mismo ~~y a los otros~~, sin beneficio para la práctica ~~de mi arte que no practico.~~ Las anécdotas
auténticas que yo he recogido de mi vida en mi vida son las que
me han probado que yo había de ser irremediablemente lo que soy, que había de conformar
~~me~~ dónde según me cuadaba. ¿Viví, gocé como yo me
había prometido en el principio de mi juventud
literaria? En seguida, me pregunto: Pero si
hubiera vivido y gozado como yo me veía en los
primeros horizontes, sería actualmente yo según
yo? No me conozco en la imagen de mi mismo, pero ya es la hora de ver y de afirmarme
en lo que soy ya recogido en mi mismo, espero
lo inesperado y de seguir caminando siempre
Amo mi arte con el amor de mi mismo. Me he creado,
me voy creando siempre como artista, con esfuerzo, ace-
lerándome, con ansiedad y con ocios. No tengo antecedentes; no soy de linaje de escritor; no
soy heredero. Dirán que mejor. Pero yo soy un tradicionalista de mí mismo. Recuerdo muebles, tacto de ropas, sabores y olores no por ellos en mi infancia sino
porque ya entonces me quedaba pensando que eran los
mismo de sangre mía. Casi todos los días me imagino

una heredad perdida, que yo nunca he visto, porque
~~la~~ ~~como~~ hacienda era de mi abuelo ~~que~~
~~tba~~ que llevo su nombre, y me dicen que ~~es~~ más viejo
~~había~~ estaba ~~manses~~ estaba nuestro nombre
y el santo. Allí quería yo recibir. Amo el paisaje
de mi comarca aunque lo han visto unas niñas que
~~se~~ fueron abuelos de mis abuelos. Todo el pasado familiar vivió ~~entre~~ y el deseo en mi tierra. No creo
que se trate de una fácil sentimentalidad; sino de
una capacidad de recuerdos, de botánica, de piedras, de
idioma, y de una incapacidad para la adquisición;
incapaz de adquirir bienes, paisaje, idioma. El arte
mismo es para mí un estado de felicidad por el ensanchamiento, por la multiplicación de mi vida, de
llegar en mi tierra a posesiones espirituales.

THE BALLAD OF *CELINOS* AT UÑA DE QUINTANA
(IN THE FOOTSTEPS OF AMERICO CASTRO)

by

SAMUEL G. ARMISTEAD

Celinos is one relatively few modern peninsular *romances* which derive directly from an epic source.[1] Its narrative is based upon an early episode of *Beuve de Hantone,* a twelfth-century *chanson de geste* which achieved vast diffusion in numerous European languages during the late Middle-Ages.[2] No Spanish text of the epic has survived, but the ballad of *Celinos,* known in a single sixteenth-century allusion and in modern version from widely separated lateral areas of the Hispanic world (Trás-os-Montes, Zamora, Castilla la Vieja, Ibiza, and various Eastern Sephardic communities), confirms that the narrative must have circulated as a *cantar de gesta.* The modern ballad is so rare and known versions are so scattered in their geographic distribution that any new text constitutes a notable discovery in its own right and is almost certain to document important and previously unrecorded details. The ballad of *Celinos* tells a barbarous tale of infidelity, treachery, and bloody vengeance. But for all its barbarism, or perhaps in part precisely because of it, it is a very effective poem. It embodies a compact, balladic honor drama, whose unvarnished violence and sanguinary character recall the somber, primitive ambience of such epics as *Los infantes de Lara* or *La muerte del infant don García.*[3]

In 1912, a youthful Américo Castro, already a distinguished philologist, carried out extensive field work on the Leonese dialect of the Province of Zamora. As in most of the linguistic *encuestas* inspired by Ramón

---

[1] Recent neo-individualist criticism has tended to minimize the relationship of the *Romancero* to its epic antecedents. See my article, «Epic and Ballad: A Traditionalist Perspective» (to appear in *Olifant*). For now, compare *La Corónica,* 10:2 (Spring 1982), 250-253.

[2] The relationship was pointed out by R. MENÉNDEZ PIDAL in *Romancero hispánico,* 2 vols. (Madrid: Espasa-Calpe, 1953), I, 261. On the different versions of *Beuve,* see S. G. ARMISTEAD and J. H. SILVERMAN: *Tres calas en el romancero sefardí* (Madrid: Castalia, 1979), pp. 70-71. We have studied various aspects of the ballad in a number of publications: «El romance de *Celinos y la adúltera* entre los sefardíes de Oriente», *ALM,* 2 (1962), 5-14; *The Judeo-Spanish Ballad Chapbooks of Y. A. Yoná* (Berkeley-LosAngeles: University of California Press, 1971), pp. 227-240; «El romance de *Celinos*: Un testimonio del siglo XVI», *NRFH,* 25 (1976), 86-94; *Tres calas,* pp. 64-77; and now, *En torno al romancero sefardí: Hispanismo y balcanismo de la tradición judeo-española* (Madrid: C.S.M.P., 1982), pp. 35-42.

[3] For another such balladic narrative, *La calumnia de la reina* (among others that might be cited), see S. G. ARMISTEAD and. J. H. SILVERMAN: *Romances judeo-españoles de Tánger* (Madrid: C.S.M.P., 1977), pp. 107-109.

13

Menéndez Pidal, it was more or less taken from granted that dialectology and ballad collecting were to go hand in hand. From graduate classes at Princeton, many years ago, I remember Don Américo's moving evocation of certain episodes of his Zamoran expedition: Travel was on horseback. Some informants, who had lived their entire lives in rural isolation, were so shy, so put off by outsiders, that Castro was obliged to write his field notes in hiding behind a screen, while the village priest read strategic questions on dialect phonology from a previously prepared list. One of a group of peasant women, at work havesting wheat, had been less reticent: «¿Usted busca cantares? ¡Pues yo le diré uno!» And she proceeded to offer an impressive rendition of *La muerte del príncipe don Juan,* that splendid touchstone of the *Romancero's* multisecular continuity: «Tristes nuevas, tristes nuevas, / que se cuentan por España...», thus bridging, in unbroken oral tradition, the nearly five centuries that separate us from the portentous death of Prince John, only son of the Catholic Monarchs, in 1497.[4] Another of Don Américo's ballad finds during his field work in Zamora was a splendid version of *Celinos.* It was this Leonese variant first collected by Don Américo, in Uña de Quintana (p. j. Benavente), in 1912, which, alone among all the ballad's modern forms, made possible our identification of a unique testimony to the poem's existence in the sixteenth-century. The enigmatic verse, «Cata las sierras de ardeña / donde brama un animal», recorded in the *Glosa peregrina* of Luis de Aranda (first printed in 1560), is indisputably linked to the motif of the bellowing stag, which has only been preserved in the modern ballad's Leonese forms.[5] Until recently Don Américo's text and another collected by Diego Catalán and Alvaro Galmés at Sejas de Aliste (p. j. Alcañices) in 1948 were the only known versions from the Leonese area. Both texts remain unedited and now part of the vast collection at the Menéndez Pidal Archive in Madrid.[6]

Over the past two decades, I have carried out a series of field trips to collect *romances* in various rural areas of Spain and Portugal, as much for the intrinsic interest which such texts inevitably embody, as to obtain an ample corpus of comparative material for the study of our extensive Judeo-Spanish *Romancero.*[7] In July 1980, I did nine days of field work

---

[4] On Menéndez Pidal's and María Goyri's dramatic discovery of the ballad, see M. GOYRI DE MENÉNDEZ PIDAL: «Romance de la muerte del príncipe D. Juan (1497)», *BHi,* 6 (1904), 29-37. Paul Bénichou's masterly study in *Creación poética en el romancero tradicional* (Madrid: Gredos, 1968) is fundamentally important.

[5] See our article in *NRFH,* 25 (1976), 86-94, or *En torno,* pp. 35-42; and v. 11 *infra.*

[6] I wish to thank Diego Catalán for his generosity in putting these and many other unedited texts at our disposal. The manuscripts of *Celinos* at the Archive were transcribed by Joseph Silverman in 1960; in 1975 we were able to obtain photocopies of the original texts.

Yet another reflection of Don Américo's work in Zamora in his perceptive reading of the «Romance de la mujer que fue a la guerra», *Lengua, enseñanza y literatura* (Madrid: Victoriano Suárez, 1924), pp. 259-280, based upon «una versión zamorana» of the famous ballad.

[7] Concerning our collection, see *Tres calas,* pp. 118-119, and, for more recent

14

in Trás-os-Montes and in Zamora, principally in villages around Puebla de Sanabria, but also at Uña de Quintana, a town to which I travelled with the specific purpose of following up Don Américo's visit of 1912.[8]

Uña de Quintana, a village of some 600 souls, stands on a level plain, about 50 kms, by secondary roads, to the west of Benavente. With its red brick construction, it projects a deceptive aura of relative modernity and offers a notable contrast to the typical, and seemingly more primitive, more archaic, stone and slate-roofed villages of the hilly Sanabrian area further to the west.[9] By its topographic situation, Uña de Quintana would not seem, at first glance, to be an ideal refuge for a relict repertoire of medieval *romances*. Against such a village of the plain, seemingly open to modernizing contacts from every side, any knowledgeable ballad collector might preferably look to some isolated hill town, tucked away in a mountain valley, and, hopefully, cut off from outside influences for centuries past. Yet things are never what they seem and Uña de Quintana, despite its apparent accessibility, proved to posses a ballad heritage which, in the rarity and archaism of its themes and the excellence of its versions, could easily rival the most vigorous and conservative traditions of Trás-os-Montes, the Azores, or Sephardic North Africa. At Uña, in less than two hours of intensive interviewing, I was to collect versions of *Le penitencia del rey Rodrigo, El príncipe don Juan, Belardos y Baldovinos, El cautivo del renegado, La buena hija,* and *La nodriza del infante,* plus a host of other, more frequently encountered *romances,* and in a majority of cases, in admirably complete versions.[10]

The first person Iapproached at Uña was Martina González, an 88 year old matriarch of imposing and seemingly reticent mien, who, it turned out, was surprisingly well travelled. Long ago she had spent sixteen years as an emigrant in Argentina, only to return once again to the Spanish village of her childhood. My approach was direct: «Mire usted, soy un profesor de Norteamérica. Estoy buscando canciones. ¿No sabría usted una que empieza...» and I cited the first verse of Américo Castro's *Celinos*: «Viniendo el conde de misa, / la condesa mala está...» To my delight, Doña Martina immediately recognized the song. She avowed she had not sung it for fifty years, but the fluency of her recitation (and two subsequent repetitions, which she patiently offered, at my insistence, to verify every reading) showed her complete familiarity with the poem. Here

statistics, our *Judeo-Spanish Ballads from New York* (Berkeley-Los Angeles: University of California Press, 1981), p. 122.

[8] Concerning this trip, see the preliminary report, «Hispanic Ballad Field Work during the Summer of 1980», *La Corónica,* 9:1 (Fall 1980), 29-36: pp. 34 ff. For more details on the work in Trás-os-Montes and a brief account of other expeditions (1963-1982), see «Una encuesta romancística: Trás-os-Montes, julio 1980» (to appear in *Quaderni Portoghesi*).

[9] For eloquent photographic documentation of what these villages were and still are like, see Fritz Krüger's classic monograph, *Die Gegenstandskultur Sanabrias und seiner Nachbargebiete* (Hamburg: L. Friederichsen, 1925).

[10] See *La Corónica,* 9:1 (Fall 1980), 36.

is Doña Martina's version of *Celinos,* based upon her three recitations of July 22, 1980 (indicated as I, II, and III in the variants):

Paseándose anda Celinos   por su palacio de real:
2 Viniera el conde de misa,   la condesa mala está,
que se la engañó Celinos   con cartas de falsedad.
4 —¿Tú qué tienes, la condesa,   tú qué tienes d'ese mal?
—Que me he hallado achacosa,   hace poco tiempo acá.
6 —Si te has hallado achacosa,   algo se te antojará.
¿Tú quieres trucha de río   o pescado de la mar
8 o carnero castellano   o vaca de Portugal.
—No quiero trucha del río,   ni pescado de la mar,
10 ni carnero castellano,   ni vaca de Portugal.
Quiero la cabeza d'un ciervo,   desde aquí lo oigo bramar.
12 Y a los montes de Celinos,   allí le irás a buscar.—
Siete vueltas dio en el monte,   sin hallar por donde entrar.
14 Y al cabo las siete vueltas,   con Celinos se fue a hallar.
—¿Tú qué buscas, el buen conde,   por éste mi monte real?
16 —Antojos de la condesa   hasta aquí me han hecho llegar.
—Antojos de la condesa   son los que a ti te han matar.
18 Con la tu mujer, el conde,   con ella me he de casar
y en la tu mulita roja,   en ella me he de pasear.
20 —Eso no será, Celinos,   eso me has de perdonar.
Saca las armas, Celinos,   vámonos a pelear.
22 —Saca las tuyas, buen conde,   las mías ya fuera están.—
A los primeros encuentros,   al conde muy malo le va.
24 Y a los segundos encuentros,   Celinos en tierra cae.
Le cortara la cabeza   y en la espada le ha'nclavar.
26 Y en el patio la condesa,   allí se la echó a rodar:
—¡Toma la cabeza del ciervo,   la que me hiciste buscar!
28 —¿Mas tú pa qué lo mataste,   si a mí no me hacía mal?
—Y ahora calla, la condesa,   si no quieres que te haga igual.[11]

In its 29 verses, our text supplements, with a number of interesting details, the splendid 27-verse variant collected by Don Américo 68 years before, while it, in its turn, adds other important details to ours. Our first verse provides a poetically effective prologue: the ominous figure of Celinos, awaiting fulfillment of his treacherous plans, paces, we may suppose impatiently, through the halls of his palace. The verse is lacking

---

[11] Variants: *5b* va de tres meses acá, *II, III*; *2b* lo *II*; *15b* I omits mi; *19a* mulita blanca *II*; *19b* montar *II*; *20a* no lo harás *II*; *20b* si *II*; *23b* malo está *I*; *24b* el conde en tierra cae *II*. This last reading is clearly a mistake. In all the ballad versions (except, possibly, some Sephardic texts from Salonika), it is Celinos, not the Count, who is killed. It would have been intolerable to the ethos of Hispanic balladry had the epic's outcome not been reversed. Yet curiously, this error has «reconstructed» the original dénouement of the *chanson de geste,* in which the conspiracy is successful: Doon kills the aged Count Gui and also puts at risk the life of young Beuve, thus launching him upon his heroic career. On the ballad's reversal of the epic's narrative, see *Chapbooks,* pp. 238-240; *Tres calas,* pp. 76-77.

in Don Américo's text, but its traditionality is fully confirmed by an essentially identical reading in an unedited version from Castillo de Rucios (p. j. Burgos): «Se paseaba Celinos / por el su palacio real...»

Our v. 3 also gives us a splendid, previously undocumented feature: Celinos has sent letters of treacherous import to the Countess. In the text from Uña, their content is only implied by the following narrative, but in versions from other areas, as also in various medieval redactions of *Beuve de Hantone,* details of the conspiracy are clearly specified: The Countess is to feign pregnancy and to insist that, as an *antojo de embarazada,* she must taste the flesh of a stag which frequents a neighboring wood, or she will lose her child. She sends her husband to hunt for the animal, while Celinos, as has been previously arranged, waits in the forest to kill him from ambush.[12] The motif of the treacherous letters, which, to my knowledge, occurs nowhere else in the modern tradition, is firmly grounded in the medieval *chanson de geste,* where an exchange of missives between the Countess and Doon de Mayence (=Celinos) leads to the plot to murder Count Gui de Hantone.[13]

At our v. 4, Don Américo's version embodies yet another important detail: To allay all suspicion, the devious Countess assures her husband that no harm will come to him because of her caprice: «De este mal que yo tengo / a ti nada te ha (d)e pasare.»

It is worth noting, at this point, that both Don Américo's text and mine make use of the widely known ballad motif of the ritualized seven turns («siete vueltas») to form a transition between the dialog of Count and Countess and the confrontation of the Count and Celinos (vv. 12-13). There can be no doubt, as we have shown elsewhere, concerning the magic associations of such numbers as *three* and *seven* and the seven turns thus serve as a ritualistic device for advancing the action.[14]

At vv. 17, 18, and 19, the 1912 text again supplements ours:

```
16   Antojos de tu condesa     la vida te han de quitare. (17)
     —Eso está de Dios, Celinos,   lo que Dios quiera será. (+)
18   —En la tu mulica roja,    me tengo de ir a paseare. (19)
     Y los tu hijos queridos   a mí «padre» me han llamare. (+)
```

---

[12] See *Tres calas,* pp. 71-76, and the abstract of the Sephardic version in S. G. ARMISTEAD et al., *El romancero judeo-español en el Archivo Menéndez Pidal,* 3 vols (Madrid: C.S.M.P., 1978), II, 78-79.

[13] See, for example, ALBERT STIMMING: *Der Festländische Bueve de Hantone: Fassung I* (Dresden: Max Niemeyer, 1911), p. 12, vv. 252 ff.; *Fassung III,* vol. I (Dresden: M. Niemeyer, 1914), 10 vv. 175 ff.; apparently, verbal messages are sent in the *Anglonormannische Boeve de Haumtone,* ed. Stimming (Halle: Max Niemeyer, 1899), pp. 4-6 (vv. 51 ff.) and its Middle English derivative, *Sir Beues of Hamtoun,* ed. Eugen Kölbing (London: Kegan Paul, 1885-1894), pp. 5-8 (vv. 72 ff.); letters appear in another English variant (p. 7, v. 119) and the Italian texts (below, n. 15).

[14] See S. G. ARMISTEAD and J. H. SILVERMAN: «Siete vueltas dio al castillo...», *RDTP,* 30 (1974), 323-326, or, amplified and up-dated in *En torno,* pp. 106-109. The «vueltas» also occur in the version from Sejas de Aliste collected by Diego Catalán and Alvaro Galmés: «Siete vueltas dio al palacio *(sic),* / sin con el ciervo encontrar. // De las siete pa las ocho, / con Cerino viene a dar.»

20   Y con la tu esposa querida,   yo me tengo de casare.— (18)
Dejara las armas viejas,   las nuevas fuera a tomare. (+)
22   A los primeros encuentros,   al conde muy mal le va. (23)
A los segundos avisos,   Zelinos en tierra cae... (24)

Here v. 17 adds significantly to the poem: Against Celinos' arrogance and treachery, the Count piously puts his trust in God. Don Américo's vv. 18-20 are much more effective than our vv. 18-19 in stressing the belligerance of Celinos' arrogant threats. In a typical tripartite pattern,[15] his verbal aggression follows an ascendant order: First he will ride the Count's mule, then adopt his children, and finally marry his wife. Celinos' implicit challenge follows a calculated gradation in usurping first chattels and them family. The reading of Don Américo's version is far superior to ours at this point and justifies an editorial change that, as we shall see, helps to clarify the structure of the poem.

Our version goes on to develop the direct confrontation of the Count and Celinos in three esential verses which are lacking in the 1912 tevt: «Eso no será... / Saca las armas... / Saca las tuyas...» (vv. 20-22).

Don Américo's v. 21 embodies a precious, but enigmatic detail: The Count has apparently taken both old and new weapons with him to the wood. One wonders why. In medieval Italian versions of *Buovo d'Antona,* the Countess insidiously dissuades her husband from going armed to the forest, since he will only be hunting game («her pigliare una vile cacciagione»).[16] The detail comes over into various versions of the Hispanic ballad:

¿Para qué queréx armas y caballos?   Ya os abasta puño endorado
(uned., Sarajevo)

Malditos sean los viejos   y quien les ha dado pan,

que para matar un ciervo   las armas ha de llevar.
(uned., Valderredible, p. j. Reinosa, Santander)

Y para matar un ciervo,   ¿armas dó(s) vas a buscar?

Con la cinta de mi rueca,   me lo obligo yo a matar.
(uned., Castrillo de Rucios, p. j. Burgos)

---

[15] On this and similar formulaic patterns, see the study by MERCEDES DÍAZ ROIG: «Un rasgo estilístico del Romancero y de la lírica popular», *NRFH,* 21 (1972), 79-94.

[16] See Giuseppe Vandelli (ed.), *I Reali di Francia di Andrea da Barberino,* vol. II: ii (Bologna: Romagnoli dall'Acqua, 1900), 328, or Giuseppe Vandelli and Giovanni Gambarin (eds.) (Bari: Guis. Laterza, 1947), p. 295; also PIO RAJNA: *Ricerche intorno ai Reali di Francia,* vol. I (Bologna: Gaitano Romagnoli, 1872), 496, vv. 106-109; Id., «Frammenti di redazioni italiane del *Buovo d'Antona»,* ZRPh, 15 (1891), 47-87, at p. 66. The motif may have had its origin in a verse of the Anglo-Norman *Boeve,* where the messenger specifies that «la dame vus enverra son seignur desarmez» (ed. Stimming, p. 6, v. 90), but, in the incident itself, the Count's being unarmed is not mentioned. Similarly, in the Midde English version, he is to be sent «with lite meini», i.e. 'with few companions' (ed. Kölbing, p. 7, v. 141).

No has de menestê es cavall,   no has d'anâ a passetjar.
Ni necessitas ses armes,   no t'has d'anâ a baraiar.
(uned., Ibiza)

But in the *romance*, in contrast to the *chanson de geste* (where the aged Count of Hantone is killed by Celinos' counterpart Doon de Mayence), the husband is not to be deceived. Despite his wife's advice that he go unarmed, he takes care to be well equipped. A lone Portuguese text, collected by José Leite de Vasconcellos in Campo de Víboras (c. Vimioso, Trás-os-Montes), in August 1883, is closest to the Uña version and shows that Don Américo's v. 21 has been misplaced and must, in some earlier form, have followed our v. 12:

—Que no monte de Selino   um serbo dizem que hay;
colheras las armas belhas,   armas nobas deix'-as 'star,
colh'um cajat'im na mano,   como que se bá passear.
—Z-num seija diabo, condeza,   que me queiras enganar:
Colherei as armas nobas,   armas belhas deixo 'star.[17]

Finally, our version improves upon the aftermath of Celinos' death. Where don Américo's text merely reads: «Le cortara la cabeza / y encomienza a caminar...» (v. 24), our v. 25 is more expressive in its truculence: «Le cortara la cabeza / y en la espada le ha'n clavar...»[18] The following verse (26), in which Celinos' decapitated head is violently hurled into the Countess' courtyard, is missing from the 1912 version, but is crucial in leading up to the Count's ironic imprecation: «¡Toma la cabeza del ciervo, / la que me hiciste buscar!»[19]

Having compared the two versions, let us now look at the poem as a whole. One feature that makes the ballad of *Celinos,* as it is sung at Uña de Quintana, such a successful poem is the almost exact symmetry of its parts. It can be divided into five segments: a Prologue (A), involving the three protagonists; the Dialogue between Count and Countess (B); at the very center, a ritualized act, which motivates further action: the magic circumambulation of the forest (C); then a second Dialogue (B'), between the Count and Celinos; and, finally, an Epilogue (A'), in which the three protagonists, even after the death of Celinos, are again juxtaposed. We must bear in mind, of course, that each rendition of a ballad

[17] J. LEITE DE VASCONCELLOS: *Romanceiro português,* 2 vols. (Coimbra: Universidade, 1958-1960), II, no. 1000 (pp. 496-497).
[18] Note similar verses in the Sephardic versions and in the lone Ibizan text: «En la punta de la lanza / allí se la fue a encolgare» (uned., Sarajevo); «Arozó él la su lansa; / la kavesa le enfilará» (*Chapbooks,* p. 228, v. 23, Salonika); «I en sa punta de sa llança / per bandera el va posar» (uned., Ibiza).
[19] It is curious to note the consistent use of the «paragogic -*e*» in Don Américo's version, over against its complete absence from the text recorded in 1980. Does this depend perhaps on the 1912 test's having been sung while ours was recited? On the arbitrary omission of the paragoge in early *romances,* see *Romancero hispánico*: «los editores... no creían necesario imprimir la -*e* añadida en el canto espontáneamente» (I, 113).

constitutes a separate, autonomous poem in its own right.[20] Were we to choose Don Américo's 1912 version as our base text, we would certainly arrive at slightly different conclusions. (Needless to say, an analysis of versions from some other geographic tradition would, again, yield an altogether different picture.) Taking the 1980 version as our base (emended at vv. 18-19 by a change in order and the addition of a single verse dictated by the text of 1912), the ballad exhibits the following structure (A represents our text; C, Don Américo's):

A. Prologue: (Celinos: absent)-Count-Countess (A1-3)

B. Dialogue: Count-Countess (A4-11)
    a. Question: ¿Tú qué tienes? (A4)
    b. Answer: Achacosa (A5)
    c. Question: Enumeration: trucha, pescado, carnero, vaca (A6-8)
    d. Negation: Enumeration: ni trucha, ni pescado, ni carnero, ni vaca
    e. Quest: La cabeza del ciervo (A11)   (A9-10)
    f. Destination: Montes de Celinos (A12)

C. Magic circumambulation (A13-14)

B'. Dialogue: Count-Celinos (A15-25+C19: hijos)
    a'. Question: ¿Tú qué buscas? (A15)
    b'. Answer: Antojos (A16)
    c'. Answer: Enumeration: mula, hijos, mujer (C18-20)
    d'. Negation: Eso no será (A20)
    e'. Challenge: Saca las armas (A21-22)
    f'. Battle: Cortara la cabeza (A23-25)

A'. Epilogue: (Celinos: dead)-Count-Countess (A26-29)

Notable are the exact parallelism and the correspondence in proportion of the poem's various segments: Prologue and Epilogue (A-A') both involve all three members of the fatal triangle, even though Celinos is physically absent in the Prologue and dead in the Epilogue; the Prologue consists of three verses; the Epilogue of four. The poem's two main segments, the two Dialogues (B-B'), each involves a confrontation of two of the three protagonists, with the victorious Count constituting, by his presence in both, a bridge between the two sections. The Dialogues embody eight and thirteen verses respectively; each consists of six parts (a-f and a'-f'); each begins with a question (a-a'), followed by an answer referring to the Countess' *antojo* (b-b'); each has as its center a formulaic

---

[20] A fundamental error of neo-individualist criticism would seem to imply that traditional compositions —the products of oral creativity— cannot (or are not worthy?) of being studied as works of art. Thus, David Mackenzie observes, in regard to the medieval epic, that «since what we have are learned compositions, ... it is quite proper to study them as works of art in their own right» (*YWRCLL*, 1978=*YWMLS*, 40). One can only wonder: And if they are not learned compositions? Then what? See also *La Corónica*, 10:2 (Spring 1892), 252, and «Epic and Ballad», n. 6.

enumerative sequence (c-c′), followed by a negation (d-d′), then by a task or challenge (e-e′), and finally by a sub-dénouement: the quest to the Montes de Celinos (f) or the fulfillment of that quest, the battle in which Celinos will die (f′). Several of these parallel segments embody similar dimensions (abc are identical in size to a′b′c′). At the same time, the final segments of the first Dialogue (B) are firmly linked to the Epilogue (A′): e. «la cabeza del ciervo» is echoed in v. 27 (¡Toma la cabeza del ciervo!), while the destination of the quest, «los montes de Celinos», is ironically linked to the destination of the decapitated head: «el patio de la condesa» (v. 26). Similarly, these linkages are confirmed by the final segment of B′: f′, «le cortara la cabeza», which likewise connects with v. 27 of the Epilogue: «¡Toma la cabeza del ciervo!» Decapitation, a watchword of the *Romancero's* iron code,[21] is clearly the unifying motif of this splendid, if truculent, poem. *Pundonor* and marital fidelity have been vigorously and bloodily reaffirmed. In the closely interlocking relationships and consistent parallelism of its pieces and parts, the poem projects a constant sense of artistic control, achieved, in the best oral tradition of ballad and epic, with a minimum of expressive baggage. A final word should be said concerning the last verse: «Y ahora calla, la condesa, / si no quieres que te haga igual.» Of the death of Celinos there can, to say the least, be no possible doubt. In this, the ballad comes to a definite close, as in the tradition of the *romance-cuento,* so prevalent in modern Hispanic balladry.[22] But in this final verse, our *romance* can, so to speak, «have its cake and eat it too». The multiple authors of oral tradition, in their gradual elaboration of the song to the form in which we know it today, have managed to give it both the clear, specific ending of a *romance-cuento* and, at the same time, to endow in with an aura of doubt and mystery recalling the intuitive style of such masterpieces as *Conde Arnaldos* or *Mora Morayma*. Will the faithless Countess be killed or, against all odds, will she somehow survive? In sum: Poetry is the art of not saying everything.

* * *

The peregrinations of *Celinos* have taken us from medieval France to distant corners of the Hispanic world. For Edumund King, *maestro y amigo,* I offer this *nótula romancística* in rememberance of personal and intellectual relationships, dear to us both, that have been and will remain a source of inspiration and are very much a part of Hispanic studies at Princeton.

University of California, Davis.

---

[21] See the many examples brought together in *El romancero judeo-español en el Archivo Menéndez Pidal,* II, 300, 320 (s. vv. *beheading* and *punishment*).
[22] On *romances-cuento,* see GIUSEPPE DI STEFANO: «Tradición antigua y tradición moderna: Apuntes sobre poética e historia del Romancero», *El Romancero en la tradición oral moderna,* ed. Diego Catalán et al. (Madrid: C.S.M.P., 1973), pp. 277-296 at 284-287.

CERVANTES AND SKEPTICISM: THE VANISHING OF THE BODY

by

ANTHONY J. CASCARDI

Near the beginning of the *Quijote,* Cervantes makes the curious observation that his hero has gone mad from too much reading, and that his brains have dried up as a result («del mucho leer se le secó el celebro,» I, 1). This is one of the first hints of his character's resistance to the idea that humans are two-part beings, made of a body *and* a mind. That view, and the philosophical problem related to it, traditionally known as mind-body dualism, is important for skepticism because it raises the question of our ability not only to be, but to know, and to be certain of what we know (indeed, even to be certain that we exist at all, that we know who we are, that *our* mind is attached to *our* body). By eliminating the mind from the hero of his novel, Cervantes disarms the very organ of skeptical doubt: Don Quijote is endowed with more certainty than could ever be needed to counter the claims or to refute the objections of a skeptic; his madness is not of doubt but of a knowledge—a certainty of the body, which is hammered home each time as he butts-up against the world—that outstrips the bounds of reason; he commits himself wholly to unquestioned truths even though others are fated not to believe him. Cervantes' acute awareness of the conditions of embodiment is not limited to the hero of the *Quijote.* It is evident throughout the novel: for Sancho, who is blanketed in Part I, and who retches after having drunk the *bálsamo de Fierabrás;* for Maritornes the prostitute in the scene at the inn, who generously ministers to Sancho's needs; for Marcela, the hard-hearted lover, incapable or unwilling to give her body as a gift, who treats it like an entirely private object, a possession; for Grisóstomo, whom she spurned, but who is himself guilty of suicide, the capital offense against the body. As this range of cases suggests, the pre-emption of mind-body dualism masks a deeper concern for the specially *human* ways in which we are made present to others and to the world about us, and for the ways in which our presence to them, and theirs to us, may be blocked or withheld. Cervantes' concern for the body shows an awareness that our potential for human community, for socialness, for publicness, is limited by our privacy, our apartness, our isolation—facts of which the body, in which each of us is sealed, is a sign.

These concerns become more explicit still in one of the *Novelas ejemplares, El licenciado Vidriera.* Here, I want to concentrate my attention on the peculiar variety of insanity that Cervantes envisions in it. The Licenciado suffers from a madness akin to acute skepticism, an affliction which is virtually the opposite of Don Quijote's. After travels in Italy and studies of law in Spain, Tomás Rodaja falls victim to the designs of a Toledan woman well-versed in «wiles and intrigue» («una dama de todo rumbo y manejo»[1]). She is amorously attracted to Tomás, but he is «more interested in his books than in other diversions,» and resists her advances. She gives him a potion, «creyendo que le daba cosa que le forzase la voluntad a quererla» *(ibíd.).* As a result of the serum, the Licenciado imagines that he is made of glass, that he is, in a sense, the exact opposite of Don Quijote—all mind and no body. Throughout, the story is laden with philosophical suggestions. The potion itself is reminiscent of the Platonic *pharmakon,* a drug whose powers were reputed to be both salutary and harmful (Cervantes' narrator explains that «las que dan estas bebidas o comidas amatorias se llaman *venéficos,* porque no es otra cosa lo que hacen sino dar veneno a quien las toma, como lo tiene demostrado la experiencia en muchas y diversas ocasiones,» *ibíd.).* Like the *pharmakon,* the serum is an inducement to thought, ostensibly a boon to philosophy's goals: it renders the Licenciado a mouthpiece of truth, capable of speaking otherwise unspeakable truths to society. That the potion is administered in the interests of love is a suggestion of the seductiveness of truth, a reminder of the deep alliance between philosophical and sexual knowledge—concerns which have been linked since at least Plato's *Phaedrus*—, a sign that the nature of the philosophical pursuit ought to be like the most intimate forms of knowing, a probing of one soul by another.

Cervantes' direct source for the germ of *El licenciado Vidriera* was probably the passage in Erasmus' *The Praise of Folly* which talks about those forms of madness in which the soul and the body split apart, where the soul breaks loose from its bodily ties («As long as the soul uses the physical organs only,» Erasmus wrote, «it is called sane; when, however, breaking away, as it were, from its imprisonment, it is called insane»[2]). But the fiction of the disappearance of the body, and the image of someone who is pure mind, or who worries that he may only be a brain awash in a vat, responding to neural stimulations, are old and recurrent themes of philosophical skepticism. The classic formulation of the disappearance of the body as a philosophical problem was stated just after Cervantes' text, in the first of the Cartesian *Meditations.* There, Descartes says «I shall consider myself as having no hands, no eyes, no flesh, no blood, nor any senses, yet falsely believing myself to possess all these things."[3] The Licenciado's madness falls precisely in line with those forms

---

[1] *El licenciado Vidriera,* in MIGUEL DE CERVANTES SAAVEDRA: *Obras completas,* II, ed. Angel Valbuena Prat (Madrid: Aguilar, 1970), p. 1042a. All subsequent references will be incorporated into the text.

[2] *The Praise of Folly,* trans. John P. Dolan, in *The Essential Erasmus* (New York: Mentor Books, 1964), p. 170.

[3] *Meditations on First Philosophy,* in *The Philosophical Works of Descartes,* I,

of lunacy from which Descartes hoped to be free (i.e. the maladies of persons «devoid of sense, whose cerebella are so troubled and clouded by the violent vapors of black bile, that they constantly assure us that they think they are kings when they are really without covering, or who imagine that they have an earthenware head or are but pumpkins or *are made of glass*,» p. 145; my italics). Descartes went on to imagine himself to be a person with no body, to consider that his idea of the body might be a case of false belief and not certifiable knowledge, because he hoped to make the certainty of his existence and identity dependent on strictly mental criteria. He wanted to sweep away any interfering material qualities and so to eliminate the possibility of sensory error. In order to know what we know with certainty—which is what the skeptic, in his rigor, asks—we must know it by mental criteria. Descartes assumed that the kind of knowledge needed to demonstrate certainty would be found in perspicuous (i.e. «clear and distinct») ideas; the fiction of the disappearance of the body is emblematic of his wish to make those ideas not only perspicuous but absolutely lucid, virtually transparent.

Descartes was particularly interested in the relationship between himself and his body because he wanted to find out whether his body was an *essential* part of him, whether his relationship to it, although remarkably close, was in fact necessary. «Nature teaches me,» he wrote, «that I am not only lodged in my body as a pilot in a vessel, but that I am very closely united to it, and so to speak so intermingled with it that I seem to compose with it one whole,» (p. 192). Is it that human beings are simply beings in human guise? *Am* I, or am I *in,* my body? As the *Discourse on the Method* makes clear, Descartes concluded that his existence was not contingent on the body; instead, he derived existence from the capacity for thought, which was made manifest in his ability to doubt: «I saw that I could conceive that I had no body, and that there was no world nor place where I might be; but yet that I could not for all that conceive that I was not. On the contrary, I saw from the very fact that I thought of doubting the truth of other things, it very evidently and certainly followed that I was; on the other hand, if I had only ceased from thinking, even if all the rest of what I had ever imagined had really existed, I should have no reason for thinking that I had existed. From that I knew that I was a substance the whole essence or nature of which is to think, and that for its existence there is no need of any place, nor does it depend on any material thing; so that this «me,» that is to say, the soul by which I am what I am, is entirely distinct from body, and is even more easy to know than is the latter; and even if body were not, the soul would not cease to be what it is,» (p. 101).

The Licenciado's madness shows some of the same traits that are marked in the Cartesian *Meditations* and the *Discourse*. Considering that he is made of glass, the Licenciado thinks that his spirit, his essence

---

trans. Elizabeth S. Haldane and G. R. T. Ross (1911; rpt. Cambridge: Cambridge University Press), p. 148. All subsequent references to the works of Descartes will be from this edition and will be incorporated into the text.

or soul, is untrammeled, that it is free from material limitations and can be known directly («el vidrio, por ser de materia sutil y delicada, obraba por ella el alma con más prontitud y eficacia que no por la del cuerpo, pesada y terrestre,» p. 1042b). The Licenciado's body of glass is the key to his intelligence and insight, the source of his enlightenment, an image which satisfies the skeptic's wish for perfect knowledge («... le preguntaron muchas y difíciles cosas, a las cuales respondió espontáneamente con grandísima agudeza de ingenio; cosa que causó admiración a los más letrados de la Universidad y a los profesores de la Medicina y Filosofía, viendo que en un sujeto donde se contenía tan extraordinaria locura se encerrase tan grande entendimiento que respondiese a toda pregunta con propiedad y agudeza,» *ibíd.*).

Glass, with its suggestion of transparency, intimates the yearning for a seamless presence to the world which the embodied characters of the *Quijote* do not know. Cervantes' purpose in the *Licenciado Vidriera* is to portray the disastrous consequences of the wish for an escape from the body and the hope of the transcendental knowledge that this might bring. Among the immediate consequences of the Licenciado's idea that he is made of glass are a fear of the finitude which the body imposes on members of the human species—a fear of death—and an aversion to others («Decía que le hablasen *de lejos,*» *ibíd.;* my italics). As if in recognition of the fact that embodiment is of mortal importance, that it is a condition necessary to being human, the transparent glass of which Tomás believes he is made is remarkably fragile; it becomes a source of division between him and the world. Thus in contrast to the perspective of a professional epistemologist, of someone like Descartes, Cervantes sees that we will *not* be made immediately present to the world simply by removing the bodily veil. Our distance, our separateness, our isolation from others, do not decrease with our denial of the body. The man of glass is wrapped in dark cloth, shielded from the world («Pidió Tomás le diesen alguna funda donde pusiese aquel vaso quebradizo de su cuerpo, porque al vestirse algún vestido estrecho no se quebrase; y así, le dieron una ropa parda y una camisa muy ancha, que él se vistó con mucho tiento,» pp. 1042b-1043a).

For an epistemologist like Descartes, the will to transcend the body is sustained by a desire to attain a knowledge uninhibited by any earthbound constraints; it is consequent on the idea that man is defined as a thinking thing, and on the wish to place the mind in a position of transcendent knowledge. *El licenciado Vidriera* proves a rather caustic commentary on such aspirations. The dream of an incorporeal existence is not sufficient to guarantee that we can possess transcendental knowledge. Cervantes finds a latent arrogance in the notion that man should be described as pure mind, or in terms of his «glassy essence,» as the phrase went,[4] and thus likened to the angels and spirits; he saw too many

---

[4] The notion has become a prominent concern in recent work on philosophy of mind, as for example RICHARD RORTY's *Philosophy and the Mirror of Nature* (Princeton: Princeton University Press, 1979). But the phrase was current among

opportunities for godliness, too easily avoided, in our embodied condition. His recognition that we are fated to inhabit our bodies should be set beside the fact of the Incarnation and what that teaches us, viz., that the Christian God was also meant to inhabit a body, that there is something divine about the bodily state, not that we achieve holiness in transcending it. Unlike the epistemologist, Cervantes is interested in the body because it is the specifically *human* condition in which we are given to know one another and the world, or to fail in that knowledge.

Cervantes finds that the skeptic's arguments (e.g. Descartes' insistence on the possibility that he may be deceived about his body) entail a retreat from the world and an avoidance of others. The miserable failure of the man of glass suggests that, unlike Descartes, Cervantes saw that there is nothing else for human beings to be (in) except their bodies, that, as a famous tag from Wittgenstein's *Philosophical Investigations* (II, 178) puts it, «The human body is the best picture of the human soul;» (Cervantes would say: not only the best picture, but the only picture). To say that the body simply *is* the image of the soul, is to say that its physiognomy, its aspects, show what it is to be human. The question implicit in Descartes' *Meditations* about my relationship to my body are thus better expressed by saying that I am bound by the body, in its possession, that the body has claims upon me.[5] If Tomás got outside his body by some sort of bewitchment, by the demoniacal lady from Toledo and her potion, then he finally gets the demon out of him—and gets himself back into his body—by something akin to exorcism («... un religioso de la Orden de San Jerónimo, que tenía gracia y ciencia particular en hacer que los mudos entendiesen y en cierta manera hablasen, y en curar locos, tomó a su cargo de curar a Vidriera, movido de caridad, y le curó y sanó, y volvió a su primer juicio, entendimiento y discurso,» p. 1051a). His body is returned by an act of mercy, as if to say that humans *can* only direct such acts toward the body, that if we want to help heal other souls, then we ought to heal their bodies.

As long as Tomás thinks he has no body, he denies the fact that man is an animal among others like him, that he is an inherently social being, not simply a sapient one. Thematically, Cervantes' view that the body is the human and social condition in which knowledge is possible provides the link between the Licenciado's mad idea that his body is made of glass and the long list of truths which Tomás sets out to preach. Much of what he has to say deals, ironically, with the specifically *social* aspects of society, with various forms of evidence of the fact that none of us lives alone. The institutions and arrangements which attract his attention center

SHAKESPEARE and BACON (in *Measure for Measure* and *Advancement of Learning*, respectively). It was first invoked for modern philosophy by C. S. Peirce, but can be traced to antique ideas (Anaxagoras) about the nature of *nous* (see RORTY, pp. 42-43).

[5] On this and related problems of embodiment and skepticism, I am indebted to STANLEY CAVELL: *The Claim of Reason: Wittgenstein, Skepticism, Morality, and Tragedy* (New York, Oxford University Press, 1979), pp. 370-496, and especially p. 383).

around the bonds of authority and control, around the tacit and explicit contraints which hold us together in groups; he is drawn to consider the relations of masters and slaves, doctors and patients, lawyers, convicts, civil servants. He points out to people that they are of necessity defined as social beings, that their existence and identity derive from their ties to others, even if those ties are not products of their own will. (A muleteer for example proclaims that he is a decent man; Tomás answers that «"La honra del amo descubre la del criado; según esto, mira a quién sirves y verás cuán honrado eres; mozos sois de la más ruin canalla que sustenta la Tierra",» p. 1046a.) Through the Licenciado's dicta, Cervantes hints at the central fact of human existence as social existence—the same fact that was later given definitive formulation by Rousseau in the *Social Contract*, viz., that «man was born free, and everywhere he is in chains.» His point, like Rousseau's, is that these two conditions *necessarily* accompany one another, that in order to free man from his bonds we must free him from society, which of course we cannot do. Like Rousseau, Cervantes sees that the social order is everywhere present, that it preexists us, is there before we are, and that we are bound to it even where it derives no apparent authority from us (i.e. where our will and our consent in the social contract are purely tacit).

The manifest irony of the Licenciado's remarks is that he tries to refuse the social aspect of his own condition. In his diatribe against the doctors, for instance, the Licenciado inveighs against the visitation of any unwanted pain or suffering on the body; the sense of what he says is that the body ought not be made subject to an alien will («El juez nos puede torcer o dilatar la justicia; el letrado, sustentar por su interés nuestra injusta demanda; el mercader, chuparnos la hacienda; finalmente, todas las personas con quien de necesidad tratamos nos pueden hacer algún daño; pero quitarnos la vida sin quedar sujetos al temor del castigo, ninguno; sólo los médicos nos pueden matar y nos matan sin temor y a pie quedo, sin desenvainar otra espada que la de un *récipe;* y no hay descubrirse sus delictos, porque al momento los meten debajo de la tierra,» p. 1047a); yet the Licenciado himself lives under the influence of the will of another, and for as long as he does, for as long as he is under the sway of the potion, resistant to the socializing influence of love, he is an ineffective spokesman of the truth. Thus, rather than bind him to others in society, the truths which Tomás recites estrange him.

What Tomás has to say—much of it draw from Scripture—may be true, but it fails to convince. This is because truth, which was Descartes' concern, matters less to Cervantes than truthfulness, the means by which we render ourselves exemplars of what we know. Authentic wisdom requires finding the right relationship to truth, recognizing that others cannot see or hear the truth in us if we do not first erect it in ourselves, build ourselves up in its image. The Licenciado had set out in life to pursue learning because he wanted specifically to make something of himself, to *become* someone («"yo he oído decir que de los hombres se hacen los obispos",» p. 1038a). But he fails to see that mere learning, the simple acquisition of knowledge, must be subordinated to the personal

28

appropriation of what we may learn: what matters is not simply to know, which is what the skeptic wants, but to be edified, to be commanded by what we know, as Don Quijote is.

This is not to say that the possession of such self-commanding knowledge will allow us to fare any better in the world, or that we will be able to erase the seams which mark our finitude and our outsideness to the world, by the simple grace of wisdom; everything about Don Quijote, as about Socrates, as about Christ, suggests otherwise. At the close of *El licenciado Vidriera,* Tomás recovers his sanity, regains possession of his body (or allows his body to retake possession of him); yet even as he becomes «at one» with himself he remains «at odds» with the world («Perdía mucho y no ganaba cosa; y viéndose morir de hambre, determinó de dejar la corte y volverse a Flandes, donde pensaba valerse de las fuerzas de su brazo, pues no se podía valer de las de su ingenio. Y poniéndolo en efecto, dijo al salir de la corte: "Oh corte, que alargas las esperanzas de los atrevidos pretendientes y acortas las de los virtuosos encogidos, sustentas abundantemente a los truhanes desvergonzados y matas de hambre a los discretos vergonzosos",» p. 1052a-b). The hard fact is that society may never be ready for the truth, that it may always resist what we have to tell it. But against this there is no recourse. At the end of the novella, where the Licenciado is in possession of his body, in command of who he is, yet deeply at odds with the world, his destiny crosses that of Cervantes' knight. As the story suggests, the condition of embodiment bears not only on knowledge but on self-understanding, on each of us knowing and being who he is. It is the basis for moral and ethical knowledge, knowledge which outstrips the rational bounds that skepticism invokes.

University of California, Berkeley.

EL CABALLERO DE OLMEDO

by

AMERICO CASTRO †

(D.ª Carmen Castro de Zubiri has kindly offered for inclusion in this volume
the following essay from her late father's unpublished papers.)

> *Que* de noche le mataron
> al Caballero...

La versión más antigua del conocido cantar comenzaba en otra
forma:

> *Esta* noche le mataron
> al Caballero...

A través de esa, en apariencia, tan simple sustitución de vocablos se
hace perceptible la forma en que Lope de Vega dispuso el movimiento
creativo de una de sus más extraordinarias construcciones dramáticas.
En la expresión «*esta* noche» el suceso se ajusta dentro de una cerrada
determinación temporal, de la cual surgirá cualquier inferencia por parte
del oyente o lector. Mas al decir *«Que* de noche le mataron...»*, la frase
se provee de una dimensión doble: aparece como resultante de fuerzas
y motivos ignotos previos al acontecimiento funesto, y también como
punto de arranque para quien desee ejercitar su fantasía, o entregarse a
la dolida contemplación del caballero arrancado a la vida cundo era «la
gala de Medina» y «la flor de Olmedo».

> Que si viene la noche...
> pronto saldrá el sole...
> Que yo mi madre, yo,
> que la flor de la villa
> me era yo...

El *que* en «Que de noche le mataron...» es «resultativo», asidero para
el clamor de quienes se prenden a tan leve palabrilla para dar aire desde
ahí a su angustiosa lamentación. Bate contra ese inicio de verso el rumor
de la alborotada gente de Olmedo: «Sabemos, dicen que le mataron».
La canción surge entonces con un *que* ponderativo, con el reflejo de una
situación inexpresada; en ella vibra el estremecimiento de quienes anuncian *que* le mataron; y para más horror, de noche. En vez de la indica-
ción temporal, sustantiva, *esta noche,* surge el adverbial *de noche,* como
una referencia a oscuridades imprecisas y sin límite.

El cantarcillo, además de sugerir el tema, infundió su tono —según después ha de verse— en la textura misma de la obra y del personaje central. De aquél emana el temblor de símbolo, latente en las palabras e incluso en el ademán de don Alonso, un héroe más lírico que épico, más expresivo de su existir que impresivo por las magnitudes de su hacer. *Medina,* con su tintineo de sonidos claros, es símbolo del querer y de la vida, y, por tanto, lugar adecuado para que en él tenga Inés su morada. *Olmedo,* con sus vocales oscuras, parece convenir a las graves llamadas del deber y de la muerte:

> En ti, Medina, vive
> aquella Inés divina,
> que es *honra* de la corte
> y *gloria* de la villa.

El dúplice encomio es congruente con «la *gala* de Medina, la *flor* de Olmedo» del cantarcillo tradicional. Mirados al trasluz de su sentido, estos sinónimos no aparecen como redundantes, como mera decoración retórica, o como balanceo del estilo, según creen algunos. La *honra* y la *gala* prestigian y exornan desde fuera; la *gloria* y la *flor* se mueven o brotan en este caso desde dentro de la misma vida; *honra* y *gloria* son objetos ideales e invisibles, mientras que la *gala* y la *flor* son materialidad tocable.

La obra, en cuanto a estructura, fue concebida como una dualidad contrapuesta, que pugna por armonizarse y por escindirse en movimientos anhelosos e indetenibles. Sería inexacto e insuficiente atribuir al llamado Barroco la plena responsabilidad de tal concepción artística. Si tales entidades fueran sólo meras trascendencias respecto de la vida, el arte concebido por ellas no sería expresivo de un vivir auténtico, ni «impresivo» para la vida sobre la cual aquel arte se proyecta. Cuando tal acontece, el arte (sea literario, figurativo o voluminoso) es simple artificiosidad, algo así como un hijo cunero que, además, tuviese la desdicha de no poder fraguarse su propio destino.

El arte de Lope de Vega no es así. Manaba de una fuente muy viva, ansiosa de cauce, y de verterse sobre campos sedientos de su irradiante virtud. Los elementos de aquel arte, explicables sin duda dentro de una tradición retórica y humanística, valen ahora en cuanto instrumentos expresivos de una situación de vida, que no era sólo individual. No diría, por eso, que fuese también ampliamente colectiva. La masa rústica —la gran mayoría de la gente española en el siglo de Lope de Vega— sentía el efecto, casi siempre material, de la situación crítica en que se hallaba, sin tener conciencia del proceso y de las motivaciones de lo sentido como oprimente realidad. Cuando no existía la forzada nivelación de este nuestro tiempo (englobamiento creado por la máquina, el dinero o el látigo), las maneras de vida muy remotas coexistían con las más recientes. La diferencia honda entre el mundo de hoy y el de la España de Lope de Vega consiste en que entonces la acción de los acontecimientos externos era muy tenue comparada con la remoción e inquietud provocadas por la conciencia del propio existir, dentro de uno mismo y del grupo social.

Sin negar la importancia de las circunstancias externas en el siglo XVI (labrar la tierra, o vivir de su renta), me parece claro que contaban más que aquéllas el cómo creer, el cómo amar, el cómo pensar o el cómo admirar y gozar lo estimado como bello. Las gentes, en consecuencia, no se encontraban ahormadas de antemano y desde fuera (por la escuela, por el modo de transporte, por el restaurante, por el periódico, por la radio, por la aspirina, etc.). El teatro de Lope de Vega se dirigía a quienes vivían trabajándose la conciencia de sí mismos; las curvas de los niveles estimativos tenían por horizonte, primordialmente, el vivir de otras personas, y no había barruntos de lo que tiempo adelante sería lo que hoy llamo «objetocracia». Era así posible estremecerse desinteresadamente cuando se clamaba que habían dado muerte a quien era «la gala de Medina, la flor de Olmedo».

Si la revolución industrial, entre los siglos XVIII y XIX, modificó en la Europa occidental los rumbos de la vida, la remoción de la conciencia personal en la España del siglo XVI dio motivo a trastornos que acabarían por hallar reflejos en los modos de expresarse la vida. Los españoles siempre habían vivido en inestable inseguridad, atribuible antes del siglo XVI a la guerra secular contra la morisma, a la superioridad económica y técnica de los judíos, muy humillante para los cristianos; a las revueltas provocadas por las ambiciones de muchos señores; a las contiendas con Aragón, amenazadoras para Castilla a lo largo de una extensa línea fronteriza, etc. Mas ahora, en el siglo XVI, ya no había tierra de moros, los judíos eran idos, Aragón era España, nadie alborotaba interiormente el reino después de Villalar (1521), y un inmenso imperio ofrecía posibilidades de expansiones y riquezas nunca antes soñadas. Y sin embargo...

Los conflictos, antes del siglo XV, se expresaban en formas de contraposición objetivada, porque la ruptura se daba fuera de la conciencia: «tus gentes contra tus gentes, e tus pueblos contra tus pueblos, e los hermanos contra los hermanos, e los padres contra los hijos» [1]. Resumiendo, en breves palabras, un proceso muy amplio y muy complejo, pudiera decirse que de la expresión de fenómenos de experiencia externa, la literatura se vuelve, a lo largo del siglo XVI, hacia la expresión de las fracturas sentidas en el fondo de la conciencia. En el siglo XIV decía don Alonso Fernández Coronel, como mensaje para el rey Pedro el Cruel, que lo mandaba matar: «Esta es Castilla, que faze a los omes e los gasta.» Y generalizaba el caso Fernán Pérez de Guzmán, en 1460: «Los que ella fizo, ella misma los desface.» Poco antes, el Marqués de Santillana iniciaba así sus Coplas a la muerte de don Alvaro de Luna:

> De tu resplandor, oh Luna!
> te ha privado la fortuna.

---

[1] Así, en la *Lamentación fecha en prophecía de la segunda destruyción de España*, del MARQUÉS DE SANTILLANA (tomo la cita de R. LAPESA: *La obra literaria del Marqués de Santillana*, Madrid: Insula, 1957, p. 242).

El gran paso dado por la expresión literaria a lo largo del siglo XVI consistía en introvertir el tema de la disyunción entre los propósitos y los fines humanos; era difícil salvar la distancia entre el impulso y la meta del existir, y era bello y apasionante transformar en expresión seductora la vivencia de ese conflicto. Con lo cual logró Lope de Vega articular las piezas de su arte dramático como un auténtico juego artístico, en el que el público participaba tensa y gravemente. Nada así en las contemporáneas Francia e Italia, o en la Europa germánica.

La dimensión artística del vivir en la literatura posee valor propio, aunque no es captada y revivida eficazmente, sino en enlace con la situación de vida de la cual es, precisamente, una dimensión. De ahí los obstáculos con que tropezamos los modernos —españoles o extranjeros— para convivir en belleza con las figuras que transitan por los ámbitos de irrealidad-real inventados por Lope de Vega. Hace medio siglo creía yo —como ciertos maestros franceses— que el teatro español «sentait trop le terroir». ¿Pero no acontece así siempre? ¿Es que la obra de Racine es plenamente gozable para quien no esté habituado al gusto del «terroir» francés? Quien no esté educado ánglicamente, con gran dificultad percibirá el cabal sentido de los dramas shakespearianos. Todo lo cual, huelga decirlo, se refiere a algo más que al *estudio* de la obra literaria, *indispensable desde luego,* aunque simple medio para captar su mensaje expresivo, en la forma que buenamente nos sea dable.

El mensaje venía de unas gentes poco dadas a construirse reposaderos para la mente, a crearse actividades que dejaran en paréntesis la conciencia de estar existiendo. El horizonte se abría en perspectivas de magnificiencia y de belleza para toda aspiración personal, y a la vez se angostaba, se le venía encima a la persona. Al familarizado con aquella época, el español da la impresión de estar siempre abriéndose a codazos el curso de su vida, tropezando con otros hombres y con resistencias misteriosas. Creencias y convicciones, no analizadas, mantenían casi inmóvil el panorama de las cosas y de las ideas.

Lope de Vega era agorero y supersticioso (una forma de creencia) porque las gentes en torno a él lo eran. El «desengaño» no fue invención de predicadores y de escritores ascéticos, sino mero resultado del ritmo pendular de quienes confiaban, plenos de esperanza, frente al ancho horizonte, y veían luego cortada su ilusión, reducida «a cisco, como tesoro de duende» *(Guzmán de Alfarache).* Se llamaba «engaño» a la ilusión fracasada: las triunfantes llevaban, en cambio, a todos los prodigios de venturas, de amor divino y humano, o alzaban a grandezas como sólo antes Roma y el Oriente habían conocido. Sí y no, maravilla y miseria, vida y muerte. La vida, en trance de ascensión y de despeño, buscó para su expresión cuantas fórmulas antitéticas y de rasgadura habían legado los antiguos y cultivaban los modernos. Lo decisivo, no obstante, era la autenticidad del vivir antitético, la tradicional inseguridad, la carencia de normas objetivadas, u objetivables, de inquietud fecunda y no inerte. Si no se tiene presente el funcionamiento y los horizontes de la vida en torno, ¿cómo puede hacérsenos comprensible el teatro de Lope de Vega?

Los personajes de Shakespeare saltaban grandiosamente sobre cualquiera barrera convencional, y aparecían como naturaleza desmandada en medio de una vida sin sentido, el «sueño de un imbécil». En un extremo opuesto el teatro de Francia aparecía sostenido, en una u otra forma, por un pensar reglado, al que servía de pentagrama el uniforme alejandrino de doce sílabas. En el mundo de Lope de Vega la vida estaba, en cambio, asentada sobre fundamentos inconmovibles, y regida por dogmas y creencias nunca objeto de podas racionales [2]. El pensamiento no puede decirse que yaciera cautivo, pues nunca sintió el español, por propio impulso, la necesidad de liberarlo. Pero cuán viva, en cambio, aparecía la conciencia de estar viviendo la propia vida. Estos personajes están abriéndose sendas a través de nieblas, tanteando su paso junto a moles confusas que atraen y amedrentan. Se vive a todo riesgo entre engaños y seducciones, mentiras y verdades, en el tris en que convergen y se equivalen la muerte y la vida. La autenticidad de aquel proceso de realización artística consistía en expresar, en efecto, el conflicto entre el frenesí de las aspiraciones —amores, grandezas, triunfos— y el riesgo y la dificultad de los logros. Todo ello sin desmán ni caos, y a la vez sin medida o claro designio. Mas sobre el frenesí de los anhelos destaca y se realza la firme y justificada conciencia de estar queriendo lo que no puede dejar de quererse. Los mayores personajes de Lope de Vega son moles voluntariosas, batidas alternadamente por el vendaval de los amores y de los horrores, azotadas por la iniquidad y redimidas por una justicia —que a veces llega tarde, y simplemente para satisfacer el ansia de vindicta en el público—. Lo cual no anula la realidad del insalvable conflicto de haber sido muerto el caballero precisamente por ser la «gala» y «la flor» de dos ciudades; o de perder atrozmente sus vidas la duquesa Casandra y Federico (en *El castigo sin venganza*) porque su bella juventud y circunstancias ajenas a su voluntad los precipitaron a la sima de su amor. Este trágico movimiento de la atracción a la destrucción ha sido encarnado en los dos personajes centrales de *El caballero de Olmedo*. El problema del destino, o, más bien, del moviente conflicto entre opuestos destinos, se convirtió aquí, de genérico o universal, en el de dos vidas individualizadas y exquisitas.

No es bastante decir que Lope se inspiró en un cantar muy difundido para idear su comedia, como en otros casos se amplía un suceso anecdótico en acción complejamente desenvuelta. El estupendo acierto fue concebir la figura del Caballero como un ser flotante entre vivir y estar ya muerto, y cuyos amores son, simultáneamente, previos y posteriores a su morir por causa de ellos. Lope no se limitó a imaginar la existencia terrena del personaje idealizado en la canción; la imagen melancólica y dolida de don Alonso —sólo existente en el aire armonioso de unos versos enternecidos— fue fundida y armonizada con la figura de un personaje

---

[2] Lmitado aquí a referirme sucintamente a lo que tendrá más cabal desarrollo en otra ocasión, recordaría la obra del sacerdote francés, contemporáneo de Lope, PIERRE CHARRON: *De la sagesse,* inconcebible en España.

que camina tenue y decididamente hacia el cumplimiento de su destino. En dos Alonso —como si dijéramos— recobra vida su estatua funeraria —como si el Doncel de Sigüenza escapara al presente intemporal de su petrificada meditación[3], y representara, como tal estatua, el pasado que habría de llevarle al futuro de su muerte. El presente en la obra de Lope envuelve un pasado y un futuro.

En la representación escultórica no cabía expresar en un movimiento coherente la intersección de las dimensiones del vivir con las de la existencia atemporal de la bienaventuranza poética. Pero el genio de Lope supo lograrlo, e introdujo así en su arte dramático una nota exquisita de melancolía —algo como un efecto de perspectiva en la obra pictórica:

> INÉS: Pena me has dado y temor
> con tus miedos y recelos...
> pero tú no has entendido
> mi amor.
>
> D. ALONSO: Ni tú, que han sido
> estas imaginaciones
> sólo un ejercicio triste
> del alma, que me atormenta,
> no celos...
> De sueños y fantasías,
> si bien falsas ilusiones,
> han nacido estas razones,
> que no de sospechas mías. (Acto III)

El pasado melancólico de don Alonso es, en realidad, posterior a su presente de figura poética, de muerto inmortalizado en belleza. Esa su doble existencia no pasó inadvertida para la mirada celosa y recelosa de su rival don Rodrigo:

> El talle, el grave rostro, lo severo,
> celoso me obligaban a miralle. (Acto II)

La comedia de Lope fue concebida y estructurada al ritmo tembloroso de unos versos, tiernos como una queja femenina o infantil; no intenta en ningún caso acordarse con la vulgaridad histórica de la persona que había perdido la vida en Olmedo, tras una disputa con motivo de unos perros de caza. El personaje de la tragedia se instalaba poéticamente sobre una figura ya poetizada:

> CONDESTABLE: A don Alonso, que llaman
> *El Caballero de Olmedo,*
> hace Vuestra Alteza aquí
> merced de un hábito.
>
> REY: Es hombre
> *de notable fama y nombre...*

---

[3] Ver *Hacia Cervantes* (3.ª ed., Madrid: Taurus, 1967), p. 83.

Don Alonso,
que por excelencia llaman
el Caballero de Olmedo...
Al que por único llaman
el Caballero de Olmedo.

La figura aparece ya de bulto, conclusa, y se hace imaginable a través de símiles mitológicos:

FABIA: Cuchilladas y lanzadas
dio en los toros como un Héctor...
Armado parece Aquiles
mirando de Troya el cerco;
con galas parece Adonis.

La vieja Fabia, en su papel de madre Celestina, habla como ésta al ponderar a Melibea las maravillas de Calixto: «En esfuerzo, Héctor; ... pues verle armado, un San Jorge; ... no era tan hermoso aquel gentil Narciso» (Acto IV). En siglos anteriores eran utilizadas libremente las obras ajenas por considerarlas parte de un común patrimonio espiritual (tal era el caso de Berceo, el de los juglares épicos). La situación ahora no era la misma. El poeta atrae hacia su personal esfera de creación cuanta materia útil yace en su conciencia-memoria, y la usa y altera para sus personales fines. A la visión de los temas como objetos flotantes en una nebulosa (el Cid, Alejandro, leyendas, lo que fuese), había sucedido la clara noción de la obra y de su autor, pertenecieran a la Antigüedad o a tiempos más recientes. De ahí que se comenten las obras de Juan de Mena, de Garcilaso, lo mismo que las de los clásicos. Las grandes obras modernas se habían hecho tan dignas de adopción como las antiguas —como expresiones personales, no como temas anónimos; había conciencia de que este mundo nuestro poseía también sus valores, y era lícito utilizarlo. La «comedia» de Lope y, en general, la literatura profana se edificaban sobre las construcciones que la acción inquisitorial no había conseguido destruir (fue en cambio imposible establecer continuidad y hábitos de pensamiento). Lope sabía que estaba usando personajes y situaciones celestinescas [4], aunque para algo sin conexión con la obra de Rojas. Fabia, con sus agüeros y hechizos, evoca el reino de las sombras misteriosas. El contraste violento en La Celestina entre amor ciego y avispada bellaquería, entre pasión justificada y un mundo adverso [5], se resuelve en El

---

[4] Cuando el criado Tello entra a casa de Inés, pregunta burlescamente:

¿Está en casa Melibea?
Que viene Calisto aquí.

ANA (criada): Aguarda un poco, Sempronio...
Lo cual es otro efecto de ambigüedad, de claro-oscuro, de ser y no ser, de vivir y morir. El autor y sus personajes saben que estas situaciones no son como las de La Celestina.

[5] «A esa lueñe tierra, mundo pusimos nombre» (SEM TOB DE CARRIÓN).

caballero de Olmedo en efectos de claro-oscuro, de juego a veces irónico entre la sensibilidad exquisita y la apicarada artimaña, entre las notas claras y las nubes sombrías. El mundo de Celestina y el de Melibea aparecen revueltos. Fabia habla a Inés y a su hermana de los enredos mujeriles de su padre don Pedro:

> Más de una vez me fió
> don Pedro sus mocedades;
> pero teniendo respeto
> a la que pudre, yo hacía
> (como quien se lo debía)
> mi obligación. En efecto,
> de diez mozas, no le daba
> cinco.

INÉS: ¡Qué virtud!

FABIA: No es poco,
> que era vuestro padre un loco:
> cuanta vía, tanta amaba.

Inés y su hermana son dos muchachas sueltas y alegres, de quienes Fabia no se recata. Antes de iniciar ella su labor de tercería, ya estaba Inés perdida de amor por don Alonso. Lo dice en claros y alegres ritmos, expresivos de la decisión a todo trance que Lope puso en una de sus más gentiles creaciones:

> Y todos dicen, Leonor,
> que nace de las estrellas...
> En el instante que vi
> este galán forastero,
> me dijo el alma: «Este quiero»,
> y yo le dije: Sea ansí».

Su hermana la llama «necia y atrevida» por acceder tan prestamente a hablar con su galán:

INÉS: ¿Cuándo el amor no lo fue?...
> Nadie del primero huye,
> porque dicen que le influye
> la misma naturaleza.

Y una vez que Inés ha entregado su amor, sabe tranquilizar a su inquieto y receloso amante, afirmando enérgicamente que no se casará con quien su padre ordene:

> No lo creas, porque yo
> diré a todo el mundo no,
> después que te dije «sí».

Tello reprocha a su amo tanta pertinaz desconfianza:

D. ALONSO: Yo, midiendo con los sueños
                  estos avisos del alma,
                  que con saber que son falsas
                  todas estas cosas, tengo
                  tan perdida la esperanza,
                  que no me aliento a vivir.
TELLO: Mal a doña Inés le pagas
                  aquella heroica firmeza
                  con que, atrevida, contrasta
                  los golpes de la fortuna.

Don Alonso es un héroe que afronta su morir decidida y melancólicamente, y a la vez vacila como enamorado frente a Inés, que, proa a la vida, todo lo arrostra, e incluso miente y arma engaños para proteger su amor. Don Alonso se reprocha sus indecisiones:

                  Bien sabe aquella noche, [6]
                  que pudiera ser mía.
                  Cobarde amor, ¿qué aguardas
                  cuando respetos miras?

Tal vez flotaba en el ánimo de Lope la impresión de las vacilaciones e incertidumbres de Calixto al comienzo de sus amores y después de la muerte de sus criados. Melibea, en cambio, podía ser evocada como una linda fierecilla ansiosa de derribar las puertas que la separaban de su amado. Fuera de eso, *La Celestina,* aludida o no concretamente, había enseñado a adquirir —por primera vez— conciencia de cómo expresar literariamente el conflicto entre los deseos y su objeto; y no en referencia a cualquier deseo, sino precisamente a los sentidos como móvil en que se cifraba la realidad y el destino de una vida.

Ahora bien, Lope de Vega no extrajo sus esquemas dramáticos de la obra de Fernando de Rojas; no hubiera sabido ni podido hacerlo. En aquélla los pobres humanos se estrellaban contra su propia humanidad, y no contra principios o fuerzas trascendentes a ella. Toda la retórica moral se hace añicos en *La Celestina* al chocar contra la marcha indetenible del curso de cada vida *deseosa,* como los sesos de Calixto se hacen pedazos contra los cantos de la calle. Buscar aquí ejemplaridad moral es tarea ociosa, pues los desastres en *La Celestina* son provocados por deflagraciones interiores. Desde el punto de vista de la moral y de la religión los amores voluntarios y consentidos por ambas partes, podrán ser deslices o pecados, no crímenes merecedores de pena capital. Las furias rencorosas de los individuos a quienes tales amores ofendan salen del círculo de la moral.

Calixto muere porque, llevado de su conciencia de caballero, se aparta de su Melibea para defender a los criados; los pies se le resbalan y

---

[6] «Noche» lo mismo que «amor» hacen aquí de sujetos personalizados.

llevan el cuerpo hacia la muerte, Melibea sacrifica su vida dentro del círculo cerrado y absoluto de su propia conciencia. Celestina muere mientras intenta proteger su vida con bravas razones; Sempronio y Pármeno se estrellan al huir, atolondradamente, acuciados por el miedo. Las moralidades y didactismos en *La Celestina* funcionan como una cantilena a destono con las acciones de la vida, para mostrar justamente su curso independiente y absoluto. Partiendo de aquí cabría llegar al arte de Shakespeare, no al de Lope de Vega.

¿Cuál es entonces la función de ciertos temas y nombres de personas celestinescos dentro de *El Caballero de Olmedo?* La intervención de Fabia para incitar a Inés no es en realidad indispensable. Ya en el comienzo declara don Alonso que los ojos de Inés

> no me miraron altivos,
> antes, con dulce mudanza,
> me dieron tal confianza
> que, con poca diferencia,
> pensando correspondencia,
> engendra amor esperanza...
> Mirándome sin hablarme,
> parece que me decía:
> «No os vais, don Alonso, a Olmedo,
> quedaos agora en Medina».

Fabia figura aquí, sobre todo, por sus conexiones con fuerzas misteriosas, diabólicas y de ultratumba:

> Apresta,
> fiero Habitador del centro,
> fuego accidental que abrase
> el pecho de esta doncella.

Y el criado Tello dice a la vieja Fabia más adelante:

> Y no me mandes tratar
> en materia de difuntos.

Al final de la obra, don Alonso ve primero una misteriosa aparición y oye luego la canción a su propia muerte:

> Que de noche le mataron,
> al caballero,
> la gala de Medina,
> la flor de Olmedo.

Piensa, el Caballero, que todo ello sea cosa de magia:

> Invención de Fabia es,
> que quiere, a ruego de Inés,
> hacer que no vaya a Olmedo.

La figura de Fabia —personaje secundario y algo borroso— se mueve en la imprecisa región en donde se confunden el mundo de ultra-tumba y el terrenal. Como reverso de la fe caballeresca o religiosa, lo demoníaco y mágico de *La Celestina* queda integrado, en cambio, dentro del proceso creado por deseos y designios en absoluto humanos; en el drama de Lope acontece lo contrario: el conflicto de los amores y de las ambiciosas codicias no se cierra y ahoga dentro de sí mismo. En Lope, el conflicto se abre hacia una trascendencia de deberes y de maldades: la filial devoción de don Alonso hacia sus padres, los celos y el despecho de un caballero de alma villana.

Dadas las preferencias hispánicas, la forma dramática exponía el choque angustioso del hacerse de la vida contra el halo de creencias e instituciones sociales que la circundaban —la familia, la clase nobiliaria, la realeza, la opinión, las ideas morales, a veces la fe religiosa [7]. En este caso del Caballero, Lope estructuró dramáticamente el encuentro de unas figuras humanas —reales en un espacio y en un tiempo— con la imagen, temblorosa de belleza y de misterio, de un personaje poético. Lo soñado y lo real interfieren mutuamente sus respectivas esferas poéticas gracias a la virtud de un cantarcillo arrebol fronterizo, fugaz y esperanzado, que a la vez separa y liga para siempre dos mundos poéticos. El caballero muerto y vivo, en los sones de su cantar, va a estarlo también en la representación de su conflictiva existencia. La pugna para lograr el amor de una linda y airosa doncella, sometida al mandato paterno y al asedio de un nada grato cortejador, esa pugna se proyecta a su vez sobre un plano en el cual se enfrentan el amador de una belleza visible y la imagen soñada de una vida que fue-es «gala de Medina, flor de Olmedo».

Tal es la realidad pluridimensional hecha de contradicciones y armonías, creada por Lope de Vega en una unidad en que se integran las visiones de lo próximo y elemental y la perspectiva de lejanías vagorosas, melancólicas e inquietantes:

> imaginaciones
> sólo un ejercicio triste
> del alma que me atormenta,
> de sueños y fantasías,
> si bien falsas ilusiones,
> han nacido estas razones...»

---

[7] Esto explicaría que la estructura del drama lopesco perdurara hasta el siglo XVIII, y que *La Celestina* y el *Quijote* quedaran como aisladas maravillas (las imitaciones de *La Celestina* no invalidan mi idea). El *Quijote* no dio ocasión a desarrollos independientes y originales antes de Pérez Galdós (en *Fortunata y Jacinta*, *Torquemada*, etc.); pero Galdós ya conocía las novelas europeas, hechas posibles por Cervantes. Habrá que pensar más en las razones interiores de los astros hispánicos que no se «constelaron»: Rojas, Vives, Cervantes, Velázquez, Goya. Ninguno de ellos hizo escuela.

EL «IR» Y «VENIR» COMO ESTRUCTURA

Las nociones de *ir* y *venir* refieren a un abstracto moverse progresiva y regresivamente, más bien que a la acción concreta de *ir* o *venir* a algún lugar. El movimiento vale aquí como actividad vacilante y no hacia metas predeterminadas. Pocas veces se muestra tan clara la dimensión artística, la función sinfónica del lenguaje en el teatro de Lope de Vega [8].

Esta obra fue concebida en clave de tránsito entre el vivir y el morir, sin hacer morada cierta en el uno o en el otro. En el cantar tomado como fondo incitante la imagen de la muerte aparecía vivificada poéticamente, salvada como «flor» y como «gala» muy humanizadas. El cero aniquilante de la nada se potenciaba en visión y melodía de vida, capaces de ser gravadas indefinidamente. El genio de Lope transformó esa porción de mínima poesía en una amplia estructura en la cual realidad y fantasía creadora se alternaban en reflejos, a su vez alternados, de vida y muerte, de esperanza y de engaño, de pasión baja y de noble y exquisita delicia, de acción justa y debida y de efecto desastroso.

Las palabras se proveen de dimensión simbólica y evocadora. *Venir* a ver a Inés es caminar hacia la vida; lleva en cambio a la muerte la acción tan loable como obligada de *ir* don Alonso a ver a sus padres. El tema de la partida y de la llegada, en sí carente de relieve, es realzado por la intensidad y la intención puestas en él.

Don Alonso describe súbitamente la belleza de Inés:

> Por la tarde salió Inés
> a la feria de Medina,
> tan hermosa que la gente
> pensaba que amanecía...
> mirándome sin hablarme,
> parece que me decía:
> «No os *vais*, don Alonso, a Olmedo,
> *quedaos* agora en Medina».

Pero dentro de la misma permanencia del quedarse rebrota, se rehace, el tema del ir y venir, constitutivo de la existencia poética de don Alonso. Encuentra éste de nuevo a Inés en la Iglesia:

> Salió esta mañana a misa
> ya con galas de señora,
> no labradora fingida...
> Miró a su hermana, y entrambas
> se encontraron en la risa...
> En una capilla entraron...

---

[8] Recuérdese cómo del soneto —en la forma dramática inventada por Lope— emana la noción de soledad; el ritmo largo de los tercetos endecasílabos refleja la importancia de las personas o de lo tratado por ellas, etc. La conciencia de vivir entre dos mundos, no siempre conciliables, suscitaba interferencias sinestéticas, cruces de dimensiones y formas procedentes de diferentes zonas de arte.

> En ella estuve turbado;
> ya el guante se me caía,
> ya el rosario, que los ojos
> de Inés *iban* y *venían*.

Recordando más tarde su encuentro, dice Inés a su hermana:

> Sus ojos causa me dan
> para ponerlos en él
> pues pienso que en ellos vi
> el cuidado que me dio...;
> Pero ya se *habrá partido*.
> LEONOR: No le miro yo de suerte
> que pueda vivir sin verte,

es decir, sin retornar a Medina.

En el mismo Acto I, cuando el Caballero cree falsamente que Inés no corresponde a su amor, da orden de partir a su criado:

> Ensilla, Tello, que *a Olmedo*
> *nos hemos de ir* esta tarde.
> TELLO: ¿Cómo, si anochece ya?
> D. ALONSO: Pues ¿qué, quieres que me *mate*?

Permanecer en Medina con la desesperación de no saberse amado equivale a darse muerte. Se preludian así los motivos del tema fundamental.

El segundo acto se inicia sinfónicamente con una llamada a la continuidad lírica subyacente a las mutaciones de la acción:

> D. ALONSO: Tengo el morir por mejor,
> Tello, que vivir sin ver.
> TELLO: Temo que se ha de saber
> este *tu secreto amor:*
> que con tanto *ir* y *venir*
> de Olmedo a Medina creo
> que a los dos da tu deseo
> que sentir, y aun que decir.

En *La Celestina*, el secreto de amor no se explica por circunstancias externas a la concepción poética. En *La Celestina*, el secreto del amor extrasocial limita el área en donde los personajes simultáneamente se labran y aniquilan sus vidas, en absoluta —o inmanente— soledad consigo mismos y fuera del círculo de sus iguales. En la obra de Lope el movimiento dramático está impulsado por circunstancias exteriores a él: el amor aquí nació y fue vivido socialmente (en una feria, en una iglesia, en casa de Inés, no en un huerto secluso). El secreto de don Alonso e Inés existe en un ámbito social muy manifiesto (el padre, fiestas públicas), existe como un peligro para Inés, destinada por su padre a otro galán, en paralelismo con las inquietantes idas y venidas de Medina a Olmedo, como rigurosa alternancia de destinos, superiores y ajenos al designio de la voluntad. El mundo poético de Lope de Vega no era como el de Rojas y el de Cervantes —o como el de Shakespeare (pasiones consuntivas de Hamlet, de Macbeth, del rey Lear).

En el mundo de la comedia, todo lo que sale al encuentro de la vida de un personaje es polarizado, o hacia su centro, o hacia la periferia; está visto y sentido en doble perspectiva, en la de un conflicto cuyos términos opuestos se proyectan recíprocamente sus sentidos, sus derechos, diríamos, a existir y a valer. En *El castigo sin venganza* esa dinámica estructura es clarísima —no la llamaría «fórmula», porque éstas son esquemas, no creaciones vitalizadas y únicas. El conflicto que da lugar a tal polarización no se plantea únicamente en el área visible de lo social (opinión, honra, autoridad), pues el genio de Lope llegó incluso a oponer conflictivamente la poetización de lo poético y la poetización de lo real. Es lo que acontece en *El caballero de Olmedo,* en donde el muerto caballero del cantar revive y endereza su alma hacia el amor de la linda Inés, la gentil labradorcilla vista en la feria de Medina. Y todo el drama consistirá en el movimiento vertiginoso de dos seres lopescos, entre el polo de la vida y el de la muerte, entre las vocales claras y alegres de Inés y Medina, y las sombrías y lúgubres de Olmedo y don Alonso (Lope, que supo de todo, también se dio cuenta de esto, y lo dice en otra obra, que las *íes* son placenteras, y las *úes* son tristes). Todo ello dispuesto armónica y sinfónicamente, con anticipos de impresiones y efectos que en el siglo XX parecían novedad en Pirandello o en Cocteau. En *El caballero de Olmedo* adquieren dimensión y virtud poéticas —es decir, un halo y un más allá problemáticos, no agotables en razones—, adquieren dimensión y virtud poéticas el ir y el venir de uno a otro punto, los ojos, las andanzas, las almas siempre transientes y nunca posadas, y, en fin, el intento esperanzado, aunque quimérico, de iniciar un amor de ultratumba, de volver de donde nadie retornó, de asirse desesperadamente a la imagen de una belleza terrena, a la cual se le dice: «por vivir os vengo a ver». Y ella no entiende, y él no comprende por qué no entiende. Ya a comienzos del siglo XVII hubo en la literatura de Europa personajes en busca de autor, que se creaban a sí mismos en el dialéctico vaivén del vivir-morir.

UNAMUNO Y ORTEGA: LEER UNA NOVELA, HACER UNA NOVELA

by

LUIS FERNANDEZ CIFUENTES

Explícitamente, *Ideas sobre la novela,* de Ortega y Gasset (Madrid, 1924-1925), es una reflexión instigada por Pío Baroja, por sus ideas literarias y su obra novelesca. Muchos de los postulados generales de Ortega habían nacido antes como graves críticas a la obra narrativa de Baroja, en «Anatomía de un alma dispersa» (1910) e «Ideas sobre Pío Baroja» (1916). Sin embargo, el antagonista más pertinaz, más radical y complejo de *Ideas sobre la novela* —y del trabajo que lo acompaña en su primera edición completa, *La deshumanización del arte*— es un texto aparecido pocos meses después, casi anulado por el destierro y la censura y probablemente escrito en completa ignorancia de los últimos trabajos de Ortega: *Cómo se hace una novela,* de Unamuno (París-Hendaya, 1924-1927).

Los avatares de la publicación y difusión de los dos textos son, en este caso, parte de su mensaje y un indicio del profundo desacuerdo que los emparentaba: *La deshumanización del arte* e *Ideas sobre la novela* no sólo alcanzaron a su público repetidamente, primero desde la prensa y en seguida desde el libro, sino que lograron también desencadenar todas las devociones y condenas que son síntoma del éxito. *Cómo se hace una novela* recorrió paralelamente un periplo laborioso y siempre desviado: se publicó, primero, traducido, en el *Mercure de France;* más tarde, en Buenos Aires, retraducido, «bastante incorrecto en la puntuación y en varios detalles lingüísticos»; y, por fin, en España, en 1950, en «versión abreviada» que omitía «poco menos de un 7 por 100» del original[1]. Esta trayectoria le privó no ya del éxito, sino de la mera y elemental audiencia.

Por esa época (1924-1927), hacía ya años que el dilatado y a veces virulento debate intelectual entre Unamuno y Ortega prescindía del enfrentamiento directo y se alimentaba de ecos, de alusiones en plural, de insultos solapados. En este nuevo encuentro, el más persistente de esos ecos remite a una circunstancia memorable y a los textos que la consignaron: en 1924 Unamuno fue desterrado a la isla de Fuerteventura por sus actividades políticas y sus ataques al gobierno de Primo de Rivera;

---

[1] Introducción de PAUL OLSON a su edición de *Cómo se hace una novela* (Madrid: Guadrrama, 1977), pp. 26 y 27. Se trata, creo, de la única edición completa y bien anotada, en la desafortunada historia editorial de este texto. A ella remiten las citas del presente trabajo.

a principios del verano logró huir a Francia y poco después comenzaba en París la redacción de *Cómo se hace una novela.* Pero Unamuno había incluido en sus críticas —sus insultos— no sólo a la dictadura, sino también a los intelectuales de *El Sol,* el periódico donde Ortega marcaba la pauta y donde acababa de publicar los primeros capítulos de *La deshumanización del arte.* Con ofendida dignidad, *El Sol* esperó a que Unamuno se refugiara en París para darle pública respuesta. En ella incluyó esta advertencia:

> Debemos decir, puesto que ahora, sin freno ya, va a lanzarse a la política, cuán perturbadora puede ser su acción en la política. España necesita, para reconstituirse, que cada cual trabaje en su propia esfera de acción. La del Sr. Unamuno está bien delimitada por sus estudios y sus aptitudes, y fuera de ella sólo puede actuar como disolvente y desconcertador [2].

Este meticuloso deslinde entre lo que pertenece a la esfera de la política y a la de las letras constituía ya entonces la base de todas las ideas de Ortega sobre el arte nuevo y la novela del momento:

> Creo que el poeta joven, cuando poetiza, se propone simplemente ser poeta. Ya veremos cómo todo el arte nuevo, coincidiendo en esto con la nueva ciencia, con la nueva política, con la nueva vida, en fin, repugna ante todo la confusión de fronteras [3].

Ortega puede dictaminar, en consecuencia, que «la voz del poeta» es «pura voz anónima [...] que sabe aislarse de su hombre circundante» [4]. Se trata de un problema epistemológico que afecta por igual al autor y al lector: «la percepción de la realidad vivida y la percepción de la forma artística son, en principio, incompatibles por requerir una acomodación diferente de nuestro aparato perceptor» [5]. En el caso de la novela, este criterio le permite, por ejemplo, aislar al «hombre Dostoievsky» del «novelista Dostoievsky». Al exponer esta dicotomía Ortega recurre al mismo término con que en otra ocasión había definido al hombre Unamuno: «Podrá ser cierto que el hombre Dostoievsky fuese un pobre energúmeno o, si gusta más, un profeta; pero el novelista Dostoievsky fue un *homme de lettres,* un solícito oficial de un oficio admirable, nada más» [6]. En último término, la distinción conduce al concepto de «herme-

[2] *El Sol,* editorial del 23 de julio de 1924.
[3] *La deshumanización del arte* (Madrid: Alianza, 1981), p. 35. Parece imprescindible citar por esta «nueva edición», puesto que, según asegura PAULINO GARAGORRI en «Nota preliminar», ha sido «revisada y corregida conforme a los originales» (p. 9).
[4] Idem, p. 36.
[5] Idem, p. 30.
[6] *Ideas sobre la novela,* en *Ideas sobre el teatro y la novela* (Madrid: Alianza, 1892), p. 32. Edición avalada con los mismos créditos que la de *La deshumanización.* En adelante, las páginas de *Ideas sobre la novela* acompañarán directamente al texto de la cita. «Energúmeno» fue el término que Ortega dedicó a Unamuno en un artículo de *El Imparcial* (27 de septiembre de 1909), recogido ahora en

tismo» con que Ortega separa a la novela de la historia (p. 47), a la novela de la vida: «el hermetismo no es sino la forma especial que adopta en la novela el imperativo genérico del arte: la intrascendencia» (p. 47), y consiste en «aislar al lector de su horizonte real y aprisionarlo en un pequeño horizonte hermético e imaginario que es el ámbito interior de la novela» (p. 44).

Esta compulsiva, persistente distinción, termina con una queja que no pudo tener entonces objeto más íntegro, inmediato y obstinado que la actitud de Unamuno:

> Hay gentes que quieren serlo todo. ¡No contentos con pretender ser artistas, quieren ser políticos, mandar y dirigir muchedumbres, o quieren ser profetas, administrar la divinidad e imperar sobre las conciencias! Que ellos tengan tan ubérrima pretensión para sus personas no sería ilícito; mas tal ambición les mueve a querer que las cosas contengan también ese multiforme destino. Y esto es lo que parece imposible. Las artes se vengan de todo el que quiere ser con ellas más que artista, haciendo que su obra no llegue siquiera a ser artística. Igualmente, la política del poeta se queda siempre en ingenuo ademán inválido (p. 47).

Unamuno respondió expresamente a la advertencia de *El Sol* y de forma indirecta a la queja de Ortega en los párrafos más airados de *Cómo se hace una novela:*

> Existen desdichados que me aconsejan dejar la política. Lo que ellos con un gesto de indefinido desdén, que no es más que miedo, miedo de eunucos o de impotentes o de muertos, llaman política y me aseguran que debería consagrarme a mis cátedras, a mis estudios, a mis novelas, a mis poemas, a mi vida. No quieren saber que mis cátedras, mis estudios, mis novelas, mis poemas son política (p. 89).

> Creer que se pueda hacer política sin novela o novela sin política es no saber lo que se quiere creer (p. 104).

Entre las citas y glosas de lecturas que son parte esencial de *Cómo se hace una novela,* predominan las de las cartas de amor de Giuseppe Mazzini (1805-1872), cuya actitud resumirá y adoptara (adaptará) Unamuno: «Política, religión y poesía fueron en él y para él una sola cosa, una íntima trinidad» (p. 88). Es una suerte de elogio que Unamuno extiende a otros autores proscritos, cuyo prestigio acaso le consolaba: Dante, Víctor Hugo, Lamartine. Paralelamente, los intelectuales partidarios del deslinde son objeto de insultos casi siempre generales («miserable escán-

Ensayos sobre la Generación del 98 (Madrid: Alianza, 1981), p. 37. El «nada más» con que Ortega termina la frase remite a otro texto de mensaje muy parecido, dedicado a Azorín en 1913, cuando se celebró su abandono de la política: «Es usted un artista exquisito que ha elaborado unas ciertas páginas egregias, cuya belleza pervivirá libre de corrupción. Nada más.» *Ensayos sobre la Generación del 98,* p. 209.

dalo», «mezquinos y menguados cotarros de hombres de letras», p. 52; «la castrada intelectualidad española», p. 84), pero a veces inequívocamente concretos: la figura de Ortega se disimula apenas en el plural de ese «sabios» y «filósofos que se alimentan en España y de España» a los que Unamuno llama «viles» (p. 89) y «prostitutos» (p. 90)[7].

La ira de Unamuno es sólo parte de un conjunto sostenido por su extraordinaria coherencia. El principio de la integración, la unidad, la indiferenciación (términos de Ortega[8]) con que Unamuno se enfrenta a las propuestas intelectuales de separación y aislamiento, origina una laboriosa teoría de la novela —*teoría* que se justifica a sí misma como *novela* (p. 58)— minuciosamente opuesta a las conclusiones de Ortega —que cabalmente abogaba porque el texto de la novela excluyera toda referencia teórica a sí mismo (p. 34).

El campo fundamental de este desacuerdo son las relaciones entre el lector, el autor y el personaje. El primer párrafo de *Ideas sobre la novela* presenta a Ortega como exclusivamente lector («lector incalificado», p. 31), por oposición a «novelistas y críticos» (pp. 15-16). Más adelante establecerá un nuevo deslinde que el primer párrafo dejaba implícito: se trata de un «lector del día» (p. 24), cuyo gusto, refinado por una larga experiencia de lecturas (pp. 18, 53) le inclina hacia la «contemplación» (pp. 36-37) y a preferir, en novelas de muy escaso y funcional argumento, la «presentación» (p. 20) de un mundo cerrado y denso de «psicologías interesantes» (p. 54). Frente a él, el «primitivo lector» (p. 21) o «lector mediocre» (p. 51) optaría aún por la «acción» (pp. 36-37) y, sin necesidad de complejos caracteres ni de forma presentativa, aspiraría a saciar su «sed de dramatismo» (p. 41) en la «narración» (p. 20) de «aventuras insólitas» (p. 43). Un último deslinde completa los dos anteriores: no cabe confundir al autor con el personaje, ni al personaje con el lector (o con la realidad del lector). En el primer caso, se trataría de una «curiosa ilusión óptica»: la que, por ejemplo, «atribuye a Dostoievsky el carácter inconsciente, turbulento de sus personajes y hace del novelista mismo una figura más de sus novelas» (pp. 31-32). En el segundo caso, «se supone torpemente que la psicología en la novela es la misma de la realidad» (p. 54).

Del aislamiento que así predicaba Ortega para los tres elementos en cuestión (autor, lector y personaje [o relato en sí]) se desprenden ciertos postulados formales: el autor del relato no puede permitirse interferencia alguna que rompa el hermetismo del texto, que delate su factura,

---

[7] Un eco más elaborado de la misma dicotomía intelectual lo recibe Unamuno en Hendaya en 1927 a través de *La Gaceta Literaria*. En el número dedicado a Góngora, Benjamín Jarnés declaraba que su poesía se aliaba con la «tranquila inteligencia» frente a «la azulada fantasía» y la «llama oscilante de la pasión». Unamuno responde: «mentira, mentira, mentira» (p. 88). Más remota y encubierta, Unamuno cree encontrar aún esta misma disyuntiva en un artículo de Azorín donde se alude al «mecanismo» de la novela: «organismo y no mecanismo», responde Unamuno (p. 106).

[8] *La deshumanización del arte*, p. 115. José Ferrater Mora prefiere hablar de «indistinción constitutiva». *Unamuno, bosquejo de una filosofía* (Buenos Aires: Editorial Sudamericana, 1957), p. 120.

que lo remita a la realidad. «Balzac, leído hoy, nos despierta de nuestro ensueño novelesco a cada página porque nos golpeamos contra su andamiaje de novelista» (p. 34). Balzac se ha vuelto «irresistible», «inaceptable» (p. 19). En cuanto a la lectura de novelas, ha dejado de consistir en una participación ingenua e indiscriminada para convertirse en un cálculo laborioso y experto al que se prestan muy pocos relatos: sólo ante las grandes novelas de Stendhal, Dostoievsky, Proust, «el lector se ve forzado a reconstruir, entre vacilaciones y correcciones, temeroso siempre de haber errado, el perfil definitivo de [las] mudables criaturas» que le presentan (p. 34). Novelas menos logradas aburren a su sensibilidad superior (pp. 18, 23). Por su parte, el relato, los personajes, se ven relegados a la invención y no cabe ya una mezcla de horizontes imaginarios y horizontes reales como la que ofrecía, por ejemplo, la novela histórica: «el intento de hacer compenetrarse ambos mundos sólo produce la mutua negación de uno y otro» (p. 47).

Rigurosamente fiel a la simetría de sus propios deslindes, Ortega aprovechará el paradigma de los pronombres para introducirla en su mismo discurso: en *Ideas sobre la novela,* «yo» es siempre, exclusivamente, el lector-Ortega; y las «ideas» que redacta aparecen protegidas por un marco de prevenciones («soy bastante indocto», p. 15) y disculpas («si yo viera que otras personas mejor tituladas... no me atrevería..., p. 15) que le permiten embozar la *autoridad* accidental de su escritura. Con el mismo objeto, el verbo *escribir* se evita a lo largo de todo el párrafo, sustituido por «decir», «meditar», «editar los pensamientos» y «enunciar a la buena de Dios» (pp. 15-16). Entre tanto, la tercera persona es, en la primera línea, un novelista concreto, Pío Baroja; luego, «novelistas y críticos literarios»; y, por fin, «algún escritor joven que está escribiendo una novela». El «yo» lector de Ortega se desvinculará expresamente de todos ellos con una confesión inequívoca: «Yo en su caso temblaría» (p. 16). Más adelante, Ortega podrá referirse con cierta frecuencia a un «lector» abstracto en tercera persona, pero cuando su discurso le obliga a enfrentar autor, lector y personaje-relato, el primero y el último serán siempre la tercera persona (la no-persona, no-presencia señalada por Benveniste), mientras el segundo se refugia en la comunidad de la primera persona del plural: «Hace falta que el autor sepa primero atraernos al ámbito cerrado que es su novela y luego cortarnos toda retirada» (p. 45); «en este sentido me atrevería a decir que sólo es novelista quien posee el don de olvidar él, y de rechazo hacernos olvidar a nosotros, la realidad que deja fuera de su novela» (p. 46). El «yo» de este perfilado lector gobierna el discurso de Ortega, un discurso del lector sobre la lectura que, si hubiera que definirlo por sus propios principios, se catalogaría dedicidamente como *no-novela.*

Entre los signos de la totalidad y la indiferenciación a que aspiraba el texto de Unamuno, la manipulación de los pronombres es acaso el más significativo. Provisionalmente, el primer párrafo introduce un «yo» que insiste en «escribir» (p. 36) y que más adelante se incluirá a veces entre «nosotros ,los autores, los poetas» (p. 63). Pero esa circunscripción será repetidamente borrada, deshecha, y el «yo» singular del comienzo acabará por dispersarse en una serie de «yos» referidos igual al autor que al lector y al personaje. El penúltimo párrafo de la novela (con el que terminan algunas de sus ediciones) lo resume así:

> Y yo estoy aquí, en el destierro, a la puerta de España y como su ujier, no para lucir y lucirme, sino para alumbrar y alumbrarme, para hacer nuestra novela [...]. Y al decir que estoy para alumbrarme, con este «me» no quiero referirme, lector mío, a mí solamente, sino a tu yo, a nuestros yos. Que no es lo mismo nosotros que yos (p. 113).

Cierto equívoco, sin embargo, permanece, porque entre yo, tú, él, ellos y nosotros, o la proliferación de «yos» que los sustituye, nunca se establece una perfecta identidad. Por parte del autor, el nombre propio que en la cubierta del libro precede al título se reproduce en el texto a la vez como «yo, Miguel de Unamuno» y como él, «al que llamamos así» (p. 65), «el Unamuno de mi leyenda, de mi novela» (p. 66). Más aún, estos yo-él del autor, que comparten los mismos shifters o indicadores, serán reducidos exclusivamente a «él» durante las ocho páginas del «Retrato de Unamuno por Jean Cassou», traducido —reescrito— por Unamuno para su propio texto con la siguiente justificación: «el lector comprenderá que si lo incluyo aquí traduciéndolo es para comentarlo» (p. 47). Y dedica las diez páginas del «Comentario» a restaurar la tortuosa identidad entre «él» y «yo». Por último, cuando ese «yo» del autor se ve obligado a proponer un protagonista para su novela, no puede distinguirlo enteramente de sí mismo: «Habría que inventar, primero, un personaje central que sería, naturalmente, yo mismo» (p. 66); pero en seguida dispersará y corregirá su nombre propio (de «Miguel de Unamuno y Jugo y Larraza» a «U. Jugo de la Raza») para desdoblar la identidad que los une, e inscribirá al personaje-yo en el relato como un él que, sin embargo, repite tantas veces las mismas palabras del yo-autor (pp. 72-73 y 76).

Al mismo tiempo, «yo» —autor o personaje— es el más voraz de los lectores: lector de un «libro fatídico» que «le gana enormemente, le saca de sí, le introduce en el personaje de la novela [...], le identifica con aquel otro» (p. 67); o lector de su propia escritura (p. 91) y de las escrituras de otros a las que adoptará/adaptará en su discurso, con una canibalización constante y declarada: «Lo propio de una individualidad que lo es, que es y existe, consiste en alimentarse de las demás individualidades y darse a ellas en alimento» (p. 55). De este modo, el «yo» de Unamuno será también —borrosamente, a través de una reescritura de sus palabras— el yo de Cassou, Mazzini, Dante, Víctor Hugo, Lamartine, Balzac. Un pronombre posesivo que el relato prodiga suele servir de puente entre los «yos» dispersados: «mi yo» (p. 113), «mi Don Quijote» (p. 75), «mi Jugo de la Raza» (p. 68), «mi Cassou» (p. 57), «lector mío» (p. 103). etc.

Ejerce así Unamuno —frente a Ortega— un derecho que le concede la teoría enunciada en su discurso: de acuerdo con ella, enajenar al autor del lector y el personaje no es más que una falacia intelectual. En primer lugar, Unamuno cancela la supuesta distancia entre el autor y el personaje reconociendo en toda forma de escritura una labor autobiográfica:

> Toda novela, toda obra de ficción, todo poema, cuando es vivo es autobiográfico. Todo ser de ficción, todo personaje poético que crea un autor hace parte del autor mismo [...]. Los grandes historiadores son también autobiógrafos. Los tiranos que ha descrito Tácito son él mismo (p. 63).

Alfonso XIII, Primo de Rivera, Martínez Anido «son otras tantas creaciones mías, partes de mí» (p. 63). Inevitablemente, el libro que lee Jugo de la Raza —y cuya lectura o abandono es el tema del relato central— es una «confesión autobiográfico-romántica» (p. 67). Se borra de este modo todo horizonte entre el interior y el exterior del relato, entre la ficción y la realidad [9]. La combatida intromisión del autor se vuelve una necesidad y «la supuesta impersonalidad u objetividad de Flaubert», una mentira (p. 63). Cassou lo formula con palabras que se dirían del mismo Ortega: en las obras «ilimitadas y monstruosas» de Unamuno «nos detienen a cada momento intervenciones personales, y con una truculencia y familiar insolencia, el curso de la ficción» (p. 43). Fiel a la autobiografía, el texto de Unamuno acabará por incluir su propio diario.

Unamuno propondrá también una clasificación de lectores que invierte limpiamente la establecida por Ortega. De una parte, «un puro contemplador, un mero lector, lo que es algo absurdo e inhumano» (p. 102); «esos lectores impenetrables [...] que no saben comerse libros ni salirse de sí mismos» (p. 54), entre los cuales contaba a los intelectuales españoles. De otra, *nosotros,* «todos los que vivimos principalmente de la lectura y en la lectura, [que] no podemos separar de los personajes poéticos o novelescos a los históricos [...]. Todo es para nosotros libro, lectura» (p. 63). Este lector es (son) Jugo de la Raza y Unamuno y el *implied reader* de su relato. *Cómo se hace una novela* es «la novela de su lectura de la novela, la novela del lector [del lector actor, del lector para quien leer es vivir lo que lee]» (p. 75. Corchetes de Unamuno). Para definir esta forma de lectura Unamuno recurre una y otra vez a un lugar común cuyo carácter metafórico había diluido la costumbre: «devorar un libro» (y el sinónimo menos convencional, «comer un libro»). La insistencia y el contexto de Unamuno restauran de golpe su vigor metafórico pero a la vez lo ponen en tela de juicio (como sucederá con otras metáforas igualmente apagadas: el libro de la vida, el teatro del mundo). «Devorar un libro» se convierte en un rito mucho más sagrado y trascendente de lo que permitía prever la metáfora popular. La escritura devora al escritor como la lectura al lector, y viceversa. Unamuno se recuerda en París devorando *Peau de chagrin* (p. 62) o las noticias que

[9] Inés Azar describe detalladamente la *mise en abîme* establecida por los tres relatos: el de Unamuno, el de Jugo y el de la novela de Jugo. «La estructura novelesca de *Cómo se hace una novela*», MLN, 85 (1970), p. 194.

llegaban de España (pp. 76, 80), pero también devorado por la escritura de sus propias cartas (p. 69) y sobre todo «devorándome al escribir el relato que titulé: *Cómo se hace una novela*» (p. 35). Para este lector-autor, la disyuntiva orteguiana de acción o contemplación resulta impertinente; sólo admitirá la «acción que es contemplativa como la contemplación es activa» (p. 104).

Unamuno anula igualmente la distancia autor-lector, acaso la más remota e irreductible de las que decretaba Ortega. La lectura de Unamuno compagina dos relaciones: una de continuidad entre autor y lector, por la que el primero prolonga su «existencia» (p. 55) en el segundo («las entrañas del organismo vivo de la novela, que son las entrañas mismas del novelista, del autor. Y las del lector identificado con él por la lectura [...]. Porque su vida íntima, entrañada, novelesca, se continúa en la de sus lectores», pp. 106-107). Otra de recreación, por la que el lector se vuelve autor de la novela con la «asistencia» (p. 55) del primero («Y así, cuando les cuento cómo se hace una novela, o sea, cómo estoy haciendo su propia novela, la novela que es la vida de cada uno de ellos», p. 57). En este proceso de indiferenciación entre autor y lector (y personaje), Unamuno llegará a interrogarse sobre el mismo problema que algunos años más tarde ha inquietado extensamente a filósofos y críticos literarios: ¿Quién es el autor? ¿Quién crea o autoriza el significado de las palabras que construyen el relato? ¿Cuál es el margen de coincidencia entre lo que uno escribe y lo que él mismo, más tarde, y otros leen? «Y oyendo los juicios que emiten sobre mis dichos, mis escritos y mis actos, pienso: "¿no será acaso que pronuncio otras palabras que las que me oigo pronunciar o que se me oye pronunciar otras que las que pronuncio?"» (p. 74)[10]. Pero él mismo admite en otro momento que esta incertidumbre es un precio voluntario por la supervivencia de su obra, «porque la hago de tal modo que pueda ser otra para el lector que la lea comiéndola. ¿Qué me importa que no leas, lector, lo que yo quise poner en ella, si es que lees lo que te enciende en vida?» (p. 50). Unamuno concluye que, realmente, escritura y lectura son un mismo y único ejercicio, puesto que toda escritura es en verdad la reescritura de uno o más textos anteriores (cuando menos, «del libro de la vida, de la historia que vivo, y del libro de la naturaleza», p. 48) y la verdadera lectura no consiste nunca en la identificación o el reconocimiento pasivo, sino más bien en una recreación del lector, incontrolable y apenas previsible para el escritor original:

> Y todo lector que sea hombre de dentro, humano, es, lector, autor de lo que lee y está leyendo. Esto que ahora lees aquí, lector, te lo estás diciendo tú a ti mismo, y es tan tuyo como mío [...]. Y no te sorprenda el que así te meta mis lecturas de azar y te meta en ellas (pp. 102-103).

---

[10] Sobre la constancia con que recurre este motivo en la obra de Unamuno véase la nota 112 de Paul Olson en la edición que cito.

La indiferenciación de autor, lector y personaje comporta un borroso, ilimitado concepto de novela: «no hay nada más que comedia y novela» (p. 93); «y no hay más que leyenda, o sea, novela» (p. 107). El término «novela» —como de hecho cualquier otro— resulta insuficiente para el concepto de Unamuno y, siendo acaso el término más prodigado en el texto (desde su mismo título), casi nunca deja de ir acompañado por otro u otros que a la vez lo desplazan y lo ensanchan: «mi novela, historia, comedia, tragedia o como se quiera» (p. 94). «Novela» se vuelve el punto de confluencia de dos coordenadas, una de trayectoria libresca (comedia, autobiografía, tragedia, libro, novela, leyenda); otra de trayectoria real, existencial (vida, historia). Unamuno no sólo rehusa distinguir entre las dos, sino que favorece los términos ambiguos, que pudieran ubicarse en cualquiera de ellas, sobre todo el de «historia». Así, mientras Ortega se ocupaba de delimitar el concepto y denunciaba con especial alarma la posible contaminación «histórica» de la novela (p. 46), Unamuno prefería sobre todos el término «historia» para construir con él el desenfocado rótulo de su discurso (pp. 57, 63, 67, 71, 76, ..., etc.).

Frente al concepto inclusivo que Unamuno tenía de la novela, el de Ortega desvela su inflexible exclusividad. En una rigurosa concatenación de deslindes, Ortega comienza por aislar herméticamente al arte de la realidad (a la novela de la vida; a la novela de la historia). Pero entre el arte en general y la novela en particular, Ortega percibirá una nueva distancia que le obliga a componer dos tratados diferentes y a menudo opuestos: *La deshumanización del arte* e *Ideas sobre la novela*. Dentro de este trabajo aislado y aislante, la novela recibirá todavía otros dos límites: uno, de tipo sincrónico, que la aísla de los otros géneros literarios (p. 36) y sobre todo de la lírica y el ensayo: la novela «no puede ser más que novela» (p. 47); otro, de tipo diacrónico, que distingue entre novelas del pasado y del presente. Ortega insiste en aclarar que sus ideas se refieren «tan sólo a la novela moderna» (p. 42), «la novela en el sentido más actual del término» (p. 43), puesto que del pasado al presente la novela no sólo ha cambiado de procedimientos, ha mejorado también de calidad: «la última perfección [...] es casi siempre una perfección de la hora última» (p. 52) y «hoy parecen pueriles [...] autores que ayer parecían excelentes» (p. 53).

Ortega consigue de este modo una extraordinaria fijación de perfiles, que afecta tanto al cuerpo de esa novela última o perfecta, como a su propio discurso. La novela iluminada por Ortega comparte con las artes en general la «perfecta claridad» (p. 17) a que aspiran sus mismas «ideas»: «la unidad indiferenciada, caótica, informe, sin arquitectura anatómica, sin disciplina regente [...] no puede continuar»[11]. Unamuno disiente una vez más: el ejercicio más meticuloso y brillante de *Cómo se hace una novela* consiste en impedir que nada, en su discurso, exista de manera fija, completa, unívoca. Ya en el «Prólogo» advierte Unamuno sobre el peligro de la «fijación»:

---

[11] *La deshumanización del arte*, p. 15.

En cuanto un pensamiento nuestro queda fijado por la escritura, expresado, cristalizado, queda ya muerto y no es más nuestro que será un día bajo tierra nuestro esqueleto. La historia, lo único vivo, es el presente eterno, el momento huidero que se queda pasando, que pasa quedándose, y la literatura no es más que muerte (p. 37).

Identificar historia y novela sería acaso el modo de redimir a la escritura, pero Unamuno tampoco alcanza esa seguridad, y es precisamente la duda —es decir, lo no fijado o decidido— lo que constituye «el tuétano de mi novela, de mi historia»: «¿Queda el escrito? ¿Se lleva el viento la palabra? ¿Tiene la letra, el esqueleto más esencia duradera, más eternidad, que el verbo, que la carne?» (p. 97). El gesto —sin principio ni fin— de Unamuno va a consistir en escribir, borrar y reescribir lo escrito, leer y reescribir lo leído, y evitar así la fijación, la inmovilidad del texto [12].

El empeño de Unamuno puede reconocerse ya en el título: un discurso titulado *Cómo se hace una novela,* que exige para sí mismo la categoría de novela, sólo puede estar postulando que el relato sea un proyecto incesante más que una acabada realización. Mediante una tortuosa estratagema etimológica, Unamuno llegará a emparentar *novela, problema* y *proyecto,* para concluir que cualquiera de los tres presuponen «no tanto una solución, en el sentido analítico o disolutivo, cuanto una construcción, una creación» (p. 104). «Y no hay más que camino», añadirá en otro pasaje (p. 100).

Todavía antes de emprender una lectura seguida del relato puede reconocer el lector un nuevo síntoma de movilización: lo que se le ofrece no es un discurso continuo o una sucesión convencional de fragmentos, sino más bien un texto descuartizado cuyas partes se reúnen en un orden equívoco, como destinado a desdibujar la imagen final más que a facilitarla. Se diría un puzzle que permite diversas composiciones, pero ninguna completa y precisa. Algunos críticos y el mismo Unamuno (p. 58) lo han comparado a las cajas chinas: no parece una imagen afortunada porque evoca el tipo de simetría que Unamuno se obstina en dispersar. Es posible que el aspecto más inquietante de esa dispersión sea un acentuado desorden temporal: el primero de los fragmentos data explícitamente de mayo de 1927; el segundo y el cuarto comparten dos fechas, la de redacción original —verano, de 1925— y la de traducción («Retrato») o retraducción («Cómo se hace una novela»), primavera de 1927; el tercero, «Comentario», data seguramente de los días del «Prólogo»; el quinto comienza el 4 y termina el 17 de junio de 1927; el sexto y último lo componen siete entradas de un diario comenzado el 21 de junio y concluido el 7 de julio de ese mismo año. Las fechas transmiten un doble, inseparable mensaje: señalan a la vez el tiempo de la escritura y el del relato. De este modo, Unamuno, que desordena los fragmentos fechados,

---

[12] El análisis que propongo inevitablemente separa y ordena sus intrincados procedimientos y no hace, por tanto, justicia, al rigor con que Unamuno los compenetra de forma inseparable.

somete también cada fragmento al presente, el aquí, el yo, el ahora: «Oigo preguntar: "¿Y qué haremos mañana?" No, sino qué vamos a hacer ahora. O mejor, qué voy a hacer yo ahora, que va a hacer ahora cada uno de nosotros. Lo presente y lo individual, el ahora y el aquí» (p. 52). Un discurso tan breve como éste se puebla así de innumerables presentes de indicativo y adverbios de tiempo («hoy» y «ahora», sobre todo), que se refieren casi siempre a momentos distintos y ni siquiera sucesivos (salvo en las páginas del diario). Sólo el fragmento nuclear del relato —«Cómo se hace una novela» (pp. 59-94)— sustituye a menudo el presente y el pasado por el condicional y contribuye así a evitar que deje de ser proyecto y se convierta en algo indeseablemente «hecho» (p. 108), «acabado» (p. 92). El desconcierto es más fácil de percibir si se compara con la ordenada reducción de Ortega: los «hoy» (pp. 51, 53, 56, por ejemplo) y los presentes de indicativo de sus ensayos se refieren todos a un mismo momento que —sin más precisiones que las aportadas por la fecha de la primera edición y por los adjetivos «moderno» (p. 42), «actual» (p. 43), «contemporáneo» (p. 52)— enfrentan el discurso al pasado y lo someten al futuro con entero reconocimiento de su provisionalidad. Unamuno, por el contrario, ofrecerá una serie de obsesivas y precisas noticias temporales que serán canceladas y renovadas en un interminable proceso —simulacro del «presente eterno» (p. 37)— sin pasado ni futuro.

El «Prólogo» con que Unamuno a la vez introduce —de hecho, reintroduce— y comienza el antiguo relato renovado, contiene fundamentalmente una promesa de infidelidad: «necesito retraducirme [pero] me va a ser imposible mantenerme fiel a aquel momento que pasó. El texto, pues, que dé aquí disentirá en algo del que, traducido al francés, apareció en el número de 15 de mayo de 1926 en el *Mercure de France*» (p. 38). Una confesión ulterior amplía y acentúa esta advertencia: «Y ahora paso a retraducir mi relato [...]. Y como no me es posible reponerlo sin repensarlo, es decir, sin revivirlo, he de verme empujado a comentarlo» (pp. 57-58). Inevitablemente, en la versión original, escamoteada ya en parte por una traducción infiel y por capas anteriores y posteriores de nueva escritura, se injerta también un discurso entre corchetes que la interrumpe, la desdice, la renueva, impidiendo su fijación.

El oficio de reescritor [13] que así ejerce Unamuno, tan difuso en sus procedimientos, tampoco tiene un límite claro en la extensión: alcanza lo mismo a los textos propios («Aquí debo repetir algo que creo haber dicho...», p. 74) como a los ajenos y, al contrario que Ortega, prescinde de la posible discontinuidad entre San Agustín y Rousseau (p. 49), San Pablo y Cervantes (p. 56), Tácito y Flaubert (p. 63), Dante y Víctor Hugo (p. 72), Guillén de Castro y Primo de Rivera (p. 81), todos ellos y el mismo Unamuno: al orden histórico y la originalidad del presente, promovidos por Ortega, opone, por una parte, «las lecturas de azar, el azar de las lecturas» (p. 103), y, por otra, el culto de la repetición: «son

---

[13] En el texto de Unamuno, el prefijo re- es una desaforada costumbre, otro aviso constante de que nada, en su discurso, se detiene.

cosas que se han dicho miles de veces, pero hay que repetirlas otros miles para que continúen viviendo» (pp. 64-65).

Con la práctica de la cita no sólo improvisa Unamuno un impaciente y borroso parentesco entre las escrituras de todos aquellos autores (junto a las de otros más recientes y oscuros), sino que las somete al mismo régimen de distorsión y comentario con que trata su propia escritura. «No ha escrito más que libros de comentarios», observa Cassou en el «Retrato» (p. 43), y comenta Unamuno: «¿Y los demás qué han escrito?» (p. 53), porque no acierta distinguir «en qué se diferencian los comentarios de los que no lo son» (p. 47). Pero en el texto de *Cómo se hace una novela,* el comentario no sólo tiene una función de revisión o de apoyo, sino primero, y más que nada, de interrupción: la imagen última del texto de Unamuno es seguramente la de un discurso constantemente interrumpido por toda clase de incursiones, pero sobre todo por citas y comentarios que suele introducir así:

En estos días he leído... (p. 62).

Acabo de recibir y leer... (p. 88).

He leído en... (p. 94).

Al releer, volviendo a escribirlo, esto... (p. 91).

En estos días ha caído en mis manos [...] un librito... (p. 98).

Hoy me llega un número de... (p. 105).

Acabo de leer... (p. 108).

Leyendo hoy... (p. 109).

El mismo núcleo del relato —«Cómo se hace una novela»— tiene su punto de partida en el encuentro fortuito del personaje con un libro («da con una novela», p. 67), de cuyo texto se transcribe una sola frase, la que augura al lector una repetición trascendental del relato: «Cuando el lector llegue al fin de esta dolorosa historia se morirá conmigo» (p. 67). A partir de ese momento, Jugo de la Raza se someterá en cierto modo a la repetición, pero sólo de forma incompleta y siempre interrumpida: «Habría recomenzado a leer el libro sin terminarlo, leyéndolo muy lentamente, muy lentamente, sílaba a sílaba, deletreándolo, deteniéndose cada vez una línea más adelante que en la precedente lectura, y para recomenzarla de nuevo» (p. 85). Unamuno ofrece en esa imagen un emblema de su propia lectura, su propia repetición.

La interrupción, la corrección, el comentario no alcanzan únicamente a los grandes fragmentos del discurso, sino también a las unidades menores, frases, enunciados, incluso palabras, en los que parecería inevitable la continuidad, la fijación. Alternativas y explicaciones introducidas por «es decir», «o sea», «o más bien», «o mejor», «o acaso», etc., imprimen al discurso un incesante movimiento de oscilación, de indeterminación: «[traducirse] es una experiencia, más que de resurrección, de muerte, o acaso de remortificación. O mejor de rematanza» (p. 37). «Un día el pobre Jugo de la Raza ya no pudo resistir más, fue vencido por la historia, es decir, por la vida, o mejor, por la muerte» (p. 71). Con esta fórmula conviven yuxtaposiciones e inversiones donde la alternativa es menos explícita y la indecisión más intensa: «se acostó como para dormir, como para morir» (p. 71); «mi historia del destierro, la historia de mi destierro» (p. 69); «en su eterna patria, en la patria de su eternidad» (p. 98).

Con todo, la expresión más cabal de un discurso que no acepta la fijación, de un relato que no se cierra, es seguramente la multiplicidad de los finales, corregida y subrayada por la negación de todo final. Curiosamente, las ideas de Ortega no incluyen ninguna observación expresa sobre el final de las novelas, por más que en esa «*forma* [...] de cosmos o mundo completo» (p. 44) que solicita para ellas podría considerarse implicada la demanda de un final resolutorio: se trata de un derecho que adquiere la novela precisamente por su enajenación y aislamiento de la vida, donde siempre algo continúa. A la hora de dar un final a su ensayo, Ortega se atiene a ese mismo derecho y lo termina de «una manera violenta» ante la amenaza de lo ilimitado:

> Y acontece que en estética, como en moral, los principios genéricos son únicamente la cuadrícula que se traza en vista de la casuística, del análisis más concreto. Donde éste se inicia comienza lo más seductor de la cuestión, pero a la vez se pone la planta en un área sin límites. Conviene, pues, aprovechar el último momento de cordura y detenerse (p. 53).

Unamuno, que postula la identidad de novela y vida, ofrece un texto definitivamente incompleto que se justifica así:

> Esta novela, y por lo demás todas las que se hacen y no que se contenta uno con contarlas, en rigor no acaban. Lo acabado, lo perfecto, es la muerte, y la vida no puede morirse. El lector que busque novelas acabadas no merece ser mi lector; él está ya acabado antes de haberme leído (p. 92)[14].

El final que Ortega descuida o da por supuesto es para Unamuno una antigua obsesión: el final del destierro, el final de la vida, el final de la lectura. Podría decirse que *Cómo se hace una novela* (y, desde luego, el núcleo central con el mismo título) se originan con la amenaza de un final y consisten en una cadena de obstáculos para impedir que ese final

---

[14] Frank Kermode observa lúcidamente que una novela como *El hombre sin atributos,* contemporánea del texto de Unamuno, «is multidimensional, fragmentary, without the possibility of a narrative end»; y ello se debe a que Musil, que hasta entonces se había atenido a «the divergence of confortable story and the nonnarrative contingencies of modern reality», al escribir su gran novela «he tries to create a new genre in which, by all manner of dazzling devices and metaphors and stratagems, fiction and reality can be brought together again». *The Sense of an Ending* (New York: Oxford University Press, 1977), pp. 127-128.

se realice. El último de estos obstáculos es la proliferación de los finales: la versión traducida del cuerpo central proponía primero un relato sin conclusión (p. 87), sugería luego la posibilidad de un accidente que permitiera al personaje olvidar «el libro, la novela, su propia vida» (p. 90) y regresaba por último a la solución anterior: «¿Para qué acabar la novela de Jugo?» (p. 90). En las prolongaciones (correcciones) sucesivas de ese cuerpo central, el autor se declara preocupado, acongojado incluso (pp. 94, 95) por el posible final de su relato y ofrece varias alternativas que tienen en común el abandono del libro y la lectura, es decir, el abandono del fin [15]: la primera es el retorno del personaje al país natal, en busca de «aquella edad en que aún no sabía leer» (p. 98) y de la «borrada» (p. 99) imagen de un padre al que sólo recuerda hablando «una lengua misteriosa y enigmática. Que el francés era entonces para mí lengua de misterio» (p. 1000) [16]. Se volvía así impenetrable la primera lengua en que se había impreso el relato que ahora reescribía. Insiste luego Unamuno en negar la necesidad de un final (p. 105), pero en los penúltimos párrafos del texto se permite otra vez la duda: «¿No sería mejor que acabase la novela de mi Jugo de la Raza haciéndole que, abandonando la lectura del libro fatídico, se dedique a hacer solitarios y haciendo solitarios esperar que se le acabe el libro de la vida?» (p. 112) [17]. Entre tanto, el texto relata que la vida de Unamuno en Hendaya oscilaba entre los solitarios y la lectura; y cada una de sus lecturas ocasiona un nuevo comentario escrito, una prolongación del texto, una dilación del final.

La casuística, escamoteada por Ortega, coopera así con Unamuno a la desviación del final definitivo. Pero en este nuevo desacuerdo se transparenta una disonancia más profunda. Todos esos finales, indecisamente sugeridos por Unamuno, comparten un mismo propósito: el de abandonar el libro —lectura y escritura— por una actividad intrascendente, por una restauración de la inocencia. Entre las repeticiones que agobian el texto de *Cómo se hace una novela,* no es la menos insistente la del horror a la lectura, el horror a la escritura: «trágica tortura» (p. 37), «agoreras cuartillas» (p. 37), «la tremenda pesadilla de la lectura del libro fatídico» (p. 95), «ese terrible vicio de la lectura [...] lleva el castigo de la muerte continua» (p. 69), «la terrible blancura» de las páginas donde se va a escribir (p. 59), «la tragedia [...] de todos los que escribimos, la de todos los que leemos, la de todos los que lean esto» (p. 65). No se trata, sin embargo, de un horror sin matices: en una ocasión aludirá al «sabroso castigo» de la lectura (p. 69); en otra, a la «sabrosa tortura» de escribir esta novela (p. 35); varias veces, al «gusto» general de leer (pp. 48, 66,

---

[15] Zubizarreta entiende que «el libro casi acabaría con la invitación al lector a que no lo lea». *Unamuno en su nivola* (Madrid: Taurus, 1960), p. 100.

[16] Sobre otras dimensiones de este retorno véase PAUL OLSON: «Unamuno's Lacquered Boxes: *Cómo se hace una novela* and The Ontology of Writing», *Revista Hispánica Moderna*, XXXVI (1970-1971), pp. 195-197.

[17] Puede además considerarse otra dilación del final en esa promesa de futuros relatos autobiográficos que completarían (y sin duda corregirían) las noticias del presente relato: «Ya las contaré en otra parte [...]. Allí contaré cómo...» (p. 95).

103), aunque «gusto» no le parezca la palabra adecuada: «habría que decir algo más íntimo y vital y menos estético que gustar» (p. 48). El verdadero «placer» es, sin embargo, patrimonio de otras actividades, precisamente las que sustituyen a la lectura y la escritura, sobre todo en el último de los finales: «mezclar los naipes y barajarlos, lo que un placer» (p. 110).

Para Ortega, por el contrario, tal intrascendencia es exactamente «el imperativo genérico del arte» (p. 47) y el que lo convierte en una fuente del *placer* tan escatimado por Unamuno: los dos ensayos de Ortega se proponen en definitiva «la delicia» [18] de reflexionar «sobre los componentes de su placer al leer las grandes novelas» (p. 37), sobre la razón del «placer novelesco» (p. 42), del «placer de leer novelas» (p. 54); o bien sobre «el goce estético», «el goce artístico», la «fruición estética», «el placer estético», «el placer inteligente» o el «sumo placer» que pueda obtenerse, por ejemplo, de la lectura de un verso de Mallarmé [19].

Princeton University.

---

[18] *La deshumanización del arte*, p. 53.
[19] Idem, pp. 16, 17, 27, 28, 32 y 35.

PELAYO AND PADILLA IN REFORMIST
AND REVOLUTIONARY SPAIN [1]

by

LEE FONTANELLA

I present this essay as a suggestion that there existed Spanish legends quite apart from the Tenorio story, for example, which can serve to define a modern Spain. The Pelayo legend might have—at least for post1700 Spain—the force of more renowned Spanish legends. I would venture to say further that the Pelayo story is superseded by another story, that of Juan de Padilla, which better served the revolutionary mentality that followed upon the heels of the Spanish eighteenth century. The Padilla story, like the Pelayo legend should rightly be the stuff of vaster considerations. Nevertheless, we shall focus, eventually, on the moment at which the Pelayo story itself seems to take on special meaning for a changing Spain, and on when the Padilla story crosses with the Pelayo story, displacing it in some degree.

The most significant details of the Pelayo history are familiar, although some background is in order concerning when, and in what capacity, the legend flourished. In reality, the Pelayo story often went hand in hand with the confused legend of Rodrigo, and if the Rodrigo legend is taken as the other side of the coin which is the Pelayo story, we can cite mention of this complex in a work dating back at least to the ninth century: the *cronicón* by Sebastián de Salamanca. In the mid-fifteenth century, Pedro del Corral wrote about the events leading up to the ruina-tion of Visigothic Spain. Apart from the early chronicle and the chivalry book by Corral, Lope de Vega's «El último godo» must have offered one of the outstanding early examples of the Rodrigo/Pelayo tale, in Spain's Golden Age. The story was cultivated little in balladry, although a few examples of *romance* did appear in the first decade of the seventeenth century, such as the «Romance de la elección del rey don Pelayo,» by Diego Suárez (1607?). The Pelayo theme became the substance of ver-sification in *octavas reales* in the same period, and this poetic form seems to have carried into the eighteenth century as the acceptable poetic standard for this heroic theme, as we shall see. Some of the more ambi-tious compositions at the time were: certain cantos of a projected Pe-layo poem by the Portuguese poetess Bernarda Ferreira de Lacerda; «La restauración de España,» by Cristóbal de Mesa; and «El Pelayo,» by

[1] The Saldueña portion of this essay was delivered, in substance, at the American Society for Eighteenth-Century Studies conference (Houston, March 1982).

Alonso López (el Pinciano). It is, to some extent, in opposition to this last example that the first memorable eighteenth-century work on the theme was composed: specifically, *El Pelayo, poema,* by Alonso de Solís Folch de Cardona Rodríguez de las Varillas, Conde de Saldueña, y de Frigiliana.[2] (He is most often referred to as Conde de Saldueña.)

The poem in twelve cantos was written in 1754 and dedicated to Fernando VI (1746-59). It bears the prefatory documents common to eighteenth-century Spanish publications. Most notable among them are the *aprobaciones* written by Torres Villarroel and by Agustín de Montiano y Luyando. Juan Manuel Crespo y Ortiz, who wrote another *aprobación* of the poem, found a dual purpose in Saldueña's undertaking, literary and political, wherefore this poet's enterprise takes on special meaning for us. According to Crespo y Ortiz, Saldueña improved upon the diction which we find in the version by el Pinciano, although the metrical scheme is the same: *octavas reales*—1019 of them, in the composition by Saldueña. To the dismay of the post-Neoclassical critical mind, this meant that Saldueña «polished» the language of el Pinciano, making it more «exquisite,» still without «disfiguring» it with Gallicisms. As Crespo puts the case, Saldueña maintained the maxims of el Pinciano, an the highmindedness of the earlier poet, but he enriched the language of that earlier poem.

The *aprobación* by Crespo added another twist, which awakens us to a further use—possibly more important—of the Pelayo tale in the eighteenth century: Crespo begged recognition not only of the so-called Sabios Poetas Españoles, but also of the Nation and of Squillace, and he thus associated the undertaking of Saldueña with current political realities in Spain. Suffice it to say that these realities were not popularist ones; the uprising against Squillace was only twelve years in the offing. Rather, they were monarchical ones, with shibboleths such as the power of the throne and a sound faith in the reform movement under the Bourbon Kings and their ministers. Saldueña's own publication procedure attested to these motives: not only did he dedicate his book to the King, which was not uncommon, but he also footed the bill for the publication, as Montiano y Luyando, in his capacity as spokesman for the King, was proud to announce in an implicitly self-aggrandizing sort of way.

Starting with the prologue to the poem, Saldueña's own text substantiates these attitudes. He is, expressly, a patrician. He will correct Pelayo's moral character from what it appears to be in the work by el Pinciano, and he will avoid the supernatural element common to chivalry books.

It turns out to be more than just apt that Saldueña should be retelling the Pelayo legend in the age of Fernando VI. That is, the legend serves Saldueña, insofar as it affords him the opportunity to comment metaphorically on the restitution of Spanish monarchy while praising by implication his own king at the same time. Most significant, from our

---

[2] Madrid: en la Oficina de Antonio Marín, 1754. I cite this edition throughout my discussion of Saldueña's *Pelayo.*

viewpoint, is canto III, wherein the monk Gundemaro prophesies the reestablishment of the Spanish monarchy, which will stem from Pelayo and his progeny. To begin with, Pelayo's daughter will marry the son of Recaredo and receive aid from Alfonso the Catholic to ward off the Saracens. Gundemaro delineates the entire royal line, right up to the era of Saldueña. In seventeen *octavas reales,* the poet traces the line of succession from Pelayo to Fernando I of León y Castilla (1035-65), and in twelve more, from Fernando I to Fernando VI. Some 300 years after Pelayo, the symbolic union of León y Castilla in the fight for reconquest, under Fernando I, meant the eventual restitution of Spanish monarchy. This historical reality supposedly reaches its culmination in the repetition of the Fernando name in the form of the eighteenth-century Fernando VI, who, by extension, is the embodiment of Spanish monarchical reform.

Gundemaro follows up his «lineage *octavas*» with sixteen more, concerning the moral substance appropriate to kingship. This typically Renaissance lesson, which, historically speaking, was perhaps a bit too enlightened even for Pelayo, is rewritten in canto X in terminology still more common the the Englightenment. Pelayo responds to Oppas, the traitorous envoy who asks him to surrender:

> Sólo me anima de la Patria el zelo,
> No fío en mi poder, sí en la justicia,
> Que espero que a mi lado querrá el Cielo
> Que batalle la Angélica Milicia:
> Desatados verás del azul Velo
> Rayos que abrasen su fatal malicia,
> Y el altivo furor de esse Armamento
> Reduciré a los átomos del viento:

«Fundaré la Española Monarquía,» is the sum total of Pelayo's response. With respect to Pelayo's obsession with *patria*—quite apart from the fact that it is anachronistic—it was current in the diction of Saldueña in 1754, as we can tell by his dedication of his poem to Fernando VI. The *patria* of Pelayo is, abstractly, that of the eighteenth century; and it has as figurehead the «Española Monarquía» reestablished.

What was unique here was not that Saldueña had used a historical incident to exemplify a matter of his own time. In reality, that was an artistic practice which would be applied increasingly in Romanticism.[3] Nor was the Saldueña example the last time the Pelayo legend would

---

[3] GEORGE BOAS, many years ago, set forth the notion that one foundation for Romanticism was, precisely, the contemporaneity between artist and subject matter («Il faut être de son temps», in *The Journal of Esthetics and Art Criticism,* I, No. 1 [Spring 1941], pp. 52-65). This argument is more credible to me, personally, than the one which argues that Romanticism uses the past to deal with the present, although it is indisputable that much early Romantic expression did resort to this latter procedure. Boas' (adopted) shibboleth would appear to define better that Romantic spirit which had departed from the Neoclassical esthetic and which looked toward the more modern offshoots of Romanticism.

be used as a commentary, by analogy, on one's own times. José Joaquín de Mora, in his *Leyendas españolas* (1840), included his version of the «Don Opas» story. As the late professor Vicent Llorens said, this was not a satire of the Spain of Rodrigo's time, rather of Mora's Spain.[4]

The same professor Llorens, whose essay «De la elegía a la sátira» suggested a portion of my essay, pointed out another curious fact, which in turn does hint at a feature that is unique about the Saldueña version of the Pelayo story. Although Llorens never did deal with the Saldueña version, nor with the Pelayo story in general, he was, customarily, immensely concerned with the figure of Manuel José Quintana. Llorens remarked that at the ceremony of Quintana's coronation as Spain's poet laureate (1855), Quintana noted: «Yo, que había invocado a mi patria con los más fervientes deseos cuando no existía, la saludé con himnos de gozo y de entusiasmo cuando la vi aparecer.»[5] In other words, for Quintana, unlike the Conde de Saldueña, there was no *patria* prior to the revolutionary spirit of Quintana's time. The Pelayo story as a glorification of the reformist period under the Bourbon Kings—despite the confluence of the name of Fernando I of León y Castilla with that of Fernando VI, of course—was utterly inconceivable for Quintana.

As a matter of fact, Quintana is the most obvious pivotal point for a change in the artistic use of the Pelayo legend. His «Pelayo» drama of 1805 came some thirty-five years after the version of the Pelayo story by Moratín padre and Jovellanos. But the difference between these two works and that of Quintana is enormous, insofar as their ultimate message is concerned. The drama by Moratín padre bears the familiar name of «Hormesinda,» as we know, and was written in 1770. (Moratín, by the way, was the first to follow the example of Saldueña by using the name Hormesinda for Pelayo's sister.) Jovellanos, who composed his play, called «Pelayo,» just one year before Moratín padre did his, uses the familiar Pelayo plot: Munuza, Moorish governor of Gijón, schemes to win the sister of Pelayo in Pelayo's absence. The return of Pelayo prompts an uprising in Gijón against the Moors, after which Pelayo's sister is saved from the clutches of Munuza, who is killed in the fray. The plays by Moratín padre and Jovellanos end with a certain optimism, with Pelayo's sister alive. The drama by Moratín looks forward, at its close, to the Reconquest, and the liberation of Spain is envisioned as virtually complete. The drama by Jovellanos is even more explicitly bright in its closing lines. It foretells of secure asylum and renascent virtue, just as Jovellanos had signaled in his prefatory resume of this plot, where the flight of the Moors from Gijón is described as «tan venturosa para la restauración y tranquilidad de aquel país.»[6]

Neither Moratín padre nor Jovellanos is far from the attitude of Saldueña, in his affirmation of faith in political restoration, at the hand

[4] «De la elegía a la sátira», in *Literatura, historia, política* (Madrid: Revista de Occidente, 1967), pp. 75-88; especially, p. 84.
[5] *Ibid.*, p. 76.
[6] GASPAR MELCHOR DE JOVELLANOS: *Obras publicadas e inéditas*, I, ed. Cándido Nocedal (Madrid: Atlas [BAE 46], 1951), p. 53.

of the Bourbon Kings. Restoration and tranquility, which together are the main conclusion in the Jovellanos version, are the vision of an optimistic academic and reformist statesman fifteen years prior to the accusations which were finally leveled against him. Paradoxically, between 1790 and 1798, Jovellanos would spend his effectual exile in his native Gijón, which, in the Pelayo stories, is liberated in the name of the nascent Spanish monarchy for which Jovellanos worked and of which he was, to a certain extent, a representative figure, for all his aristocratic inclinations. So, from the viewpoint of 1769, it is quite simple to see why Jovellanos would have been the natural author of a Pelayo drama, by whose plot the wrongful governor, Munuza, is ousted from his seat and replaced by rightful Spanish lineage. From the vantage point of the 1790's, however, it is hard to picture Jovellanos prognosticating restoration and tranquility with regard to the homeland in which he finds himself in effectual exile.[7] The symbolism of Gijón, or Asturias, as reformed monarchy is difficultly imaginable for Jovellanos in the 1790's.

It was in this atmosphere, more or less, that Quintana conceived of his «Pelayo.» When, in 1855, he noted that he had invoked the *patria* when it did not exist, he was not referring so much to the political nation itself, as some would have it, rather to the fact of current realities in Spain, specifically in the 1790's, I would guess. This same poet, who sang «A la Paz entre España y Francia en 1795», and who, by virtue of this poem, extolled Godoy for the Paz de Basilea, would, by May 1797, compose «A Juan de Padilla,» an embittered vision of a nonfatherland:

> ¡Patria! Nombre feliz, Numen divino,
> eterna fuente de virtud, en donde
> su extinguible ardor beben los buenos;
> ¡Patria! ... La vista atónita no encuentra
> Patria en torno de sí, ni el labio implora
> con voz tan bella al simulacro yerto
> que se muestra en su vez...[8]

By the 1826 composition of Quintana's «(Romance) a Somoza,» the situation had only gotten worse, as Llorens indicated, following the poet's disillusionment with the loss of the promising triennium, during which he was assigned to effect truly significant measures under the new constitutional government. Thus, the aforementioned *romance* was a paradoxical creation, by which he claimed that he could not sing verses to Somoza in 1826, although Somoza had asked him to do so; this of course, while the poem became a realization of verses sung to Somoza.

In the meantime, between 1797 and 1826, Quintana wrote «A la invención de la imprenta» (1800) and «El panteón del Escorial.» (This poem

---

[7] See Angel del Río, ed., JOVELLANOS: *Obras escogidas,* I (Madrid: Espasa Calpe, 1965), pp. xlv, ff.

[8] For most of the dates pertaining to Quintana, and for the poetic text, I rely on Albert Derozier, ed., MANUEL JOSÉ QUINTANA: *Poesías completas* (Madrid: Castalia, 1969).

was written in the very year of his «Pelayo».) All of these poems, «A Padilla,» «A la invención de la imprenta,» and «El panteón del Escorial,» reflect in no uncertain terms the critical attitude which Quintana must have sensed as he composed his «Pelayo.» The plot of this play unravels in a way similar to the Moratín and Jovellanos versions, except for the disastrous note of the death of Hormesinda. But Quintana's play does not present the conciliatory, optimistic vision of a reformed fatherland under a reinstated Spanish monarchy. Unlike the versión of Jovellanos, Quintana has Pelayo himself speak to close the play, and he uses the closing lines as a call to arms. Once the people are rid of the tyrant Munuza, there should be no further examples of the same. Furthermore, Quintana wants there to be relentless battle against tyranny. Munuza was only the first of many examples; he is not the end of an age and the beginning of another brighter one, as he was in the Moratín and Jovellanos versions. Quintana's Pelayo character says at the end:

> Muerto el tirano veis: ya no hay reposo;
> Siglos y siglos duren las contiendas;
> Y si un pueblo insolente allá algún día
> Al carro de su triunfo atar intenta
> La nación que hoy libramos, nuestros nietos
> Su independencia así fuertes defiendan,
> Y la alta gloria y libertad de España
> Con vuestro heroico ejemplo eternas sean.[9]

To Quintana, it was clear from the examples in his own day that the end of tyranny, much less the enlightened practice of Spanish monarchy, had not come with the death of Munuza in the eigth century.

With one notable exception (Espronceda), the anti-tyrannical Pelayo legend and the revolutionary Padilla story were not normally cultivated in Spaing during the reign of Fernando VII. Perhaps this is one reason why the story of Pelayo by Pedro de Montengón appeared in Naples, not in Spain.[10] Whatever the case, this epic poem, *La pérdida de España reparada por el rei Pelayo,* recultivates mainly the Rodrigo legend which Montengón had written about in 1793, in his novel *El Rodrigo.* The poem in fourteen cantos is primarily concerned with an atmosphere of conniving and disintegration among the Visigoths, and with the legend involving the vengeance of Count Julian against King Rodrigo. It is only

---

[9] MANUEL JOSÉ QUINTANA: *Obras completas* (Madrid: Atlas [BAE 19], 1946), p. 73.

[10] LUIS A. RAMOS-GARCÍA discussed the novel *El Rodrigo. Romance épico* (Madrid: Sancha, 1793) in his thesis «Pedro Montengón: Proceso de la novela en el siglo XVIII» (December 1975). The novel, apparently, did not make much of the Pelayo figure. The Naples publication was, in contrast, an epic poem, titled *La pérdida de España reparada por el rei Pelayo* (Naples: Battista Settembre, 1820). RAMOS-GARCÍA, a doctoral student at the University of Texas, is currently studying the works on this fascinating writer, about whom too little has been written. He will unravel serious confusions which have arisen concerning the Rodrigo/Pelayo publications by Montengón.

secondarily concerned with Pelayo. Still, ñhen Pelayo is present, all the
epithets customarily appertaining to him are there. Amidst a Spain «en
su total ruina» (p. 152), there appears the «Salvador de España» (p. 173).
He is an epic hero in the fashion of Lukács; he is representative among
his troops, which come from all over Spain (p. 230), a modern, demo-
cratic epic hero. Ultimately, after a light in the sky foretells a redeemed
Spain, the poet adopts the optimistic stance of a Jovellanos or Moratín.
The poem ends:

> En la ruina universal de España,
> Abatido su trono, y destruida
> La goda monarquía; en don Pelayo
> Pone sus ojos la Cantabria, llenos
> Del resplandor de su virtud, y gloria,
> I cómo a su señor, le erige el trono,
> Que el destino le tuvo reservado,
> Como merecedor, y sólo digno
> De restaurar la ibera monarquía (p. 255).

Was Quintana's revolutionary ardor, in the cultivation of his Pelayo
story, a historical anachronism? Or were the examples which followed,
such as that of Montengón, retrogressive products of a tyrannized land,
basing themselves attitudinally in literary tradition, rather than reflecting
political actuality? Certainly, since Montengón had already cultivated
his Rodrigo tale in a particular way in 1793, he could have justified his
traditionalistic use of Pelayo as a relatively simple, epithetical, secondary
figure in comparison to the more intriguing Rodrigo. All of these are
possibilities, we may suppose, but the curious fact is that the Pelayo
which Quintana had begun to develop, so pertinent to his time, was
becoming something else in the age of literary Romanticism, and in the
shadow of Fernando VII. Although Juan de Dios de Mora would retain
the optimistic, epithetic value of the Pelayo figure, in his historical
novel, *Pelayo,* which appeared in 1853 and enjoyed several editions, the
Pelayo legend—even the Rodrigo legend—was becoming feminized, just
as was the don Juan legend in the hands of José Zorrilla (1844). In
«Florinda» (1824-1829),[11] an epic in five cantos, the Duque de Rivas
focused not only on the Rodrigo legend, to the near exclusion of the
Pelayo figure (Pelayo appears momentarily, in canto V); his eye is on
the female character, now, and on affective aspects of the story.[12]

There is no more clear example of the feminizing of the Pelayo story

---

[11] I surmise the dates from comments by Enrique Ruiz de la Serna, ed., ANGEL
DE SAAVEDRA, DUQUE DE RIVAS: *Obras completas* (Madrid: Aguilar, 1956), pp. 28-30.
[12] The approach to the Rodrigo story was not entirely new in 1824. CADALSO,
probably half a century before Rivas, composed a poetic «Carta de Florinda a su
padre el conde don Julián, después de su desgracia» (*Poetas líricos del siglo XVIII,*
I, ed. Leopoldo Augusto de Cueto [Madrid: Atlas (BAE 61), 1952], pp. 251-252).
Of course, this does not have to do with the Pelayo figure, strictly speaking.

than the play by Juan Eugenio Hartzenbusch, «La madre de Pelayo.» [13]
This little known play has certain of the trappings of a classical tragedy,
as we might expect from Hartzenbusch, but it does not amount to that
in the end. Luz, the mother of Pelayo, almost fatally judges her son, who
is unrecognized by her, because he has a false identity and, to some,
a mysterious birth. Also, we are led to think, for a while, that Pelayo
was the unwitting killer of his father, Favila. This story evades the
customary Rodrigo/Pelayo question, obviously, and focuses on the personal trials of Pelayo and his mother, prior to his fame as savior of
Spain. In the end, the threat of Rodrigo's kingship looms, and there is
a clear prognostication of Pelayo's subsequent salvation of the country.

In 1824, just following the failed effort of the liberal triennium, Rivas
had begun his «Florinda» in London, around the same time he was
writing «El sueño del proscrito,» for which he is better known.[14] In 1824,
it must have been as natural to write about the psychical degeneration
of Spain (Florinda»)—however metaphorically—as it was to write about
one's exile («El sueño del proscrito»). After all, the date is not long prior
to Quintana's paradoxical denial of verses to his friend Somoza. In fact,
it was just one year before another iconoclast, perhaps the most icono-
clastic of Spain's young Romantics, José de Espronceda, began his epic
poem on the Pelayo subject. Although this might be considered merely
an early poetic exercise based on a traditional subject, possibly under
the guidance of Alberto Lista, it could also have been much more.[15] Seen
in the light of Rivas' composition and Quintana's magnificent *romance,*
it could have meant the continuation of the Quintana tradition, whereby
the symbol of Spanish reformism and political restoration was to become
a revolutionary voice in the form of a call to arms. After all, that would
not have been out of character for Espronceda. We shall never know, it
seems, since the nearly completed epic remains unknown except in fragmentary form. Nevertheless, the possibility is especially likely for the
young firebrand whose secret society of «Numantinos» was politically
dissolved, only weeks before he undertook the *Pelayo.*[16]

If the 1824 (post-triennium) era prompted reconsiderations of the Pelayo story in terms of psychical degeneration, or in terms of the revolutionary spirit which grew out of that degeneration, the years following the death of Fernando VII also lent themselves to the revival of the
story. If we read the review of a production of Quintana's «Pelayo,»
written by Larra around 1835, we find that he disliked the production
because of the lead actor (Puchol), but he seemed to accept the play

---

[13] «... drama en tres actos en verso» (Madrid: Imp. de José Repullés, March
1846).
[14] See Enrique Ruiz de la Serna, *op. cit.,* p. 28.
[15] Dates for the *Pelayo* poem are based on Robert Marrast, ed., JOSÉ DE ES-
PRONCEDA: *Poesías líricas y fragmentos épicos* (Madrid: Castalia, 1970), pp. 10,
80-81. ALBERTO LISTA showed special interest in this poem, in his comments (1840)
on Espronceda's poetry («Poesías de D. José de Espronceda», in *Ensayos literarios
y críticos,* II [Sevilla: Calvo-Rubio, 1844], pp. 82-85).
[16] Marrast, *op. cit.,* p. 10.

as still valid for a modern Spain of his own revolutionary mentality.[17] In 1835, *El Artista* announced that the new poet Espronceda had prepared portions of some cantos of the aforementioned Pelayo epic. In the years when Espronceda wrote his truly modern epic, *El diablo mundo*, Domingo Ruiz de la Vega wrote his epic poem *Pelayo* (1839-40). It becomes sometimes difficult to pinpoint the motives for the cultivation of the Pelayo legend in the mid-nineteenth century. In December 1842, Zorrilla wrote «El puñal del godo,» in one act. But for this play, he had a rather private motive, or so the story goes: it was the result of a bet with his friend and playwright Tomás Rodríguez Rubí, concerning how quickly he could write the play. In any case, «El puñal del godo» is not a Pelayo story, rather one of Rodrigo, whereby this character is now enhanced psychologically and seen in a somewhat different light than tradition would allow.

Possibly the publication of Quintana's works in the Biblioteca de Autores Españoles in 1852, the restaging of his «Pelayo» in September 1854, and the coronation of the poet in the following year prompted more works of this title. We can say, at least, that this was the receptive atmosphere in which Juan de Dios de Mora published his first edition of the novel *Pelayo* (1853), which we have already mentioned. Subsequent to mid-century, the Pelayo story would appear in a variety of literary modes. Although A. Tejeros wrote another historical poem named «Pelayo» in 1857, in the same year Antonio Arnao would try his hand at a new genre, using the same familiar title; he wrote a *drama lírico*, as he did for other topics of erstwhile epic proportions. A «Loa a Pelayo,» written in 1864 by S. Alvarez, was titled «Covadonga.»

While in 1805, Quintana was able to adapt Pelayo, a traditionally symbolical figure of reformism, to one more suitable to his own time, Juan Meléndez Valdés could not bring himself to sing of Pelayo at all. His Epístola IX («Al doctor don Plácido Ugena, prebendado de la iglesia catedral de Valladolid, sobre no atreverme a escribir el poema épico de Pelayo»), probably written around 1800, during his years of exile and political disgrace, is no call to arms.[18] On the contrary, it is quite unlike the Quintana play, insofar as it amounts to an expression of the security of peaceful forgetfulness. The comparably moderate, rational posture of Meléndez, even in moments of serious tribulation, keeps him rooted in Neoclassicism, despite the realities which oppress him. Since Meléndez could not bring himself to sing of a reformed Spain, because of those bitter realities, he could not treat of the Pelayo story, precisely because of its reformist implications. This is not to denigrate this superb poet, who was artistically and philosophically advanced beyond many of his

---

[17] «Salida del señor Nicanor Puchol en 'Pelayo', tragedia de don Manuel José Quintana», *Obras de D. Mariano José de Larra (Fígaro)*, ed. Carlos Seco Serrano (Madrid: Atlas [BAE 127], 1960), pp. 239-241.

[18] In *Poetas líricos del siglo XVIII*, II, ed. Leopoldo Augusto de Cueto (Madrid: Atlas [BAE 63], 1952), pp. 210-212. The situation of Meléndez in the final years of the eighteenth century is described by Pedro Salinas, ed., MELÉNDEZ VALDÉS: *Poesías* (Madrid: Espasa Calpe, 1965), pp. xxii, ff.

contemporaries, certainly; rather, it is to point out the procedural contrast between his poem and the ending of Quintana's «Pelayo,» or between his poem and the «Romance a Somoza,» where Quintana used poetry to do what he said he could not bring himself to do.

Meléndez, around the turn of the century, could not bring himself to alter the traditional meaning of Pelayo, although in 1805, Quintana could. However, even Quintana resorted to the figure of Padilla, not of Pelayo, in 1797, when earlier he felt the need to write rebellious political verses. Perhaps like Meléndez, Quintana was reluctant at first to use a work about Pelayo as a vehicle for rebellious message. If so, in avoiding that option, Quintana set in motion the trading off of one national myth for another—Pelayo for Padilla—although we now know that he would resort again to Pelayo for a rebellious message, thus altering the future significance of that figure. The line of demarcation between the use of one legend and the use of another is, of course, not sharply clear. We can only state it in general terms: Spain was shifting from a reformist attitude to one of revolt.

Enrique Gil y Carrasco found the Guerra de las Comunidades, which is represented, of course, by the spirit of Padilla, questionable as a revolutionary fact.[19] But this opinion surely did not reflect the way in which the Padilla story was told and applied in a variety of artistic and societal media in the nineteenth century. In 1821 (within the historical limits of the liberal triennium), the «Comuneros Granadinos,» who were a group of *liberales exaltados,* called their periodical publication *El Amigo de Padilla.*[20] Also in 1821 (?), Bartolomé José Gallardo established the group called «Hijos y Vengadores de Padilla.» Gisbert painted the «Ejecución de los Comuneros.» In 1840, José Quevedo, librarian at El Escorial, published his Castilian translation of Juan Maldonado's sixteenth-century account of the uprising *(El movimiento de España, o sea Historia de la revolución, conocida con el nombre de las Comunidades de Castilla),* which was later reviewed by Gil (see note 19), but which was first announced by the *Semanario Pintoresco Español.*[21] The brief review is especially curious, since it hints to us that in 1840, the Spanish public would see in Maldonado's account certain revolutionary interest:

> Los curiosos pormenores referidos por Maldonado con suma sencillez, y con todo el aspecto de la más severa imparcialidad, del levantamiento de las ciudades de Castilla, como también, aunque con más brevedad, de las germánicas de Valencia, hacen sumamente interesante ese libro a cuantos desean conocer a fondo los móviles ocultos, los que parecen más insignificantes en los sucesos de im-

---

[19] Review of the translation by José Quevedo of JUAN MALDONADO's *El movimiento de España* (1840). Included in *Obras en prosa de D. Enrique Gil y Carrasco,* II, eds. Joaquín del Pino and Fernando de la Vera e Isla (Madrid: Viuda e Hijo de E. Aguado, 1883), p. 168; originally, in *El Pensamiento,* I, No. 8 (1841).

[20] Ref. ANTONIO GALLEGO Y BURÍN: «Una colección de periódicos del reinado de Fernando VII (1820-1823)», printed in separata by Jaime Ratés (Madrid, 1927); precise pagination for this issue unavailable to me.

[21] In No. 42 (October 18, 1840), p. 335.

portancia, y que, sin embargo, contribuyen poderosamente a promover y acelerar el curso de las revoluciones.

By the 1840's, Padilla was topical, both as legend and as comparably historical account. *España Pintoresca, Artística, Monumental, Literaria y de Costumbres,* a Mexican publication on the order of the *Semanario Pintoresco Español* of Madrid, and which often took its material from this periodical, published two historical articles, at least the second of which was by Leopoldo Augusto de Cueto: «Juan de Padilla», «Padilla y los Comuneros».[22] Ferrer del Río wrote his *Historia de las Comunidades* (1850), and not long after, V. García Escobar composed «El castillo de Torrelobatón», wherein he relates the story of Juan de Padilla.[23] The *Semanario Pintoresco Español* seemed proud to announce, with a near full-page engraving, a new historical novel by Vicente Barrantes: *Juan de Padilla.*[24] Nor was the subject dying toward the end of the century. Miguel de Palacios published his «Noche de Villalar» (1884), and Manuel Danvila y Collado published his *Historia crítica de las Guerras de las Comunidades* (1897), to name two late-century examples of this theme.

In the politically charged atmosphere of the Cortes de Cádiz, Francisco Martínez de la Rosa composed «La viuda de Padilla,» to which he added his own historical account and commentary on the Guerras de las Comunidades.[25] Although Eugenio de Ochoa once claimed that this play enjoyed relatively little success in Madrid, it remains one of the most memorable of the Padilla stories.[26] In a sense, this is the consummate legendary depiction, in which the hero, Juan de Padilla, does not appear, naturally, since he had died before the play began, and he is present here only in spirit. In this play, as in reality, Spain was moribund («expirante patria»). In this way, Martínez's Padilla story matches that of Quintana fifteen years before.

The modern age has done this play enormous injustice, possibly because modern critics inherited all of the vituperations which had accrued to Martínez, an ultimately rejected political moderate who, in the vibrant age of the Cortes de Cádiz, had shown himself to be one of the more liberal and promising statesmen of his fatherland. Without entering into the matter of the political adversity which Martínez de la Rosa came to face, «La viuda de Padilla,» was denigrated because it too much reflected formal Neoclassical preoccupations, which did not

[22] Respectively, in I (1843), pp. 546-547 (written by «A. G.»); and in II (1844), pp. 13-17.

[23] García Escobar, in *Semanario Pintoresco Español,* No. 27 (July 3, 1853), pp. 210-213.

[24] In No. 43 (October 21, 1855), p. 344.

[25] Madrid: Imp. que fue de García, 1814. Aprrpriately enough, the historical introduction by Martínez de la Rosa has been preserved in more modern editions of the play, for example that by Jean Sarrailh, the biographer of this statesman-author (*Obras dramáticas* [Madrid: Espasa Calpe, 1954]).

[26] «Don Francisco Martínez de la Rosa», in *España Pintoresca, Artística, Monumental, Literaria y de Costumbres,* I, No. 1 (México, 1843), p. 9.

jibe with the rebellious note which the play conceivably contained. The criticism is foolish, in the end, and this play remains one of complexity beyond what has customarily been thought.

«La viuda de Padilla» itself does what certain of the versions of the Pelayo and Padilla stories achieved as a group. It is a story about the practicability (or impracticability) of different modes of political rhetoric. It depicts in different instances figures which might have been a politicized Quintana, a reformist Pelayo or a vengeful Pelayo, a moderate Martínez de la Rosa, a willful Padilla, etc., at the same time that it exalts the female character, in the personage of the widow. The play is charged with implications regarding the effectiveness of political rhetoric and activity, and Martínez's position on this matter may not be as sharply defined as modern criticism would make it out to be. Is this a play which predicates the tragic downfall of exalted politics? By extension, if so, what must Martínez de la Rosa have thought of Quintana's version of the Pelayo story? Perhaps the most fruitful response to the play would rest in an unimpassioned criticism which saw a great variety of political and rhetorical modalities represented here. After all, was not Martínez de la Rosa, a *moderado,* the most likely to compose such a play?

«La viuda de Padilla» is an appropriately complex play, which reflects the political and artistic complexities of its time. Just as it (perhaps unwittingly) tests the range of political potentialities, it reminds us of the confluence of the Pelayo and Padilla legends, and of the morphology of the former. The morphology of the Padilla figure and its function in art and social realities of Spain's nineteenth century should clarify still further the stance of the cultured Spaniard in this confusing period of history. Considerations such as these should render results as fascinating as the morphology of the don Juan myth, at least with regard to a definition of Spain in the eighteenth and nineteenth centuries.

University of Texas at Austin.

"LA AMARGA REALIDAD" AND THE SPANISH IMAGINATION

by

E. INMAN FOX

Against all the efforts over the past two or three decades to marshall evidence in support of Spain's participation in European culture of the eighteenth and early nineteenth centuries, remains the overriding fact that the most significant currents of European thought—Rationalism, the epistemological ideas deriving from Locke on how the human mind understands or apprehends reality, and Idealism—were at best only marginal in the shaping of the Spanish mind. This, along with other factors, led to a sort of abortive Romanticism in Spain, so perceptively interpreted by Edmund King in his 1962 essay.[1]

It is my purpose here to use the now widely accepted evaluation of the lack of profound spiritual, intellectual, or cultural experience behind the Romantic attitudes expressed in Spain, not to further insist on the fact that Spanish Romantic literature was more rhetorical than expressive, but as a point of departure to explore what significance it might have in explaining the eccentricity of the modern Spanish imagination in the European context.

Since literary imagination is a way of perceiving or «knowing» reality (or perhaps even another text), it threfore has an epistemological foundation which is bound to be determined by our ideas with respect to man's intellectual powers of imitating reality (or of perceiving it) or of creating a different reality. And since Romanticism was in fact particularly epistemological in nature because of its special interest in the creative imagination, a review of the developments in the philosophy of knowledge during the eighteenth century is pertinent to any serious consideration of how it was received in Spain.

We owe the notion of «the mind» as a separate entity in which «mental processes» occur to Descartes; and we owe the notion of a «theory of knowledge» based on an understanding of «mental processes» to Locke. Rejecting the traditional doctrine of innate ideas, Locke believed that the mind is a *tabula rasa* upon which the physical world describes itself through the experience of the five senses. Knowledge arising from sen-

---

[1] «What is Spanish Romanticism?», *Studies in Romanticism*, II, No. 1 (Autumn 1962), 1-11. Many of the ideas I put forward here have their origins in Professor King's work on Spanish Romanticism and modern Spanish literature, which influenced a whole generation of his students. To him and to his intellectual and personal generosity we are indebted in more than one way.

73

sation is perfected by reflection, thus enabling man to arrive at such ideas as space, time and infinity. Our mind was held to have the power to order received sensations, or to associate them. This associative power was what Addison called Imagination. The preoccupation with how the mind works passed through various other stages of interpretation, including the platonic theory which saw the mind capable of reflecting or creating natural order through experience, until it arrived at the Romantic idea that the mind is able to create its own experience through the imagination, which can mediate not only between sensation and perception, but also between perception and thought. This was made possible by Kant's attack on empiricism in which he contended that we organize knowledge through categories which are *a priori* to the mind. Man progressed from being seen as a mere receiver or recorder of the laws of nature to one who in fact formulated and imposed these laws.

One of the key concepts of eighteenth century European thought was that the rational shaping of human existence through man's knowledge and creativity perfects human life and leads to improvement and progress. Voltaire, for example, saw evil in the world, but he believed that man's response must be characterized by equanimity. His dictum, «Il faut cultiver notre jardin», is an exhortation to impose civilization on the chaotic, resulting from his belief that culture is not only a possible, but a necessary ordering of human existence. Another invention of the eighteenth century mind was a new way of looking at history, no longer conceived of as a simple narrative whose purpose was to illustrate morality, but rather as an effort to make abstractions or to theorize on the nature of human events. The ideas on progress and decadence of civilizations, for example, were products of this new approach. Poulet has said that the great discovery of the eighteenth century was the phenomenon of memory and its capacity in the form of history to permit man to transcend time, to gain access to the atemporal in an act of conscience.[2]

Whatever the case may be, it can be seen that throughout the eighteenth century there was growing confidence in Europe concerning man's intellectual capacity to give shape to reality. Because of the close alliance between philosopher, poet, and critic—an alliance which seems to be a constitutive element during important epochs of high culture—, this led in literature and literary theory to a striking change under Romanticism in the evaluation of the role of the creative imagination. Instead of simply serving as the apparatus of memory or the propagator of adornment as allowed by Hobbes and others, the imagination became an integral and essential part of the work of art. In his brilliant book, *The Mirror and the Lamp*, M. H. Abrams demonstrates how from Plato to the eighteenth century the mind had been considered a mirror, a reflector of external objects, while for the Romantics it became a lamp, a radiant projector. Abrams sees this change from an imitative concept to an expressive one as a decisive rupture in the continuity of aesthetic theory. For the first time a clear distinction was outlined between two aspects of the imagina-

---

[2] *Études sur le temps humain* (Paris: Plon, 1950), pp. xxx-xliii.

tion: on the one hand, the power to recall, more or less in detail, experiences already gone by; and on the other, the power to *create,* to construct mental images of events and things merely suggested. It is in this last sense that the Romantics interpreted the role of the imagination; for them it was not so much the capacity to form images of reality as the faculty to create images which go beyond reality, images seen by an intimate eye which transform existential reality into a higher reality of dream or song.

From these brief considerations it can be concluded that the origins of what we might now call the modern European way of understanding or interpreting reality evolved significantly during the eighteenth century in particular through a complicated process of influences and correspondences between English, French and German thought and at a time when literature and philosophy marched hand in hand. What is most notable in the case of Spain is not so much its lack of contribution to the process, but the fact that Spanish writers and intellectuals seemed little aware of or little receptive to, these developments.

We are of course familiar with the cultural and historical reasons for Spain's marginality with respect to eighteenth century Europe: the War of Succession and the dismemberment of Spain, the Inquisition, the opposition to the secularization of the State, and the enlightened despotism's fear of the French Revolution, etc.; in summary, Spain's relative historical isolation from the rest of Europe effectively restricted the impact of mainstream European thought on the Spanish imagination. A cursory review of Spanish literary theory from Luzán (1737) through Capmany (1771), «Philoaletheias» (1787), to the so-called Romantic statements by Martínez de la Rosa (1822), Alcalá Galiano (1833) and Larra (1836), indicates that not only were the Spaniards not following the epistemological turn taken by philosophy, but that they remained in many ways essentially Aristotelians in their prejudices: Art should be imitative of Nature rather than creative, with the intention of making an intellectual statement of moral precepts. As for theories of the mind or the role of the imagination, none seems to go beyond a simplistic acceptance of Lockian ideas.

All of this leads of course to the striking aspect of the Spanish literature of the period: intellectual distance from reality or the material under question is rarely achieved, the facts of life and history are rarely raised to abstraction or universality, or related to the fixed point of view of an ideal. Cadalso, whom some have chosen untenably to promote as the first Spanish European Romantic, is, I believe, a case in point. In the *Cartas marruecas,* he, like Voltaire, points up the evils of society for future betterment. He is unable, however, to transcend his concrete observations and criticisms of Spanish society. As Glendining has pointed out, although the ideas he uses are current in eighteenth century French and English thought, Cadalso seems to be closer to the Spanish moralists of te preceding century than to the imaginative, philosophical satirists of his own like Swift and Voltaire.[3] But even in the case of Quevedo, man is being criticized *sub specie aeternitatis,* while Cadalso limits him to his membership in Spanish society, often in a context which is *costumbrista* in nature. And the fact that he does not advance any abstract ideas on the relationship between man and society leads to a focus on Spanish society rather than on man as a social being. Nor do Cadalso's analyses of Spanish history in the *Cartas marruecas* allow for any reflection on the meaning of history itself.

If, then, widespread inquiry into theories of the mind and the close relationship between philosophy and literature were to radically alter the European imagination and if Romanticism («where the creation of order out of the artist's inner self replaces the imitation of pre-existent external order») [4] was indeed an outgrowth of this set of cultural circumstances, the Spanish imagination remained on the whole decidedly different. The oddity of the grounds on which Romanticism itself was debated in Spain provides alone ample evidence that the Spanish were little sensitive to the real import of the intellectual and artistic revolution which was taking place elsewhere. Even Larra, one of the principal protagonists of Spanish Romanticism, seems untouched by the philosophical constructs propagated in the rest of Europe. Moreover, what is important about Larra are not his Romantic attitudes, but the fact that he was the most lucid, and corrosive, observer of his times.

It is perhaps Espronceda, the finest lyric poet of Spanish Romanticism, who appears to most readily challenge the strange lack of «inwardness» I have alluded to in early nineteenth century Spanish literature. For this reason an analysis of his case is instructive, because he too finally rejects the importance of the poetic imagination and its power to transform reality. In *El Diablo Mundo,* the only truly Romantic poem in Spanish according to Robert Marrast,[5] the rebellion against reality obeys a profoundly vitalistic and even metaphysical impulse. It appears that the Poet's dream or vision might serve to transcend, or allow an escape from the painful awareness of the deep-seated dualism and discord evident in the earthly condition. But such does not turn out to be the case.

From the outset, in the introduction to *El Diablo Mundo,* the Poet is confused by the Muses and tormented by the voices of poetic inspiration. And it is suggested that poetry only exists in some undefined space between hope and memory, between illusions and pleasure and bitterness and suffering, between fantasy and truth. The spirit of poetry promises no more than to create illusions or lies which allow man only to pretend that he is not bound by material reality.

Poetry then can only suspend the ineluctable metaphysical anguish. The poet is not conceived of as one who through special powers of the imagination can create a vision which goes beyond commonplace reality.

---

[3] *Historia de la literatura española. El siglo XVIII* (Barcelona: Ariel, 1977), pp. 89-90; and in the prolog to the edition of *Cartas marruecas* (London: Támesis, 1966), pp. xxvi-xxx.

[4] KING, *op. cit.,* p. 8.

[5] See the Introduction to his edition of *El estudiante de Salamanca* and *El Diablo Mundo* (Madrid: Castalia, 1978).

He is at best a dreamer whose dream is but a deceitful respite from the unrelenting pressures of reality. *El Diablo Mundo* is structured around a series of dreams which become true is one sense or another, like Adam's dream in the garden of Eden, but in the case of Espronceda reality always overpowers the dream. The old man in *El Diablo Mundo*, who awakes from his dream transformed into the vigorous, generous and innocent Adam, finds that his garden of Eden, filled with injustice and cruelty, turns into a prison. Adam's own later dream of seignorial life among beauty and riches takes on the possibility of reality during the incursion into the Palace of the Countess of Alcira, but the experience degenerates into nothing more than a failed robbery and flight to a brothel. As a contrast in Romantic attitudes, it is worth noting that Keats explored more deeply the logic of «Adam's dream» («he awoke and found it truth»): he saw it as suggestive of the transforming power of the aroused imagination, as an empyreal reflection of the repetition of human life.[6] But Espronceda finds no spiritual or intellectual resolution between «la ilusión que es mentira» and «la amarga realidad».

Even the disillusionment Espronceda sees as a constant in affairs of the heart does not appear to stimulate metaphysical disquisitions in *El Diablo Mundo*. It becomes rather a metaphor for the ills of society. In fact, Espronceda tells us in Canto I that his intention is to offer us a poem which is «de nuestro mundo y sociedad emblema». What finally shapes Espronceda's best lyric poetry is a denunciation—admittedly underlined by the Romantic concepts of independence and rebellion—of the defects, evils and conventionalities of contemporary society as reflected in concrete political or social institutions like the system of justice or mercantilism.

It would seem, then, that Spanish culture and thought had been almost impervious to powerful notions like the Cartesian transcendental ego or the Romantic creative imagination, that the Spanish mind did not become imbued with the self-consciousness and self-confidence which emanated from the gradual acceptance in the rest of Europe during the eighteenth and nineteenth centuries of philosophy-as-epistemology, of a nonempirical «science of man». This left the Spaniard with the propensity for a ready, unquestioned acknowledgement of the historical nature of human existence.[7]

It is true that such a view of the Spanish imagination tends to devalue its literary accomplishments, to emphasize the limitations of Spanish Romanticism, to explain the peculiar timing and longevity of *costumbrismo* in Spain. But it is also central to an understanding of how the Spanish writers and intellectuals of the early twentieth century (Baroja,

---

[6] Cf. Keats' famous letter to Bailey of 22 November 1817, in *The Letters of John Keats*, 1814-1821, vol. I (Cambridge: Mass., 1958). Keats' ideas of the meaning of «Adam's dream» are central to as interpretation of «Eve of St. Agnes» and «The Fall of Hyperion».

[7] PHILIP W. SILVER develops similar ideas to explain Ortega's aesthetics and Guillén's poetry in «Jorge Guillén, 'Amigo de mirar': Breve prehistoria de una idea crítica», *Cuadernos hispanoamericanos*, No. 318 (December 1976).

Azorín, Unamuno, Machado, Ortega, etc.)—not just incidentally the first generation of Spaniards in over a century to be thoroughly engaged by current European thought—became, paradoxically, the harbingers of the modern European temper. When faced by a heightened awareness of rampant materialism and demeaning historical circumstances at the turn of the century, the Spanish mind, particularly susceptible to the philosophical pessimism of the times, responded with a raw, almost natural existentialist view of reality, different from the self-deception of Romanticism. Later, as philosophy in the rest of Europe seemed to repudiate the idealistic tradition, to turn away from epistemology, from the attempt to constitute itself a tribunal of reason, the foundation for a new creative imagination in which ontology, irrationality and absurdity became defining concepts of art had already been laid in Spain.

Northwestern University.

LAS ALMENAS DE TORO: POETRY AND HISTORY

by

STEPHEN GILMAN

> «Taurus simplicibus dotabit rura co-
> lonis pacatisque labor veniet; nec prae-
> mia laudis sed terrae tribuet partus
> summittis in astris colla iugumque suis
> poscit cervicibus ipse. Ille suis Phoebe
> portat cum cornibus orbem militiam
> indicit terris et segnia rura in veteres
> revocat cultus...»
>
> MANILIUS: *Astronomica*, IV, 140-145

The title of a classic monograph by my former colleague, Claude Anibal — «The Historical Elements of Lope de Vega's *Fuenteovejuna*» [1] — suggests the risks involved in comparing Lope's history plays to those of Shakespeare. Does not the former pick out a few «elements» which suit him and then go on to embroider them with poetic caprice? Is he not unconcerned (as the latter was concerned) with the recorded sequence of known events? Do not his portraits of past monarchs (for example, the several versions of don Pedro) correspond less to a perception of them as historical characters than to the thematic needs of individual plays tailored to the contemporary audience's taste for variation and novelty? Since these questions, however valid, suggest their own answers, it is not surprising that those who ask them generally agree that Lope uses history as a mere springboard, that his medieval characters are in no way different from those plays dealing with his own time, and that his occasional efforts to suggest past milieux are two-dimensional. The authoritative affirmation of these views by such major scholars as Vossler and Parker [2] has been greatly influential and is echoed most recently in Francisco Rico's dismissal of history from *El caballero de Olmedo*: «No hay, por supuesto, reconstrucción arqueológica o psicológica del ambiente de antaño; quitadas unas cuantas referencias de historia política, todo —lenguaje, modas, maneras— es de días de Lope.» [3]

Rico's observation that Lope does not «reconstruct» history archaeologically or psychologically is irrefutable, but at the same time, it

---

[1] PMLA, XLIX, 1934, pp. 657-718.
[2] *Lope de Vega y su tiempo*, Madrid, 1932, p. 257 and *An Approach to the Spanish Drama of the Golden Age*, TDR, IV, 1959, p. 55.
[3] *El caballero de Olmedo*, ed. Francisco Rico, Salamanca, 1967, p. 45.

leads him to overlook that other pathway back through time which is characteristically Lopesque: love for and a gift for intuitive re-creation of poetry inherited from the Spanish past. Our 17th-century playwright is clearly not Sir Walter Scott, nor does he attempt to recreate epochs which were according to Musset, «forever destroyed» by the French Revolution and its Imperial aftermath.[4] Let us avoid, therefore, confusion of history with 19th-century historicism and recognize instead its living presence for Lope in the words ot poets long dead.[5] In the specific case of *El caballero de Olmedo* the 15th century literally breathes in the «cantinela» with its mortal assonance in «e-o,» in the «morir-vivir» rhetoric of the «cancioneros,» in *La Celestina,* and in the nostalgia of Jorge Manrique for «damas,» «galas,» «armas,» and «torneos.»[6]

This notion of the identity of poetry with history in plays dealing with the Spanish past is derived from the traditionalist reading of Menéndez Pelayo and in one important way justifies comparison with Elizabethan drama. Like Calderón who presents world history as a «comedia en tres jornadas,»[7] both Lope and Shakespeare present their respective nations as having lived through a poetic drama in three acts: primitive virtue, intermediate decadence, and salutory restoration under Henry Tudor and his heirs and Ferdinand and Isabella and theirs. In the case of Lope even more clearly than in that of Shakespeare this age-old moral triad (a myth inherent in temporal collectivity) provides an indispensable means of classification for the immense number of such compositions. Thus, the plays which take place during the first «jornada» represent a frontier Golden Age at once primitively rude and innocently pastoral, an indomitable society capable of withstanding the threats of Moors, wild animals, and outbreaks of instinctual misbehavior. Then in the second, raw «virtue,» in both senses of the word, and the mission of reconquest are forgotten; it is the time of Fortune when «hombría» has degenerated into «machismo» and the «measured» loyalty of the Cid has been replaced by over-reaching greed, unrestrained violence, superficial pomp, and shameless self-service. A period of historical sin! And finally, with the accession of the Catholic Monarchs, redemption, rededication to the providential crusade, and that recovery of social cohesion defined in *Fuenteovejuna* as «amor» bring almost eight centuries of national drama to their appropriately «comic» ending.[8]

[4] *Memoires d'un enfant du siècle,* 1835, Chap. I. This remark is taken to symbolize the fundamental revolution in historical consciousness which separates us from our ancestors (including Lope) who perceived time as cyclical.

[5] This is not to deny the importance of chronicles, at times followed faithfully, at times points of poetic departure. Lope was clearly fascinated by their language, the poetic suggestiveness and the primitive comedy of which delight us in *Las famosas asturianas.*

[6] There are admittedly no direct references to *Las coplas* comparable to those to *La Celestina.* However, Lope certainly knew the *Coplas* and in this dramatic poem he reveals the same ambivalent regret.

[7] A phrase of «el Mundo» at the opening of *El gran teatro.*

[8] «Comic» in the sense of a happy ending, and not because in his contemporary plays he tends towards comedy.

The triad, of course, was not invented (or reinvented) by Lope. He had inherited it from the long tradition of prophetic Castilianism most eloquently exemplified by Juan de Mena.[9] And it served him well. It was, however, far too schematic and unambiguous for a sensibility superbly gifted for intuition of individual life in its immediate «ambiance.»[10] In each of the three larger «jornadas» a series of major plays illustrate the complexity of personal existence within an historical milieu by means of a melange of disparate and even antithetical tones, themes, and motifs. The 15th century in provincial Medina del Campo is at once tenderly festive and bleakly tragic, while Charles the Fifth's 16th-century sojourn in France combines Imperial celebration with broad erotic burlesque and political skepticism. Indeed — with the partial exception of *Fuenteovejuna*[11] — I can think of no play among the 100 or so I have read which portrays the national past with the simplicity and the unadulterated moral rigor of conventional historical interpretation. History for Lope was neither rigorously factual nor morally categorical. As a manifestation of individual and communal life, it was above all poetically unique.

Turning now to *Las almenas de Toro,* we may best begin by considering it in terms of what archaeologists would call a «typology» of the plays corresponding to its «jornada»: that framed roughly by *Las famosas asturianas*[12] and the lost *Conquista de Andalucía.*[13] What is more or less typical therein is intentional cross-breeding of the rustic with the courtly, of nature with history, of «alabanza» with «menosprecio.» But Lope's binary opposition, although related to both, is not identical to that of Guevara — effete corruption versus innocent simplicity — nor to that of the pastoral tradition — artificiality versus lyrical sincerity. Rather the chronicled savagery (dynastic murder, treason, revenge, pride, unrestrained ambition and sexual aggression) inherent in institutional consciousness of rank and role is contrasted to and intertwined with the sheer unmediated humanity of primitive frontier existence. Lope does utilize recognizeable folkloric elements taken from the «intrahistorical» Spain of his time, but in addition to crusty country «hidalgos,» amorous shepherds, and simple «villanos,» in such plays as *Los Benavides, Los prados de León, El testimonio vengado,* or *El príncipe despeñado,* the

---

[9] See R. B. TATE: *Ensayos sobre la historiografía peninsular siglo XV,* Madrid, 1970.

[10] See VOSSLER cited above, p. 267.

[11] «Partial» insofar as the Comendador is a bit pathetic in his incomprehension of the moral revolution which destroys him.

[12] Lope's «últimos godos» are not Spaniards in the sense that the characters of *Las almenas de Toro* are. In the «tragicomedia» dealing with the sin of Rodrigo, Pelayo's closing apostrophe to España, like the prophecy of the Duero in *La Numancia,* clearly presents history as future. As for the «godos» themselves, their names and genealogies catalogued at the beginning sound as comic and alien as they do to Spanish school children now. The savagery and superstition of the legend also become part of the ambiance. Lope's combination of poetical and historical insight here predicts that of Américo Castro.

[13] A play apparently dealing with the end of the medieval frontier mentioned in both *Peregrino* lists.

population of the «Green World» inevitably also includes an assortment of abandoned scions of high estate ignorant of their ancestry as well as royal refugees and other well-born cast-outs forced into exile from history. Pristine «hombría,» unadulterated by social restraints, and emergent from the combination of exalted «race» [14] and prehistoric «milieu,» insures their victory over all usurpers and entrenched adversaries. Noble savages in a literal sense, their direct confrontation with the corrupt and vicious courtly variety provides Lope with his most effective scenes.

As is apparent in *Las almenas de Toro,* the term «hombría» should not be interpreted anachronistically as medieval male chauvinism. When early in Act I the heroine, doña Elvira, confronts the Cid (his only extant personal appearance in the Lope corpus) from the walls of Toro, he is almost embarrassingly on the defensive. He begins by justifying his presence and message (the King wants you to open the gates) with the traditional «disculpa del embajador» and ends by warning her against his own liege lord: «Guardaos, Elvira, quel rey / no está bien aconsejado.» [15] In other plays belonging to the «jornada» of initial reconquest, the «hombría» of such women as «las famosas asturianas» or Elena and Clara in *Los Benavides,* who defend family honor with challenges to armed combat, is presented with a mixture of admiration and rueful amusement. In this one, however, Lope celebrates a woman as indomitable as she is beautiful, as clever in exile as she is stalwart in battle. Characteristically he takes full advantage of both the masculine («toro de lidia») and feminine (the sign of Taurus ruled by Venus) connotations of the titular town to elevate her poetically. Bullfighting was presumably more familiar to the «vulgo» than astrology, but, as we shall see, it is the latter skein of complex imagery which converts her into a «deidad que anda.» For example, her brother Sancho, the turbulent and doomed young king of epic and ballad, begins by exclaiming: «Si es estrella es la de Venus / ques de los amores reyna.» But he ends by discovering that the astrological «detriment» [15] of that planet is Mars: «Dele el dios Marte su encina...»

In this role she brings Act I to an end with a triumphant «romance» that must have brought the audience to its feet. With imprecations worthy of Raoul de Cambrai, Lope brings back alive the savage exultation of her primitive «hombría»:

> ¿Qué pensaban las gallinas,
> que era arroyuelo ese foso?
> Pues, haránle un mar de sangre,
> y será mar, que no arroyo,

[14] Lope has the historical insight necessary to comprehend that the myth of Old Christian equality (expressed in ROJA's title, *Del rey abajo ninguno*) did not apply to the nation's earlier centuries.

[15] I am citing Thomas E. Case's critical edition, University of North Carolina Studies in Romance Languages and Literatures, no. 104, Chapel Hill, N.C., 1971.

[16] The «detriment» according to NICHOLAS DE VORE (*Encyclopedia of Astrology,* Totowa, N.J., 1976) is «placement of a planet in the opposite sign from that which is said to be the ruler», p. 110.

> y entonces berán rodando
> del muro sus cuerpos troncos,
> qué doncella se pasea
> por las almenas de Toro.

Within a play centered on such a heroine as this, the Cid's demotion to a mere supporting role («even in his presence, she prevails» the audience is supposed to realize) is intentional.

Role-reversal and legend-making are crucial to the play as a whole, and in both stellar imagery is operative. Elvira, though living in a ballad world, is more than a traditional ballad character; she is a marvellous rhetorical creature, like Athena seemingly born spontaneously and fully armed from Lope's endless «ingenio»: «Así pintaban a Palas.» Hers was the Spain of the Cid, of Sancho and Urraca, of Vellido Dolfos and Arias Gonzalo, individuals whose words, deeds, and misdeeds were so time-honored and so much a part of the lives of the public that they offered minimal room for creative freedom. Guillén de Castro, to whom the play is significantly dedicated,[17] might have allowed them to repeat their traditional lines to the audience in a quest for direct recognition. But Lope as usual went to work his own way. Rather than representing on stage the siege of Zamora, that «historia archisabida» is relegated to an off-stage «relación» in Act III, while the seed from which is new play burgeons in uninterrupted surprise is a little know single ballad substantially remodelled and re-experienced in its passage through oral tradition. The air of mystery and the capacity of beckoning to the auditory imagination which Menéndez Pidal sees as the fruit of this process of continual re-creation is manifest in the suggestive initial image of a star in mourning:

> En las almenas de Toro
> allí estaba una doncella
> vestida de negros paños,
> reluciente como estrella...

Who is the damsel? The ballad singers seem to have forgotten, since her name does not appear in the lines which follow. However, the mention of Toro and the «negros paños» were sufficient for Lope to surmise that the fanciful events recounted bore remote reference to Elvira's loss

---

[17] Lope does not mention Las mocedades, but instead with the same tone of false modesty audible in the Arte nuevo praises Guillén de Castro's Dido for following the rules of tragedy as contrasted to his own mixture of genres and «rudos versos». He also sounds a bit patronizing when he praises the «caballero valenciano» for honoring «nuestra lengua con sus escritos». That he had read Las mocedades is evidenced by his concern to distinguish his more astute and more «mesurado» (Lope's term is «desapasionado») portrait of the Cid from «el soberbio castellano». Then too in the character of Don Vela (a relative and counterpart of Diego Laínez) he plays with the theme of youth and age which had been deadly serious in the Castro play. Don Vela is not only an old hero but a «viejo verde» who woos Elvira. One is reminded of Lope's amused creation of Celestina replicas.

of that recent legacy to her brother, Sancho el Fuerte, an incident presented in the *Primera crónica general* as a preliminary match or warm up for the «Cerco de Zamora». In addition, as is apparent in his amplifications of the ballad, Lope also realized that the substitution therein of Alfonso VI («pasara el rey Alonso») for his brother reflected oral contamination with *En Santa Gadea de Burgos*.[18] And, knowing that this would not make sense to an audience well aware of Sancho's rash sibling rivalry, he returned him to his original role. What remained was conserved in the climactic scene of Act I which is the poetic nucleus of the whole: the monarch smitten by the beauty of the «doncella» is determined to possess her, whether as wife or concubine; he is informed that she is «vuestra hermana» and reacts by ordering his «ballesteros» to murder her; and, in conclusion, that black deed is prevented by the Cid.

Thus, the creative imagination of generations of singers converted what in the original «cantar» seems only to have been a brief anticipation of the siege of Urraca in Zamora into an open doorway into the past. The ballads having to do directly with those events, like those celebrating the youth of Rodrigo, toe the line of epic and chronicle. But that which provides the title of the play, precisely because it was fancy-free, because its traditional reelaboration had broken loose from tradition, allowed Lope to capture alive the unbridled lust and the impetuous temper of the young king and to communicate time gone by in its pulsating immediacy. The audience is led to comprehend unrestrained preterite passion not just through recognition of verses known since childhood but in direct communion with Lope's creative communion with the words of king, sister, and vassals. Two changes do the work: background and foreground trade places; and the epic «then» of irrevocable deeds is resuscitated by the «now» of oral transmission. The «romancero» not only furnished Lope with an abundance of legend possessed in common with his audience (and so propitious for dramatic irony)[19] but also it taught him how to evade the grasp of legend by «making it new,» how to discover in poetry what man had been and felt. Which is to say, history.

This juncture of Lope's sensibility with that of oral tradicionality meant, in the first place, freedom to make up stories. How did Elvira lose Toro? What happened to her in the green wilderness after her escape? How did she contrive to recover her heritage? But it is equally important to notice that it allowed him to explore realms of human existence inaccessible to epic and derived chronicle. As just suggested, these deal perforce with what happened: events over with, deeds accomplished, «res gestae» in an eternal preterite or timeless aoristic. Spanish «romances,» however, can project out of the dramatic presence of each oral performance implicit, open futures. They can create suspense by telling us of events — the

---

[18] At the close of the *Toro* ballad Alfonso sends the defiant Cid into exile, as in *Santa Gadea*. Lope in turn alludes to the latter by imitating the terms of the oath. Sancho cries out: may she marry a «villano» who has never sat astride a horse, donned spurs, or worn a shirt.

[19] See the excellent disseration of SONIA HARRISON JONES: *The Devices of Foreshadowing in Lope de Vega's «comedia»*, Harvard dissertation, 1971.

assassination of Elvira — that could occur, potential happenings provocative of hope or fear. And even more, with lyrical imagination they can communicate what their passionate speakers wish might happen: the embarkation of Conde Arnaldos, or the wedding of Juan II with Granada, or the punishment of Alfonso VI should his oath prove false. If history is poetry and poetry is history, all is possible, all is available, all is alive, all is now, or may be later.

As Marsha Swislocki recently has pointed out,[20] it is in the amplification of the fierce reverie of Sancho (what he wishes might happen) that Lope most strikingly demonstrates his genius for incorporating «lo inventado por él... en el fondo de la tradición.»[21] The original consists of four sparse lines with verbs in the conditional: «Dice: —Si es hija de rey / que se casaría con ella, / y si es hija de duque / serviría por manceba.» In the play, however, Lope derives therefrom some 39 of his own in the future tense which celebrate eloquently the plasticity of oral fantasy: «carroza de plata,» «lazos de nácar,» «el más rico estrado / que moro o cristiano tenga, / donde no se echan de ver / con los diamantes las telas.» All will be hers if the still unidentified «doncella» should prove worthy of becoming the queen of the impetuous monarch. But it is when Lope imagines Sancho imagining the alternate possibility of making her his mistress that he is most historically perceptive and poetically suggestive:

> haré que por celosías
> mire las públicas fiestas,
> juegos de cañas y toros,
> torneos, justas, libreas;
> yremos los dos a caça
> por los montes y florestas;
> gauilán que lleve en mano
> de oro tendrá las pigüelas.[22]

The celestial orb will be brought down and emprisoned within jalousies as if she were a Moorish concubine. And then, if the pageantry she will witness through the interstices will not provide sufficient relief from the tedium of confinement, alone with her royal lover she will roam through the Castilian counterpart of Sherwood Forest: the semi-savage «vega» of Toro which a moment before had also ignited Sancho's tinder-dry imagin-

---

[20] *Lope, the «romancero» and the «comedia»*, Harvard diss., 1976.

[21] M. MENÉNDEZ PELAYO: *Estudios sobre el teatro de Lope de Vega, Obras completas*, 31, Madrid, 1949, p. 375.
Precisely because Don Marcelino understood that Lope «se inspiraba en la poesía nacional», the historical validity of such «comedias» (even when they ignore or change «facts») was more or less taken for granted by him. He did not, in other words, have to contend with Parker, Vossler, and Rico.

[22] He goes on to imagine future provision for his bastard children. The eldest will be given the fiefs of Carrión and Palencia, the daughters will be dowried, and the younger sons invested with bishoprics. It would be difficult to overestimate the historical preceptivity of Lope's amplification.

ation: «Tal campaña, ni tal vega / tal dispusición di sitio, / tales campos y arboledas, / no las e bisto en mi uida.»

The horizontal juxtaposition of the court («torneos, justas, libreas») with «montes y florestas» is, as we have suggested, typical of «comedias» of the first «jornada.» But what is unique in both the ballad and this play is the vertical juxtaposition of the soaring «almenas,» representing history, with the heavens, nature's ultimate boundary. Sensing this, Lope modified the opening lines of the ballad in a way which, as we shall see, was to be crucial to the poetic structure of the whole. There the «doncella» was compared to a shining star, but Lope chooses to delay that comparison for a few lines and to begin with the sun. Sancho, who has never before seen his sister, begins to recite his own version of the «romance» — as if he were its initial composer:[23]

> Por las almenas de Toro
> se pasea una doncella
> pero dijera mejor
> quel mismo sol se pasea.

Why the change — a change that must have surprised those in his audiences who had heard or real the original — from «the twinkling star» to «the sun itself»?[24] Part of the answer, of course, has to do with degrees of brightness and the consequent overwhelming effect on the smitten king. Then, too, there is the obvious relationship of sunligt to the fertility of the «campos y arboledas.' The sun reigns over the natural world in which Elvira is soon to find refuge. Tempt her — Vellido Dolfos typically advises Sancho — to abandon her protective «almenas» and then capture her: «Salga del muro a estos prados, / quel sol a bordar comiença...»

Nevertheless, abundant textual evidence indicates a more profound and poetically suggestive reason for the alteration. To begin with there is repeated stress on the verb «pasearse,» suggesting not diurnal rise and fall (the «carrera» of Phaeton as Lope often calls it) but the measured annual passage of the sun through the heavens. Elvira walking around the circular wall is an emblem of that ever-repeated solar journey, but then she pauses and the confrontation begins: «ya se pára a berte en ellas / en una almena la mano.» The sun has arrived in Taurus, and the king, as we mentioned earlier, immediately connects the ascendency of that sign with its «ruler» — and his — Venus. And if we had any further doubts, they are dispelled by Sancho's subsequent comments:

> Digo que la sutileza
> con que allá la astrología
> pinta figuras diversas

---

[23] MARSHA SWISLOCKI (see n. 20) emphasizes the frequency of this device with remarkable examples from many ballad plays.

[24] The omission of the «negros paños» is more easily explained. In the ballad image the star was swathed in the night sky, but once the sun was substituted, mourning made no visual sense. To Lope, Rimbaud's «Soleil noir» would have seemed absurd.

> en el manto azul del cielo,
> me ha hecho agora que crea
> que muchas imaginadas
> deben de ser verdaderas.

As Sancho looks up at her, the «doncella» is the sun,[25] and Toro has become Taurus. It is hard to resist the temptation — though Lope is not so explicit — to go on to visualize the pointed «almenas» as «las armas de su frente.»

But why again? Are these astrological references mere rhetorical decoration designed to alleviate the legendary grimness of the ballad background? Or does Lope have a further poetic purpose? A positive reply is suggested by Nicholas de Vore in his recent *Encyclopedia of Astrology:* «The sun's entry into Taurus was celebrated as a Feast of Maya (Maia) — our May Day — the Sun represented as a white bull with a golden disk between his horns, followed by a procession of virgins, exemplifying the fecundity of Nature in Spring.»[26] In view of this, the soliloquy of don Vela (an imaginary aged uncle of the Cid who has retired into the country and who later offers refuge to Elvira in peasant disguise) which immediately follows the frustrated assassination takes on added meaning:

> Montes que el Duero baña,
> y en cadenas de yelo
> os tiene por verdes pies atados...
> Bega de Toro hermosa...
> por donde alegre pasa
> Duero que quiebra yelos,
> y cuyas ninfas ban cantando a coros
> haciendo que los poros
> de la hermosa ribera
> brotan las altas cañas,
> anchas como espadañas,
> de trigo fértil, la mançana y pera,
> y el racimo pesado
> con verdes hilos al sarmiento atado...

This is to be the setting and season of the rest of the play: that time of annual celebration of revived fertility which Góngora salutes in the opening lines of the *Soledad de los campos.* Natural time and historical time, the life-giving splendor of the sun at the beginning and the literally «dark» deed of Vellido Dolfos at the end, complement each other poetically as the play progresses in the collective mind of the audience. Lope, with the effortless outpouring of his «ingenio,» exploits the verticality of the ballad invocation (as well as the name of Toro) as a means of uniting

---

[25] He goes on to mention the constellations of Andrómeda and Ariadna, two feminine constellations on either side of Taurus.

[26] See n. 16, p. 363 as well as the initial citation from MANILIUS.

poetically domains which in other frontier plays are antithetical. Sancho is not only a foredoomed victim of «history»; he is also a passionate lover of nature. And its seasonal time is also predetermined. Or, listening at a further distance, we may propose that Lope's use of astrological imagery corresponds to the theme of predestination. That of the tale («Ya se canta por ay / y hasta en la cama se duerme / el niño con las canciones / que se an hecho a las almenas / de Toro y estarán llenas / de tu historia mill naciones»)[27] is joined to that of the stars and to that of the immutable «paseo» of the sun. The three acts are full of surprises, disguises, and wild coincidence, but they are held together poetically and historically by threefold necessity.

In conclusion, we may ask, what about Elvira herself, at once a person and a personification, presiding visually and rhetorically at the center of intrigue? Not only Sancho but also Sancha (his feminine counterpart in slavery to passion[28], and the Cid identify her — at least metaphorically — with the sun.[29] But she, like the Caballero de Olmedo and the Santo Niño de La Guardia, seems to be at once unaware and aware of her astral self — what Sartre might have termed her mythological «être pour autrui.» As far as unawareness is concerned, it is apparent in her remarks about the sun as another being to whom she is grateful or which she fears. In Act I dawn alerts Toro to its present danger: «que la encubierta celada / el sol con sus rayos puros, / nos dixo luego quel alba / en su acero amaneció.» And later she predicts — correctly we assume knowing the fate of her brother García — that if she surrenders she will be imprisoned in «un escuro calaboço / de alguna torre, en que pase / mi bida, sin ber mis ojos / la luz del sol para siempre.» Finally, when in hiding and a servant girl called «Sol» (apparently for the sake of wordplay) is summoned, she cries: «Miedo me da, / porque si el sol biene acá / me descubrirá por fuerça.» She is not the sun, but she senses its special significance for her in given situations. If don Alonso Manrique senses his poetic affinity with night, in Elvira's case it is the sun.

After the loss of Toro in Act II («Industria de Bellido»), Elvira flees to the country, disguises herself as an Asturian servant girl with suitable clothing and accent. Yet her brilliance shines through. In the climactic duet with her lover, Enrique (a scion of the house of Burgundy also in disguise) she hears herself directly identified with the sun: «Si eres sol,

---

[27] Since the speaker is Vellido Dolfos the irony is double.

[28] Not only her name but her intense jealousy of Elvira-Pascuala and her threat of violence indicate the comparison.

[29] In the play the Cid is the first to see her on the wall, and he reacts like the king: «... sale... al muro un sol». But then, perhaps because of Jimena, he admits he fears the mortal brilliance of her «llama». Again in Act II Sancha, bringing food to farmhands at dawn, discovers Elvira just after her escape from Toro and cries with spontaneous admiration: «Truje sol; sol esta aquí.» There are any number of other references slyly inserted but none so explicit. For example, when Enrique and Elvira, both still disguised as peasants, elope, Don Vela asks where the former is and is informed: «Al campo se fue...» Whereupon he exclaims: «En este tiempo me admira / que el sol encendido abrasa.» As usual in Lope, irony extends beyond events into dialogue.

porqué te encubres?» That is, why do you hide from me? She answers
that indeed she is of noble birth and can never be his. Enrique is not
surprised:

> Bien me lo pensaba yo,
> bien me lo dixo tu cara,
> el resplandor de tu honrra,
> lo graue de tus palabras,
> la autoridad de tus obras;
> que, como luz que traspasa
> el vidrio, el alma te ui...

Even in her assumed name, Enrique detects her identity with the Christian celebration of Spring: «Mas, Pascuala, o quién tu eres, / que en fin
no serás Pascuala, aunque serás la de flores, / si por ventura eres Pascua.»
Enrique goes on to reveal his own noble birth, and again begs Elvira
to correspond. This time she promotes herself to the next social grade:
«pues siendo una pobre hidalga, / no podemos tratar cosa / conque mi
honor satisfagas.» It doesn't convince him for the same reason: «¿Cómo
no, si tu hermosura, / executoria en la cara, / es calidad de los cielos, /
que no calidad humana?» Whereupon she reveals her full awareness of
her mythological fate:

> Toda estoy turbada.
> Ramiro, yo tengo un nombre
> cuyos ecos tiran, matan;
> vivo en un signo del çielo,
> de quien mi sangre me aparta;
> no puedo decirte más.

He misunderstands: «Bamos. Adios, la del nombre / que tira y mata, que
estaua / por dezir que es el león / el signo de v[uestr]a casa.»[30] Not at
all: «Engañaste, que más çerca / de la primavera esmalta / el campo de
varias flores, / de suelta nieve las aguas.» She is the Sun whose rays not
only give life but also like the arrows of Apollo «tiran y matan»;[31] and
her «blood» brother has deprived her of her «sign,» Taurus or Toro. The
fatality of history and the fatality of poetry are one. She is a creature
of sunlight who can no longer conceal from others and from herself the
coincidence of the «claridad» of her lineage and of her image.

---

[30] Meaning, of course, that she is of royal blood.
[31] Case would dispute this: «The sum of the clues, then, seems to involve
those born under the sign of Taurus, subject to a violent nature, the bull itself
who violently throws and kills with its horns, and the conclusion, the city of
Toro», op. cit., p. 26. He does not consider the fact that Taurus is the «sign» but
not the identity. Furthermore, he does not take into account the Cid's remark
to the «ballesteros»: «... que las damas / son las que tiran las flechas». There is
also at least one direct reference to the Iliad. Accusing Elvira of being a fugitive
adulteress, Sancha terms her an «Elena». Helen too, as we remember, shone like
a goddess (Venus in both cases?) from the walls of Troy during a siege which
ended with an «industria».

The poetic climax is not, as it is in *El caballero de Olmedo,* the dramatic climax. The play goes on; the intrigue is tangled and untangled; the epic tales is retold down to its last grim syllable. And then when the lovers are about to flee the green world in order to reclaim Elvira's urban patrimony, Lope reveals his own poetic secret to those members of the «vulgo» who only had been concerned to satisfy their auditory appetite for rustic comedy, rousing oratory, repeated surprise, and intense confrontation. Don Vela confides in Sancha his desire to marry Elvira:

SANCHA:	¿Cómo? ¿Sin sauer quién es?
	Aunque ella, señor, dezía
	que allá en un signo uiuía...
DON VELA:	¿Del çielo?
SANCHA:	Del çielo pues.
DON VELA:	Los viejos en la experiencia
	son sabios; guardó el decoro
	a su patria, y de que es Toro
	lo tengo por çierta çiencia
	que el toro es signo del çielo,
	que el sol por mayo calienta.[32]

Harvard University.

---

[32] In case this was disregarded, Lope spells it out even more clearly when the runaways arrive in Toro: «Pascuala, si en Toro uiues / este es el signo del çielo.»

RAMON GOMEZ DE LA SERNA'S FADED IMAGE

by

MIGUEL GONZALEZ-GERTH

In my opinion, contemporary literary historians and critics for the most part have misjudged Ramón Gómez de la Serna's overall achievement. Ramón is not mere imagery, as some would have us believe, though to be sure his imagery is dazzling. At the core of his work there is, apart from the purely esthetic, an intellectual or spiritual substance, the equivalent of the qualities so much admired in the members of the Generation of 1898 but, of course, of a different temper. All one has to do is carefully read his more recondite essays, such as «Las cosas y el "ello"» and «Las palabras y lo indecible,» to comprehend some of the notions and concerns which lie behind his dynamically imagistic writing. But critics have been either too harsh or too timid, literary historians too flaccid, and scholars in general have felt more secure in taking a lofty position when not knowing how to assess the torrential output of a man who was not a clown, though he may have indulged in some clownish acts, who was a writer through and through, perhaps the most natural Spanish writer in recent times. My contention is that, though much of his work may appear dated now (whose does not?), Ramón's best writing and his achievement as precursor of the avant-garde in Spain deserve continued notice among literary stock. Though some critics have remarked that nothing in art ages more rapidly than do forerunners, at least equally true is the fact that without them no innovation is possible nor esthetic evolution so visibly detected.

A symptom and a consequence of the foregoing is the relative unavailability, the lack of historical and anthological prominence of Ramón's work. The main problem encountered today in approaching such a situation consists in that his former public image as humorist and literary lion and his final and multiform achievement have become critically confused. Some have emphasized a single aspect of his work while completely neglecting others, and some have denounced him for traits and positions they simply do not like for themselves, traits and positions which have nothing to do ultimately with the office of literature.

Ramón has been acknowledge as a major writer in many genres including the novel, but most critics have concentrated on the *greguerías* and few have had anything to say about his penultimate major novel, *El hombre perdido,* published in 1947. Even if Ramón had not written some truly unique works, he deserves an obvious place in Spanish literary history because of his enormous creativity and prophetic vision. He not only coincides with the European avant-garde, he sometimes anticipates it. It cannot be denied that one of his outstanding contributions, one he consciously cultivated, is an extremely brief, esthetically poignant kind of text which he defined as a combination of metaphor and humor. But these *greguerías* are strictly the hallmark of his overall style, the verbalized perceptions achieved through intuition which reflect his understanding of reality. Critics who stop with them misjudge the range of Ramón's originality and tend to restrict his vision to the period between the two World Wars, when in fact *El hombre perdido* turns out to be the unapparent result of Ramón's later vision of his life, in other words, his literary response to a turning point in the twentieth century.

Criticism sometimes has ways of repeating its errors. Among his novels Ramón had published *El incongruente* in 1922, *El novelista* in 1923, *¡Rebeca!* in 1936, and *El hombre perdido* in 1947. These constitute a tetralogy in technical and structural progression. As early as 1924 Ramón complained about the lack of attention paid to *El incongruente*. Even the following year Guillermo de Torre, then the spokesman for the Spanish Peninsular avant-garde and much later Ramón's best though limited critic, praised the metaphorical qualities of Ramón's production but said nothing of his novels. The critics of that period were apparently not prepared to recognize such innovative techniques in novel-writing. Of course, by 1928 Breton's *Nadja* quickly became a favorite among the snobs. It is interesting to note that Joyce's *Ulysses* also appeared in 1922 and was not universally regarded in all its greatness until much later. Certainly *El incongruente* does not approach the artistic mastery and complexity of Joyce's novel, but by the time Ramón's tetralogy reaches its fourth stage (and there is reason to believe that the initial composition of *El hombre perdido* dates back to the twenties), it is not surprising that the text, though culturally different, is just as enigmatic and labyrinthine as the Irishman's and the principal themes, instead of reflecting carefree playfulness and lighthearted absurdity, as in *El incongruente*, have become those of guilt and exile in a world of ultimate estrangement and frustration, a world whose social and technological environment is conducive only to spiritual vacuity.

When I first read Wylie Sypher's *Loss of the Self in Modern Literature and Art*, I was amazed by how well so many of his observations apply to *El hombre perdido*. Sypher presents the reader with a general scenario. Around the middle of this century, three forces have impelled artists and writers to search for «selfless» creations: 1) the liquidation of collective romanticism, including orthodox religion, from the realm of art, 2) the almost inevitably parallel development of art and science as world-views in which anthropomorphic and anthropocentric values have been significantly diminished, and 3) the creation through technology of a mass consumer society, in which individual human identity is blurred to near extinction and replaced by dehumanized figures much like statistical data.

As impossible to condense as Joyce's *Ulysses* or *Finnegans Wake*, *El hombre perdido* manifests a slight and obscure central story told in the first person by an apparently nameless protagonist-narrator who early on refers to himself obliquely as «a lost man,» having neither home nor family, only a «brother» and an «uncle» appearing once. On various occasions the reader is presented with some intriguing female characters, but one cannot be sure whether they are real or figments of the narrator's desire and, if they are «real,» whether they are different women or merely different aspects of the same ideal woman, since toward the end of the book the narrator abruptly suggests being married. This narrator-protagonist is never seen at, going to or coming from work, though from time to time he mentions either being or having been a wine salesman. He seems to spend his time wandering aimlessly, preoccupied with finding the meaning of life, some proof of his being truly alive, and an explanation of his sense of guilt.

All this, I think, is a distillation of Ramón's previous character motivations, infused almost certainly with a good dose of personal feeling and confession as stemming from the period of its final composition. In earlier novels, with the exception of El incongruente, there is thematic cohesion within the apparently chaotic medium, owing to the fact that the protagonists, whether male or female, are singleminded in their lifestyle. El incongruente sets all human experience free, and the expression of that experience is sheer imagery, happy and unconcerned imagery. El hombre perdido projects that imagery and its corresponding attitude and vision into the middle of the twentieth century. Without a doubt we have here contemporary man as seen in contemporary art. Sypher offers many precedents and parallels of the Lost Man: Diogenes Teufelsdroeckh in Carlyle's Sartor Resartus, Frédéric Moreau in Flaubert's L'Education sentimentale, and above all Ulrich in Robert Musil's Der Mann ohne Eigenschaften. Of course, we must not forget Leopold Bloom and Stephen Dedalus in Ulysses and Humphrey Chimpden Earwicker in Finnegans Wake. For his part, Sypher even more than to Kafka seems partial to Beckett and the practitioners of the nouveau roman. In any case, whether wanderers or men entrapped, the protagonists of all these novels (not to mention the earlier guilt-ridden ones of Dostoevski's) are questers who end up lost, at least culturally, psychologically, or metaphysically.

Ramón's protagonist-narrator in the novel under discussion ends up even more lost. After numerous misadventures experienced either by him, or in the company of others lacking any clear significance in his life, he goes wandering again in the outskirts of town where he had previously found a deserted railroad spur. He says (and I translate): «I had always looked forward to that interval between life and travel with the unexpressed desire of someday taking refuge there.» Such is the out of the way place, the spiritually comfortable nook where he can get away from working, from waiting, from all the novelties of human progress. Relieved yet apprehensive because he remembers hearing that a hobo had been maimed somewhere by a passing train, he carelessly lies down on the tracks, confident that the use of the facility has been long since discontinued and, feeling his bones rearrange themselves within his body, he goes to sleep. The book closes with the impersonal facsimile reproduction of a newspaper clipping reporting the discovery of an unidentifiable human body smashed to pieces by a train unexpectedly sidetracked for loading at that very spur. The machine has become an instrument of chance, a tool of destiny, and the word for «travel» turns out to be a metaphor, as it has often been, of death.

In more than two hundred pages replete with metaphorical description of persons and things, there is no definite access to the identity of the protagonist-narrator. Only after finishing the novel can the reader discover an overall design by applying the principle of reflexive reference. In this narrative, means of locomotion such as trains and motion itself are symbols of material instability. Similarly, the various female figures in the protagonist's life, despite the thematic quest for true love, betray his emotional instability. Then there are his homelessness, his lack of vocation, and his apparent fatal uprootedness. Most importantly, the human figures which appear in this novel can be seen as symbols of spiritual instability. It turns out that, from the beginning, certain fleeting characters are curiously compared to the Lost Man, among them a vagrant whose name is gradually given as Gonzalo Herreros. He is actually a double, wraith or Doppelgänger of the protagonist-narrator who, having looked for his identity in life, remains without it even in death and, if the careful reader has found it out, is no longer of any consequence to him.

To be sure, *El hombre perdido* has a theme: that of the «new» human condition. But apart from such a theme being dismally negative, it is hardly exploited in the narrative itself. What little actually happens in the book is inconsequential in terms of realistic or even psychological novels. It is only a mood sustained by the author's use of metaphor, with a tenuous design superimposed on the text for symbolical reasons, a framework which ultimately brings together the referential action of the many discontinuous episodes. In effect, there is no story. The reader finds himself before what some would call an anti-novel. This is in general terms what Sypher likes about Beckett. But there is really no such thing as anti-literature any more than there is anti-art or anti-form. There are only new concepts of form and new forms which reflect, as Octavio Paz has pointed out, occasional breaks with tradition.

With respect to Ramón the man, he comes very close to fitting John Stuart Mill's self-evaluation as it emerges, according to Sypher, from the fifth chapter of his *Autobiography:* «He seemed to have nothing personal left to live for; his life no longer seemed to be really his, but only a derivation of the institutions that modeled it. He felt, in brief, like a hollow man, one whose spirit is empoverished, one whose self is merely a byproduct of social laws ... [He] had ... a depressing sense that all his pleasures, his passions, his virtues were undermined. He saw that he had been working towards ends for which he had no real desire, for they would make him a man without qualities...» The parallels with themes of T. S. Eliot and, of course, Robert Musil are not surprising. Indeed, as Sypher points out, this represents a crisis in romantic-liberal thought and, we might add, this applies quite particularly to the artists and writers. If it sounds like Ramón's protagonist-narrator in *El hombre perdido* it is no coincidence, for he has these words to say about himself (and I translate): «I was beginning to turn into a man who is expected by all to sit and write, but I only wished to achieve a definite situation where I could spend some time in meditation, perceive the elusive woman when she approaches, and enjoy lounging in the sun parlor of a grand hotel, where I could watch those who meet for lunch and act as if they own the world.» Candor, irony, and humor are fused in this confession. It is undoubtedly the author's own confession. Paradoxically, the more abstract the work of art, the less dependence on traditional form and, therefore, the greater the artist's personal investment in it. *El hombre perdido* is a sublimation of Ramón's life, I am convinced of that, and hence it is more essentially autobiographical, closer to his inmost being, than his official autobiography entitled *Automoribundia* and published in 1948.

El hombre perdido takes up thematically and structurally where *El incongruente* left off, but it turns the author's world upside down, as the real world was turned upside down by the Second World War. The later novel is imbued with a sort of nihilistic existentialism, the inevitable refuge for the once young and optimistic avant-garde artists and writers when they feel old and war-weary. Ramón seems to have deliberately ceased to be what he once was. Sypher quotes Carlyle asking this most important question: «Who am I? The being who calls himself I?» A literary alternative is for the self to go in the opposite direction and attempt to objectify the first person by turning it into a third as so many writers have done. The danger is that this third person can now become anybody and then nobody, which is what symbolically happens in *El hombre perdido*. The self or existential core of being functions as a differential of will and understanding. When essential objectives and means of understanding become totally uncertain, then the self ceases to function and becomes useless and, therefore, lost. This did not really happen in the work of Ramón, only in the inattention and superciliousness of so many literary critics and historians. It is error and injustice that account for Ramón Gómez de la Serna's faded image.

University of Texas at Austin.

LA LOZANA ANDALUZA
AND THE COMEDIA JACINTA [1]

by

JOHN B. HUGHES

Retrato de la lozana andaluza and *Comedia Jacinta* are works that differ radically in genre, tone and meaning, but, as an introduction to my subject, I wish to point out certain obvious features they have in common. Viewed from a convenient distance, the two works share a common subject matter and theme. Each centers upon a heroine, the city of Rome and the relationship of the Spanish *converso* colony to both. The lady, an elegant and/or earthy courtesan, is the embodiment of the life and style of Rome in both works. In both, the heroine and the city are celebrated in essentially lyrical terms.

If the above is more clearly a description of Torres Naharro's play and much other commentary must be added to adequately characterize the *Lozana andaluza,* it is none the less true that Francisco Delicado, like Torres Naharro in the *Comedia Jacinta,* portrays Rome as a «patria común» and a refuge against the fires of the Inquisition and his heroine, like the city, however corrupted and corruptible, as an admirable symbol of freedom, grace and humanity in a still more corrupt and dangerous world.

Both works are self-consciously experimental and both authors are aware that they are presenting the public with a reality that is socially and aesthetically new, contemporary and topical. *Comedia Jacinta* and *Retrato de la lozana andaluza* are written from perspectives which are partially satirical and ironical and must be read, in part, as social criticism and social commentary. Irony, existential anguish and low comedy achieve a unique blend in each. Both works exude an air of virtually unrestrained sexuality: the *Comedia Jacinta* by implication, allusion and the use of idealized, symbolic and convoluted language, the *Lozana* through narration, the direct presentation of sexual experience in dialogue, and the lyrical, crude and imaginatively transformation and celebration of obscenity in all forms. Both works consistently display considerable virtuosity

[1] All references to the two texts concerned are to: FRANCISCO DELICADO: *Retrato de la loçana andaluza,* edición crítica de Bruno M. Damiani y Giovanni Allegra (Madrid, Ediciones José Porrúa Turanzas, 1975) and BARTOLOMÉ DE TORRES NAHARRO: *Propalladia and Other Works of Bartolomé de Torres Naharro,* edited by Joseph E. Gillet (Bryn Mawr, II. Collected Plays, 1946), *Comedia Jacinta,* pp. 325-365. In the case of *Comedia Jacinta,* references are to *jornada* and verse rather than page numbers.

in deliberate ambiguities and double-meanings with regard to political, social and religious matters, and above all, in endowing the most innocuous of everyday language with a wide variety of direct sexual allusions and erotic overtones.

Some of the more sombre aspects and tone of *Retrato de la lozana andaluza,* published in Venice in 1528, must be laid, not only to it's more «realistic» aesthetic, but also to the horrendous sack of Rome in 1527 by the troops of Charles the Fifth which led both Delicado and the heroine in his proto-novel to seek refuge in the islands of the Adriatic: Venice-Lípari. The intermittent note of elegy occasionally sounded in the *Lozana andaluza* is, at least, in part, a lament for the loss of precisely that worldly paradise which is simultaneously celebrated and satirized in the *Comedia Jacinta*.[2]

This essays seeks to demonstrate:

1. That Bartolomé de Torres Naharro, Francisco Delicado and Juan del Encina, three Spanish *conversos* known to be in Rome in 1513, knew each other and knew the «Lozana andaluza» who was first depicted in literature as «Divina» in Torres Naharro's play *Comedia Jacinta;*

2. that Torres's play is an «oeuvre à clé» in which the characters can be identified as follows:

Divina	Lozana
Pagano	1. Rampín
	2. Torres Naharro (dramatic voice)
	3. Pseudo rustic, loutish *cristiano viejo*
	4. Pre-gracioso, theatrical device
Jacinto	Torres Naharro (lyric voice)
Precioso	Juan del Encina
Phenicio	Francisco Delicado;

3. that to be fully understood, the play must be read as an ironic «semi-cypher» in which the lyric celebration of the central and explicit themes, i.e. *Eros,* woman (women) and the city of Rome, and the exalted vow of friendship in adversity of the three pilgrims, and by implication of all the characters, are analyzed against the backdrop of the work's

2 Both works were conceived from the essentially ironic perspective of the «half-outsider». I have chosen the term used by Claudio Guillén to describe the perspective of the narrator-protagonists and authors of picaresque fiction («Toward a Definition of the Picaresque», in *Literature as System,* Princeton University Press, 1971, pp. 72-106), advisedly, but I would not restrict its use to the Picaresque. My analogy lies rather with the broader range of possibilities open to the *converso* of which the perspective of the *pícaro* was surely one. Both Bartolomé de Torres Naharro and Francisco Delicado were within the fabric of Spanish Society, however marginal they may have been to its majority objectives. Each had the capacity to view his society and himself from without and from within at the same time. The «half-outsider» is equally a «half-insider» and not infrequently an «inside-dopester» (witness Pagano). For such writers, as for many *conversos,* partial alienation provided the dual advantage of ironic distance and a heightened awareness of themselves and others in confrontation with their surroundings.

wealth of historical, «realistic» and topical allusion, and in terms of it's frequently ambiguous and convoluted language;

4. that such a reading reveals an elaborate and self-conscious juxtaposition which would have been perfectly obvious to the public for whom the play was written, namely the presence of a transparent vulgar farce behind the lyrical aristocratic façade in which the noble *señora del castillo,* the three *caballeros* and *Pagano, criado de Divina* are clearly perceived to be a well-known prostitute, her «court» of *converso* clients and admirers, and her pimp;

5. that one of the play's significant levels of meaning is as an «in-joke» for a *converso* public in Rome in which the dominant Old Christian Society of Spain is severely criticized and parodied at the same time that the livelier *converso* sub-world of the author and his friends is simultaneously mocked and exalted;

6. finally, that this reading of the play, in conjunction with his other works, suggests, in addition to his importance in the development of the Spanish theater, that Bartolomé de Torres Naharro should be included among the significant creators of the Spanish secular novel in the great tradition stemming from the *Celestina* and leading to the *Quijote.*

It follows that the *Comedia Jacinta* (1513-17) and *Retrato de la lozana andaluza* (1524-28) are intimately related texts. A critical understanding of each is much enhanced by a close reading of both. Although one might have been tempted to read the *Lozana* in terms of its predecessor, undoubtedly known to Delicado, I have preferred, for the most part, the reverse procedure and have analyzed the *Comedia Jacinta* in terms of the *Lozana andaluza.* My reasons are twofold: 1. my essay is not an influence study; 2. Francisco Delicado is much more explicit in his intent and *Retrato de la lozana andaluza* does not depend to the same degree on «outside» knowledge for a critical exegesis. On the other hand, it could be maintained that the scheme applied in this essay is fundamental to a critical understanding of the meaning and structure of the *Comedia Jacinta,* which, however much admired for its undeniable literary merits, has always remained something of an enigma to all of its critics.

I am obliged to admit that «absolute proof» for some of the hypotheses contained in this essay is lacking and may never be available. However, I am convinced, as I hope the reader will be, that the «coincidences,» parallels, suggestions, analogies and glimmerings contained in the two texts and adduced in my essay are such as to make the interpretation presented overwhelmingly probable, if not absolutely certain. Finally, I would like to suggest that in criticism of this type, as in literature itself, some tautology is inevitable. I have attempted to justify it in context as best I could.[3]

[3] There are many bits and pieces of supporting evidence to reinforce the hypotheses presented in this essay. In Delicado's novel, Lozana's arrival in Rome coincides with the coronation of Pope Leo X in 1513 (Mamotreto VI, p. 96). In both works the lady arrives following extensive travels in Africa and the Levant. 1513 is the year when Juan del Encina's *Egloga de Plácida y Victoriano* is performed

Although the *Celestina* is clearly Francisco Delicado's literary point of departure and his *Retrato de la lozana andaluza,* shows traces of other literary sources, among them, the *Comedia Thebaida* and Torres Naharro's *Comedia tinelaria* and *Comedia soldadesca,* the author insists that his heroine is based upon a figure drawn from real life, well known to him and many others. His realistic aesthetic as protonovelist in his fictional recreation of a woman, a city and a style of life, in some respects akin to that of the reporter and the social historian, takes the form of the «portrait.» Like the painters he gives as models «porque quando hazen un rretrato procuran sacallo del natural, e a esto se esfuerçan,» Delicado has sought above all to be faithful to his subject and he is confident that others, who, like himself, knew Lozana, will recognize the original in his verbal recreation.

> Y porque este rretrato es tan natural, que no ay persona que aya conoscido la señora Loçana en Roma o fuera de Roma, que no vea claro ser sacado de sus actos y meneos y palabras; y assimismo porque yo he trabajado de no escrevir cosa que primero no sacase en mi dechado la lavor, mirando en ella o a ella (p. 74).

at the home of Cardinal Arborea with the author in attendance. At this performance according to witness Stazio Gadio in a letter to the Duke of Mantua: «E più puttane spagnuole vi erano che homini italiani» (BENEDETTO CROCE: *La Spagna nella vita italiana durante la Rinascenza,* Bari, 1917, p. 74), 1513-1515 are the probable dates of composition of the *Comedia Jacinta.* There are references to both Juan del Encina and Torres Naharro in *Retrato de la loçana andaluza.* An obscene quotation in Catalan is attributed to Juan del Encina by Rampín's mother (Mamotreto XI, p. 114). Torres Naharro is accorded much better treatment. The *Comedia Tinelaria* is ranked among Lozana's favorite works, among those she requests her old friend and client Silvano to read to her: «... porque quiero que leáys, vos que tenéys gracia, las *Coplas de Fajardo* y la *Comedia Tinelaria* y la *Celestina,* que huelgo de oyr leer estas cosas muncho» (Mamotreto XLVII, p. 329). In a little known article, first published in 1917, «La garza Montesina (Retrato Imaginario)», (*Obras completas de Alfonso Reyes,* México, Fondo de Cultura Económica, VI, 1957, pp. 249-256) Alfonso Reyes suggests, not only that Delicado and Juan del Encina knew each other but that Delicado's character, the *Garça Montesina* may be the same person alluded to in Juan del Encina's *villancico* «Montesyna es la garça». The fact, not alluded to by Reyes, that the poem is an acrostic on the name Montesyna (JUAN DEL ENCINA: *Poesía lírica y cancionero musical,* edición de R. O. Jones y Carolyn R. Lee, Madrid, Castalia, 1975, pp. 150-152) makes it virtually certain that the poem referred to someone known to Juan del Encina. Montesina is an Italian name and the lady of the poem as clearly a courtesan as Delicado's character. Our findings make the hypothesis so modestly put forward by Reyes, namely, *that the Garza Montesina* whom Juan del Encina may have known in his youth *is perhaps an aging courtesan in Delicado's novel and therefore all the more dependent on Lozana's cosmetic preparations* (prior to her pathetic death in the plague following the sack of Rome), *that much more convincing.* Menéndez Pelayo admired this particular composition and attributed it to Juan del Encina's «trato y comercio con la musa vulgar». Nor is it difficult to relate Torres Naharro to the same world. In the opinion of contemporary Juan de Valdés in his *Diálogo de la lengua:* «assí como escría bien aquellas cosas baxas y plebeyas que passaven entre gente con quien él más ordinariamente tratava, assí se pierde quando quiere scrivir lo que passa entre gente noble y principal, lo qual se vee largamente en la comedia *Aquilana*».

Although today's critic may never be able to identify the historical person behind Delicado's Lozana and should surely be advised, in any event, to concentrate his energies and analysis upon the fictional character as she appears in the pages of the *Retrato de la lozana andaluza*, Delicado's words carry the weight of conviction and make it virtually impossible for the reader to doubt that such a person, did, in fact, exist and served as his model.

In spite of widely divergent interpretations of the work's meaning, the historical, topical and «realistic» dimension of the *Lozana andaluza* has been accepted by the majority of Delicado's critics from Gayangos and Menéndez Pelayo to the present. Because the *Comedia Jacinta* is a more playful and partial statement of the human condition, its message more indirect and implicit and its language more elevated and lyrical, it has produced a still greater variety of interpretations and an understandable confusion among critics, both as to the author's intent and the work's meaning, and with regard to its undeniable personal and topical allusions. The one area of general agreement among the critics has been in identifying the play as an «obra de cámara» in which the characters on stage represent persons or values which go beyond themselves, and virtually all criticism to date, including this essay, has attempted to solve the riddle of the play's meaning by identifying the off-stage persons (or values) for whom the characters stand.

The play consists of an «Introito y argumento» in which a crude and obscene rustic, presumably Pagano, after alluding to a series of rudimentary sexual games he once played «con las moças del rencón», introduces a «breve comedieta» in which he finds it advisable to insert «un pedaço de argumento.» The bare bones of this most minimal of plots are provided in a few succinct verses. Three *caballeros*,

> «sus aventuras buscando
> todos tres van sospirando
> sin prazer y sin dinero,
> cada qual por sí quexando,
> quexosos mui por entero,
> *de señores el primero,*
> *y de amigos el segundo*
> *y el otro de todo el mundo.»* (Verses 100-107)

Their names respectively are Jacinto, Precioso and Phenicio.

> «Pasando por tal lugar
> todos tres ya tardecillo» (Verses 109, 110)

they are seen by Divina «la señora del castillo» who sends her servant Pagano to intercept them. She orders them to wait

> «con este que havéis oydo
> y ella les baxó a hablar
> por seguralle el partido.

101

Como a todos tres los vido
tan onestos cortesanos,
tomó a los dos por hermanos,
y al uno por marido.» (Verses 114-120)

The fame of the lady is well known to all:

«La qual por ser de tal fama,
dada a tan nobres prazeres,
se dirá bien de mugeres,
y mal de quien las disfama.» (Verses 129-132)

If the lady's name Divina were not meant to be an ironic transformation akin to, let us say, Celestina, these last verses would surely have been unnecessary. The first three acts *(jornadas)* are merely the presentation in turn and in detail of each of the *caballero's* complaints and their confrontations with Pagano. In *jornada* IV, with Pagano gone to fetch Divina, the three swear a bond of eternal friendship. In *jornada* V, after requestioning them, Divina resolves all problems and offers to share all she has with them: «en mí no cabe sino placer y alegría.» All swear allegiance to Rome, God and Divina. Pagano exhorts them to sing a «villancico.» Divina provides the subject: «del placer que aquí se toma,» and the play ends with a «villancico,» omitting all mention of God but glorifying Rome and Divina. There is a mysterious incident in which Pagano, by a veiled allusion, threatens the visitors with the smoke and flames of the Inquisition and is punished for his discourtesy by being slapped in the face by Divina.

The undramatic simplicity of the plot makes it clear that the play requires several levels of interpretation to be fully understood or indeed to possess real literary interest. As has been remarked, a number of critics have already attempted to unmask the disguised identities in the play, correctly perceiving in it an «obra de cámara» directed toward a limited audience—one specially prepared to understand whatever allusions it might contain—as was generally the case with the pastoral novel and the pastoral comedies of the early Spanish theater.

Menéndez Pelayo, who thought highly of the play, identified all three travelers directly with the author:

En rigor, estos tres personajes se reducen a uno solo, que es el propio autor, hablando por boca de todos ellos: y de aquí nace el interés psicológico de esta ingenua fábula... Estos diversos estados de su alma se reflejan con más sinceridad que artificio en los fáciles y elegantes versos de esta composición, escrita con más gravedad y decoro que todas las restantes del poeta...[4]

---

[4] MARCELINO MENÉNDEZ Y PELAYO: «Estudio crítico de Bartolomé de Torres Naharro y su *Propalladia*». In BARTOLOMÉ DE TORRES NAHARRO: *Propalladia* (Madrid, II, 1900), p. CXVI.

As will he shown, properly read and understood, the «fábula» is in no way «ingenua.» However, although the work is «autobiographical» in Menéndez Pelayo's interpretation only in the sense that all literature may be said to be so, Torres Naharro does speak to the reader directly through one of the travellers, Jacinto, and through Pagano. Finally, as was often the case, even when wrong, Menéndez Pelayo reveals a critical sense and a literary intuition of a very high order.

J. P. Wickersham Crawford («Who is the Character of Divina in the Comedia Jacinta?») in an understandable misreading of the play considered it «highly probable» that Divina was the celebrated Isabella d'Este, the Marchioness of Mantua, who visited Rome in 1515.[5] Although expressing reasons for doubt, Joseph E. Gillet, surely the scholar who has contributed more than anyone else to our knowledge of Torres Naharro, accepted Professor Crawford's conjecture as possible. Much more alarming is the uncritical acceptance of Professor Crawford's conjecture as fact by Otis Green, John Lihani and D. W. McPheeters.[6] Professor Gillet repeatedly identified Jacinto as Torres Naharro himself, but also found reason for suspecting that the rustic servant Pagano was also the playwright's spokesman.[7] My interpretation fully bears this out.

In a penetrating study «Retratos de conversos en la Comedia Jacinta de Torres Naharro,» Stephen Gilman neither accepta nor rejects any specific identification of the characters but attempts to bring out the substance which lies beneath the play's façade and to characterize the tone and attitudes expressed. I am in profound agreement with the symbolic meaning he assigns to Divina, the city of Rome and the play itself.

> Divina puede o no ser Isabella d'Este, pero ciertamente es —en otro nivel de significación— Roma misma, acogiendo en sus brazos abiertos a todos los refugiados que huyen del fanatismo periférico. Conversos de toda especie encuentran protección, o al menos la tolerancia y el anonimato reconfortante que necesitan, en ese abrazo verdaderamente «católico». A un público compuesto de esos refugiados, y a sus amigos y protectores italianos que hablan o entienden el español, Torres Naharro parece decirles que sólo en Roma

---

[5] J. P. WICKERSHAM CRAWFORD: «Two Notes on the Plays of Torres Naharro», *Hispanic Review*, V, 1937, p. 76.

[6] GILLET, III, 1951, pp. 601-602. See also IV, 1961 (completed by Otis H. Green). JOHN LIHANI: «New Biographical Ideas on Torres Naharro», *Hispania*, LIV (1971), p. 835. D. W. McPHEETERS: «Introducción», *Comedias, Soldadesca, Tinelaria, Himenea* (Madrid, Castalia, 1973), p. 11.

[7] He is supported in the latter by John Lihani who concludes by rejecting the attribution of Jacinto altogether and who further suggests that Pagano and therefore Torres Naharro is a morisco convert from Islam, p. 829, p. 834. Lihani also attempts to correct Professor Green by insisting that Divina really selects Phenicio as «husband» rather than Jacinto as has usually been maintained. Divina is seen by Lihani to represent the Church «in which some conversos as Phenicio sought refuge. Hence he "marries" the Church, i.e., Divina. Divina seems to be a triple metaphorical representation: Ciudad Roma, Religión=Iglesia, Isabella d'Este», p. 835.

puede reencarnarse, en esos momentos, la secular tradición hispánica de coexistencia de las tres «religiones del libro».[8]

Gilman further specifies that «por lo menos dos de estos personajes son judíos conversos» (Precioso and Phenicio).[9] According to my reading of the play, all of the characters are conversos and primarily conversos from judaism, which would modify somewhat Professor Gilman's more ecumenical view in which Jacinto may be seen as a «cristiano viejo» and Pagano as a «morisco,» «moro» or at least someone of Islamic ancestry. It is possible to conceive of both a Judaic and an Islamic background for Pagano and therefore Jacinto-Torres Naharro and also for Lozana, whose real name of Aldonza, like Dulcinea's, is derived from Arabic, and for Rampín whose father's noble *apellido* of Jumilla derives from the predominantly Moorish territory of Murcia. But because of the enormous Spanish colony of Jews and *conversos* from Judaism in Rome at this time, following the expulsion of 1492 (were there Moriscos in Rome and more significantly, *Morisco writers* in Rome?) and above all, my reading of the three writers who appear as characters in the *Comedia Jacinta,* the aggressiveness of their self-awareness within Spanish society, I incline toward the view that their *most recent* «conversions» were from Judaism. Pagano is the most difficult of all the characters to deal with in as much as he plays so many roles. There are clearly times when his «dramatic functions» as Old Christian Rustic and «Pre-Gracioso» are in conflict with the historical persons —Rampín and Torres Naharro— for whom he may be considered an allusion. I interpret his «¡A ello, juro a Mahoma!», *jornada* V (Verse 301) as a light-hearted disclaimer of all vows before such a public and in such a place where allegiance to God is subtly dropped in favor of Rome and Divina, rather than an affirmation of Islamic faith, but it may be an allusion to a remote—as I believe—or more recent Islamic background as well.

Divina

In the course of the play, Divina is described no less than three times by the adjective «lozana» always placed in a strategic position of stress. The first occurs in the first verse of the «argumento»:

> Una dama mui *loçana*
> de gran vertud y nobreza,
> tenía una fortaleza
> d'un camino muy cercana.
> Poníase a la ventana
> muchas veces a prazer;
> con voluntad y con gana
> de nuevas nuevas saber. (Verses 85-92)

---

[8] STEPHEN H. GILMAN: «Retratos de conversos en la *Comedia Jacinta* de Torres Naharro», *Nueva Revista de Filología Hispánica,* XVII (1966), pp. 35-36.
[9] GILMAN, p. 23.

The fact that the lady's fortress is «muy cercana,» her habit of «placing herself in the window» with its double meaning is an allusion to the custom of prostitutes and courtesans «advertising their wares» by showing themselves to their clientele (as Lozana remarks to Rampín, her lover, servant and pimp: «A vos quiero que seays mi gelosía que no tengo de ponerme a la ventana», p. 172). The great curiosity which one associates with Lozana to know everything that is going on and all the latest news, «nuevas nuevas saber,» are sufficient to alert any careful reader of the *Lozana andaluza*. It is probable that the combination of the two «nuevas» refers specifically to news from Spain and Rome concerning *New* Christians since «new news» concerning them was constantly forthcoming at this time.

This view is reinforced by Precioso's statement in *jornada* V concerning the latest news from Rome:

Pues en Roma a la sazón
más nuevas no se dezían
sino que algunos huhyan
de la Sancta Inquisición. (Verses 85-88)

Pagano characterizes the lady to Jacinto in high blown language and biblical references, all of which tend to exalt her sexual prowess and to suggest the habits and life style of the courtesan or madam of a house rather than an aristocrat, model of virtue or person of royal birth. There are also veiled allusions which closely correspond to details in the biography of the «Lozana andaluza» as it is later portrayed by Delicado:

qu'esta dueña, mi señora,
te dará remedio, ¡y tal!
Porqu'es persona rëal
y de excelente valor
como el águila, señor,
que comiendo al más sabor
suelta las presas suaves
para que coman las aves
que le están en derredor.
Es dueña tan acabada
que bondad no le fallece,
y en sus cosas me parece
Semíramis la nonbrada,
más que Judic esforçada,
segunda Dido Africana,
Pantasilea estimada
y amazona muy *loçana*... (*Jornada* I, Verses 184-200)

The eagle, a bird of prey, suggesting skillful rapacity as expertise, is not a usual term of comparison for a great and noble lady. Her generosity, while herself «comiendo al más sabor» in releasing the «presas suaves» to be enjoyed by the other birds around, suggests the action of the madam of a house who is also an enthusiastic practitioner. This des-

105

cription is completely consistent with Pagano's further characterization of Divina. «En sus cosas,» in itself a suggestive phrase, she is compared to Semiramis, the legendary Assyrian Queen, known for her voluptuous and sensual life, lack of scruples, feverish activity and infidelity, as opposed to Judith, model of austerity and chastity. One may be permitted to doubt that such allusions, however couched in mythological and literary language, could really have been applied to Isabella d'Este, a lady universally esteemed for her virtue and freedom from scandal. Penthesilea, Queen of the Amazons, is a warrior and leader of other female warriors. The unmistakable impression given is that the warfare in question is primarily erotic and amatory. This is also implied in the reference to Divina as an «amazona muy loçana.»

Francisco Delicado is more explicit in making the analogy between physical love and warfare when he has Lozana advocate the establishment of a «taberna meritoria» for retired prostitutes in accordance with the treatment given to military veterans.

> No sé, por mí lo digo, que me maravilla cómo pueden bivir munchas pobres mugeres que an servido esta corte con sus haziendas y honras, que nos las bastavan puertas de hierro, y ponían sus copos por broquel y sus oídos por capaçetes, combatiendo a sus espesas y a sus acostamientos de noche y día. (Mamotreto XLIII, página 316.)

Rafael Alberti used these lines and others as the basis for his transformation of the end of Delicado's novel in his play (*La lozana andaluza,* Madrid, 1961) in which he portrays Lozana as the heroic leader of a band of courtesans determined to «save Rome» at the time of the famous sack of 1527 by engaging the conquering army with their bodies.

The adjective «loçana,» as used by Pagano, has precisely the same resonances of meaning in the *Comedia Jacinta* as in Delicado's novel, i.e. beautiful, extraordinary, exhuberant, lively, lusty, agile, «sexy,» etc.

Pagano's other references, with minor embellishments, can be applied directly, if ironically, to crucial details of Lozana's biography, as it was later narrated by Delicado. She is a «segunda Dido Africana» in that she is, in a sense, a «widow,» abandoned by her lover the merchant Diomedes, through no fault of her own, but because his father had kidnapped her and ordered her put to death. At a later point, Pagano states that Divina is «la más merecedora que hay de Levante a Poniente» (Jornada II, Verses 89, 90). And if this is an all-inclusive cliché, it also makes the reader think of Lozana's travels with Diomedes in the Levante and elsewhere. And could not «merecedora» be associated by word play with «meretriz»?

Divina does not appear to owe her position to wealth, fortune or noble anscestry, nor indeed to anyone except herself and her own actions. Pagano portrays her as an «hija de sus obras.»

> Y si muchas más subieron
> en favor de la fortuna

> no deve nada a ninguna
> de todas quantas nacieron.
> Con essos que la siguieron
> tales cosas ha sembrado,
> que a contallas como fueron,
> quedarías espantado. (*Jornada* I, Verses 205-212)

If the early verses seem to relate Divina to figures like Lozana or Lazarillo de Tormes, the last four lines could hardly be more suggestive or ambiguous. It is not what Divina has inherited or collected but what she has «sembrado.» Finally we have Pagano's announcement of the lady's coming to all three travelers at the end of *jornada* IV:

> ¡Ho d'allá! Steis en buen ora.
> Nuestrama viene a hablaros
> con ganas de motejaros,
> porqu'es muy gran dezidora.
> Sabel de habrar agora,
> pues presumís de señores,
> a tan honrada señora
> que viene como las flores.
> Hazeros ha mil favores
> ora que viene de gana,
> chapada, linda, *loçana,*
> para mataros de amores. (*Jornada* IV, Verses 205-216)

Again the language used and the qualities attributed to Divina are better suited to a courtesan or prostitute of spirit that to an aristocrat. Specifically, the description exactly corresponds to Delicado's Lozana: «gran dezidora,» «hazeros ha mil favores,» «mataros de amores.» Lozana is known, like her pallid literary descendent, the Pícara Justina, for her colorful language, the custom of bestowing «motes» upon all and sundry, for rewarding her friends and attacking her enemies. The location of the adjective «loçana» here, following two others and coming before the last verse could hardly be more strategic or emphatic.

However, in case any doubt remains as to the lady's genuine talents and lest what has come before be taken for metaphorical gallantries, the following passage, still from Pagano, in spite of its «euphemisms,» convoluted language and comic overtones, could scarcely be more deliberately, crudely obscene and scatological nor more explicitly sexual. There is here a convoluted and perversely «literary» malice as well as a kind of vulgarity totally lacking in *Retrato de la lozana andaluza:*

> Pues si sabéis rebolver
> vuestro fuego con su estopa,
> dom'a Dios qu'es buena ropa
> y amiga de tal prazer.
> Poco afán es menester
> para que presto se enceste,

sino que avéis de tener
un aviso, y es aqueste:
que entre vos se manifieste
quál es más enpercotibre,
porque sería posibre
repuxalle el cagameste. (*Jornada* IV, Verses 217-228)

One of the many advantages to be derived from a close reading of the *Lozana andaluza* is its richness in double meanings and specifically its use of antiphrasis and other distortions of normal language in order to express an erotic or scatological meaning.[10] Partially a device to frustrate censorship, the application of this principle to Torres Naharro's verses makes manifest, beyond any shadow of doubt, the vulgar farce behind the high-sounding and poetic language of Torres Naharro's play. Little commentary is required for the first four verses. At the level of maximal academic abstraction, the last eight are elegantly transposed by Professor Gillet to read «les aconsejo que averigüen primero cuál de Vds. es el más listo, porque aun éste es posible que le venza la señora.»[11] On a more direct and literal level, only the most «enpercotibre» (penetrating) of the travelers should have sexual intercourse with the lady because she might well «fuck the shit out of him.» Obviously «afán» (desire), «se enceste» (to enter sexually), enpercotibre (penetrating), «repuxalle» (to shock, frighten, clean out) and «cagameste» (anus) are loaded words. The mysterious rustic «gracioso» Pagano indulges in a kind of poetic license not permitted to the other essentially straight characters of the play.

Undoubtedly one of the reasons it has taken so long for scholars to recognize the close relationship between the two works is the different rolle played by the heroine in the aesthetic structure of each. Of the one hundred twenty five characters in *Retrato de la lozana andaluz,* only three are important, Lozana, the author Francisco Delicado and Rampín, and of these three—all present in the *Comedia*—in every sense, the novel belongs to Lozana who appears on nearly every page. The work is centered on Lozana's way of speaking, acting and relating to every person and situation she confronts. Everyone else, even Delicado to a considerable extent, is a foil to reveal Lozana's personality. In a structural sense within the work, her role is closer to Pagano's than to Divina's. Divina has less personality than any of the other characters in the *Comedia Jacinta* and, for the most part, is characterized from without and in terms of her symbolic role. She does not appear on stage until the last *jornada* and even then her symbolic role as woman and patroness is emphasized. Divina's speech has not a trace of Pagano's (or Lozana's) vulgarity nor would the aesthetics and decorum of Torres Naharro's play have permitted it, but a glimpse into the person behind the symbol is vouchsafed in the revelation of her relationship to Pagano.

---

[10] See MANUEL CRIADO DE VAL: «Antífrasis y contaminaciones de sentido erótico en *La lozana andaluza*», *Homenaje ofrecido a Dámaso Alonso*, Madrid, I, pp. 437-57.
[11] GILLET, III, p. 622.

Pagano

Pagano, the man of many masks, is the most mysterious and complex character of the play. Leaving aside his role in the «Introito» as *villano,* Torres Naharro's transformation of Juan del Encina's Rustic as foul-mouthed and loutish *cristiano viejo,* he performs his other three roles simultaneouly or as it suits him throughout the work. In the least important of these, he is a definite allusion to Rampín: 1. he plays the role of *alcahueta* or *rufián* with regard to Divina in following her instructions and waylaying the three travelers; 2. more important, he enjoys a special relationship with Divina which suggests the one described in Delicado's novel where Rampín is at once Lozana's pimp, servant and lover; 3. Pagano projects a mysterious «underworld» background and knowledge, certainly Judaic, but possibly Moorish as well, similar to that inherited by Rampín from his mother, and which coincides in kind with that displayed by Lozana in the novel.

The first point requires no illustration. Limitations of space will not allow me to develop the third here. Concerning the second, it is clear that Pagano is both servant and pimp to Divina throughout the play and in *jornada* V, there are unmistakable allusions to the effect that the relationship does not stop at this point. From the beginning, Pagano's manner has been overly familiar, both in his way of addressing the three travelers and in the liberties he has taken in describing his mistress. In *jornada* V, when he oversteps in public by threatning the visitors and particularly Phenicio with the smoke of an *auto da fe:*

> «hazeros ver mundo nuevo
> y andaros los ojos llenos,
> y en poco rato, a lo menos,
> con una yerva que sé,
> si quijerdes, os haré
> que tireys dozientos truenos.» (Verses 187-193)

he is punished by being slapped in the face by Divina.

DIVINA:	¡Toma! villano, ahorcado.
PAGANO:	O mezquino, desdichado,
	¿Cómo stoy sin me matar?
	¿Pues qué? ¿Quánto he trabajado
	me lo han así de pagar?
DIVINA:	Pues, si no quieres callar,
	te daré otra bofetada.
PAGANO:	Mas pagadme mi soldada,
	dexad de me castigar.
DIVINA:	*En casa te pagaré*
	por cuenta de tus bondades. (Verses 209-218)

Whatever has happened in public, Divina clearly intimates that she will make it up to Pagano in private. But it is not only the absence of a regular salary and the payment at home «por cuenta de tus bondades» which elevates Pagano above the lesser roles of pimp and servant, but his presumption throughout the play and the deference shown him. The uniqueness of the relationship presented by Delicado is sufficient to allow the reader to recognize it however transformed or disguised in the *Comedia Jacinta*. At the end of the play, when Divina agrees to take two os the travelers as «brothers» and one as «husband,» Pagano immediately asserts himself, as if demanding some sort of recognition.

> PAGANO: Ora, pues, todos habremos.
> ¿Yo me quedo por mojón? (Verses 290-291)

Jacinto graciously and euphemistically tells him that he will be «nuestro patrón.» (Verse 292)

Pagano and Jacinto

At this point in my analysis, it is convenient to consider Pagano together with Jacinto because it is between these two that the *Comedia Jacinta* is structured and acquires its special flavor. Both make autobiographical confessions directly attributable to Torres Naharro. Pagano is surely one of Torres Naharro's greatest discoveries. As a *pre-gracioso,* endowed with the artistic self-consciousness and «agudeza» of his author, his uninhibited questioning of the three travelers serves to create such dramatic interest as the play may be said to possess. As Stephen Gilman puts it:

> Es él el encargado de reunir a los tres meditabundos e intro-
> vertidos caminantes, estimular un diálogo y ayudarles a proyectar
> teatralmente, ante un público expectante, sus cuitas líricas persona-
> les. Un papel de esta índole exige precisamente la combinación de
> perspicacia, atrevimiento, agudeza, cinismo y humor desenfadado
> que tiene Pagano.[11]

However, if Pagano provides drama, low comedy, spectacle and conflict, Jacinto, «primer galán», «gentilhombre», provides the lyrical tone and resolution of *Comedia Jacinta,* and the play takes its name from him. Jacinto early emerges as the spokesman for the three travelers and is the triumphant bridegroom who «marries» Divina. His name, Hyacinth, both as flower and as color—coral red—simbolize the celebration of pleasure. Divina provides the theme and Jacinto the refrain of the *villancico:*

> Una tierra sola, Roma,
> y un Señor, un solo Dios,
> y una dama sola, vos. (Verses 301-303)

---

12 GILMAN, p. 35.

At which point Pagano inserts «¡A ello, juro a Mahoma!» and the *villancico* is sung concluding

«no se hallan tales dos:
ni otra Roma, ni otra vos.» (Verses 316, 317)

Pagano and Jacinto are the only two characters to appear in all five *jornadas* and it is appropriate that once again, a dialogue between the two voices of Torres Naharro should bring the play to its lyrical conclusion.

In marked contrast with his brutal treatment and interrogation of Precioso and Phenicio and his allusions to their Jewish origins and precarious *converso* status, Pagano and Jacinto hit it off extraordinarily well from the moment of their first encounter in *jornada* I and throughout the play. Pagano's first words to Jacinto are to call him an «¡honbre de pro!» (Verse 109) and on receiving Pagano's advice on how he should speak to Divina in *jornada* IV, Jacinto tells Pagano that he is «más philósopho que pastor.» (Verses 267-268) The most telling piece of textual evidence may be Pagano's immediate understanding of Jacinto's problem and the following speech:

No te pongas en cuidado,
que me duele tu dolencia,
porque veo en tu presencia
que deves ser hombre onrrado.
Tú vienes muy congoxado,
yo te seré buen amigo
que me cuentas de tu grado
dónde vas sin ti contigo; (Verses 121-128)

This is of course a conceit, but, if, as Professors Gillet, Lihani and others maintain, Torres Naharro played the role of Pagano, the last line, through the familiar process of *double entendre,* would seem to link the playwright indissolubly with both characters.

In *jornada* V we are presented with the following dialogue between Jacinto and Divina:

JACINTO: Señora, no puede ser
    que sea quien es Pagano
    porque no son de villano
    su argüir y responder.
DIVINA: Nunca vistes tal sabor
    para grossero pastor
    que puede dar que hazer
    a qualquier predicador.
JACINTO: Téngole por tan doctor
    y que entiende y sabe tanto
    que no vi so tan ruin manto
    yazer tan buen beuedor.
DIVINA: Ponelde cualquier questión

111

y algunas dudas dudas dudosas
y veréis a todas cosas
cómo os da buena razón. (Verses 109-124)

«Tal saber» and «tan doctor» suggest a university education. In an earlier exchange in *jornada* I, Jacinto tells him bluntly that «para quien eres, me pareces muy letrado» and Pagano replies:

No te engañes *si te engañas;*
que si tengo algún saber,
primero hu bachiller
que pastor de las montañas,
y he quemado las pestañas
mejor que tú por ventura. (Verses 215-226)

The assumption of the pastoral role after having been a «bachiller» is probably the most direct allusion in all of Torres Naharro's writings to his own *converso* origins. This is made clearer when related to the verses of Juan del Encina's song:

¿Quien te traxo cavallero—,
aquesta montaña escura?
Yo cuidé que eras Bartolo
un pastor d'Estremadura.[13]

It is generally conceded that Bartolomé de Torres Naharro, like Juan del Encina, had been a student at Salamanca.

The assumption that all of Jacinto and one of the many selves of Pagano are both projections of Torres Naharro himself provides a rationale for many lines, for example «No te engañes, *si te engañas*» and turns others into in-jokes: «y he quemado las pastañas mejor que tú por ventura.» There is never any friction between Jacinto and Pagano and if my interpretation is correct, that is, if Phenicio (Francisco Delicado) is openly and explicitly a *converso* and Precioso (Juan del Encina) a *crypto-converso* anxious to hide his origins, Jacinto-Pagano (Torres Naharro) is still more careful but cannot resist the clever device of revealing his *converso* status indirectly through the more than half disguised voice of Pagano, whose other selves will surely throw the uninitiated off the track, while at the same time allowing his friends to enjoy the joke with him.

Jacinto

It is through Jacinto however that the major complaints of Torres Naharro as man and as writer are expressed. Jacinto transcends lyrically the resentment disguised as modesty of the author's problematical con-

---

[13] JUAN DEL ENCINA, p. 324.

fession and complaint in the *Prohemio* of the *Propalladia:* «toda mi vida *siervo*, ordinariamente pobre, y lo que peor es, *ipse semipaganus*, etc.» (Vol I, p. 140). Jacinto complains of masters and everything known of Torres Naharro indicates that he was a «servant» in search of a good «master» and that his expectations were invariably defrauded. This is the major theme in Spanish prose fiction running from the *Celestina* to the *Quijote*. It is not an accident that the *Propalladia* should have been published jointly in one edition with *Lazarillo de Tormes*, nor that Torres Naharro's *Comedia tinelaria* and *Comedia soldadesca* should have found new ways of releasing obliquely voices of protest from the bottom as well as serving as a model for Francisco Delicado in reflecting the Babylonic confusion of Italian and Spanish spoken by the lower orders of Spanish society in Italy.

Jacinto does not reveal his origins and hence might seem to pass for a *cristiano viejo*, but his complaints are definitely *converso* complaints and very bitter ones. Again, a fuller exposition must be postponed but a sample may suffice:

> y vemos por bien servir
> de los más venir a menos... (Verses 31-32)

> *y en lugar de los leales*
> *suceder oy los parleros;*
> *que los grandes caballeros*
> *estiman en sus secretos*
> *los traidores por discretos*
> y los buenos por grosseros... (Verses 43-48)

> *Y a la corta o a la luenga*
> *reniego del mejor d'ellos,*
> *pues he de servir a ellos*
> *y buscar quien me mantenga.*
> *Por lo qual quiero llorar*
> *todo el tiempo que serví,*
> *pues veo que lo perdí*
> *para nunca lo cobrar...* (Verses 58-64)

> *que he perdido en esta cuenta*
> *los mis años más floridos,*
> *que fueron como escojidos*
> *desde los quinze a los treinta,*
> *Pues o tiranos traidores,*
> *los que mandáis y tenéis,*
> *¡quán sin vergüença bevéis*
> *de los ajenos sudores...* (Verses 69-76)

> *Sabrás que desde la cuna,*
> *sin un punto de reposo,*
> *no me acuerdo vez alguna*
> *poderme llamar dichoso...* (Verses 137-140)

113

> Sabe Dios quánto holgara
> *de saber algún oficio...* (Verses 145-146)

> Pero ¿quién jamás pensara,
> donde son tantos señores
> que un señor no se hallara
> para buenos servidores?
> Aquellos somos traydores
> que dezimos las verdades
> y los que ensayan maldades,
> susceden en los favores... (Verses 149-156)

> Tienen puestos sus cuidados
> en contino atesorar,
> *sacando algunos ducados*
> *que se gastan en caçar...* (Verses 161-164)

In the context of my essay, Jacinto's complaints speak for themselves. He is as self-evidently a *converso* as are his two companions, and for that matter, as are their «benefactors,» Divina and Pagano. This is no mere Renaissance *Topus*. What is expressed here *as personal experience* is precisely «the fall of Fortune» so acutely felt by the generation of Juan Luis Vives, Fernando de Rojas, Juan del Encina, Francisco Delicado and many others, masterfully characterized by Stephen Gilman in *The Spain of Fernando de Rojas* and elsewhere.

A sense of radical personal alienation permeates these verses. The impotent vengeance of the Pícaro, from Pármeno and Areusa to Lazarillo, is contained in the definitive «reniego del mejor d'ellos». It is not merely unappreciated «service» which is being complained of here, but the forced service of a caste, condemned to serve and then to suffer for having served. The passages in italics underline both the hopelessness of such feelings and the specifically *converso* nature of the problem. The *conversos* were precisely the servants and administrators of the «grandes caballeros» who are seen here as ruthlessly exploiting their vulnerability as New Christians by listening to the «parleros» in order to be able to appropriate their servant's possessions and squander their goods and lives. Torres Naharro alludes specifically to the cruel trap baited exclusively for *converso* servants by their Old Christian masters: «Qu'estos amos con sus redes *nuestra* muerte y sus mercedes nos ordenan todo junto» (verses 98-100).

It is significant that Jacinto (Torres Naharro) should think in terms of learning «algún oficio» —a profession— as a means of combatting the situation, a concern which would hardly have occurred to a *cristiano viejo*. It is equally revealing that «they» should spend the «ducados» gained from a process of «contino atesorar» «en caçar», an identifiably non-judaic activity traditionally associated with the Old Christian landowner. It is not one of these indices alone but the presence of all of them in conjunction in the context of this play which I consider conclusive.

I concur with Professor Gillet in attributing verses 69-72 and those immediately preceding to Torres Naharro. As he says «It is difficult to admit that such definite details should not correspond to actual facts, and if we may recognize an intensely personal accent in these lines..., they may well be facts in the author's own life».[14]

In short, the nature and tone of Jacinto's complaints reveal the same sense of victimization, helplessness and by implication, caste allegiance, openly expressed by Phenicio and indirectly revealed by Precioso. This is the reason for the pact of friendship proposed by Phenicio and eagerly accepted by Jacinto and Precioso. That this sense of a *Judeo-converso* community in adversity should be implicit rather than explicit is entirely understandable. Without the ambience of freedom of Italy it would not have been presented at all.

Precioso

Precioso is the most removed or «disconnected» of any of the characters of the play. He is not directly involved or linked by the author with any other character, nor does he play as central a role in the play's structure or denouement as either Jacinto or Phenicio. Nevertheless, he does provide a necessary structural function in the work and his complaint and voice are distinct from those of his two companions. His is the sharpest satirical commentary on the intrigue and corruption of Rome and it is he who provides the only «nuevas nuevas» so eagerly asked for by Divina.

As has been suggested earlier, Precioso's status as a *converso* lies somewhere in between that of Phenicio, overtly judaic and in the process of converting to Christianity and a religious life, and Jacinto, who makes no specific allusions to his own background nor is alluded to by Pagano. In Precioso's case we are given a sufficient number of clues, not only to identify him as a *converso* but to indicate what kind of *converso* he is. Precioso links his fate with the children of Israel by biblical allusion:

> ¿Dónde voy con *tanto afán?*
> desdichado, ¿dónde iré?
> Que por do los pies porné
> las yervas se secarán
> las piedras se partirán
> con la carga de mis pies,
> según el mar y el Jordán
> por mandado de Moysés. (*Jornada* II, Verses 1-8)

After he has finished his opening monologue, there follows a series of sharp exchanges between Precioso an Pagano in which Pagano, showing his response to Precioso's pretensions and at the same time implying that he is a *converso* refers to him as «el escudero». Only Precioso will reveal

---

[14] GILLET, III, 604.

such an awareness of self-importance or by implication link his fate with that of an Old Testament Prophet. Precioso scornfully responds by calling Pagano a «villano grossero» (Verses 61-64).

In *jornada* V, when Precioso cynically, and, as if from above, describes the situation of the conversos who have come to Rome to flee the Inquisition:

> Muchos juegan de esgarrón
> *y se afufan con el cayre,*
> que no queda remendón,
> abad, ni monje ni flayre;
> vellos yr es un gran donayre
> derramados en gran suma
> como manojo de pluma
> que la soltáis en el ayre. (Verses 89-96)

Pagano cannot resist jumping to the conclusion that Precioso should be numbered among them: «¿Vas tú huyendo también, que habras muy ahotado?» (Verses 99-100). The exchange which follows defines Precioso's covert status as a *converso*:

> PRECIOSO: Sabe Dios que me ha pesado
> por no ser marrano fino,
> que por faltarme un costado
> bivo pobre de contino.
> PAGANO: Pues no te burles, hazino,
> *que muchos y muy ufanos*
> *dizen mal de los marranos,*
> *y ellos no comen tocino.* (Verses 101-108)

It is at this point that Jacinto remarks to Divina «no puede ser que sea quien es Pagano». Precioso does not answer Pagano's last jibe and Jacinto's subsequent conclusion about the wisdom of Pagano says something about the inside knowledge and *agudeza* as well as the almost certain *converso* status of all three. It is highly significant in the previous quotation that Precioso should join the frequently *converso* occupations of *remendón, abad, monje,* and *flayre* with the flourishing underworld of prostitution. *El cayre* is precisely money made from prostitution. We have here another irrefutable linkage with the world of Lozana, Rampín and Francisco Delicado. As in the *Lozana andaluza,* the assumption is made that prostitution in Rome (and by implication, in Spain as well) is in the hand of Jews and *conversos*. (This is undoubtedly Delicado's reading of *La Celestina* and his interpretation of Rojas' character.)

Precioso's concise worldly summary of life in Rome is another perspective on the world of the *Lozana andaluza*:

> De Roma no sé qué diga
> si no que por mar y tierra
> cada día ay nueua guerra,

nueva paz y nueua liga,
la corte tiene fatiga,
y el Papa s'está a sus vicios,
y el que tiene linda amiga
le haze lindos seruicios,
los ricos con sus officios
triunfan hasta que mueran,
y los pobres desesperan
esperando beneficios.
En Roma los sin señor
son almas que van en pena;
no se haze cosa buena
sin dineros y favor.
Quál vive muy a sabor;
quién no tiene que comer;
vnos con mucho dolor,
y otros con mucho plazer.
Dos cosas no pueden ser
de plazeres y dolores
ni peores ni mejores
que son Roma y la mujer. (*Jornada* V, Verses 61-84)

Although his description has a satirical edge, Precioso stops short of condemning the situation.

What began as fruitful speculation has ended in virtual certainty: Precioso is Juan del Encina. My reasons are: 1. his name which means beautiful and corresponds with Juan del Encina's «real» name of Fermoselle derived from the name of the town, or as it was hispanized by his brother Pedro, Hermosilla; 2. the fact that he claims to come from Rome; 3. the nature of his complaint which centers on the betrayal of friends; 4. the knowledge of Roman corruption and intrigue contained in his verses; 5. the worldly and petulant tone of his complaint; 6. the character of Precioso as portrayed by Torres Naharro in the play, which, all in all, coincides with what is known about Juan del Encina.

It is the judgement of all his biographers that Juan del Encina was obsessed with status and prestige and that he was constantly seeking and failing to find a patron.[15] Having failed at the court of the Duke of Alba and ultimately having been rejected for the cantorship of the Cathedral of Salamanca in favor of his apprentice Lucas Fernández because of the good connections and machinations of the latter, Juan del Encina was happiest and most successful in Rome where he was strongly supported first by Pope Alexander VI and later by Julius II and Leo X. From the time of his first visit (1499?) until 1523 when he assumed the priorship

---

[15] See particularly J. RICHARD ANDREWS: *Juan del Encina, Prometheus in Search of Prestige* (Berkeley and Los Angeles: University of California, 1959) and R. ESPINOSA MAESO: «Nuevos datos bibliográficos de Juan del Encina», *Boletín de la Real Academia Española,* VIII, 1921.

of León acquired for him by Leo X, Rome was his principal base of operations and one which he used to attempt to reinstate himself in the peninsula and to take vengeance on those who had betrayed him. Precioso's anger in his complaints in *jornada* II is directed precisely against those whom he had befriended and helped when he was «on top» and who had subsequently conspired against him (Verses 13-24, 49-52). This is a clear allusion to Lucas Fernández and company against whom Juan del Encina had his brothers initiate suit in 1502, armed with a Papal Bull claiming for himself the appointment as *cantor* he had lost in 1498. The same rivalry and resentment of former friends is openly expressed in Juan del Encina's own verses, of which the verbal skirmish between Juan del Encina and Lucas Fernández, as portrayed by shepherds Juan and Mateo may be found in Egloga I, and the allusions made concerning Encina's chances of succeeding to the cantorship of Fernando de Torrijos in the Cathedral of Salamanca in Egloga IX, may serve as conspicuous examples.

Of the three writers, only Juan del Encina took on a new name to erase the memory of his former one of Fermoselle (as a place name a confession of an earlier name change) choosing Encina perhaps because it seemed to suggest local Old Christian ancestry and because Salamanca is a land of *encinas*. Torres Naharro is playing with this name change as well as the personality of Juan del Encina when he has Precioso say: «Yo señor, aunque grossero, tengo por nombre Precioso» (*jornada* IV, verses 177-178).

Phenicio

The most conclusive parallels in the play and *Retrato de la lozana andaluza* are those which link Phenicio to Francisco Delicado and to his character Lozana. He is identified: 1. as unmistakably a *judío* or *converso*; 2. as the victim of an unspecified secret disease, by implication, syphilis; 3. as one who chooses to enter the Church and end his life in her service; 4. as one who is conscious of leaving one religion, or one life style for another; 5. by his way of speaking which closely parallels that of the narrator and character of *autor* in *Retrato de la lozana andaluza* and who employs exactly the same language to depict his entering the Church as is used by Lozana in the Novel to describe her retirement from prostitution to the Island of Lípari; 6. finally, by the total personality revealed and by his relationship with all the other characters in the play. The last point is strengthened by emphasizing that the *Comedia Jacinta* presents essentially the same *ambiente* and world of experience as the *Lozana andaluza* although from a different vantage point and with a different aesthetic.

The first point could not be more clearly established. Of all the characters in the play, Phenicio is singled out. He could not possibly *not* be a *converso*. His name, the fact that he comes from Spain, innumerable allusions in the text, his exchanges with Pagano who singles him out for his roughest jests, and in *jornada* III calls him one of «aquellos de la Tora» (verse 157), all lead to this conclusion. This is a fundamental point when one remembers the strong judaic overtones of *Retrato de la lozana anda-luza* and the extent to which, in striking contrast to *La Celestina, Laza-rillo de Tormes* or even the *Comedia Jacinta,* the *Lozana andaluza* is an explicitly *converso* book. Phenicio is the only explicitly *converso* figure in the *Comedia Jacinta.* This is all the more striking in view of the fact, that, as we have seen, all of the other characters of the play are almost certainly *conversos* or *crypto-conversos* as well.

Pagano must somehow have known beforehand of Phenicio's disease, since only in his case does he speculate as to whether the traveler is or may be a victim of syphilis:

> «o tu vas percutido
> de secreta enfermedad» (*Jornada* III, Verses 79-80) [16]

and Phenicio gratuitously confirms this in *jornada* IV when he expresses his gratitude to a lady (Lozana?) who helped or cured him.

> Jamás pagarle podría
> sin mucha dificultad
> lo que en una enfermedad
> me sirvió una amiga mía (Verses 45-49)

Lozana's claims as *curandera* are of course greater than her medical knowledge but one may remember the case of the «canónigo» whom she does cure and who repays her by making her pregnant. (Mamotreto XXIII)

Phenicio's motivation in entering the Church would seem to be prima-rily, if not solely, as a means of self-preservation. In the desperate straits in which he finds himself, he has nowhere else to go. Both the elegiac tone and his sententious way of speaking correspond to those of the character of the *autor* in the *Lozana andaluza.* I have already alluded to the parallel between Phenicio's words in choosing to enter the Church and those of Lozana in abandoning a life of prostitution. In both instances, the decision implies a sort of «forced conversion».

> Qu'este mundo todo es viento,
> pues de pobres ni de ricos,
> ni de grandes ni de chicos
> ninguno bive contento.
> ¡O, loco el honbre o muger,
> con quanto puede afanarse,
> que piensa de contentarse
> por más averes aver!
> Que si bien por carescer
> se duele la pobre gente,
> no veo que por tener
> algún rico se contente;

---

[16] As Gillet points out, the «enfermedad» referred to is probably the *mal fran-cés, III,* p. 611.

porque en el siglo presente
muy más grande ser conviene
el temor qu'el rico tiene
qu'el dolor qu'el pobre siente.
Pues, vista la perdición
qu'este mundo nos procura,
no será poca cordura
procurar nuevo patrón:
quiero entrarme en religión
y acabar mi vida allí,
do daré cuenta y razón
de quanto a Dios ofendí;
y al mundo que trata ansí,
ganemos honrra con él,
que quiero dexalle a él
antes qu'él me dexe a mí (Jornada III, Verses 45-72)

Phenicio's complaint is total and refers, as least, in part, to the human condition; but his comments concerning «el siglo presente» refer directly to what was happening in Spanish «Christian» society at the time. In contrast to Jorge Manrique's leveling of rich and poor beyond the grave, Phenicio warns the rich that they have more to fear in the probable loss of their «averes» in this life than the poor. This is surely a reference to the plight of the *conversos* whose goods were subject to confiscation by the Inquisition, should they be found guilty of being *judaizantes* and is almost certainly Phenicio's plight as well. In view of which «no será poca cordura procurar nuevo patrón... y al mundo que trata ansí, ganemos honrra con él». Phenicio's motives are entirely justifiable but they are only minimally religious, if indeed, they are religious at all. The Church was the safest haven of all for a potential victim of the Inquisition.

Pagano leaves no room for doubt:

¡Hideputa fanfarrón!
¿Tú piensas que no te entiendo?
¡Dom a Dios que vas huyendo
de la Santa Enquesición! (Verses 145-149)

The author and Lozana abandon the dangers of Rome for the peace and security of the Islands Venice-Lípari. As Lozana tells Rampín and the reader: «Estarme he rreposada, y veré mundo nuevo, *y no esperar que él me dexe a mí sino yo a él.*» (p. 419) The humane *but notably secular* goa's for which Francisco Delicado, not entirely safe, even in his refuge in Venice, prays, are «buen fin y paz y sanidad a *todo el pueblo cristiano (Read both Old and New Christians),* amén» (p. 442).

The portrayal of Phenicio reveals him to be an original and compassionate man who has not allowed his many problems to destroy him or his spontaneity. He has reached an acceptance of his fate which is both philosophical and opportunistic. Phenicio, like Francisco Delicado an his

Lozana, is ardent, generous and outspoken. He is as resourceful and exhuberant a character as his circumstances will allow. In the curiosity, irony, resignation and underlying directness with which he bares his soul to Divina and the others, Phenicio strongly resembles the author who opens his life and problems to the reader, along with his character, as few have done before or after him in the pages of *Retrato de la loçana andaluza*. Finally, it is Phenicio who proposes the moving pact of friendship, warmly embraced by the three pilgrims:

> Yo, señores, he pensado,
> si os paresce cosa tal,
> *que pues Dios nos ha juntado*
> *nos juntemos por igual;*
> *dexando todo lo ál,*
> *nos demos la fe y las manos*
> *de sernos buenos hermanos*
> *para bien y para mal.* (*Jornada* IV, Verses 185-192)

Further development of my argument and further documentary proof for the assertions here contained will have to await the publication of my book *From the «Celestina» to the «Quijote»*. I am particularly grateful to the editors for my inclusion in this *homenaje* to my friend, teacher and colleague, Professor Edmund L. King, who, among his many other achievements, was the translator, editor and lifelong friend of Don Américo Castro, without whom few of the «discoveries» of many contemporary hispanists, including —needless to mention— the modest contents of this essay, could have been made.

New York University.

121

9-

FIGURATIVE DISPLACEMENTS IN A PROSE POEM
OF LEZAMA LIMA: A COMMENTARY
ON *PESO DEL SABOR*

by

JAMES IRBY

> Hay quienes se sobresaltan tontamente cuando leen en Tristan Tzara: *el pensamiento se hace en la boca.* Y no se sobresaltan necesariamente cuando encuentran en Santo Tomás de Aquino: *La sabiduría es una emanación de la boca de Dios.*
>
> (LEZAMA LIMA: *Exámenes*)

I

As even casual readers can see, the texts of José Lezama Lima (1910-1976) are fabulously difficult. Fabulous as in the magic of fable. Fabulous as in fabulously rich. Difficult as in *difficult,* with the exuberance of those often quoted opening words of his lectures in *La expresión americana:* «Sólo lo difícil es estimulante.» Julio Ortega has recently summarized with admirable eloquence and insight the extreme nature of Lezama's displacements of poetic meaning, the force of his originality as poet and as *genius loci* of a tropical America. (Tropical: trope, turning point.) Ortega has shown also how refractory Lezama's writing is to the usual «balances críticos», but even so, he adds, «hay que proceder a esos balances pacientes para ir recorriendo con más detalle las evidencias de su mundo [...], [hay] que proceder a levantar los paradigmas poéticos, las operaciones textuales, el funcionamiento de sus figuras, la valencia connotadora de sus imágenes...».[1] For the most part, even elementary verifications are still lacking. Trying to make sense of Lezama, in the present state of affairs, is like trying to make sense, say, of Blake or Rimbaud or Mallarmé without any of the rich superstructure of annotation, concordance, biography and exegesis by the aid of which they are now available and precious to us. Lezama is of their kind. But in a New World.

So far, what detailed analyses of Lezama's writing we do possess have mostly preferred his fiction, especially the novel *Paradiso.* Very few of his many poems have ever been scrutinized closely to see how they function as texts. Ortega rightly notes that in his published work Lezama appears from the start as an accomplished poet, seeming never to show

---

[1] JULIO ORTEGA: «Prólogo» to his anthology of texts by Lezama, *El reino de la imagen* (Caracas: Biblioteca Ayacucho, 1981), p. xvii.

«los inicios de un aprendizaje». But this is not to say that there are no formative processes to be seen in his early work. By early I mean prior to his founding of the epoch-making magazine *Orígenes* in 1944, which was when Lezama also began to act more concertedly, with fertile and lasting results, as mentor to a younger group of Cuban writers. For the enigmatic Lezama offers us the additional enigma of always having sustained a genial, convivial dialogue with others. Ortega observes, «Lezama debe ser paradójicamente el escritor hermético que más ha buscado hacerse comprender», adding that «su voluntad de comunicar y comunicarse es también la búsqueda de ese conocimiento en el espacio de un diálogo que le resulta esencial a las demandas de su poética».[2] And it was precisely with the beginning of *Orígenes* that Lezama also began to move in his essays from pieces on individual authors toward a series of substantial speculations, which were to extend over the rest of his life, on poetics in general or, as he soon called it, «un sistema poético del mundo» (AR, 229).[3] Central to these speculations then and later was, of course, Lezama's peculiar Catholicism, his peculiar identification of the power of poetry (that is, the power of poetry of extreme difficulty, the power of extreme imagination over natural order) with the power of resurrection, that *quia absurdum* of early Christianity: «la muerte devorada por la sistematización de un nuevo absurdo poético», in a system that would be «la más segura marcha hacia la religiosidad de un cuerpo que se restituye y se abandona a su misterio» (AR, 229). In these few quoted words, I would stress the paradox of a system of the absurd, the oral metaphor of devouring and the restitution of a body as especially significant for what I want to develop here now.

In this transitional period, between his long essay on Julián del Casal of 1941 and the first of his general essays on poetics, the dialogue «X y XX» of 1945, Lezama wrote a remarkable set of ten prose poems that later came to form the middle section of his collection of otherwise mostly verse poems, *La fijeza*. This volume came out in 1949, but the prose poems are of earlier date, having first appeared in print between September 1942 and March 1944, one in each of the ten issues of another of Lezama's magazines, *Nadie parecía,* in exactly the same order in which they are found in *La fijeza* and in the later *Poesía completa* (this matter of their order or progression is very important, as we shall see).[4] Lezama's texts never quite resemble anyone else's, but these prose poems stand apart even in his own writing for their extraordinary energy and density, for their almost inextricably compacted clashes of many textual

---

[2] *Ibid.,* p. xxiii.

[3] All quotations from Lezama's writings are followed by abbreviations and page numbers referring to these editions:

AR   *Analecta del reloj* (Havana: Orígenes, 1953).

PC   *Poesía completa* (Havana: Instituto del Libro, 1970).

[4] For my attempt at an English translation of these prose poems, see José Lezama Lima: «Ten Prose Poems», *Sulfur,* I, 3 (1982), pp. 40-51. For the date of each poem's original appearance in *Nadie parecía,* see Pedro Simón (ed.), *Recopilación de textos sobre José Lezama Lima* (Havana: Casa de las Américas, 1970), pp. 353-4.

strands, both imagistic and discursive, in which each individual word takes on an enormous weight and an almost opaque materiality. Poems of intricate physical process alternate with sermon-like transports on ultimate paradoxes of the Resurrection, in an overall progression toward greater and greater enigma and fervor. The first few poems trace vivid images of corporeal form and motion: the silver shark suddenly taking shape, emerging from a primordial churning of waters like liquid lead, and the human arm steeped for years in the pounding tides of the ocean, growing for itself a whole new improbable body. However, as the set unfolds, any sense of recognizable contour and setting, indeed any sense of mimesis at all, disintegrates in what could be called, borrowing the title of the penultimate poem, an «éxtasis de sustancia destruida». That is, as their religious emphasis grows, the poems become more difficult, more dense in their *poiesis,* more impenetrable in their shaping of verbal bodies. Now part of this density is self-scrutiny or self-representation: these are poems also about their own processes. In fact, when seen closely alongside other texts of Lezama, especially the essays of those years, these poems appear as the most complete compendium of his early poetics, both in action and in speculation. From my notes for an extended analysis of all ten poems, I extract for presentation here a commentary on the fifth poem, «Peso del sabor», stressing the fact that this commentary is still a draft, a fragment of work in progress. But before explaining the reasons for choosing this poem and before considering at length the details of its functioning, I must mention a few more general features of the whole set.

These are strongly apocalyptic poems, both in the biblical sense and in the broader sense in which Northrop Frye has defined the apocalyptic as a basic variety of archetypal imagery. Three of the poems in particular I would call apocalyptic in the more strict, biblical sense. They are the fourth, seventh and ninth of the set, «Pífanos, epifanía, cabritos», «Procesión» and «Extasis de la sustancia destruida». These are the poems of sermon-like cast and inflection. The first and last of these explicitly quote *Revelation* as they conclude. All three end with prophetic references to resurrection and the final union of man with God. All three juxtapose pre-Christian concepts of man and the world to Christian ones in a sharply paradoxical way, simultaneously evoking and denying the sense of before and after, of temporal sequence and logical causality, the power of resurrection being seen here as a force shattering such orders. And a sense of shattering, of physical impact and dislocation is increasingly embodied in the verbal texture of each of these poems, with abstract and concrete terms violently wrenched from their normal contexts and thrown together in disconcerting new orders. Another poem, «Resistencia», the last one of the set, though of different configuration and only indirectly religious in its terms, partakes of this sense of the apocalyptic with its concluding quotation from Columbus' journal on the eve of sighting land in the Antilles, telling of a branch of fire falling into the sea, like the biblical burning bush. The final gesture of the whole set of prose poems is prophetic, suggesting the imminence of some

125

vast epochal change akin to the emergence of America, another shattering of orders: «Son las épocas de salvación y su signo es una fogosa resistencia» (PC, 179).

The apocalyptic in Frye's sense involves the extreme transformation of nature by human desire, «the imaginative conception of the whole of nature as the content of an infinite and eternal living body,» with the attendant effect of «animal and vegetable worlds identified with each other and with the divine and human worlds as well, [as] in the Christian doctrine of transubstantiation,» and symbolic transmutations of the four natural elements.[5] To these notions I would add others from Frye's commentary on Blake's *Marriage of Heaven and Hell:* the apocalypse and the resurrection as man's «return to the titanic bodily form he originally possessed» before the Fall, with «no natural laws which the risen body must obey and no compulsory categories by which it must perceive».[6]

The other six poems of the set seem bent on postulating and creating various tangencies, intimations, of such an infinite «titanic body.» They can be divided into two groups of three each. The first group is comprised by the first three poems of the set, «Noche dichosa», «Censuras fabulosas» and «La sustancia adherente», which I would call, borrowing a phrase from Lezama's essay «Sierpe de don Luis de Góngora» (1951), poems of «metamorfosis ácuea» (AR, 202). Here the images of the shark («Censuras fabulosas») and the arm («La sustancia adherente») appear. Each of these poems traces the change or formation of a body—human, animal or composite—as it moves though the ocean's waters or is acted upon by the waters' own motions. The space here is the organic space of seascape, of flux and flow. The bodies are organic as well, undergoing growth, accretion, osmosis, but the whole interaction of diverse substances evolves entities that more and more exceed natural limits.

The fifth, sixth and eighth poems, «Peso del sabor», «Muerte del tiempo» and «Tangencias», are what I would call poems of anti-physics. Here the space is more that of sheer extension, of trajectory and mass, of number, velocity and gravity, where both organic and inorganic bodies coexist. But at the same time, the movement of these bodies in this space, though strongly marked, is more and more violently interrupted, scattered, negated, generating an extreme tension of opposing or intersecting forces, thematicized in «Muerte del tiempo» by the express train accelerating to an infinite velocity that is also an infinite stasis. The concluding poem of the set, «Resistencia», though akin to the sermon-like apocalyptic poems by virtue of its discursive configuration, also partakes of the tendency of the anti-physical group, by virtue of its explicit opposition of *poiesis* and physics and its insistent transformation of the term *resistencia,* which normally connotes passivity, into an active, disruptive force that breaks into various physical and psychic conti-

---

[5] NORTHROP FRYE: *Anatomy of Criticism* (Princeton: Princeton University Press, 1957), pp. 119, 143, 145.

[6] NORTHROP FRYE: *Fearful Symmetry: A Study of William Blake* (Boston: Beacon Press, 1962), pp. 194, 195.

nuities. It is very striking that in the concluding poem of such an apocalyptic set there are no clear, central references to God's powers. The ubiquitous mover is, instead, *resistencia*. Now in Lezama's essays of that time, *resistencia* and *resistente* are always linked to *poiesis,* as when he speaks of «los poetas tejedores de la gran resistencia» (AR, 214). Discontinuity, the disruption of strong progressions, the leap to terms defying relation, are for him so essential to that weave of poetry that at one point he wonders whether a poem is a unit at all: «¿La poesía tiene que ser discontinuidad o un ente?» (AR, 145). In this sense, the prose poems end with a celebration of a power more poetic than divine.

II

Here is the text of «Peso del sabor» (PC, 171-2):

Sentado dentro de mi boca asisto al paisaje. La gran tuba alba establece musitaciones, puentes y encadenamientos no espiraloides. En esa tuba, el papel y el goterón de plomo van cayendo con lentitud pero sin causalidad. Aunque si se retira la esterilla de la lengua y nos enfrentamos de pronto con la bóveda palatina, el papel y la gota de plomo no podrían resistir el terror. Entonces, el papel y la gota de plomo hacia abajo son como la tortuga hacia arriba mas sin ascender. Si retirásemos la esterilla... Así el sabor que tiende a hacer punta, si le arrancásemos la lengua, se multiplicaría en perennes llegadas, como si nuestra puerta estuviese asistida de continuo por dogos, limosneros chinos, ángeles (la clase de ángeles llamados Tronos que colocan rápidamente en Dios a las cosas) y crustáceos de cola larga. Al ser rebanada la esterilla, convirtiendo el vacío en pez preguntón aunque sin ojos, las cuerdas vocales reciben el flujo de humedad oscura, comenzando la monodia. Un bandazo oscuro y el eco de las cuerdas vocales, persiguiendo así la noche a la noche, el lomo del gato menguante al caballito del diablo, consiguiéndose la cantidad de albura para que el mensajero pueda atravesar el paredón. La lámina de papel y la gota de plomo van hacia el círculo luminoso del abdomen, que tiende sus hogueras para recibir al visitante y alejar la agonía moteada del tigre lastimero. La pesadumbre de la bóveda palatina tritura hasta el aliento, decidiendo que el rayo luminoso tenga que avanzar entre los estados coloidales formados por las revoluciones de los sólidos y los líquidos en su primer fascinación inaugural, cuando los comienzos giran sin poder desprender aún las edades. Después, las sucesiones mantendrán siempre la nostalgia del ejemplar único limitado, pavo real blanco, o búfalo que no ama el fango, pero quedando para siempre la cercanía comunicada y alcanzada, como si sólo pudiésemos caminar sobre la esterilla. Sentado dentro de mi boca advierto a la muerte moviéndose como el abeto inmóvil sumerge su guante de hielo en las basuras del estanque. Una inversa

costumbre me había hecho la opuesta maravilla, en sueños de siesta
creía obligación consumada —sentado ahora en mi boca contemplo la oscuridad que rodea al abeto—, que día a día el escriba amaneciese palmera.

This is one of the more difficult poems of the set, though not the
most difficult. I chose it for analysis because it offers a particularly
striking example of how mimesis is destroyed in these poems by
intricate rhetorical means and, at the same time, because of its powerful
sense of a transformed body. In the first three poems of the set, a continuing outline of body seen amid a seascape is discernible, though less
and less distinct in each poem. As long as such an outline remains
distinct and continuing, there is also at least the illusion of a literal
ground of reference figuratively elaborated or varied to one degree or
another. Here the opening sentence refers a body in a setting to the
first person singular (rare in these poems), lending it the emphasis of
that form of utterance. But no sooner are these initial givens stated, a
complex process of figurative displacement begins to recombine them
so radically with other elements that the body, setting and person lose
any possible status as literal grounds of reference. Furthermore, whereas
in the earlier poems the movement was of a single body through a space,
here there are many movements of many bodies through the body posited
initially, in such a multiple way that finally there is no sense of separate
space and body left at all. It is this complex process of figurative displacement that I want to trace in detail here. As part of that process,
I will also point out some symbolic equivalences suggested by passages
in essays by Lezama, equivalences that make it possible to read the
poem as the allegory of a poetics.

A significant division of the poem into three main segments is suggested by the way the opening sentence —«Sentado dentro de mi boca
asisto al paisaje»— is repeated twice at the end, in the last two sentences, with variations and added elements. The first segment is the
opening sentence itself, the third its repetition and variation, and the
second the longer segment lying in between. This division is corroborated
by the way semantic classes of important words are distributed throughout the poem. To recognize these classes it is essential of course to recognize as well a variety of what I will call for the moment «figurative»
substitutions, though, later on, when in the main part of my commentary
I trace in detail those substitutions, it will become evident how problematical any distinction between «figurative» and «literal» is with regard to
this poem. The most important semantic class is made up of terms
relating to the mouth and throat, which appear in all segments but
according to the following variation. In the first and third segments,
boca alone appears. In the second, there is instead a series of metonyms
or synecdoches: *lengua, bóveda palatina, sabor, cuerdas vocales, abdomen*
and *aliento,* some of which are repeated several times. The *paisaje* of the
opening sentence has its synecdochic counterparts at the end in *abeto*
(twice), *estanque* and *palmera.* The second segment has no vegetation or

other landscape element strictly speaking, but on the other hand it has a large number of other living beings that can be classed as «God and a hierarchy of His creatures» (or «God and a full range of His sentient creatures, mortal and immortal»), among which animals are the most frequent: *tortuga, dogos, limosneros, ángeles, Dios, crustáceos, pez, gato, caballito del diablo, mensajero, tigre, pavo real* and *búfalo,* no member of which class is repeated. The second segment also has a distinctive component in the repeated pair *papel / plomo,* to which perhaps, *humedad, estados coloidales, sólidos* and *líquidos* could be assimilated in a class of «substances.» Another semantic distribution distinguishing the three segments of the poem is the varying sense of space in each. Here again a «figurative» substitution is important. The opening sentence provides the matrix. No matter whether we consider the landscape to be inside or outside the mouth, the words *dentro, boca, paisaje* and *asisto* imply an inside / outside distinction of some sort reinforced by an observer / observed distinction. Now if we substitute for *boca* a word like *casa* we obtain a «non-figurative» statement, a fact not without consequences, since throughout the second segment of the poem a sense of house or dwelling coexists with that of mouth, body, etc., which is an aspect of the blurred or disappearing sense of inside / outside characteristic of this segment. In the final segment, the initial spatial distinction reappears only to be juxtaposed to an erasure of that distinction in the last sentence, as I will show later. One other feature differentiating the three segments is the use of first person pronouns, *yo* at the beginning and end, *nosotros* in between. All these distributions have some significant exceptions to be noted later, but for the moment they provide useful entry into the poem's processes.

Before looking more closely at those processes, however, a further overall sense of the relationship between the three segments of the poem can be gained by noting how certain of its key terms —*boca, plomo, retirar, siesta*— were also used by Lezama in two essays written at about the same time. By calling attention to these other uses, I do not intend to reduce the poem's meaning to that of the essays, since, aside from the fact that their meaning is no easy matter to establish either, the differences, as we shall see, are as suggestive as the similarities. The immediate contexts in the essays where these terms appear all have to do with defining poetry. First of all, there is this passage toward the end of «Julián del Casal». After speaking of Casal's introduction into Cuba of a poetry of what Lezama calls «evaporación», represented in Europe by Baudelaire, he then mentions another kind of poetry introduced by Martí:

> El poeta, dice Claudel, en su boca sin hablar siente las palabras por su sabor. Tenía Martí el sabor de las palabras, aunque en ocasiones masticaba demasiado deprisa. Había llegado por esa salvadora pesantez del verbo a una danza, más tumultuosa que de ballet, en que el paladar intervenía directamente en la sabiduría. Claro está que así como Casal no llegó a una total recepción entre la

129

imitación y la onda como Baudelaire, Martí tampoco había de llegar a la total rumia, salvadora gota de plomo o buey junto al establo, de Unamuno, Claudel o Peguy. Ya que el sabor no es una prueba deliciosa, como el desprendimiento de la sustancia, sino poema incorporado, como lo es también la respiración. Y esa danza nocturna en que la palabra en una innumerable ley de gravitación gira sobre el secante de la lengua que absorbe con una lentitud que es casi un irradiar. Y el cielo del paladar cayendo, triturando casi la oscura ley del verbo, muy semejante al otro cielo sobre nosotros mismos (AR, 94-5).[7]

Rather than an externalization, a bringing forth, here poetry is a taking in, an oral incorporation, a chewing, savoring and transmutation of words as if they were physical substances, having their own gravitation and weight, their own dark density. And this incorporation is also a wisdom (*sabor* and *sabiduría*, in fact, derive from the same root) and a salvation, which, judging by the Catholicism of the European poets chosen to exemplify the plenitude of such poetry, must be a Christian redemption. The drop of lead is mentioned only once, but it is obviously an image of that paradoxical «salvadora pesantez del verbo». And the way it is equated to another kind of heaviness represented by the ox (aside from the stable and its possible allusion to the Nativity, note here the equivalence of incorporator and incorporated) seems parallel to the way, in the poem, a whole parade of animals and other creatures alternates with the paper and lead in a (partly) oral space. The poem never declares any correspondence between *palabra* and *gota de plomo,* of the kind it does state between *esterilla* and *lengua.* Its series of words clearly implying verbal communication —*musitaciones, llamado, preguntón, mensajero, escriba*— seems overshadowed by other series. But the insistent combination of the lead with paper (thereby forming the paradox of a light substance and a heavy one both falling in the same way) does suggest the materials of writing or printing. The most striking difference between the essay and the poem, however, is that, in «Peso del sabor», instead of absorbing the lead / word / wisdom / poem, the tongue is repeatedly, violently *removed,* and that the falling of the paper and lead, which is concurrent with a proliferation of creatures and other substances (akin to the *innumerable ley,* the *danza,* the *irradiar,* in the essay), seems to take place precisely as a result of that removal.

The idea of removal or withdrawal, along with some other important elements found in the poem, occurs in another essay, «X y XX». At

---

[7] The statement by Claudel must be from his *Art poétique*: «Pour comprendre les choses, apprenons les mots qui en sont dans notre bouche l'image soluble. Ruminons la bouchée intelligible» (PAUL CLAUDEL: *Oeuvre poétique,* Paris: Bibliothèque de la Pléiade, 1957, p. 149). When Lezama's essay was reprinted after the Cuban Revolution in the centenary edition of Casal's works, the reservations here about Martí were all replaced by expressions of praise, and the names of Emerson and Whitman were added to those of Unamuno, Claudel and Péguy (see JULIÁN DEL CASAL: *Prosas,* I, Havana: Consejo Nacional de Cultura, 1963, p. 89).

the end of a long passage which speaks about sleep, death and «la voluntad de penetrar con la forma de la persona en ese cuerpo oscuro que ya no es el cuerpo nuestro», comes this:

En el Trópico todo depende del estilo de la siesta. Y que en la misma siesta piense usted en el suicidio. Después sale de esa siesta con sus sentidos iluminados. Todos los días en la siesta, como ejercicio de ascesis, piense en la muerte. Eso fortalece su sensualismo, lo hace más verdadero. En la poesía, en su sustancia, es como la voluntad logra manifestarse con más dignidad, se hace totalmente invisible. Hay allí una lucha entre los retiramientos y los números concordes. Un poema va avanzando en la concordancia de los números, es decir, el ritmo, pero de pronto aquella impulsión gratuita vacila y ya nada más que percibe que no puede continuar, porque para esperar el nacimiento de una palabra hay que aislarla con una violencia desusada de su impulsión anterior, de su eco y del metal con que se apuntala momentos antes de extinguirse (AR, 136-7).

Here, rather than the oral elements of the middle segment of the poem, we find the main elements of the conclusion: the tropics (implied by the contrast between fir and palm), the *siesta*, the evocation of death, with, of course, the variation that in the poem death is seen in the landscape and the dream omits death. In «X y XX», as in the Casal essay, there is a wisdom —the illumination of the senses— and a salvation, a liberation from the power of death. More importantly, in both essays these clusters of images illustrate modes of *poiesis*. *Retiramientos* are the breaks in continuity in a poem, breaks that depart from clear harmonious sequences (*números concordes*) and violently isolate words so they may be «born». Since *retirar* is used twice in the poem for the removal of the tongue and then followed by the more violent *arrancar* and *rebanar*, it would seem that such an insistent destruction of the natural organ of articulation, accompanied by the multiplication of other elements, represents those productive discontinuities of *poiesis*, which, as I have suggested earlier, are consubstantial for Lezama with the unending miracle and power of resurrection. As he says later in «X y XX», «la discontinuidad es la única manera de aproximarnos a la reaparición incesante» (AR, 149).

The third essayistic passage relevant to particulars of «Peso del sabor» is also found in «X y XX». Disagreeing with Rilke's notion of a death of one's own (*muerte propia*), Lezama writes:

Pero la muerte que quisiera ser propia es en realidad sucesiva. La forma en que la muerte nos va recorriendo pasa desapercibida, pero va formando una sustancia igualmente coincidente, actuando como el espacio ocupado como un poema, espacio que muy pronto deviene sustancia, formado por la presencia de la gravitación de las palabras y por la ausencia del reverso no previsible que ellas engendran. El tamaño de un poema, hasta donde está lleno de *poiesis*, hasta donde su extensión es un dominio propio, es una resistencia

131

tan compleja como la discontinuidad inicial de la muerte. Es decir, no hay el poema propio, sino una sustancia que de pronto invade constituyendo el cuerpo o la desazón sin ventura. La forma en que hay que tocarla o respetarla, abandonarla o poseerla, descarga en lo inmediato una cuantía tan inefablemente contraída que es imposible revisarla por el propio sujeto. El poeta es como un copista que al copiar prefiere hacerlo en éxtasis (AR, 146).

This is a more complex passage and only a few things in it can be noted here. Again there are intimations of death inseparable from the substance of poetry. But there are variations. Earlier it was discontinuity / rebirth, now the necessary complement appears: discontinuity / death. Again the gravitation of words, again their substance as the substance of *poiesis,* not a substance fashioned by the poet as his own, but an invading substance received and transcribed. The use of *copista* here clarifies the use of *escriba* in «Peso del sabor». And the notion of death going through us like a substance through a space, or leaving a substance, just as the verbal substances move through the space of a poem, could help explain why so many living creatures mingle with the lead and paper in «Peso del sabor», since they are, for the most part, *mortal* creatures.

In the light of all these passages it becomes possible to suggest a correspondence between the three segments of «Peso del sabor». The beginning and end use *boca* as a vantage point from which to perceive a landscape and transform it. The middle segment uses orality to incorporate substances and beings and words and transform them. Both transformations are transformations also of the body into an organism that is vaster and more inclusive and more multiple and more powerful («titanic» in that sense). And all these transformations are complementary, converging, modes of *poiesis.*

Let us now look more particularly at the sequences and discontinuities by means of which «Peso del sabor» is fashioned. Like other prose poems in the same set, especially those I called poems of anti-physics, its progressions are marked by extreme tensions. There is a simultaneous sense of the densely *compacted* and the intensely *disjunctive.* On the one hand, there is an effect of strict concatenation of syntax and of objects named: the patterns of «if this then that» and «as this is done that happens,» along with the physical contiguity and contact of objects in close interaction. On the other hand, there is a bewildering eruption of successive varieties of new terms so distant from one another as to seem complete non-sequiturs. To this sense of distance and of tension, two other tendencies strongly contribute. One is the repeated switching back and forth between «literal» and «figurative» in intricate accumulations. For example, elements introduced as «figurative» terms of a comparison or hypothesis then come to function like «literal» terms in subsequent comparisons or hypotheses, and so on. Variants of this tendency are the plays on more or less «literal» or more or less «abstract» or «concrete» repetitions of certain terms. The other tendency is the repeated use of paradox or oxymoron as the axis of relationship. The paradoxical or contradictory building of figure upon figure (and figure within figure) becomes especially complex in the closing two sentences of the poem.

Just after the opening sentence, the passage about the *gran tuba alba* initiates one of the main series of repetitions in the middle segment —that of the paper and lead— and seems to contain implications about the status of words in the poem:

> Sentado dentro de mi boca asisto al paisaje. La gran tuba alba establece musitaciones, puentes y encadenamientos no espiraloides. En esa tuba, el papel y el goterón de plomo van cayendo con lentitud pero sin causalidad.

«Sentado dentro de mi boca...» and «En esa tuba...» are precise in their spatial sense: something or someone located *inside* something else. But where is the *tuba* located: in the mouth or in the landscape? And what is this *tuba*, which never reappears later? An instrument of sound, obviously, and in that sense analogous to the mouth, but is it a metaphor for the mouth? Subsequently, the paper and lead which it contains intermingle with parts of the mouth, literally so named or identified by the metaphor *esterilla de la lengua*. But the *tuba* cannot be so clearly situated or equated in the poem. Recalling that passages from *Revelation* are cited or evoked in other prose poems of this set, that near the beginning of *Revelation* the *tuba* or trumpet first appears as a metaphor for the divine voice, which directs the speaker to write down what he will see,[8] and that both *tuba* and the color white are frequent throughout *Revelation*, one could conjecture that this unlocatable, founding instrument containing the materials of writing that fall into the body suggests that supernatural and impersonal origin of the word, that «sustancia que de pronto invade» spoken of in «X y XX». The *tuba* establishes mutterings, linkages. The lead and paper fall without causality. Immediately after this, however, a causality, a linkage, an articulation begins to be traced.

Two important series begin in the next few lines, series that closely alternate and interlock with one another and with the series of the lead and paper, begun just before. One is the series of the mouth, or rather of its synecdoches or parts, of which the tongue is the most notable because of the repeated insistence on its removal and the consequences thereof and also because of the particularly obvious play on the «literal» and the «figurative» it forms part of. Tongue and palate are synecdoches for the mouth, but *esterilla de la lengua* and *bóveda palatina* are metaphors that make explicit the implied double sense of mouth as mouth and mouth as house in the opening sentence. They are also metaphors that display both the «literal» and «figurative» terms of their comparison. *Bóveda palatina* is a lexicalized metaphor that remains constant, *esterilla de la lengua* an invention of Lezama's that subsequently becomes just

---

[8] I refer to *Revelation* 1: 10-11: «I was in the Spirit on the Lord's day, and heard behind me a great voice, as of a trumpet, / Saying, I am Alpha and Omega, the first and the last: and, What thou seest, write in a book...»

esterilla (with one exception to be noted later). The stages in the tongue's removal can be schematicized as follows:

(A) Aunque *si se retira la esterilla de la lengua* y nos enfrentamos de pronto con la bóveda palatina, el papel y la gota de plomo no podrían resistir el terror.

(B & C) *Si retirásemos la esterilla...* Así el sabor que tiende a hacer punta, *si le arrancásemos la lengua,* se multiplicaría en perennes llegadas [...]

(D) *Al ser rebanada la esterilla,* convirtiendo al vacío en pez preguntón aunque sin ojos, las cuerdas vocales reciben el flujo de humedad oscura [...]

The «terror» could be the release of possibilities by removing natural articulation. Included in those possibilities is the plurality of *nosotros* instead of the initial *yo.* In a metonymical shift, the terror is felt, not by us, but by the verbal materials themselves. The whole series comprises three suppositions about the results of removing the tongue, followed by an assertion of what happens as it *is* removed: a move from the hypothetical to the assertive, from the «figurative» to the «literal». With increasing violence a paradox is repeated: a removal, a mutilation, causes an abundance, a proliferation. At (B & C), just as the removal is seen as violent and its result as multiplicative, there is another metonymical shift adding another «figurative» degree: if the *flavor's* tongue were torn out... (but tongue, the «literal» term, returns).

Another series involved here is that of animals and creatures, whose first two appearances are introduced by two other «figurative» shifts, a simile and a hypothetical comparison, an «as if». Just after (A), comes this as another result: «Entonces, el papel y la gota de plomo hacia abajo son como la tortuga hacia arriba mas sin ascender.» To the «literality» of the invariant lead and paper, a «figurative» comparison is attached, a comparison which is also an oxymoron, a logical impossibility. And yet, the tortoise so introduced is the first of many creatures, many animals, to follow, so in that sense the «impossible» trope becomes a bridge to the reality of an invading, proliferating series. Then, just after the complex hypothesis at (B & C), as an amplifying illustration, but also as yet another hypothesis, comes this: «...como si nuestra puerta estuviese asistida de continuo por dogos, limosneros chinos, ángeles (la clase de ángeles llamados Tronos que colocan rápidamente en Dios a las cosas) y crustáceos de cola larga». (*Puerta* here continues the sense of house, as will *paredón* later.) Hypothesis upon hypothesis, figured level upon figured level, but the series of creatures extends, now encompassing God and angel and man and animal, and it will later become even more widely established, with animals recurring even more (here there is also a kind of *mise en abyme:* into the mouth / house space are placed the same kind of angels that put things in God). When the tongue series ends with the assertion of effects concomitant with the slicing away of that

134

organ, a transformation is added, turning an emptiness into a fish (and a blind and verbally inquisitive one at that): «... convirtiendo el vacío en pez preguntón aunque sin ojos...».

(Before tracing this process any further, I should point out that each of the above figures introduced by *como* or *como si* has a symmetrical counterpart later in the poem. The simile «la muerte moviéndose como el abeto inmóvil...», like the simile of the tortoise, is an oxymoron concerning movement and, like it also, introduces a «figurative» term —the fir— that immediately then takes on the effectiveness of the «literal». The hypothetical comparison « como si sólo pudiésemos caminar sobre la esterilla» closing the middle segment of the poem, unlike the earlier multiplicative use of *como si,* now proposes in the form of a contrary-to-fact supposition a limitation, a reduction of the *lengua / esterilla* metaphor to only one «literal» term. I will note other implications of both these comparisons later.)

The end of the tongue series initiates this part of the middle segment:

> Al ser rebanada la esterilla, convirtiendo al vacío en pez preguntón aunque sin ojos, las cuerdas vocales reciben el flujo de humedad oscura, comenzando la monodia. Un bandazo oscuro y el eco de las cuerdas vocales, persiguiendo así la noche a la noche, el lomo del gato menguante al caballito del diablo, consiguiéndose la cantidad de albura para que el mensajero pueda atravesar el paredón. La lámina de papel y la gota de plomo van hacia el círculo luminoso del abdomen que tiende sus hogueras para recibir al visitante y alejar la agonía del tigre lastimero.

The continuing series of animals now includes varieties inhabiting land, air and water. The addition of *hogueras* provides the fourth basic element —fire— as well. Another part of the oral cavity —*cuerdas vocales*— appears twice, adding to the verbal series begun earlier —*musitaciones, llamados, preguntón, mensajero*—, which will culminate later with *escriba* (and there is sound also: *eco, monodia*). Amid these increases in substances and the verbal, the paper and lead reappear for the last time, moving toward the center of absorption in the body (but which has fires for visitors, like a house). The predominant substance or element is water and there is also a repeated stress on darkness and light. All of these, especially the latter, have roles in the important transformations occurring at the end of the poem. Finally, throughout the passage quoted above, there is a vigorous concatenation of physical movements and contacts: receiving, beginning, pursuing, attaining, going through, going toward, keeping away.

The final part of the middle segment of the poem contains a major set of variations which introduces a metalinguistic dimension:

> La pesadumbre de la bóveda palatina tritura hasta el aliento, decidiendo que el rayo luminoso tenga que avanzar entre los estados coloidales formados por las revoluciones de los sólidos y los líquidos en su primer fascinación inaugural, cuando los comienzos

135

giran sin poder desprender aún las edades. Después, las sucesiones mantendrán siempre la nostalgia del ejemplar único limitado, pavo real blanco, o búfalo que no ama el fango, pero quedando para siempre la cercanía comunicada y alcanzada, como si sólo pudiésemos caminar sobre la esterilla.

The heaviness, previously implied by the lead and attached in the title to *sabor,* here is attached to the palate, in a metonymical transfer rather like the earlier tearing out of the flavor's tongue. But, more strikingly, the grinding up effected by the palate (there are no teeth in this poem of orality) leads to a new mode of designation, a new order of relationships. What the grinding up determines is that the ray of light moves not into specific substances like those named before (lead, paper, dampness) but into general types of substance, more abstractly designated (colloids, liquids, solids). And their movements are defined with a sudden concentration of another kind of abstract vocabulary hitherto all but absent from the poem, a temporal and numerical vocabulary: *primer fascinación inaugural, comienzos, aún, edades, después, sucesiones, nostalgia, ejemplar único limitado, siempre.* Previously there seemed to be a movement toward digestion. Now there is like a primordial swirl, a genesis, with cosmic ages to follow. But it is also as if what had previously unfolded in the poem —the emergence, interaction and progressive multiplication of substances and creatures— were now being reconsidered abstractly. And precisely when that sense of reconsideration appears, movements of pro-gression and re-gression are named: *sucesiones, nostalgia* (from Greek *nostos,* return). Earlier, I suggested that this shift from concrete to abstract is akin to the shift from «literal» to «figurative».

Also, amid these abstractions, there are still more animals, concretely named: *pavo real blanco, búfalo que no ama el fango.* Why are they «unique limited specimens», why will successions maintain nostalgia for them? Perhaps unique because atypical, perhaps seen with nostalgia because, as such, they remain *hors série.* But then what is the «nearness communicated and attained» and how is this like «only walking on the mat»? In the first passage quoted earlier from «X y XX», Lezama speaks of the progression of a poem as «una lucha entre los retiramientos y los números concordes» (AR, 136). In another essay, «Exámenes» (1950),[9] there is a long and very difficult passage (AR, 225-7) concerning another kind of struggle in a poem, a struggle between its longing to return to its point of origin («deseos de reingresar en el acto que lo exhaló», AR,

[9] Rather than a continuous text, «Exámenes» is a mosaic of fragments (AR, 215-29) which contains at its conclusion Lezama's first formulation of the idea of «un sistema poético del mundo». Immediately preceding that formulation, several of the prose poems are paraphrased and one is quoted (the last sentence of «Peso del sabor») without, however, explaining to the reader in any way what texts are being referred to or who wrote them. Also, in the middle of «Exámenes», four verse poems by Lezama are inserted with no comment. These poems are not found in any of his volumes of poetry.

225), which is called a «nostalgia», and its impulse towards an «incesante proliferación de las sugerencias» (AR, 226), an «incesante suma de nacimientos» (AR, 227), driven by «otros deseos de religación que no eran la constante de su materia trabajada» (AR, 226). If we see «nostalgia» here as meaning not just a desire to regain the initial creative moment but also a desire to remain faithful to the initial image, to effect some kind of continuing mimesis of it as the poem unfolds, then perhaps that meaning can elucidate the passage in question in «Peso del sabor». But, of course, what is «same», what is «different», what is «mimesis», what are for that matter «literal» and «figurative»? The «unique specimens» evoked are animals and, as such, belong to a series already established in the poem. But they are *different* from all the others and it also happens that, whereas *esterilla / lengua, cuerdas vocales, bóveda palatina* and *papel* and *plomo* are all repeated literally or with slight variants in the poem, no animal or creature is repeated, *all* of them are different. An approximation of sameness, this passage seems to say, can be gained —«cercanía comunicada y alcanzada»— but what follows as a seeming illustration of this is «como si sólo pudiésemos caminar sobre la esterilla»: we can suppose (but it isn't so) the mat is only a mat to walk on. And following that «return» of a previous figure, the initial sentence of the poem also «returns», but how?

Here is that initial sentence with the two variants of it found at the close:

(A) Sentado dentro de mi boca asisto al paisaje.

(B) Sentado dentro de mi boca advierto a la muerte
moviéndose como el abeto inmóvil sumerge su guante
de hielo en las basuras del estanque.

(C) Sentado ahora en mi boca contemplo la oscuridad
que rodea al abeto.

The main verb changes, but the sense of witnessing or perceiving remains constant. *Paisaje* is replaced by longer phrases, but a sense of landscape continues, organized around *abeto* as a repeated synecdoche. The third sentence, like the first, can be seen as a «non-figurative» statement with one «figurative» substitution, that of *boca* for another term like *casa*. The second, however, introduces as landscape a complex figure, itself made of both «literal» and «figurative» elements, the «figurative» ones being *muerte* placed as something perceptible in a spatial context and the implicit personification of *abeto*. As in the simile used earlier in the poem, a new element —*muerte*— is introduced by way of an oxymoron, the difference here being that not all terms naturally belong to the realm of movement / stasis (whereas before *tortuga, papel* and *plomo* all did). A main effect here is to insert «death» by a symmetrical variation of figures into a context of perceptible external space, linked to cold, darkness and a certain tree.

But the sense of this progression is drastically altered by the larger

137

sentence into which the third variant is inserted as a parenthetical member:

> Una inversa costumbre me había hecho la opuesta maravilla, en sueños de siesta creía obligación consumada —sentado ahora en mi boca contemplo la oscuridad que rodea al abeto—, que día a día el escriba amaneciese palmera.

Along with the sense of insertion, of containment (so pervasive in this poem, even in the midst of so much scattering), there is also the sense of a mirror image, coming from the preceding suggestion of the fir reflected in the pond and the insistence here on inversion. This larger sentence also works its variations on the basic members of the others:

sentado dentro de mi boca+   advierto   +muerte moviéndose como abeto
↓   ↓   ↓

sentado   ...   en mi boca+   contemplo   +oscuridad que rodea abeto
↓   ↓   ↓

en sueños de siesta   +creía obligación +escriba amaneciese palmera
                                consumada

The vantage point becomes an activity unlocatable in space (dreaming), the perception becomes a belief (moreover, belief in a fulfilled obligation), and the spatial relationship of landscape elements becomes a relationship of metamorphosis (a scribe awakens as a palm). These changes are reinforced by further shifts from earlier patterns in the poem. Previously, the present tense had been the only one used. Now the past perfect and imperfect appear in a sharp contrast further marked by the pair *inversa costumbre* / *opuesta maravilla* and the addition of *ahora*. Surrounding the last variant of the poem's beginning, there is a retrospective evocation of some prior continuity other than the one hitherto traced by the text. The chiasmus «una inversa costumbre me había hecho la opuesta maravilla...» on one level joins both perception and dream as customs producing marvels (another oxymoron), but on another level it separates them, playing on the similarity of *inversa* and *opuesta* to produce a marvel opposite to the perception of death. In dreams, day after day, the scribe awakened as a palm: a metamorphosis contrary to the darkness and cold and death here clustered around the northern fir, contrary too to the separation of perceiver and perceived in space (the space that Lezama once called «el demonio de lo extenso, donde es imposible la participación metafórica», AR, 228). This metamorphosis seems to partake of the force of natural sequences of change: the passage from night to day and from sleep to waking, the growth of a tree. The *yo* throughout is passive, limited to contemplation and dreaming; other forces act upon it, displace it. Categories previously kept separate in the other segments of the poem now converge and the transformational energy built up throughout the various interlocking series in the middle segment is drawn upon again in this close. «Creature» and «tree» (= landscape) up to now belonged to separate segments of the poem. Now a new instance of one class (scribe) is transformed into a new instance of the other (palm), with various earlier connotations of the verbal and of writing returning in *escriba*.

A few concluding remarks, some of them about conclusions. «Dense» I have repeatedly called Lezama's prose poems. (Density: the degree to which anything is filled or occupied, the amount of something per unit measure.) I have tried to show what that means, the incredible concentration of rhetorical displacement, the incredible expansion, too. Ortega has spoken of «hiporfiguración» in Lezama, explaining:

> ... la figura en Lezama está lejos de poder ser codificada desde aquellos repertorios [de las retóricas tradicionales], porque las distancias que ella establece entre sus términos, en el impulso de la hipérbole, no están soldadas por un discurso no-figurativo, cuya excepción sería el instante de la figura; al contrario, es el cuerpo mismo del poema una figuración, y, de ese modo, un rebasamiento de los doblajes, alusiones, coberturas y sustituciones, de la figura retórica estable.[10]

I have tried to show how this occurs in a given text and in its dialogue with a few others. One of the difficulties in understanding Lezama's texts lies in the difficulty of seeing them as processes leading by functional stages to a definite *end*. These prose poems, however, though difficult, usually close with a gesture of religious affirmation which, explicitly or implicitly, is charged with a sense of resurrection. «Peso del sabor» certainly follows this pattern. Robert Graves has pointed out that both the fir and the palm are «birth trees» signifying, since very ancient times, eternal life.[11] Lezama, of course, makes his scribe the tropical variant.

Princeton University.

---

[10] JULIO ORTEGA, p. xxxvi.
[11] ROBERT GRAVES: *The White Goddess* (London: Faber and Faber, 1962), p. 190.

NOTES ON THE VALUE AND MEANING
OF SENSE EXPERIENCE IN THE NOVEL:
MONTEMAYOR TO MIRO

by

WILLARD F. KING

No reader of Gabriel Miró can fail to remark the wide, complicated, and original use he makes of sensory experience and the demands he makes on his reader to absorb his text through the senses. We are compelled to see, hear, taste, feel, touch not only the Levantine landscape but the moral and emotional aura of the characters who people it: not only the quality and aroma of the breeze that ruffles trees or raises dust, the dazzle of sun on irrigation ditches, the aroma of tuberoses or the fetid smell of flooded rivers, but also the form and shape of the lived moment and the physical weight and feel of human joy or fear or pain.

To Ortega y Gasset, who in his 1914 *Meditaciones del Quijote* irritably condemned the Mediterranean artist for his «sensualismo» and delighted representation of the «apariencia de las cosas,» Miró must have seemed the ultimate «impressionist» and «illusionist.» [1] Unhappy even with Goya for his shimmering impressionism, «frenético dinamismo,» and lack of Northern European profundity and solidity, Ortega characterizes Latin artists as «meros soportes de los órganos de los sentidos: vemos, oímos, olemos, palpamos, gustamos, sentimos el placer y el dolor orgánicos... Con cierto orgullo repetimos la expresión de Gautier: "El mundo exterior existe para nosotros".» Never, he cautions, can sense impressions give us «lo que nos da el concepto, a saber, la forma, el sentido físico y moral de las cosas.» [2]

It should then have come as no surprise that Ortega, when faced with the task of reviewing in 1927 Miró's *El obispo leproso,* found the novel not to his taste. Brilliant, in that «superficial» Mediterranean way, so much so that the images almost blinded him («recamado de luces y de imágenes, hasta el punto que casi ha de leerse con la mano en visera, amparando los ojos»),[3] yet not a good «novel,» perhaps because, like the canvases of Goya, it lacked «conceptos»—although, to be sure, in this

[1] José Ortega y Gasset: *Meditaciones del Quijote y La deshumanización del Arte* (Buenos Aires: Espasa Calpe, 1942), p. 72.

[2] *Meditaciones,* pp. 84, 73, and 81 respectively. For an explanation of Ortega's apparent animus against impressionism and plea for «conceptos», see Philip W. Silver: *Ortega as Phenomenologist: The Genesis of Meditaciones on Quijote* (New York: Columbia Univ. Press, 1978).

[3] «El obispo leproso», por Gabriel Miró: *Obras completas,* 6th ed., III (Madrid: Revista de Occidente, 1966), 545.

fretful and uncomfortable review Ortega appears mostly dissatisfied with the development of character.

Whether we agree or disagree with Ortega's criticisms of Miró (perhaps they should not be taken too seriously, since he confessed in the same review to being a «pésimo lector de novelas,» p. 544), Don José does, as usual, stimulate thought and direct our attention, in this review and in the earlier *Meditaciones,* to an important question, namely, the role of sensory experience in the novel. In truth, it would seem that, from the beginning, for the novelist—whether Latin or Northern European, and much more than for the poet or the dramatist—the apprehension of the «mundo exterior» through the senses and the representation in words of the world outside the self have always been a central problem. Consciously or unconsciously, the novelist himself must grasp directly through his senses the external forms and manifest how his characters perceive their world in the same way. He may judge sense experience to be untrustworthy, fallacious, dangerous or beautiful, beneficial, illuminating; but, whether he assigns a positive, negative, or neutral value to sense experience, it is the basic stuff of which his work is fabricated.

It is no doubt significant and not purely coincidental that the new genre of the novel arises precisely in a sixteenth-century Spain which in every way took more obvious delight in sensual experience and paid much more attention to the power of the senses than it had in previous centuries. The essential role of sense experience in strengthening and confirming religious faith was made explicit in San Ignacio's famous *Ejercicios espirituales,* which ask the penitent to recreate imaginatively with all five senses and in minute and painful detail the principal moments of Christ's Passion. Perspective painting deceived and pleased the eye. Gentlemen and ladies paid immense sums for the velvets and laces and satins of their court dress; austere castles became sumptuous palaces with rich gardens. The magnificence of Baroque (often Jesuit) architecture compelled the viewer's awe and admiration. All this lavish gratification of the senses is nowhere better summed up than in five unusual canvases, each dedicated to a different sense, executed by Jan Brueghel in 1617-1618 *(La vista, Alegoría del oído, Alegoría del olfato, Alegoría del gusto,* and *Alegoría del tacto);* they charm and overwhelm the spectator with their display of musical instruments, burnished armor, heaped platters, objets d'art, and luscious female nudes.[4]

Furthermore, the «new» philosophies of the century, Neoplatonism and Skepticism, though diametrically opposed in many ways, both called attention to the dominant role of the senses in man's life. While affirming that divine beauty, the ultimate reality, is knowable only through the *spiritual* senses of the human intellect and soul, Neoplatonism still places great emphasis on the two *corporeal* senses of sight and hearing, for they perceive the reflection of divine beauty in all created things—the eyes

---

[4] These canvases, now in the Prado, are discussed and illustrated in Spain, Ministerio de Cultura, Dirección General del Patrimonio Artístico, Archivos y Museos, *Pedro Pablo Rubens (1577-1640): Exposición homenaje* (Madrid: Aro Artes Gráficas, 1977), nos. 108-112.

apprehend the radiance of form, reflection of the divine intellect; the ears apprehend order, harmony, and concord, reflection of the divine soul. To be sure, the eyes and ears are only messengers, carrying sense information inward; it is the soul which *knows* corporeal beauty. And if a man's soul is greatly impeded by the «rudeza y grosedad»[5] of the corporeal matter in which it is sheathed, he will be deaf and blind to spiritual as well as physical beauty: «las ánimas que conocen dificultosamente las hermosuras corpóreas... son asimismo difíciles en conocer las hermosuras espirituales... conviene a saber, las virtudes, ciencias y sabiduría» (León Hebreo, p. 285). Thus, for all its emphasis on the infinite superiority of the invisible idea over the created form, Neoplatonism creates an intellectual atmosphere that encourages sensory appreciation through the eye and the ears of the world and its beauty. Indeed, the spiritually elect alone *can* perceive and appreciate them.

Only against this background can the pastoral novel in general and Montemayor's *Diana* in particular be comprehended. The *Diana* is thickly populated by men and women whose souls have been instantly captivated by beauty of face and voice perceived through their senses of sight and hearing. Belisa first falls in love with Arsileo after hearing one night his «suave canto» which, like that of Orpheus, «suspendía y ablandaba» the hearts of all his auditors;[6] Arsileo shortly afterward falls as hopelessly in love with Belisa after one glance at her beauty (puso los ojos en mí... y quedó tan preso de mis amores...,» Montemayor, p. 154). Sireno loses his heart wholly to his shepherdess at their first meeting, when he had seen «la hermosura, gracia, honestidad de la pastora Diana, aquella en quien naturaleza sumó todas las perficiones que por muchas partes avía repartido» (Montemayor, p. 10). The stimulus of sense experience transforms the souls and lives of all the characters; and though the love engendered by beauty causes pain as well as joy, it is universally accepted that the person most sensitive to external beauty possesses the most excellent soul. Sensory experience in the pastoral novel is the source of spiritual enrichment. Nowhere is there a suggestion that the wise and good man should steel himself in stoic fashion against the siren face and song of beauty, nor is there an intimation that the beauty perceived is fraudulent or deceptive.

Skepticism, on the other hand—so prominent a philosophical stance among sixteenth-century intellectuals from Erasmus to Montaigne—in its drive to demonstrate that man cannot achieve through his own faculties any certitude about the nature of reality, attacks the reliability of all the senses. We can at best know accidents through them but never essences, because the data they convey to the mind are affected by the circumstances under which an object is perceived, by the inherent limitations of the sense organs, and by the physical and mental state of the perceiver

---

[5] LEÓN HEBREO: *Diálogos de amor,* tr. Garcilaso de la Vega el Inca (Buenos Aires: Espasa Calpe, 1947), p. 284.
[6] JORGE DE MONTEMAYOR: *Los siete libros de la Diana,* ed. Francisco López Estrada, 2nd. ed. (Madrid: Espasa-Calpe, 1954), p. 150.

himself. Such a conviction does not, however, reduce the importance of sensory experience but enhances it; however faulty the senses may be, they remain our one mode of contact (other than faith and revelation) with the world outside ourselves, whose existence or importance the skeptic does not necessarily deny. That most radical of skeptics and doubters, René Descartes, opens his treatise on optics with the flat assertion that «[t]oute la conduite de nostre vie dépend de nos sens...»[7]

Novelists operating generally within the skeptical framework may, like Alemán or Quevedo or Gracián, find support in skeptical arguments for their underlying ascetic or stoic beliefs, multiplying examples of how our senses deceive us, of how we apprehend only appearance, which is always false, but not truth and virtue. To do this, however, they must and do present a richly perceived world of appearance, and their characters (Guzmán de Alfarache, Pablos of the *Buscón,* Andrenio of *El Criticón*), assaulted by sense experience of all kinds, revel in the pleasures it may bring.

Guzmán de Alfarache, remembering the freedom from responsibility he had enjoyed as a beggar on the streets of Rome, speaks with special eloquence of the freedom to use to the fullest all five senses: «¿Quién hay hoy en el mundo, que más licenciosa ni francamente goce dellos que un pobre, con mayor seguridad ni gusto?»[8] Then he proceeds to tick them off one by one:

Y pues he dicho *gusto,* comenzaré por él, pues no hay olla que no espumenos, manjar que no probemos...

El *oír,* ¿quién oye más que el pobre?... durmiendo en plazas y calles ¿qué música se dió que no la oyésemos? ¿Qué requiebro hubo que no lo supiésemos? Nada nos fué secreto y de lo público mil veces lo sabíamos mejor que todos, porque oíamos tratar dello en más partes que todos.

Pues el *ver,* cuán francamente lo podíamos ejercitar sin ser notados ni haber quién lo pidiese ni impidiese. Cuántas veces me acusé que, pidiendo en las iglesias, estaba mirando y alegrándome. Quiero decir, para mejor aclararme, codiciando mujeres de rostros angélicos...

Oler, ¿quién más pudo oler que nosotros, que nos llaman oledores de casas ajenas? Demás que, si el olor es mejor, cuanto nos es más provechoso nuestro ámbar y almizcle, mejor que todos y más verdadero era un ajo... preservativo de contagiosa corrupción...

El *tacto* querrás decir que nos faltaba, que jamás pudo llegar a nuestras manos cosa buena. Pues, desengañaos... Los pobres tocan y gozan cosas tan buenas como los ricos... Y ¡cuántas veces algunas damas me daban de su mano la limosna! No sé lo que los otros

[7] «De la dioptrique», *Oeuvres de Descartes,* ed. Charles Adam and Paul Tannery, V (Paris: Librairie Philosophique J. Vrin, 1965), 81.

[8] MATEO ALEMÁN: *Guzmán de Alfarache,* ed. Samuel Gili y Gaya, II (Madrid: Espasa-Calpe, 1963), 210.

hacían; mas yo con mi mocedad trataba della con las mías y en modo de reconocimiento devoto no la soltaba hasta habérsela besado. (Alemán, pp. 210-211; emphasis mine.)

There may well be some irony in this catalogue of the limited sensual gratifications available to the poor, but we cannot mistake the avidity with which the pícaro absorbs life into himself through the senses. Nor can we mistake the negative value placed upon that experience sinful and distracting from the path of virtue. If the classical pastoral novel may be said to seek beauty and virtue through sense experience, the classical picaresque novel cautions against succumbing to the temptations of the material world presented to us so attractively through the senses. This radical difference in the evaluation of sensory experience is one of the cluster of characteristics which marks off one genre from the other.

Finally, in *Don Quijote,* Cervantes examines more thoroughly than any other novelist before or after him the basic skeptical problems—can man know the external world around him, what is the role of the senses in the perception of that world, and what causes error in the interpretation of sensory data? The *Quijote* presents, as Ortega remarked long ago, a magnificently visualized world («potencia de visualidad... literalmente incomparable,» *Meditaciones,* p. 71), in which Sancho and Don Quijote, if they are to make their way successfully, must interpret correctly the sensory data brought to them by eyes, ears, hands, nose. Don Quijote's sensory organs are in excellent condition, but he rejects the information they bring him because of an intense psychological need to make external reality conform to his own preconceptions of it derived from the world of books. Let us look at one of many examples. In the darkness of an inn at night, deprived of the use of his sense of sight, he falls into grievous error, however comic it may be for the reader. Imagining that the daughter of the lord of the castle, sick with love for him, has come to visit him in the attic, he seizes upon the gross Maritornes, come to her assignation with a muleteer, and,

> Tentóle luego la camisa, y aunque era de harpillera, a él le pareció ser de finísimo y delgado cendal... Los cabellos, que en alguna manera tiraban a crines, él los marcó por hebras de lucidísimo oro de Arabia... Y el aliento, que, sin duda alguna, olía a ensalada fiambre y trasnochada, a él le pareció ser que arrojaba de su boca un olor suave y aromático... Y era tanta la ceguedad del pobre hidalgo, que el tacto, ni el aliento, ni otras cosas que traía en sí la buena doncella, no le desengañaban, las cuales pudieran hacer vomitar a otro que no fuera harriero; antes le parecía que tenía entre sus brazos a la diosa de la hermosura (I, 16).

Reality is not unknowable here; the senses would perform their functions satisfactorily, if the perceiver had not distorted their data. In other cases, when the Duke and Duchess arrange chivalric adventures for Don Quijote, or when the «dreamed reality» of the Cave of Montesinos proves impenetrable to sensory probing («el tacto, el sentimiento, los discursos concertados que entre mí hacía, me certificaron que yo era allí entonces [en la cueva] el que soy ahora,» II, 23), the perceiver's task is more difficult. Sensory experience provides no absolute truth, as in the pastoral novel, nor is it always to be viewed suspiciously, as in the picaresque. It is valuable, necessary, omnipresent, but must be interpreted with discretion.

Granted, then, that sensory experience has been a major concern of the novel from its inception, it is nonetheless clear that Gabriel Miró intensifies and heightens that experience far beyond any of his predecessors, even the slightly older generation of *modernistas,* with their cult of sensuous beauty—an aesthetic attitude best exemplified by the *Sonatas* of Valle-Inclán and by the latter's 1908 definition of the modernist creed: «es ciertamente un vivo anhelo de personalidad, y por eso, sin duda, advertimos en los escritores jóvenes más empeño por expresar *sensaciones que ideas.*» [9]

Certainly the *modernistas* taught the young Miró a great deal. He like them valued artistic sensibility and learned from them that a valid literature could be created out of the writer's highly personal view of the world, based on his sensual apperception of it, rather than out of more general concepts, the property of all men.

Yet his sensationalism from the beginning is joined to ethical concerns in a way which recalls the linkage between ethics and aesthetics in Neoplatonism and the pastoral novel. In his first artistic manifesto, written in 1901 when he was only twenty-one, aesthetic sensibility is exalted not only because it recognizes beauty but because the capacity to do so is incompatible with selfishness and contempt for the other. Nature, he says, hides her treasures from no one:

> ... por todos se engalana con flores en primavera, y luce hermosos paisajes en estío, y crepúsculos tristes pero bellos en invierno; y sin embargo, no todos se extasían contemplando sus gracias, no todos admiran sus colores, su luz, ¿por qué?, porque falta lo principal, lo necesario, falta el sentimiento del arte, y sin él no hay artista.
>
> ¡Si todos los hombres lo fueran! Desaparecería el crimen, el egoísmo, la maldad, porque no comprendo que exista el arte que lo sublima todo en un corazón ruin. [10]

---

[9] As cited by MELCHOR FERNÁNDEZ ALMAGRO: *Vida y literatura de Valle-Inclán* (Madrid: Taurus, 1966), p. 110; emphasis mine. The original version of these remarks had been published in 1902. To be sure, by 1914 in *La lámpara maravillosa* Valle-Inclán claims to have adopted a new aesthetic based on gnostic mysticism which rejects sensations and sensory data: «Colócate fuera de los sentidos... fuentes de error más que de conocimiento» (*Obras completas*, I [Madrid: Rivadeneyra, 1944], 786-787). Beauty resides only in the eternal, wihch is not accessible to the senses. It is fruitless to seek consistency in Don Ramón's thought.

[10] GABRIEL MIRÓ: «Domingo Carratalá», in *De mi barrio,* ed. E. Mendaro del Alcázar (Alicante: Imprenta y Litografía de Tomás Muñoz, 1901).

While the ethical concerns expressed here remain in the mature Miró, the wispy, sentimental, modernist images of spring flowers and «crepúsculos tristes,» which try to capture the fleeting beauty of seasonal change, soon disappear in his prose. He comes more and more to conceive that the senses can authentically probe into nature's substance, that man has the unique gift and duty of apprehending—and *comprehending*— through the senses the substantial reality outside himself, whether it be of landscape or the soul of his neighbor. The percept has a power all its own and can give us not only the flesh of things but—pace Ortega— their form and physical and moral meaning.

For himself he had discovered what the philosopher Xabier Zubiri calls «la inteligencia sentiente.» Intelligence *is* the apprehension of reality in all its fullness through the senses:

> Inteligir es formalmente aprehender realidad, y aprehenderla en su mera actualidad de realidad con todo su contenido. Y en este respecto la aprehensión primordial de realidad no solamente es más rica que la intelección según los modos ulteriores [*logos* and reason, in Zubiri's terms], sino que es la intelección por excelencia, pues es en ella en la que tenemos actualizado en y por sí mismo lo real en su realidad... Por esto, pese a su enorme volumen y riqueza, la intelección según los modos ulteriores es indeciblemente pobre respecto del modo como la aprehensión primordial aprehende la realidad.[11]

Thus Miró turns outward to the world through his senses, escapes the modernists' tendency toward solipsism, *ensimismamiento,* and self-indulgence, and struggles with the brilliant sensory images of his prose to show us reality in all its variousness. «Conceptos» there are in his work, and powerful ones, but they themselves are also sentient and spring from the primordial sensory intellection. All thought, all feeling, and all will, the whole of man's life, flow *from* «la inteligencia sentiente,» and not inversely.[12]

Thus too the ethical necessity of sensory sensitivity. The heroes in Miró's novels are those who seize their world most fully through the senses. In the memorable sketch from *El humo dormido* (1919) significantly entitled «Don Jesús y la lámpara de la realidad,» Don Jesús, the most intelligent, sympathetic, and charitable of the members of the *tertulia* which meets at the canon's house, irritates the others, content to sit in semidarkness, by his insistence on turning up the kerosene lamp to

---

[11] XAVIER ZUBIRI: *Inteligencia sentiente* (Madrid: Sociedad de Estudios y Publicaciones, 1980), pp. 266-267.

[12] Cf. ZUBIRI, pp. 282-285. A somewhat similar attitude was expressed by William von Humboldt at the end of the eighteenth century, when he warned against the suppression of sensuality; a culture which fails to bring it «into creative tension with reason can never realize its highest possibilities, for while reason 'gives direction' to energy, 'sensuality is the source of all vital energy'» (statements cited and commented upon by LIONEL GOSSMAN: «Literature and Education», *New Literary History,* 13 (1981-82), 350.

flood the room with light, and shocks them all by proclaiming: «Nadie burle de estas realidades de nuestras sensaciones, donde reside casi toda la verdad de nuestra vida. Yo hasta me las atraigo, aunque no me lo proponga.»[13] As a result of this vigorous absorption of outside reality, he finds palpitating with life the provincial town seen as inert and dead by all the others. Uncomprehending and suspicious, one man objects that «la realidad... era una para todos los hombres.» Don Jesús «se lo contradijo» (Miró, *Humo,* pp. 106-107). He is not, however, committing himself to the perspectivist doctrine which affirms that reality is different for each observer and that, consequently, all views are equally valid; rather he argues for the necessity of an «inteligencia sentiente» which apprehends the plenitude of reality.

Throughout the two great final novels of Miró, *Nuestro Padre San Daniel* and *El obispo leproso,* those characters who open themselves to the world through the senses are shown as morally superior to the sensorially limited and ascetic. The most odious character in the novels is Father Bellod, the torturer of rats, priests, and parishioners. Bellod is blind in one eye, and his face is constantly scarred by the daily wounds inflicted as he shaves without soap or a mirror, using an ancient blade employed afterwards to cut bread «para socorrer a sus mendigos.» «No fumaba, no tenía olfato, y el mejor manjar y gollería para su gusto eran los salazones, principalmente el cecial y cecial de melva.»[14]

Our moral guide throughout the novels, on the other hand, is the highly sensual priest Don Magín, avidly investigating the physical world through all his senses, especially the sense of smell, delighting equally in the aroma of chocolate, cinnamon, flowers, cooking food, and wine barrels—but also, for the same reason, open to, and able to read, the suffering and loneliness of Don Alvaro or Cara-rajada.

For Miró, lack of charity in human relationships and ethical defects in general unfailingly stem from lack of aesthetic and sentient powers, the failure to use that *inteligencia sentiente* which is man's unique gift and which allows him to possesses the substance, the complexity, and the constantly renewed freshness of the world. He who does not use his senses fully closes himself off within the prison of the self and denies his essential nature as, to use Zubiri's term, the *«animal de realidades»* (*Inteligencia sentiente,* p. 284). This generous openness to the reality of the world «out there» and the other recalls the profound vision of Cervantes and sets Miró's fictional universe off sharply from that of most of his contemporaries: the turbulent but shadowy spiritual landscapes of Unamuno's *nivola;* the flat world of appearance in Baroja; the grotesque gesturings of Valle-Inclán's puppets; the monotonous repetitiveness of Azorín's Castile.

The complex interplay between the *inteligencia sentiente* and reality is nowhere better expressed than in the following passage from *El humo*

[13] Ed. Edmund L. King (New York: Dell Publishing Co., Inc., 1967), pp. 109-110.
[14] *Nuestro Padre San Daniel, Obras completas* (Edición conmemorativa), X (Barcelona: Tipografía Altés, 1945), 30.

dormido: the *hombre desconocido* who walks through the nameless town is an emblem of the artist whose *inteligencia sentiente* in its hard, sometimes painful, contact with reality reveals the world anew to us; Miró's language conveys the general concept through sensory images. We leave the last and best words to Miró himself:

Pasó el hombre desconocido. Caminaba como si se dejase todo el pueblo detrás; y casi todas las gentes, aunque les rodee el paisaje, caminan como si siempre pisaran el polvo de una calle; y él no; a él se le veía y se escuchaba su pie sobre la tierra viva, su pie desnudo aun a través de una suela de bronce. Seguía el mismo camino de los otros, y semejaba abrirlo; levantaba la piel y el callo de la tierra; y sentía la palpitación de la virginidad y, en lo hondo, la de la maternidad; pies que dentro de la huella endurecida de sandalias o de pezuñas hincan su planta, troquelan el sendero y sienten un latir de germinaciones. Todo breñal en torno de sus rodillas lo que es asfalto liso para los otros hombres que llevan en sus talones membranas de murciélago o la serrezuela de la langosta...

Siempre se alza ese hombre entre el humo dormido... Y el rumor de sus pisadas trastorna las palabras del *Eclesiastés,* porque sí que hay cosa nueva debajo del sol, del sol y de la tierra hollada; todo aguarda ávidamente el sello de nuestra limitación; todo se desgarra generoso y se cicatriza esperándonos...[15]

Bryn Mawr College.

---

[15] *Humo dormido,* pp. 60-61. In his Introduction to this book, pp. 44-52, Edmund King examines the linguistic methods Miró evolved to transmit his vision. These pages are indispensable reading for anyone who wishes to understand Miró's unique art and artistry.

TRES POETAS ANTE LA SOLEDAD:
BECQUER, ROSALIA Y MACHADO

by

RAFAEL LAPESA

Una vez más me propongo contrastar la poesía de tres grandes figuras de la lírica intimista española. Creo que el tema de la soledad, capital en los tres, está concebido por cada uno de manera distinta y puede servir para destacar aspectos esenciales de sus respectivos modos de sentir, poetizar y representarse el mundo.

I. BÉCQUER [1]

Inevitablemente imaginamos a Gustavo Adolfo Bécquer deambulando a solas, entre sombras y a la luz de la luna, por los rincones de Toledo, atento a la lámpara transparentada por las vidrieras de una iglesia y en espera de identificar una voz entre las del coro de las monjas; o vagando, contemplativo y soñador, por Veruela o las cercanías de Soria. Sin embargo, la palabra «soledad» no aparece en sus *Rimas;* pero la situación y el sentimiento que ella implica están presentes en algunos de sus más intensos y estremecedores poemas. Sólo está el poeta, aunque no nos lo diga, cuando «mudo, sombrío, la pupila inmóvil / clavada en la pared», pasa entre llantos y maldiciones la noche en que «la embriaguez horrible del dolor» le ha hecho envejecer (XLIII); solo también cuando se enfrenta con los elementos enfurecidos —olas gigantes, ráfagas de huracán y nubes tempestuosas— pidiéndoles que lo arrebaten para huir de sí mismo:

> Llevadme, por piedad, adonde el vértigo
> con la razón me arranque la memoria...
> ¡Por piedad! ¡Tengo miedo de quedarme
> Con mi dolor a solas! (LII)

Pero la compañía del dolor puede ser salvadora, antídoto vital contra el tedio acarreado por la monótona sucesión de días vacíos:

> ¡Ay, a veces me acuerdo, suspirando,
> del antiguo sufrir.
> Amargo es el dolor; pero siquiera
> padecer es vivir. (LXVI)

[1] Cito según *Rimas.* Primera versión original, 3.ª ed., Buenos Aires, Pleamar, 1948.

Bécquer ha expresado con fuerza y sobriedad inigualables el sentimiento de soledad provocado por la insolidaridad ajena:

> Llegó la noche y no encontré un asilo;
> ¡Y tuve sed!... Mis lágrimas bebí.
> ¡Y tuve hambre! ¡Los hinchados ojos
>   Cerré para morir!
> ¿Estaba en un desierto? Aunque a mi oído
> De las turbas llegaba el ronco hervir,
> Yo era huérfano y pobre... ¡El mundo estaba
> Desierto... para mí!   (LXV)

En otro poema se imagina muriendo sin tener quien esté a su lado,
sin mano amiga que estreche la suya y cierre sus ojos, sin nadie que
rece por su alma, sin nadie que se acuerde de él al día siguiente (LI). En
la rima LXVI da una respuesta desconsolada a las preguntas «¿De dónde
vengo?», «¿A dónde voy?»: viene del «más horrible y áspero / de los
caminos», y se dirige, cruzando «el más sombrío y triste / de los pára-
mos», hacia la tumba, señalada por una «piedra solitaria / sin inscripción
alguna», allá «donde habite el olvido». En la rima II, presumiblemente
anterior, dice de sí, comparándose a la saeta y a la ola, que se mueven
sin conocer su rumbo:

> Ese soy yo, que al acaso
> Cruzo el mundo, sin pensar
> De dónde vengo, ni a dónde
> Mis pasos me llevarán.

Es posible que en las dos rimas haya un eco lejano de las *Fragen*
de Heine:

> O löst mir das Rätsel des Lebens,
> Das qualvoll uralte Rätsel...
> ....
> Sagt mir, was bedeutet der Mensch?
> Woher ist er kommen? Wo geht er hin?
> Wer wohnt dort oben auf goldnen Sternen?...[2]

Pero en ambas rimas las preguntas se limitan al pasado y futuro del
poeta en su vida terrenal, sin ninguna referencia trascendental. No es
que en Bécquer falten muestras de la inquietud romántica por el origen
y destino de los humanos; tales problemas figuran en la rima IV como
una de las realidades que por sí mismas considera poéticas:

> Mientras la humanidad, siempre avanzando,
>   No sepa a dó camina;
> Mientras haya un misterio para el hombre,
>   ¡Habrá poesía!

---

[2] HEINRICH HEINE: *Buch der Lieder*, Die Nordsee, 7, en *Werke*, Hamburg,
Hoffmann und Campe, 1956, s. 147.

Lo que no parece haber es conexión entre estas cuestiones y el tema de la soledad según lo plantea Bécquer. Tampoco parece que el sentimiento de ella esté en relación con vacilaciones de fe religiosa: Bécquer hubo de tenerlas, pues deja escapar alguna manifestación de escepticismo y algún reconocimiento de sus dudas; por saber lo que su amada ha pensado de él, daría «esta vida mortal, y de la eterna / lo que me toque, si me toca algo»; y en otra ocasión declara:

> En el mar de la duda en que bogo
> Ni aun sé lo que creo.

Pero añade a continuación:

> ¡Sin embargo estas ansias me dicen
> Que yo llevo algo
> Divino aquí dentro...! (VIII)

Reflexionando sobre la brevedad de la vida, ve la gloria y el amor como «sombras de un sueño» cuyo «despertar es morir» (LXIX); pero también, contemplando en un sepulcro gótico la estatua yacente de una bella mujer, siente avivada «la sed de lo infinito, / el ansia de esa vida de la muerte / para la que un instante son los siglos» (LXXVI) y expresa anhelos de supervivencia imprecisos, pero suficientes para provocarle repugnancia por lo solos que se deja a los muertos en el camposanto (LXXIII). Es la única vez que la idea de la soledad rebasa en Bécquer los linderos de la vida mundanal. Bécquer, en suma, expresa la radical soledad del hombre como realidad inmediata, como vivencia personal, con impresionante autenticidad; pero ni teoriza ni la relaciona con ninguna actitud o creencia respecto a los problemas últimos del ser humano.

Ahora bien: hay en las Rimas de Bécquer una ventana abierta explícitamente hacia el misterio del más allá, hacia lo que Dámaso Alonso llamó «trasmundo» del poeta: el limbo del duermevela, en que la mente vaga, «cambian de forma los objetos», se enciende el mundo de las visiones y se oyen rumores, llamadas semejantes a «una voz delgada y triste» que al despertar se reconocen como anuncio de que ha muerto algún ser querido. O la evasión, en sueños, del espíritu, «huésped de las nieblas», para encontrarse con otros espíritus y compartir con ellos la risa, el llanto, el odio y el amor. Es el mundo de los sueños habitados donde Bécquer se escapa de su soledad terrena.

II. ROSALÍA [3]

Más vario, hondo y complejo es el enfrentamiento de Rosalía de Castro con la soledad, eje de su poesía, donde se presenta como dramática experiencia personal y con angustiado planteamiento de interrogantes sobre el sentido y fin último de la vida. Así lo han puesto de relieve,

[3] Cito según *Obras completas*, I, *Obras en verso*, Madrid, Aguilar, 1977.

entre otros, Domingo García Sabell, Ramón Piñeiro, Juan Rof Carballo y Marina Mayoral [4]. En las páginas que siguen trataré de subrayar la precocidad, continuidad y enriquecimiento del tema en la lírica rosaliana, sus imbricaciones con otros temas y la variedad de aspectos que ofrece.

* * *

En 1857, Rosalía de Castro publicada en Madrid, con el título de *La flor,* un folleto de cuarenta páginas que contenía cinco poemas y dos *Fragmentos* de otro. Sus versos mostraban juvenil inexperiencia y abrumador influjo de Espronceda. No era de extrañar, pues la autora apenas tenía veinte años, hacía pocos meses que había llegado a la capital desde su rincón gallego y no había tenido tiempo de conocer la tendencia, que entonces empezaba a apuntar, hacia una lírica de sentimiento condensado y expresión contenida; recordemos que fue en ese mismo año 1857 cuando aparecieron en el *Museo Universal* los 16 primeros Lieder de Heine traducidos por Eulogio Florentino Sanz. El tono, el estilo, el léxico y hasta los ripios de *La flor* son ostensiblemente esproncedianos. Pero bajo este ropaje hay en la obra primeriza de Rosalía rasgos muy personales que se perpetúan en *Follas novas* (1880) y *En las orillas del Sar* (1884). Para nuestro actual propósito son de especial interés los dos *Fragmentos,* que recuerdan a cada paso el *Canto a Teresa* y están escritos, como éste, en octavas reales. No debe importarnos que a la primera estrofa le falte un verso y a la decimoquinta el final de otro, ni que encontremos muchas veces desarrollos retóricos manidos en lugar de la palabra exacta: son fallos de principiante que no atenúan la intensidad penetrante de su lamento ni ocultan la hondura y trascendencia con que plantea el tema de la soledad. Entresacaré los pasajes más representativos:

1   Cuando miré de soledad vestida
    la senda que el Destino me trazó,
    sentí en un punto aniquilar mi vida.

    ....

5   Cuando, infeliz, me contemplé perdida
    y el árbol de mi fe se desgajó,
    tuvieron, ¡ay!, para llorar mis ojos
    de amargura y de hiel tristes despojos.
    La nada contemplé que me cercaba,
10 y... al presentir mi aterrador quebranto,
    miré que, solitaria, me anegaba
    en un mar de dolores y de llanto.
    Nadie ni amor ni compasión cantaba,
    ni un ángel me cubrió bajo su manto;

[4] Domingo García Sabell: «Rosalía y su sombra», en *Siete ensayos sobre Rosalía,* Vigo, Galaxia, 1952, 41-46; Ramón Piñeiro: «A saudade en Rosalía», *Ibid.,* 95-109; Rof Carballo: «Rosalía, Anima Galaica», *Ibid.,* 111-149; Marina Mayoral: *La poesía de Rosalía de Castro,* Madrid, Gredos, 1974.

15   sola mi voz mi corazón oía
     de la última ilusión que se perdía...
     ....

25   La risa y el sarcasmo por doquiera
     que fuera yo mi corazón palpaba,
     y doquiera también que me escondiera,
     ¡ay! la risa sardónica encontraba...
     ....

45   Luego al Cielo exclamé puesta de hinojos,
     y el Cielo mis clamores no advirtió;
     y sola combatí con mis pesares
     ¡lágrimas tristes derramando a mares!
     ....

55   Sola era yo con mi dolor profundo
     en el abismo de un imbécil mundo.
     ....

65   La Soledad... Cuando en la vida, un día
     circunda nuestra frente su fulgor,
     un mundo de mortal melancolía
     nos presenta un fantasma aterrador...
     ....

105 Las horas que soñé desparecieron
     cual la flor que un torrente arrebató
     y allá en la nada del no ser se hundieron...
     ....

121 ¿Qué es este miedo aterrador que siento
     y esta congoja inalterable y fría,
     que cuanto más desvanecer intento,
     más se burla, mordaz, del ansia mía?
     ....

     ... Y la acritud de un pensamiento triste
     me grita sin cesar: «La fe perdiste».
145 Y perdida la fe..., la fe perdida...,
     roto el cristal de esa belleza oculta,
     el cielo encantador de nuestra vida
     entre pálidas nubes se sepulta...
     ....

157 ...Porque esa flor de mis jardines muerta,
     nada..., en nada no más se ha convertido.
     ¿Y quién la nada en algo convirtiera?
     ¡Sabio fuera, en verdad, quien lo dijera!

Perdónese la longitud de la cita. Creo importante señalar en sus versos
una serie de rasgos fundamentales para comprender la actitud de Rosalía
ante la soledad. Los numeraré para su ulterior estudio: [1] la soledad
le ha sido impuesta a Rosalía por el Destino, y es la realidad que envuelve
y ha de envolver su decurso vital (vv. 1-2). [2] La conciencia de tal realidad le ha llegado por súbita iluminación (vv. 1-3 y 65-66), a cuya luz

un fantasma aterrador le ha descubierto un mundo de mortal melancolía (vv. 66-67); [3] La hostilidad y burlas de los humanos (vv. 13 y 25-28). [4] así como el silencio y desamparo por parte del Cielo (vv. 14 y 45-46), han contribuido a revelarle la soledad a que está predestinada. [5] Sola combate con sus pesares (vv. 47 y 55) y se anega solitaria en un mar de dolores y de llanto (vv. 11-12). [6] Perdida la fe (vv. 6 y 144-148), [7] se da cuenta de que la nada la rodea (v. 9), ve en la nada —«La nada del no ser»— el paradero de todas las ilusiones (vv. 105 y 155-159), y siente que su vida misma queda aniquilada (v. 3). [8] Tiene miedo, «aterrador» también, [9] que no puede apartar de sí y que se mofa de ella (vv. 121-124).

Si no supiéramos que la serie precedente corresponde a los *Fragmentos* de *La flor*, podríamos creer que extractaba poemas de *Follas novas* o *En las orillas del Sar*, pues la configuración del tema de la soledad en estas obras de madurez no difiere en nada fundamental de la que le había dado la poetisa veinteañera. He aquí las coincidencias y semejanzas:

[1]. *Soledad por destino.*—En sus dos libros de plenitud Rosalía atribuye repetidamente a sí misma, a imaginarios dobles suyos o, en general, a las víctimas de la desgracia, la predestinación al dolor (OC., pp. 348, 373, 394-395, 407, 409, 579, 588-592, 698, 761-762); frecuentemente el dolor de los predestinados va unido a la soledad, explícita (301, 351, 407) o implícita (723, 762, etc.). En los *Fragmentos* la soledad impuesta por el Destino está emparejada con el dolor (vv. 11-12, 47 y 55).

[2]. *Fantasma aterrador.*—Son varios los fantasmas temibles que aparecen en *Follas novas:* el «fantasma pavoroso dos meus remordementos» (367); «ese fantasma horribre» de la desgracia, «que a desesperazón da por remate» (377); otro sin identificación expresa:

> ¡Mar!, cas túas aguas sin fondo,
> ¡ceo!, ca túa inmansidá
> o fantasma que me aterra
> axudádeme a enterrar...

Es más grande y poderoso que el mar y que el cielo, «impracabre, bulrón e sañudo»,

> i amenaza perseguirme
> hastra a mesma eternidá (325).

Rosalía deja sin identidad a este fantasma, que así cobra la densa imprecisión de un símbolo. Sería aventurado establecer correspondencias —que nunca podrían considerarse rigurosas— entre él y conceptos definibles. Cabría pensar, no obstante, que el poema situado inmediatamente después en *Follas novas,* «Cava lixeiro, cava», fuese continuación del que nos ocupa: en aquél se habla de enterrar la memoria del pasado. La secuencia prosigue con «Cando penso que te fuches, / negra sombra que me asombras», el poema simbólico de interpretación más controvertida en toda la lírica rosaliana.

[3] *Indiferencia, hostilidad y burlas por parte de los hombres.*—Es uno de los motivos más constantes en la obra poética de Rosalía; podría

reunirse toda una antología con sus protestas contra la insolidaridad respecto a los desdichados:

> Ladraban contra min, que camiñaba
> cásique sin alento,
> sin poder co meu fondo pensamento
> i a pezoña mortal que en min levaba.
> I a xente que topaba,
> ollándome a mantenta,
> do meu dor sin igual i a miña afrenta
> traidora se mofaba. (319)

Esa antología acusadora incluiría *A xusticia pola man* (332), *A desgracia* (375-376), *Los tristes* (588-592), la serie que empieza con «Los que a través de sus lágrimas» y continúa con «Pensamientos de alas negras» (673-677), etc. La hostilidad del hombre, «enemigo del hombre» (613), convierte en yermos la vida y el mundo en desierto (575).

[4] *Silencio e impasibilidad del Cielo;* [5] *soledad y desamparo ante el dolor;* [6] *pérdida de la fe.*—Todo ello se encierra en la pregunta que corona una sucesión de interrogaciones donde se enumeran inexplicables contrastes entre el pretérito estado de ánimo de la autora y el que ahora tiene:

> ¿Por qué, en fin, Dios meu,
> a un tempo me faltan
> a terra i o ceo? (321)

Sintiendo esa falta, Rosalía, con dramática referencia a su soledad y abandono, invoca a poderes celestiales que no la asisten: el Ángel de la Guarda (cf. «ni un ángel me cubrió bajo su manto», *Fragmentos,* v. 14), la Fe y la Esperanza:

> ¿Dónde estades, en dónde,
> cando o que en vós confía
> soio, en loita coas ansias de agonía [5],
> orfo, vos chama, e naide lle responde? (407)

En ninguna de estas dos ocasiones se rebasan los límites de la experiencia personal. Pero en un sobrecogedor poema de *En las orillas del Sar* (que en adelante mencionaremos como «poema agónico») Rosalía se plantea el problema de la supervivencia humana y suplica ahincadamente a Dios el recobro de su fe; desoído el ruego, la fe se le desmorona, y ella se siente invadir por la angustia ante el vacío de la nada:

> 1   Una luciérnaga entre el musgo brilla
>   y un astro en las alturas centellea:
>   abismo arriba, y en el fondo, abismo:

---

[5] Cf. *Fragmentos,* vv. 11-12 y 47.

¿qué es al fin lo que acaba y lo que queda?

....

    Arrodillada ante la tosca imagen,
10 mi espíritu abismado en lo infinito,
impía acaso, interrogando al Cielo
y al Infierno a la vez, tiemblo y vacilo.
    ¿Qué somos? ¿Qué es la muerte? La campana
con sus ecos responde a mis gemidos
15 desde la altura, y sin esfuerzo el llanto
baña ardiente mi rostro enflaquecido.
    ¡Qué horrible sufrimiento! ¡Tú tan sólo
lo puedes ver y comprender, Dios mío!
    ¿Es verdad que lo ves? Señor, entonces,
20   piadoso y compasivo
vuelve a mis ojos la celeste venda
de la fe bienhechora que he perdido,
y no consientas, no, que cruce errante,
    huérfana y sin arrimo,
25 acá abajo los yermos de la vida,
más allá las llanadas del vacío.
    Sigue tocando a muerto; y siempre mudo
    e impasible el divino
rostro del Redentor, deja que envuelto
30 en sombras quede el humillado espíritu.

....

35   Todo acabó quizás, menos mi pena,
    puñal de doble filo;
todo, menos la duda que nos lanza
de un abismo de horror en otro abismo.
    Desierto el mundo, despoblado el cielo,
40 enferma el alma y en el polvo hundido
    el sacro altar en donde
se exhalaron fervientes mis suspiros,
    en mil pedazos roto
    mi Dios cayó al abismo,
y al buscarlo anhelante, sólo encuentro
la soledad inmensa del vacío... (574-757).

En los *Fragmentos* de *La flor* la angustia de Rosalía tenía su origen en la penosa experiencia vital de la adolescente marginada; en el «poema agónico» la angustia nace de la inquietud por la supervivencia tras la muerte. Salvo esta diferencia inicial, el proceso anímico es el mismo, descrito con ingenuo zigzagueo en *La flor,* con ordenada maestría en la obra madura. En ésta se da entrada a la intervención de «la duda que nos lanza / de un abismo de horror en otro abismo». El término del proceso es común a los dos poemas: quiebra de la fe y descubrimiento de la nada. (Luego trataremos de explicar el «happy end» que clausura el «poema agónico».)

[7] *La nada; sus equivalentes léxicos y simbólicos.*—Frente a la insistencia con que los *Fragmentos* emplean la palabra «nada», ésta no aparece en el «poema agónico», que usa en lugar de ella «el vacío» (vv. 26 y 46), «lo infinito» (v. 10) y «(el) abismo» (vv. 3, 38, 44). La cercanía semántica de todas estas designaciones se comprueba en *Predestinados,* composición póstuma donde «el abismo» y «el vacío» atraen irresistiblemente a un suicida cuyos ojos «se fijan en lo infinito / que él cree imagen de la nada» (760-761).

El «aterrador quebranto» presentido en *La flor* ante la contemplación de la nada circundante tiene su paralelo en el «horrible sufrimiento» que en el «poema agónico» hace temblar, vacilar y gemir a la autora, y que baña en lágrimas su rostro enflaquecido. Pero la nada presenta aspecto menos espantable a quien busca en ella la paz definitiva: el alma que desea liberarse de recuerdos oprobiosos «quisiera en el no ser desvanecerse» (669); Rosalía se dirige así a los meses del invierno:

> Chegade, e tras do outono
> que as follas fai caer,
> nelas deixá que o sono
> eu durma do non ser.
> E cando o sol fermoso
> de abril torne a sorrir,
> que alume o meu reposo,
> xa non o meu sofrir. (404)

Más tarde, cuando sus pasiones duermen ya «el sueño de la nada», no quiere que resuciten, aunque el placer y el dolor que proporcionan se alimenten de la vida y a su vez la sostengan (682, 601). Ya hemos visto la vehemente atracción que la nada ejerce sobre el protagonista de *Predestinados,* uno de los varios suicidas que desfilan por las páginas de Rosalía. Si en ese caso la nada atrae como infinito, vacío y abismo, en otros la representa el mar, cuya inmensidad sugiere infinitud y cuya hondura es abismal: una mujer, presa de tristeza «negra coma a orfandá», desaparece un buen día en el arenal de una playa solitaria, y devuelta por las olas, «soia enterrada está» (351); un hombre, «con ánimo forte» se lanza al mar en vertiginosa carrera «cal si a atraisón do abismo misteriosa / con forza estraña o conduxese á morte» (409); otro, ansiando «de la muerte / la soledad terrible» se sepulta en lo profundo «del abismo inmenso», tras proclamar que lo único cierto es morir, « y todo lo demás mentira y humo», cosa que Rosalía comenta ambiguamente:

> Lo que encontró después posible y cierto
> el suicida infeliz, ¿quién lo adivina?
> ¡Dichoso aquel que espera
> tras de esta vida hallarse en mejor vida! (725-726)

Sean recuerdo de sucesos reales, sean entes imaginarios, estos personajes reflejan la tentación experimentada por la autora misma:

Co seu xordo o constante marmurio
atraime o oleaxen dese mar bravío
cal atrai das sirenas o cantar.
«Nesta meu leito misterioso e frío
—dime— ven brandamente a descansar».
El namorado está de min, ¡o deño!
i eu namorada del.
Pois saldremos co empeño,
que si el me chama sin parar, ¡eu teño
unhas ansias mortás de apousar nel...!   (295)

Pero ni Rosalía se suicidó ni llegan a hacerlo todos los que en sus poemas lo intentan. Uno de ellos desiste al oír la voz consejera de un ser invisible (409); otra es salvada por un mariñeiro (519-522); un cazador despeñado revive y abre su alma a la dicha bajo el ardor de unos ojos brillantes que, por voluntad de Dios, ahuyentan de su corazón el frío de la muerte (711-712). En el «poema agónico» no hay tentativa de suicidio, pero la orante ha llegado a la más absoluta desesperanza cuando oye a los ángeles explicarle el silencio divino: Dios —le dicen— no escucha «el insolente grito» de un corazón que idolatra la materia (575-576). La primera impresión del lector ante estos finales ortodoxos y felices es considerarlos palinodias insinceras y añadidas *a posteriori*; pero, aunque se tratara de adiciones, cosa no probada, podrían responder a algo auténtico: la contienda interior entre dudas y rebeldías, por una parte, y por otra el afán de conservar o recobrar una fe quebrantada o perdida, pero nunca renunciada.

La misma infinitud positiva y plena del Dios creador, contrapuesta a la pequeñez del hombre, sugiere a Rosalía la idea de la nada como último fin de su existencia; pero la Pasión y promesas de Jesús, el Dios que padeció por amor a los hombres, la conmueven y le dan esperanzas de vida eterna (672).

[8] y [9]. *El miedo y la burla*.—La medrosidad aparece como rasgo característico en la obra poética de Rosalía, que siente miedo aldeano al doblar las campanas, al entrar en el templo oscuro y silencioso, al creer que la miran los monstruos esculpidos en los capiteles catedralicios o al oír el ladrido de los perros. Otras veces su miedo es premonitario, como cuando pregunta en *La flor*: «¿Qué es este miedo aterrador que siento...?», o en una de las *Vaguedas* de *Follas novas*:

¿Qué pasa ó redor de min?
¿Qué me pasa que eu non sei?
Teño medo dunha cousa
que vive e que non se ve.
Teño medo á desgracia traidora
que ven e que nunca se sabe ónde van.   (282)

Si en los *Fragmentos* de 1857 el «miedo aterrador» se burla, mordaz, del ansia que le produce (v. 124), el fantasma que la aterra en *Follas novas* es —repitámoslo— «impracabre, bulrón e sañudo» (325); y la

«negra sombra» que la espanta se mofa de ella junto a los cabezales de
su lecho (327).

* * *

Hasta aquí hemos podido ver cómo la conciencia y sentimiento de la
soledad expresados por Rosalía en 1857 se mantienen sin alteración esencial en obras suyas publicadas veintitantos años más tarde e incluso en
poemas que dejó inéditos. Asimismo perduran las conexiones de la
soledad con el rechazo social, la crisis de la fe y la revelación de la nada.
El árbol ha robustecido tronco y ramas, pero sigue siendo el de antes.
No por eso ha dejado de echar vástagos nuevos: en *Follas novas* y
En las orillas del Sar la soledad presenta, además de su aspecto más hondo
de angustia existencial, otras facetas complementarias. Una es la soledad
buscada por quienes huyen de sí mismos, de sus recuerdos, remordimien-
tos y congojas, sin conseguir librarse de su compañía:

> Camiño, camiño branco,
> non sei para dónde vas.
> ....
> ¡Qué ojallá en ti me perdera
> pra nunca mais me atopar...!
> ....
> Nin fuxo, non, que anque fuxa
> dun lugar a outro lugar,
> de min mesma naide, naide,
> naide me libertará.   (506-507)

> ... Mais seica fuxindo
> de min mesma iña...   (519)

> Alma que vas huyendo de ti misma
> ¿qué buscas, insensata, en las demás?
> Si en tí secó la fuente del consuelo,
> secas todas las fuentes has de hallar.   (598)

> Díme a marchar, huyendo de mi sombra.   (662)

> ¿Adónde irei comigo?... ¿Dónde me asconderei
> que xa ninguén me vexa i eu non vexa a ninguén?
> ....
> ... Mais non, dentro te vexo,
> fantasma pavoroso dos meus remordementos!   (366-367)

Complementaria de la soledad atraída por los abismos de la nada es
la soledad del alma donde se alberga la noche perdurable del dolor o
donde existen vastedades sin llenar:

> Só en min mesma, buscando no oscuro
> i entrando na sombra,
> vin a noite que nunca se acaba
> na miña alma soia.   (310)

161

> Cuando en las noches tristes y solas
> que están llegando
> brille la luna, ¡cuántos sepulcros
> que antes no ha visto verá a su paso;
> Cuando entre nubes hasta mi lecho
> llegue su rayo,
> ¡cuán tristemente los yermos fríos
> de mi alma sola no irá alumbrando? (721)

Ya en *A mi madre* (1863) había descrito Rosalía su alma como «vasto páramo», «abrasado desierto», «mar que nunca se acaba» (56). Ahora bien, con el tiempo descubre que el vacío interior no se llena con risas ni contentos, sino con los «froitos do delor amargos» (287); echa de menos la pena que había logrado arrancar del corazón (286) y reconoce en el dolor el compañero que anula la soledad:

> No va solo el que llora.
> No os sequéis, por piedad, lágrimas mías;
> basta un pesar al alma,
> jamás, jamás le bastará una dicha.
> Juguete del Destino, arista humilde,
> rodé triste y perdida;
> pero conmigo lo llevaba todo:
> llevaba mi dolor por compañía. (723)

Junto a la dominante visión sombría de la soledad, no es raro que en la poesía rosaliana de madurez aparezcan aspectos más atractivos de ella. La soledad esperanzada, e incluso la triste y conflictiva, ahorran al espíritu preocupaciones mundanas:

> Detente un punto, pensamiento inquieto:
> la victoria te espera,
> el amor y la gloria te sonríen.
> ¿Nada de esto te halaga y encadena?
> —Dejadme solo y olvidado y libre;
> quiero errante vagar en las tinieblas;
> mi ilusión más querida
> sólo allí dulce y sin rubor me besa (581)

> Yo prefiero a ese brillo de un instante
> la triste soledad donde batallo
> y adonde a nunca a perturbar mi espíritu
> llega el vano rumor de los aplausos. (717)

Los paisajes solitarios comparten las penas y alegrías del alma, que los siente afines y proyecta sobre ellos su propio estado de ánimo:

> ¡Oh, mi amigo el invierno!
> Mil y mil veces bien venido seas,
> mi sombrío y adusto compañero. (616)

Blanca senda, camino olvidado
—¡bullicioso y alegre otro tiempo!—
del que, solo y a pie, de la vida
va andando su larga jornada: más bello
y agradable a los ojos pareces
cuanto más solitario y más yermo... (621) [6]

Un manso río, una vereda estrecha,
un campo solitario y un pinar,
y el viejo puente, rústico y sencillo,
completando tan grata soledad.
¿Qué es soledad? Para llenar el mundo
basta a veces un solo pensamiento.
Por eso hoy hartos de belleza encuentras
el puente, el río y el pinar desiertos.
No son nube ni flor los que enamoran:
eres tú, corazón triste o dichoso,
ya del dolor y del placer el árbitro,
quien seca el mar y hace habitable el polo. (580)

No siempre se produce la ósmosis afectiva entre la naturaleza y el alma, que a veces, invadida por el dolor, se cierra al luminoso júbilo universal, y a veces, entregada a la ilusión, cree oír en la naturaleza contrapuntos burlones:

No ceo, azul crarísimo;
no chan, verdor intenso;
no fondo da alma miña,
todo sombriso e negro... (331) [7]

Dicen que no hablan las plantas, ni las flores, ni los pájaros,
ni el onda con sus rumores, ni con su brillo los astros.
Lo dicen, pero no es cierto, pues siempre, cuando yo paso
de mí murmuran y exclaman: —Ahí va la loca, soñando
con la eterna primavera de la vida y de los campos,
y ya bien pronto, bien pronto, tendrá los cabellos canos,
y ve temblando, aterida, que cubre la escarcha el prado. (668)

En el secreto lenguaje que la Rosalía otoñal sabe descifrar, la natuleza no emite sólo comentarios malévolos a cuenta de la soñadora: rumores, reflejos, piar de aves pasajeras y aromas llevados por el viento le traen el mensaje de que

---

[6] Véase también «Ya que de la esperanza para la vida mía...» (568).
[7] En *A pena ó lombo* (530) se describe un paisaje primaveral y tranquilo; sólo se oye el piar de los pájaros y el lamento de una mujer, acompañado por el murmullo de un regato; y Rosalía comenta: «¡Que tristeza tan doce! / ¡Qué soidá tan prácida! / Mais para un alma en orfandá sumida, / ¡qué soidá tan deserta y tan amarga!»

mundos hay donde encuentran asilo
las almas que al peso
del mundo sucumben   (583).

Más modestos, sin halo estético ni voz trascendente, los ruidos más triviales acompañan al alma que ha buscado la serenidad en el apartamiento y se siente invadir por el miedo a la soledad; es lo que ocurre a Rosalía después de haber alejado de sí la «vitalidade inquieta» de la juventud:

I ó fin soia quedei, pero tan soia,
que oio da mosca o inquieto revoar,
do ratiño o roer terco e costante,
e do lume o *chis chas,*
cando da verde ponla
o fresco zugo devorando vai.
Parece que me falan, que os entendo,
que compaña me fan;
i este meu corazón lles di tembrando:
«¡Por Dios!... ¡non vos vaiás!»
¡Qué doce, mais qué triste
tamén é a soledad!   (290-291)

Junto a la soledad amarga hay, pues, en *Follas novas* y sobre todo *En las orillas de Sar,* la soledad agridulce y la plácida. Esta ampliación habrá de relacionarse con la vaga espiritualidad que apunta crecientemente en el último libro de Rosalía. La autora «comprende» entonces la imagen inefable de la eterna belleza y se anonada en sus abismos (643). Luz y calor más vivos y dulces que los del sol penetran en su alma y abren sus ojos, cegados por el dolor (659). Busca en todo la hermosura sin nombre (660) y cree encontrarla contemplando la imagen de Santa Escolástica, esculpida por Ferreiro en la iglesia compostela de San Martín Pinario: «¡Ya yo no estaba sola!», exclama al verla iluminada antes de proclamar con entusiasmo: «¡Hay arte! ¡Hay poesía!... ¡Debe haber cielo: hay Dios!» (666-667). No podemos asegurar que tan exultante serie de afirmaciones fuese definitiva: si el orden con que figuran los poemas de *En las orillas del Sar* responde a la cronología —cosa que no sabemos—, algunos de los últimos volverían a reflejar atormentado pesimismo. De todos modos es indudable que la esperanza no se había dejado oír con tanta fuerza en los libros anteriores.

III. ANTONIO MACHADO [8]

A diferencia de Bécquer, Antonio Machado emplea muchas veces en su poesía la palbra «soledad», y da el título de *Soledades* a su primer

---

[8] Cito según *Obras. Poesía y prosa,* ed. Aurora de Albornoz y Guillermo de Torre, Buenos Aires, Losada, 1964. (A veces uso la abreviatura *OPP.*)

libro de versos; como su antecesor sevillano, vaga solo por callejas y plazas desiertas, paseando recuerdos y esperanzas. Como Rosalía, y aún más, explora las solitarias galerías de su propia alma, o suma su soledad de caminante a la de los campos; y, como Rosalía también, relaciona su sentimiento de la soledad con la sed de Dios y el vacío de la nada; pero en vez de presentar la continuidad de un mismo y prolongado conflicto, cambia la orientación de sus inquietudes, intenta crearse una fe y una metafísica personales, y finalmente acepta la nada como la última de las postrimerías. Difiere asimismo de Rosalía en no sentirse víctima de la burla, hostilidad, indiferencia ni olvido de sus semejantes: su soledad proviene de sí mismo, de su carácter retraído y soñador; lo sabe, y su disconformidad con la sociedad en que vive no se traduce en queja personal, sino en invectivas políticas a favor de «una España implacable y redentora», «la España de la rabia y de la idea» (197).

Este hombre «misterioso y silencioso», como lo calificó Rubén Darío, ama la soledad, que invita al ensueño y a la evocación. De niño empezó a soñar, instado por el tedio y al son de un piano monótono, en el salón de su casa, amplio cuarto sombrío (92, 99); y se habituó a envolver en mágica nebulosa el pasado y el presente, que con la distancia atenúan sus colores y suavizan sus aristas:

> ... Y todo en la memoria se perdía
> como una pompa de jabón al viento. (104)

> ... Tener algunas alegrías... lejos
> y poder dulcemente recordarlas. (111)

> Tengo a mis amigos
> en mi soledad;
> cuando estoy con ellos,
> ¡qué lejos están! (267)

La soledad favorece reflexiones que hacen ver la falsedad de aparentes evidencias:

> En mi soledad
> he visto cosas muy claras
> que no son verdad. (255)

Y sobre todo permite sondear el misterio del alma, ahondar en sus recovecos y oír allí las llamadas de la buena voz y el rebullir de fieras enjauladas (105). Pero la alucinante indagación puede llevar a laberintos de espejos donde el poeta no halle respuesta satisfactoria a sus preguntas sobre la propia identidad. Y en el retablo de sus sueños, «siempre desierto y desolado», el único poblador es su fantasma, su «pobre sombra triste / sobre la estepa y bajo el sol de fuego» (80). En fin de cuentas, la soledad suele aparecer asociada al hastío, al cansancio y al dolor:

Tú venías solo con tu pena, hermano;
tus labios besaron mi linfa serena
y en la clara tarde dijeron tu pena.
Dijeron tu pena tus labios que ardían;
la sed que ahora tienen, entonces tenían.   (60)

Suena en la calle sólo el ruido de tu paso;
se extinguen lentamente los ecos del ocaso.
¡Oh, angustia!, pesa y duele el corazón...   (68)

... Y quizás el cenit de un nuevo día
amenguará tu sombra solitaria.
Mas no es tu fiesta el Ultramar lejano,
sino la ermita junto al manso río.   (75)

Recuerdo que una tarde de soledad y hastío,
¡oh tarde como tantas!, el alma mía era
bajo el azul monótono un ancho y terso río
que ni tenía un pobre juncal en su ribera...
....
... Y se alejó en silencio para llorar a solas.   (95)

... Mal vestido y triste
voy caminando por la calle vieja.   (110)

Voy caminando solo,
triste, cansado, pensativo y viejo.   (177)

Machado —otra diferencia con Rosalía— no dice que la soledad le haya
sido impuesta por el Destino; bien es verdad que en su obra poética
sólo excepcionalmente habla del destino[9]; no recuerdo que mencione
siquiera la fatalidad ni la desgracia. Pero simboliza a la soledad como la
«virgen esquiva y compañera» que ha de ir a su lado durante todo el
camino de la vida (76)[10]. La contradicción entre los aspectos tristes y
plácidos de la soledad hace que el poeta dude si es su enemiga o su ena-
morada, la sed o el agua, misterio que no llega a resolver. Otra compañera suya es, desde la infancia, una angustia inexplicada en que Machado reconoce después[11] la soledad producida por no haber encontrado
a Dios:

[9] Lo hace en el poema dedicado a Martínez Sierra: «Maldiciendo su destino /
como Glauco, el dios marino...» (69); y en la *Muerte de Abel Martín*: «Mas si
un igual destino / aguarda al soñador y al vigilante, / ... al fin sólo es creación
la pura nada» (346-347). En ambos casos la palabra significa lo determinado por
un Poder superior, no el Poder mismo, como el Destino en Rosalía.
[10] Inducen a creerlo así las coincidencias con el soneto «¡Oh soledad, mi sola
compañía!» (286), publicado en las *Nuevas canciones* de 1917-1924.
[11] Desde la 4.ª ed. de las *Poesías completas* (1936) se reúnen en este poema dos
composiciones que desde las *Soledades, Galerías y otros poemas* (1907) venían apareciendo seguidas, pero con numeración independiente; la primera, «Es una tarde
cenicienta y mustia», y terminaba con el verso «—Sí, yo era niño, y tú mi compañera», cuarto de nuestra cita.

La causa de esta angustia no consigo
ni vagamente comprender siquiera;
pero recuerdo y, recordando, digo:
—Sí, yo era niño, y tú, mi compañera.

Y no es verdad, dolor, yo te conozco,
tú eres nostalgia de la vida buena,
y soledad de corazón sombrío,
de barco sin naufragio y sin estrella.

Como perro olvidado que no tiene
huella ni olfato y yerra
por los caminos, sin camino, como
el niño que en la noche de una fiesta
se pierde entre el gentío
y el aire polvoriento y las candelas
chispeantes, atónito y asombra
su corazón de música y de pena,
así voy yo, borracho melancólico,
guitarrista lunático, poeta
y pobre hombre en sueños,
siempre buscando a Dios entre la niebla.   (112)

La busca fue larga y hubo de tener penosas alternativas. En un poema de *Soledades* (1903), «daba el reloj las doce, y eran doce / golpes de azada en tierra», el poeta cree llegada su hora final, pero «la voz del silencio» le tranquiliza:

—No temas:
dormirás muchas horas todavía
sobre la orilla vieja,
y encontrarás una mañana pura
amarrada tu barca a otra ribera.   (72) [12]

Esa confianza en la otra vida seguía alentando cuando entre 1903 y 1907 la muerte cortó un amor juvenil: aunque los ojos del poeta no verán ya a la amada, su corazón la aguarda, lo que implica que, igual que todos los autores de poemas «in morte», cree en la supervivencia o la ve, al menos, posible [13]. Pero en 1907 o poco antes, al prolongar un libro de Martínez Sierra, se expresa en términos de radical y rebelde pesimismo, comparables al «brutto / poter che, ascoso, a comun danno impera» de Leopardi:

Él sabe que un Dios más fuerte
con la sustancia inmortal está jugando a la muerte

---

[12] Véase DÁMASO ALONSO: «Muerte y trasmuerte en Antonio Machado», *Revista de Occidente*, 3.ª época, n. 5/6, marzo/abril 1976, 11-24.
[13] Remito a «Amor y muerte en tres poemas de Antonio Machado», *Homenaje a Antonio Sánchez Barbudo*, University of Wisconsin, Madison, 1981, 81-87.

cual niño bárbaro. Él piensa
que ha de caer como rama que sobre las aguas flota,
antes de perderse, gota
de mar, en la mar inmensa.   (70)

En 1912, la muerte de Leonor, su joven esposa, le hizo experimentar
una «segunda soledad», más dura que la anterior [14], y atravesar una crisis
decisiva para su pensamiento y sentido de la existencia. Machado se ve
de pronto, desamparado por Dios, frente a los enigmas de la muerte y de
la nada, y grita:

> Señor, me cansa la vida
> y el universo me ahoga.
> Señor, me dejaste solo,
> solo, con el mar a solas.   (745) [15].

Tal es el primer esbozo del poema, cuya redacción definitiva suprime
la referencia al mundo y añade la expresión de una protesta impotente:

> Señor, ya me arrancaste lo que yo más quería.
> Oye otra vez, Dios mío, mi corazón clamar.
> Tu voluntad se hizo, Señor, contra la mía.
> Señor, ya estamos solos mi corazón y el mar.   (176)

Su espíritu se resiste a admitir la desaparición total de Leonor. En
una carta a Unamuno declara: «Tengo a veces esperanza. Una fe negativa es también absurda... En fin [Leonor] hoy vive en mí más que nunca,
y algunas veces creo firmemente que la he de recobrar» [16]; y en otra de
sus fluctuaciones dice: «Vive esperanza: ¡quién sabe / lo que se traga
la tierra! (177; también en 176). En algunos cantares enviados por entonces a Unamuno parece estar cerca de hallar a Dios, por lo menos en
el deseo:

> O Tú y yo jugando estamos
> al escondite, Señor,
> o la voz con que te llamo
> es tu voz...

> Por todas partes te busco
> sin encontrarte jamás,
> y en todas partes te encuentro
> sólo por irte a buscar.   (745)

El anhelo de un Dios amoroso le hace soñar la «bendita ilusión» de
tenerlo albergado dentro de sí como manantial de nueva vida, colmena

---

[14] «Esta segunda soledad me aterra», escribe en la versión original del poema
dedicado a Xavier Valcarce (972), compuesto en 1912.
[15] Esta cuarteta, que Antonio Machado envió a Unamuno, no se publicó en
vida del autor.
[16] MANUEL GARCÍA BLANCO: «Cartas inéditas de Machado a Unamuno», *Revista Hispánica Moderna*, XXII (1956), 105-106.

que melifique sus amarguras y ardiente sol que le dé calor, lo alumbre y le haga llorar (101) [17]; pero el anhelo no se convierte en fe ni la ilusión en creencia; de ahí la

> amargura
> de querer y no poder
> creer, creer y creer! (184)

Lee con avidez libros de filosofía, sin encontrar en ellos solución satisfactoria. En el hastío de Baeza, solo y enfrascado en Bergson, comenta: «¿Todo es / soledad de soledades, / vanidad de vanidades / que dijo el Eclesiastés?» (186). La razón y el corazón están en pugna (212-213), y la crisis desemboca en una «Profesión de fe», según la cual Dios es el Criador, está en su creación y es a la vez hechura de ella; pero de todos modos es inencontrable (212). Rehúsa la fe sin caridad, piensa en el hombre hermano (205 y 212), y en el Elogio a la *Castilla,* de Azorín, formula así su nuevo credo:

> Creo en la libertad y en la esperanza,
> y en una fe que nace
> cuando se busca a Dios y no se alcanza,
> y en el Dios que se lleva y que se hace (220)

A pesar de todo, el enigma del más allá le sigue acechando, como lo prueban estas dramáticas preguntas que se hace por los mismos años:

> Morir... ¿caer como gota
> de mar en el mar inmenso?
> ¿O ser lo que nunca he sido,
> uno sin sombra y sin sueño,
> un solitario que avanza
> sin camino y sin espejo? (207)

Los dos primeros versos de este cantar condensan, con notorias coincidencias verbales, lo que Machado había dicho seis años atrás al prologar el libro de Martínez Sierra; pero entonces la aniquilación del ser individual en la mar de la nada aparecía como certeza, como solución única (no sabemos si en el pensar del prologuista, del prologado o de ambos); ahora forma parte de un dilema cuyos dos términos son poco halagüeños. Intentemos explicarnos el que se le opone: el poeta se resiste a ser «uno», innominado, despersonalizado, sin individualidad ni caracterización; «sin sombra», esto es, sin el otro yo, sin el hombre que va siempre con él, dentro de él, y con el cual conversa, el que le sirve de puente para dialogar con los demás, comprenderlos y amarlos; y «sin sueño», sin capacidad para crear el mundo mago de los recuerdos, imaginaciones y esperanzas. Después, como aclaración, niega haber sido

---

[17] El poema «Anoche, cuando dormía», aunque desde las *Poesías completas* de 1917 está incluido entre los de *Soledades,* no figura en la primera edición de éstas (1903), ni en la primera de *Soledades, Galerías y otros poemas* (1907), ni en *Campos de Castilla.* Debió de componerse, pues, entre 1913 y 1917.

«un solitario que avanza / sin camino y sin espejo»: no niega su solitariedad, harto ostensible en toda su producción, sino haber carecido de camino y de espejo; «camino», orientación hacia una meta, ruta que vamos abriendo con nuestro mismo andar; «espejo» puede simbolizar el mundo de los recuerdos, como variante del «sueño» del verso anterior; pero también cabe entenderlo variante de «sombra», es decir, «el otro yo», «el yo complementario»; y, por último, es susceptible de una tercera exégesis, «el otro», «el prójimo», autorizada por proverbios de 1923-1928 y con antecedentes en la atención al «hermano» señalada líneas arriba en los proverbios de 1913-1917 [18]. He aquí los textos de 1923-1928:

> Todo narcisismo
> es un vicio feo
> y ya viejo vicio.

> Mas busca en tu espejo al otro,
> al otro que va contigo.

> Ese tu Narciso
> ya no se ve en el espejo,
> porque es el espejo mismo. (253)

> Busca en el prójimo espejo,
> pero no para afeitarte
> ni para teñirte el pelo. (259)

> Poned atención:
> un corazón solitario
> no es un corazón. (263)

Jugando a la paronomasia diríamos que «solitario» se deprecia [19] y «solidario» se valoriza, aunque Machado no empleara aquí el segundo adjetivo. El poeta antes introvertido se orienta hacia los demás y ve narcisismo vitando en la introspección que tanto había practicado. Tal cambio repercute en su actitud frente a la soledad, según se patentiza en el soneto IV de *Los sueños dialogados:*

> ¡Oh soledad, mi sola compañía,
> oh musa del portento que el vocablo
> diste a mi voz que nunca te pedía!
> Responde a mi pregunta: ¿Con quién hablo?

[18] Para estas interpretaciones véase lo que digo en «Sobre algunos símbolos en Antonio Machado», *Poetas y prosistas de ayer y de hoy*, Madrid, Gredos, 1977, 264, 283-284 y 287.

[19] No está clara la valoración de este adjetivo en el *Recuerdo infantil* de Juan de Mairena (372): «el niño Juan, el solitario» representa allí al poeta puro tal como lo entendía entonces Machado, a saber, como aquel para quien la poesía es «palabra en el tiempo»; pero en la gestación del poema la variante «Pequeño Onán» implica sugerencias evitadas en la versión definitiva; véanse los *Apuntes inéditos* publicados en la ed. del *Juan de Mairena* con prólogo y estudio de Pablo del Barco, Madrid, Alianza Editorial, 1981, 27-28, 49, 51, 53 y 58. Libre de tales implicaciones parece estar «Martín, el solitario», que permanece en su rincón, alejado de la algazara infantil (*Muerte de Abel Martín*, 345).

Ausente de ruidosa mascarada,
divierto mi tristeza sin amigo
contigo, dueña de la faz velada,
siempre velada al dialogar conmigo.
Hoy pienso: este que soy será quién sea;
no es ya mi grave enigma este semblante
que en el íntimo espejo se recrea,
sino el misterio de tu voz amante.
Descúbreme tu rostro: que yo vea
fijos en mí tus ojos de diamante. (286)

La «virgen esquiva y compañera», innominada en 1903, tiene ya nombre en 1924, «soledad», inspirando por ella misma al poeta que nunca se lo había preguntado. Sus ojos negros y ardientes antaño se han transformado en ojos diamantinos, de frío y pétreo fulgor. Aunque su voz sea «amante», no ha revelado su secreto al poeta, que sabe cómo se llama la «dueña» —ya no doncella— de la faz velada, pero ignora cuál es su ser. Y esto es lo que precisamente le interesa: quien veinte años antes preguntaba si su acompañante le era propicia o adversaria y, perdido en un laberinto de espejos, dialogaba con la noche amiga sobre la autenticidad de las propias lágrimas, desdeña ahora semejantes cuestiones, concentrando su inquietud en el misterio de la soledad en sí, en la esencia de la soledad.

Cuando Machado escribió este soneto ya debía de estar esbozada en su pensamiento la metafísica que entre burlas y veras había de atribuir a Abel Martín y Juan de Mairena en 1926 y 1928. Era un intento de eludir la opción entre dos concepciones que niegan la supervivencia del individuo: desechada la idea de un Dios personal, le quedaba, o bien la solución panteísta, con la absorción de todo ser concreto en el insondable océano de la divinidad, en el Todo universal, o bien la «fe empirista» (205), con la sola perspectiva de la desaparición en la nada. Para sortear el dilema, Antonio Machado imaginó que Dios, «el Ser que se es», creó la nada para poder pensarse, y así de un «fiat umbra» brotó el pensar humano. Como manifestaciones del no ser, de la nada, son también creaciones de Dios la ausencia y la distancia [20], generadoras de soledad, que, sin mencionarse, está implícita en ellas. No se la nombra, y sí a la ausencia y la distancia, en las *Ultimas lamentaciones de Abel Martín,* aunque el protagonista desee alcanzar la desasida soledad de las águilas en vuelo:

¡Oh, descansar en el azul del día
como descansa el águila en el viento,
sobre la sierra fría,
segura de sus alas y su aliento! (329)

En cambio, «solitario» y «soledad» figuran, cargados de significación, en la *Muerte de Abel Martín,* el amargo y asombroso poema en que

[20] Véanse el soneto *Al gran Cero* y el poema *Siesta* (311 y 313).

171

Machado imagina las postrimerías del hombre como progresivo despojo hasta sumirse en el no ser. Abel, solitario cincuentón, viendo el revoloteo de los vencejos al atardecer, rememora el niño solitario que fue, retirado en su rincón mientras los otros niños gritaban, saltaban y reían. Ahora la algazara vital le perturba; su espíritu, vacío por obra de la razón, busca para salvarse la distancia, la ausencia y el olvido, esperando protegerse de la mortífera mirada de Dios gracias a la sombra proyectada por la mano divina: ««ahógame esta mala gritería, / Señor, con las esencias de tu Nada». Su deseo se cumple: el ángel que sabía el secreto de Abel lo saltea y se queda con el dinero —el contenido anímico de dolores, recuerdos e ilusiones— que el peregrino hacia la muerte llevaba consigo. Se acallan los gritos, pero el alma, antes llena, queda vacía; y la sombra que había deseado lo oculta a los ojos de Dios; así padece doble soledad:

> Aquella noche fría
> supo Martín de soledad; pensaba
> que Dios no le veía,
> y en su mudo desierto caminaba.

Descubre al fin que la nada es destino común del soñador y del racionalista, siente angustia y fatiga, y al comprobar que Dios no lo ve porque ni siquiera lo mira, lleva con serenidad a sus labios el vaso letal, «de pura sombra —¡oh pura sombra!— lleno» (345-347)[21].

* * *

Cada uno de los tres poetas ha dado un tratamiento distinto al tema de la soledad. La versión de Bécquer, sobria y densa, se ciñe a situaciones primarias en que lo vivido por un hombre es valedero para todos: embriaguez obsesiva del dolor, miedo de quedarse a solas con él, desamparo del hambriento sin asilo, mirada a un desolado vivir pretérito y a un olvido futuro, inquietud ante la enfermedad y la muerte desatendidas. El máximo personalismo y la máxima desnudez de estos poemas desgarrados los hacen universalmente humanos. En Rosalía el sentimiento de la soledad, enraizado en su condición de hija espuria y en el consiguiente recelo a la murmuración y la burla, agranda sus dimensiones vinculándose con la predestinación al dolor, la hermandad con las demás víctimas de la desgracia, la crisis de la fe y la presencia de la nada —pavorosa y atrayente, motivo de rebeldías y espantos, pero imán de suicidas—. En una etapa tardía (sea o no la última) de su recorrido poético, junto a esta visión amarga de la soledad se abren paso sentimientos de afinidad y complacencia en ella, concordes con ráfagas de espiritualidad antes insólitas. En Machado la soledad soñadora, melancólica e introspectiva de sus libros juveniles está unida, ya entonces, a la busca de Dios y a fluctuantes actitudes respecto a la otra vida. La muerte de Leonor le hace experimentar la soledad ante la nada, enciende sus ansias de super-

---

[21] Remito a «Las *Ultimas lamentaciones* y la *Muerte de Abel Martín*», *Poetas y prosistas de ayer y de hoy*, 300-327.

vivencia y aguija sus intentos de acercamiento a Dios; pero la fe le es inaccesible, y las soluciones racionales no satisfacen su exigencia vital de perduración. Sus elucubraciones filosóficas le conducen, de una parte, a un humanitarismo combativo, y de otra, a aceptar la nada como término de la existencia. La soledad ante la nada, vivida por Antonio Machado al morir su mujer, es en la *Muerte de Abel Martín* la consecuencia de una construcción teórica que el poeta sitúa en la mente y en la agonía del más entrañable de sus sosias.

Real Academia Española.

CUADRA'S *MAR DULCE*

by

FRANCISCO LASARTE

Pablo Antonio Cuadra's *Cantos de Cifar y del Mar Dulce*[1] is a loosely arranged cycle of poems of deceptive simplicity. Ostensibly a poetic biography, that of the sailor Cifar Guevara, and a tribute to the Mar Dulce, or Lake Nicaragua, whose waters Cifar fishes and navigates, the *Cantos* are also the creation of an autonomous poetic world, where people and the natural setting have been endowed with a myhtical aura. The book's title, with its ambiguous *de*, suggests that *Cantos de Cifar y del Mar Dulce* could be read not only as poems *about* Cifar but also as poems *by* Cifar. And it suggests, for the same reason, that it is made up not only of songs *about* the Mar Dulce but also of songs of the kind one is likely to hear sung by the people of its shores. In other words, the reader expects Cuadra to conjure up his poetic landscape through the voice of one or more folk personae and in the language of the people. The reader's expectations, however, are only partially fulfilled. There are indeed poems where we are told that the speaker's voice belongs to Cifar (or to one of his fellow lake dwellers), and Cuadra deliberately strives for a poetic diction approximating the spoken word. But the *Cantos* contain much more than this. Cuadra, clearly a learned man, chooses not to efface himself in his poems but instead allows his erudition —and especially his knowledge of the Greek and Latin classics— to show through, so that the folk persona turns out to be a charming deception. The texts which make up *Cantos de Cifar y del Mar Dulce* are thus a skillful blend of the popular and the learned, of local lore and classical myth. In Cuadra's poetic evocation Cifar transcends his Nicaraguan origins to become a kind of universal epic hero, with the Mar Dulce as the mythical setting for his adventures.

From the very first Cuadra explains that his *Cantos* are based on actual people and events. He dedicates the book to his brother Carlos, to Cifar Guevara himself, and to others, «todos finados, que en paz descansen, compañeros de mi juventud navegante» (p. 7). Of course, the dedication could itself be a fiction. Cifar is by no means a common name, and it becomes even more unusual when one hears in it an echo of the medieval *Cavallero Zifar*. Is this the first of many erudite allusions in Cuadra's

---

[1] PABLO ANTONIO CUADRA: *Cantos de Cifar y del Mar Dulce*, 3.ª ed., aumentada (Managua: Academia Nicaragüense de la Lengua, 1979).

poetry? Perhaps. Elsewhere, however, Cuadra has also written of Cifar as a real person, identifying him as the sailor whose death by drowning he witnessed some forty years earlier, when he was «un joven poeta, que llevaba en el bolsillo una gastada edición de la *Odisea,* miraba todo aquello y abría su corazón a lo que veía».[2] Thus, the *Cantos* have their genesis in a memory from long ago. By the time of the book's composition, Cifar and the other lake folk have no doubt acquired the poetic patina which memory—especially a poet's—overlays on the past. And as I intend to show, what separates the real Cifar from his counterpart in the *Cantos* is more than forty years of historical time. Memory and the imagination conspire to make of Cifar and his lake the stuff of myth, so that one can argue that the poems have a temporality (or, if one wishes, atemporality) all their own.

Just as the name Cifar has literary connotations and reminds one of epic and chivalrous deeds, the name Mar Dulce strikes the uninformed—in this case non-Nicaraguan—reader as a poetic image, as Cuadra's own name for an otherwise prosaic Lago de Nicaragua. However poetic, the name Mar Dulce is nonetheless historic, for it was the name originally given to the lake by the *conquistadores.* José Coronel Urtecho, in his prologue to Ernesto Cardenal's *El estrecho dudoso,* a book of poems about the arrival of the Spaniards in what is today Nicaragua, writes that «Gil González descubrió el Gran Lago llamado luego de Nicaragua, que los indios llamaban Cocibolca y él llamó la Mar Dulce».[3] Mar Dulce, then, is a name that recalls a time of adventure and epic deeds, which, even if historic, are not all that far removed from the deeds of a fictional character such as the *Cavallero Zifar.* Thus the happy conjunction of Cifar and Mar Dulce in the book's title prepares us for what is to follow, namely the portrait of a man and of a geographical region transfigured, the one into an epic hero of sorts, and the other into a realm of poetry and myth.

If Cuadra does not efface himself in his poems, he does not make his presence obtrusive either. Instead, what we have in the *Cantos* is a subtle blend of voices, a poetry delicately poised between the two extremes of popular song and the poems of an educated man. The various «singers» —Cifar himself, the unidentified men or women who sing of Cifar and the natural setting (or address Cifar directly), the occasional collective *nosotros,* the oracular Maestro de Tarca—occupy that middle range. Rarely does the language of the poems lose its fundamental coherence. The variation among individual voices is not so wide-ranging that it destroys the integrity of the *Cantos'* own particular diction. Save for a

[2] PABLO ANTONIO CUADRA: «Cifar», *Cuadernos Hispanoamericanos,* 296 (febrero de 1975), 253. All direct quotations from Cuadra followed by a page number higher than 200 have been taken from this article. Otherwise, the passages cited belong to *Cantos de Cifar y del Mar Dulce.*

[3] JOSÉ CORONEL URTECHO: «Carta a propósito del *Estrecho dudoso*» in ERNESTO CARDENAL: *El estrecho dudoso* (Madrid: Visor, 1966), p. 33. All other direct quotations from Coronel will be identified by a page number referring to this edition.

couple of poems, *Cantos de Cifar y del Mar Dulce* maintains the illusion that the texts which make it up are songs from the Mar Dulce, albeit a Mar Dulce that is Cuadra's own recreation of the lake and its people.

Only on two occasions does Cuadra disturb that illusion. The last poem of the book, entitled «Mujer reclinada en la playa» (and set apart in italics from the poems which precede it), is clearly the work of a learned poet. In it Cuadra calls the woman of the title «Casandra» and then corroborates our suspicion that her name is an allusion to the Cassandra of Greek mythology when he goes on to say: «Todo parece griego. El viejo Lago / y sus hexámetros» (p. 125). Of course, one could argue that the use of italics excludes «Mujer reclinada en la playa» from the *Cantos* as songs from the Mar Dulce. But the book's first poem has also been set in italics, even though Cuadra identifies it as a «barcarola marinera» and its language clearly groups it together with the «songs» immediately following.[4] The first and last poems of the book aside, only one of the remaining seventy-seven contains a break in the illusion of popular song. The poem in question is «Marcela, muchacha paladina,» where Cuadra for one brief moment drops the disingenuous role of the lake singer and takes on a different voice, the voice of seomeone with a folklorist's interest in the Mar Dulce and its people. There is a bit of the *costumbrista* in the poet who, having told the story of Marcela, concludes his poem in this fashion: «Son leyendas / isleñas, son consejas / de mujeres cuando ven a los hombres / partir con dinero hacia los puertos» (p. 77).

Although the title of the book suggests we should think of the *Cantos* as oral poetry from the Mar Dulce, a close look shows they could hardly be that. Cuadra's diction may approximate spoken language and it may abound in colloquialisms from the area of Lake Nicaragua, but this does not necessarily make folk songs out of his poems. The *Cantos*, in fact, could only be the product of a modern poet. For one thing, their meter hardly fits the more or less regular octosyllabic pattern which invariably turns up in oral poetry. Quite the contrary. Cuadra writes the sort of free verse we find everywhere in the work of contemporary poets. Moreover, he plays with the typography of his poems, much in the manner of his fellow Nicaraguan (and cousin) Ernesto Cardenal. (A striking example of this technique is to be found in the poem «Anades» [p. 83], where the lines «vuelan / en / V» are centered on the page so that their sequence becomes a graphic representation of the letter V.) And the wide variation in the use of imagery—some poems are practically devoid of tropes while others rely heavily on them—stands is sharp contrast with popular poetry and its stock imagery.[5] Finally, in a couple of the *Cantos*

---

[4] More about this later. The *Cantos* can also be seen as an elegy for a world vanishing under the influence of 'culture' and 'civilization'. Thus, framing the cycle between a 'barcarola marinera' and a learned poem would be another way of underscoring the changes which have been taking place.

[5] Some of Cuadra's poems are remarkably free of poetic imagery, so much so that their language can no longer be mistaken for ordinary speech, which does

one can actually hear the learned poet speaking through his surrogate the folk singer. A case in point is «Eufemia,» where Cifar complains about a woman who both plagues and captivates him. His complaint, in the form of an apostrophe, sounds suspiciously like an epigram in the manner of Martial. For example: «Cuánto mejor aguantar / tus gritos, Eufemia; cuánto mejor / tu cólera, tu desgreñada / ira en la madrugada / que esta furia de las olas y estos gritos / bajo los rayos y los vientos» (p. 30).[6]

«Marcela, muchacha paladina,» which shows Cuadra stepping back from his folk persona, points out in another way, too, the fundamental difference between popular poetry and the deceptive *Cantos de Cifar y del Mar Dulce.* Even as he tells his own version of Marcela's story, Cuadra cites three lines of a *corrido* which someone, presumably one of the lake folk, has composed about her. The contrast between the two songs is striking. In the fragment from the *corrido* we see many of the formal characteristics of oral poetry: «Espera que te espera / solitaria en su isla / pendiente de una vela» (p. 76). The meter is regular, with an assonant rhyme scheme, and in the first line we have a poetic formula which is typical of popular song. Cuadra's own «song» about Marcela could not be more different. It is made of lines which vary significantly in length; it has no rhyme other than a few stray assonances in e-a; and it contains a good number of enjambements. With his *Cantos de Cifar y del Mar Dulce,* then, Pablo Antonio Cuadra has «composed» highly original «songs» which one must approach as the formulation of a virtually autonomous poetic realm, a place within a poet's imagination where reality, myth, and several literary traditions fuse in a remarkable way.

Cifar Guevara, the subject of Cuadra's poetic biography and a figure emblematic of the lake folk, is an example of such a fusion. Cuadra introduces him right away, in the «barcarola marinera,» as a man whose song has a powerful and mysterious hold over the listener: «Baja el marinero velas, / se detiene el remero. / Es Cifar solitario, a la deriva / dejándose llevar de la música y del viento» (p. 9). In several poems Cifar is given an epithet—*el navegante, el arpero, el cachero*—and this rhetorical device, though here neither as frequent nor as elaborate as in epic poetry, suggests something mythical or heroic about the man. (*Cachero* is a local word meaning «importunate» or «deceitful» and thus the epithet lays bare a less than admirable side of Cifar's character.) In any case,

---

make use of 'unconscious' imagery. The result of Cuadra's efforts in a poem such as «Angelina en el acantilado» is the creation of a different and highly poetic language.

[6] Here Cuadra gives the show away by attaching a Latin epigraph to the poem: «Et Merito, Quoniam Potui Fugisse Puellam...» Cuadra does not identify the author of the passage, and my efforts to find it in Martial led nowhere. In the rest of the *Cantos* one finds two more epigraphs from classical writers. One, a transliteration from the Greek into Spanish, remains unidentified. The other is a translation into Spanish of a brief passage from Lycophron's *Alexandra.* Cuadra's use of epigraphs is, as we can see, quite eccentric.

Cuadra has mostly admiration for the sailor, as we see in the following passage from his article on Cifar:

> Cifar Guevara fue un juglar (le llamaban «el poeta del lago»), un marinero que tocaba admirablemente el arpa y la guitarra, un peón de las aguas con alma aventurera y bohemia, un revolucionario que se metió en el abordaje de los vapores del lago en una guerra civil, un impenitente enamorado, un inquieto navegante. Sin embargo, aun con toda su exhuberante [sic] capacidad de aventura, Cifar no pasó de ser un pobre Odiseo frustrado (p. 235).

Cuadra immediately questions the validity of his last statement («¿Será cierto lo que digo?») and then tries to arrive at an answer in a couple of pages of speculations on the similarities between life on the Mar Dulce and on Homer's Aegean. I say «tries» because his answer is ambiguous (and complex). Even if Cifar is an «ilusionado y pobre Odiseo» (p. 257), Cuadra nonetheless conceives of him as a version of the Homeric hero. Odysseus and the Nicaraguan sailor converge and become one in the poet's evocation.

The Mar Dulce undergoes a similar poetic transformation, as it becomes the setting for myth and adventure. In Cuadra's eyes, the Mar Dulce is to Cifar what the Aegean is to Odysseus. His essay on Cifar compares life in both places and comes up with remarkable similarities. A ship leaving, say, the port of San Miguelito could, in the poet's imagination, be about to sail with a Nicaraguan Telemachus on board. Cuadra then gives a reason for the fundamental resemblance between the Homeric Aegean and his own Mar Dulce. Seafaring people everywhere—Polynesia, the Mediterranean, the waters off Galicia, the North Sea, Lake Nicaragua—give rise to analogous legends and folk tales. As he explains:

> El misterio de las islas y de las aguas, las condiciones del hombre que navega en el peligro de las olas, de los vientos y las distancias, producen en todas partes mitos y temas de literatura popular similares. El mito de Circe, por ejemplo, casi no hay región acuática con islas que no lo tenga en una u otra forma (p. 254).

Geography is therefore at the root of Cuadra's mythopoetic recreation of Lake Nicaragua. His own experience of the lake, during his «juventud navegante» and at a time when he carried «una gastada edición de la *Odisea*» in his pocket, together with subsequent reflection on the nature of folklore and myth, yield what we now have as the *Cantos de Cifar y del Mar Dulce*.

Cuadra's source of myth and epic material is not limited to Homer and the classical world. In the *Cantos* one also finds odds and ends from other traditions. For example, the poem «El Gran Lagarto,» where Cifar battles the huge «monstruo» which has been terrorizing a lake village, can be seen as a combination of the Christian myth of Saint George and the Greek myth of Perseus. Unlike his ancient counterparts, however, Cifar fails to kill the monster. The villagers who had gone along, «gente huer-

179

tera inútil a las aguas, / ranas que no se apartaban de la orilla» (p. 53), lose heart, and in the panic that ensues the sailor almost loses his life. This ironic outcome exemplifies, I suppose, the sort of frustration the poet attributes to Cifar and his heroic undertakings. For, as Cuadra has written, «la mayoría de los cantos de Cifar son motivados por intensas fascinaciones, pero siempre sus finales o sus regresos quedan impregnados de una dolorosa frustración» (p. 257). For this reason—and for other reasons I will single out later on—Cuadra's Mar Dulce turns to be less than perfect as a realm of myth and epic deeds. Reality intrudes. But it is through such flaws and imperfections that the poetic enclosure obtains its complexity and deeper significance.

The *Cantos* also draw from local Indian legends and from the heroic —or, for many, not so heroic—deeds of the Spanish *conquistadores,* with no apparent ideological contradiction resulting from the use of such disparate sources.[7] After all, the Mar Dulce is primarily a setting for myth and poetry, not history. Thus, the poem «Caballos en el lago» describes several horses of «estampa antigua» wading into the lake and dreaming of past glories: «Entonces sueñan / —bulle / la remota osadía— / se remontan / a los días heroicos, / cuando el hierro / devolvía al sol sus lanzas / potros blancos / escuadrones de plata / ...» (pp. 12-13). The image «caballos en el lago» probably alludes to the discovery of Cocibolca by the Spaniards, when Gil González rode his horse into the lake to verify that the vast body of water was indeed a «mar dulce» and not the salt-water ocean he had imagined.[8] And if here the vision of horses in the lake water becomes in the poet's imagination a reenactment of a legendary past event, elsewhere it is Indian mythology that which captures the poetry of the Mar Dulce. In the poem entitled «Las islas» (and dedicated to Ernesto Cardenal), Cuadra has the Maestro de Tarca, a Nestor-like figure given to gnomic utterances, say these prophetic words:

> —En Solentiname,
> archipiélago de las codornices
> pereció Tamagastad
> contra los escollos de la Venadita.
> Allí lloró la tribu a su héroe.
> Allí todavía lloran los que pasan
> esperando una antigua promesa.
> Allí dice la leyenda
> que ha de volver a su pueblo
> con una palabra nueva (pp. 119-120).

Tamagastad, who was the Nicaraguan counterpart of Quetzalcoatl, thus lives on in the legends of the lake folk.

---

[7] One suspects, however, that Cuadra's sympathies lie with the conquered Indians. In the poem «Las islas» Tamagastad, the Nicaraguan version of Quetzalcoatl, appears in the role of a future conqueror and redeemer.

[8] This fact —or is it legend?— is mentioned by JOSÉ CORONEL URTECHO in his «Carta», p. 33.

In Cuadra's poetic Mar Dulce, then, we see legends and myths from various places and times in a subtle and effective combination. Some are native to the region, derived from historical events and from pre-Hispanic mythology. Others are clearly the result of Cuadra's own erudition. But the reason for it all is the lake, which the poet sees as a privileged place, as a locus for poetry and folklore, as a kind of Nicaraguan omphalos. As he tells it:

> Desde su primitiva significación mítica ya el lago perfila nuestro destino, porque el lago es nuestro mar interior, es el corazón de nuestro país, pero, simultáneamente, sus aguas son camino de conquistas, codicias e invasiones. Para el indio, el Gran Lago es el nido de la serpiente. Pero entonces el español rodea al lago con nombres de santos que combatieron a la serpiente (p. 250).

Historically, Cocibolca first becomes «la mar dulce» in the astonished words of a Spaniard and the the Lago de Nicaragua of the atlases. Poetically—in Cuadra's Cantos de Cifar y del Mar Dulce—the lake becomes a point of convergence for fact and fiction, for history and myth. And it becomes, above all, the subject matter of song.

The songs of the lake tell of a life of adventure and peril, the sort of life which, for Cuadra at any rate, is the inevitable result of living on the water: «El agua es destierro, exige un abandono de la seguridad, un desasimiento de lo terrestre para vivir la maravilla de la aventura» (p. 257). And the Cantos show Cifar and his fellow sailors risking their lives in a variety of ways. The dangers to be met are manifold: monsters such as the Gran Lagarto or the equally dangerous fresh-water sharks; the lake's unpredictable weather, which can leave a boat dead in the water during a «calmura» or subject it to «las olas furiosas y los vientos negros de Octubre» (p. 30); the women of the islands, some of whom lure men with their siren songs and bewitch them; the life of personal violence which can lead to deaths (and indeed, in Cifar's case, sends him to jail for having killed someone in a «desgracia»); the vaguely presented civil war which involves Cifar and takes the life of Tomasito el Cuque. Danger, however, has its attractions, particularly for a man like Cifar, who, as his mother puts it, prefers «lo temerario a lo seguro» (p. 17). We have proof of this in the poem «El miedo,» which explains that on the lake fear arises not «cuando el Lago / irritado / y pardo / puma / ruge» (p. 72) but «cuando / terso / susurra brisas» (p. 72), because the there is the danger of never setting sail at all.

In the Cantos Cuadra wants to recover a sense of adventure lost to the modern world:

> La aventura verdadera ha sido descalificada por la mitología moderna y comercial que hace tiempo compró los moldes de sus héroes y campeones. [...] La aventura ha descendido al sótano de la pobreza. Sus hazañas pertenecen a una épica humilde y el poeta tiene que acertar con un lenguaje muy desnudo y simple —a nivel

> muchas veces del hombre y de la frustración— para contar, para
> narrar —porque la narrativa es oficio también del poema— la
> odisea de los que siguen luchando por lo «imposible» (p. 252).

And the Mar Dulce miraculously affords its people the opportunity to
live a life resembling that lost «aventura verdadera.» Cifar may be something of a frustrated Odysseus and his deeds may amount to an «épica
humilde,» but the sense of adventure is nonetheless there, on the water
with its «potencia de aventura, fecundidad y sueño» (p. 265). Regardless
of what Cuadra may say about «bargain basement» adventures on Lake
Nicaragua, there is nothing of the bargain basement about the *Cantos*
and their «plain» diction. Through the language of his poems the poet
redeems what he otherwise sees as a world degraded and frustrated by
«modern» concerns. His backward glance to a more heroic time, both in
history and myth, transforms the Gran Lago into a poetic Mar Dulce
which is at the same time the Aegean, Cocibolca, and «la mar dulce» de
Gil González.

Cantos de Cifar y del Mar Dulce in part resembles a quest narrative.
The lake folk—Cifar especially—recognize (and heed) the call to embark
on a search for the «imposible.» As Cifar himself explains in a poem
entitled «El mal»: «¿Qué me pide partir? / Los dedos en el arpa / y ya
me empieza / el mal de lontananza» (p. 15). Song and the quest go hand
in hand on the lake, where the urge to sail over the horizon is practically
a compulsion. In «La partida» Cifar categorically rejects his mother's
entreaties that he keep to the safety of the shore by saying «El lago es
aventura,» «Prefiero lo extraño a lo conocido,» and «El hombre es
nave» (p. 17). And in the poem's conclusion, the narrating voice suggests that a man of the lake is not really born until he sets sail. It describes Cifar raising anchor and then adds: «Otra vez un niño / salía del
vientre / de su madre / al mundo...» (p. 18). For Cuadra, to be afflicted
with the «mal de lontananza» is also to be drawn to a kind of poetic
experience. The poem «La llamada» has a speaker who addresses Cifar
directly thus: «Cifar / calla tu canto. / Cifar / no recubras de música tu
oído: / Ese ilimitado / Azul / te llama» (p. 29). Through the unmistakable
allusion to the *azul* of the *modernistas,* Cuadra conjures up yet another
Nicaraguan legend, the poet Rubén Darío, an Odysseus of sorts in the
literary world. So, Cifar must hush his own song so that he may listen
to the lake's poetry and then, one assumes, once more take up his harp
to compose songs of his brush with the «infinito» of poetry and adventure. The lake is a locus of poetry. And this poetry—the mysterious
«ilimitado Azul»—is to be found everywhere in the lake's deceptively
pedestrian reality. In another poem Cifar, having followed the Maestro
de Tarca's advice that he go out looking for «la isla desconocida,» complains to the Maestro that the island, once he had found it, turned out
to be quite familiar. By way of an answer, he gets the following Delphic
statement: «Lo conocido / es lo desconocido» (p. 39). And without going
too far, I think, one can see in the Maestro's words a commentary on
the creation of the *Cantos.* Cuadra's nostalgic and endearing vision of

the lake turns «lo conocido»—a place degraded by la «mitología moderna y comercial»—into a world of poetry and mystery.

If the *Cantos* resemble a quest narrative, they also resemble a pastoral—or, to be more precise, piscatory—idyll. There is something of the *locus amoenus* of classical literature in Cuadra's Mar Dulce. Right off, in the poem telling of Cifar's birth, we find an island portrayed emblematically as a bountiful refuge:

Hay una isla en el playón
pequeña
como la mano de un dios indígena.
Ofrece frutas rojas
a los pájaros
y al náufrago
la dulce sombra de un árbol (p. 11).

The season associated with plenty is summer, for it is then that nature offers itself most generously. The poem which lists the different kinds of lake fish one can catch and feast on also has the Maestro de Tarca explain that during the summer, «toda aventura te permite / el espejeante lago / todo alimento te ofrece / (aunque teme / siempre / su inmotivada furia)» (p. 68). In the Maestro's last words we see that even in the most bountiful time of year danger is never too far away. The *locus,* then, is not completely *amoenus.*

Cuadra's Mar Dulce, in the first half of the *Cantos* at least, is a land of plenty. But so, it seems, are the islands of the real Lake Nicaragua. Here I turn once more to José Coronel's prologue to *El estrecho dudoso,* where he writes:

La pobreza no impide, sino al contrario, hace la vida fácil en esas islas —basta un niño con un anzuelo para garantizar el almuerzo de la familia— y en realidad resultan aún más paradisíacas que las otras del lago. Además de que abundan en sus canales todas las variedades de peces comestibles que se conocen en la zona, la tierra de las islas, donde todo está a mano —casi ninguna de ellas es demasiado grande ni pequeña— sirve sin gran trabajo para el cultivo de toda clase de verduras y frutas tropicales... (pp. 21-22).

Coronel is actually describing the Archipiélago de Solentiname, but what he says about its islands easily fits Cuadra's poetic isles. Moreover, Coronel comes to a conclusion regarding life on the archipelago that is equally applicable to the world of the *Cantos.* He singles out «la tentación de lo paradisíaco, que no es únicamente la de la vida fácil, sino más bien la tentación de no entrar en la historia o de evadirse de ella» (p. 22). To a large degree, Cuadra's evocation of the Mar Dulce—in its backward-looking blend of legend and myth, in its view of the lake as «ese ilimitado Azul»—is a yielding to that temptation, an effort to escape history.

History—and its ally, time—do intrude, however. As we read on in the *Cantos* we notice a gradual erosion of the privileged poetic enclosure. A sense of disillusionment with the quest sets in, and in the end the idyllic vision is subverted, even if not altogether lost. The early poems, those which set up the Mar Dulce as a *locus amoenus* and as a place of adventure, already contain subtle signs of the destructive changes to come. For example, the poem about Cifar's birth ends with the image of his mother throwing the bloody afterbirth over the boat's side, «mientras giraban en las aguas / tiburones y sábalos / atraídos por la sangre» (p. 11). The sharks lurking underwater suggest that the island haven is actually surrounded by danger, much in the same way as the calm waters of the summer lake hold the potential of destruction. In «Caballos en el lago» the vivid evocation of a heroic epic past immediately gives way to a more humble present: «Pero vuelven / (Látigo / es el tiempo)» (p. 13). The horses may still be young and vigorous, but the dream of bygone glories has vanished. Time, the bringer of history, has asserted itself. At the end of the book we encounter once more the image of the horse, only in this case as an illustration of the effects of time as bearer of death. The poem in question is «El caballo ahogado,» and in it we are told of the dread felt by the people who discover the dead animal: «Sintieron / como un extraño / presagio / y vieron / una corona / de gaviotas blancas / en el viento» (pp. 115-116). What we have here, of course, is a premonition of Cifar's own death by drowning. But we also have more: an intimation of the death and disappearance of an entire way of life. In this sense, then, the drowned horse as foreteller of doom anticipates the image of Cassandra which closes the *Cantos*.

The quest motif undergoes a similar change, since towards the end of the book the «mal de lontananza» carries a much heavier stress on «mal.» In the poem «Lo que escribió Cifar sobre su hija Ubaldina» we hear the sailor addressing God in this fashion:

> Me diste, ¡oh Dios! una hija con el espíritu
> de la barca
> en que crucé las aguas
> enfurecidas del tiempo.
> No permitas, Señor, que el viento
> la arroje como a mí
> a lo insaciable (p. 112).

God should instead give her a «bahía mansa.» There is more here than the words of a man fearing for the safety of a woman. The taste for adventure has soured, for «ese ilimitado Azul» has become «lo insaciable.» And «aguas enfurecidas del tiempo» sets up the lake as a metaphor for human existence. A much older Cifar, however compelled to continue his life of adventures, now sees the quest in quite a different manner. Time and the frustrations of life on the lake have subdued somewhat Cifar's passion for adventure.

Just as the *Cantos de Cifar y del Mar Dulce* tell or Cifar's birth, life, and death, they show other elements of the Mar Dulce—the emblematic island, for example—following an analogous process of degeneration. In «El cementerio de los pájaros,» for instance, we have an island which is strikingly different from the island of «El nacimiento de Cifar.» Instead of life we have destruction and death, what at the end of the poem is called «el cementerio del canto» (p. 122). Cifar reaches the island tired and sick, looking for «el descanso de un árbol» (p. 121). But, as he immediately remarks: «No vi tierra / sino huesos. / De orilla a orilla / huesos / y esqueletos de aves, / plumas calcinadas, / hedor de muerte / ...» (p. 121). The dead birds on this island contrast sharply with the birds portrayed in «Anades,» where the poet describes them in flight: «recuperan / en la altura / el orden / la libertad / y el canto» (p. 83). Now, rather than life, movement, and song we have a dead landscape and «graznidos de agonía, / trinos tristes / y alguna trémula / osamenta / aún erguida / con el pico abierto» (pp. 121-122). Images of death and desolation abound towards the end of the *Cantos.*

Something else which threatens the Mar Dulce's idyllic nature is the arrival of «civilization» and its attendant evils, social and economic injustice. For the most part Cuadra's protest against such injustice —there is no questioning his awareness of the problem—appears in an understated and oblique way. In the *Cantos,* at least, the recreation of a mythical and largely idealized Mar Dulce occupies center stage at all times. Certain texts, however, contain remarks that are like cracks or fissures on the surface on the idyllic and heroic vision. In «Viento en los arenales» we read of «gentes de adentro / con lámparas y hambre» (p. 74) who come by to pick up the sardines which the tide has left stranded and stinking up the beach. And elsewhere the Maestro de Tarca pronounces: «En el rencor del Lago / me parece oír / la voz de un pueblo» (p. 84). The people are seen here as a natural force, presumably as vigorous and as eternal as the lake and its anger. One assumes, given the history of Spanish America, that the hunger afflicting the «gentes de adentro» stems from the inequalities of an economic system based on the exploitation of the poor. The lake folk too, despite their independence and bountiful lake, have cause to feel wronged. The poem «In memoria» is a kind of history of the Moras, long-time inhabitants of Zapatera Island, but as Cuadra (or Cifar) points out: «Siglos / de habitar la isla / pero / nunca dueños» (p. 106). A civil war—its causes and outcome are never shown—eventually reaches the lake, involving Cifar as a gun-runner and rebel simpathizer and causing the death by torture of Tomasito el Cuque, but the conflict is only marginally and hazily portrayed. Modern political strife, then, hardly enters the Mar Dulce and, even when it does, Cifar's participation in it can be seen as just one more of his adventures.

Only one poem in the entire *Cantos* contains a direct attack on «civilization,» which Cuadra sees as a degrading influence, a threat even to the «épica humilde» of the Mar Dulce. It is called «La isla de los "Gavilanes"» and relates the story of three firshermen, the «Gavilanes»

185

of the title, who left their island and their ship «La Sirena» to live in Managua. After depicting their former life, Cuadra goes on to say:

Hoy Juan maneja un taxi
en Managua y cobra
un peso por carrera
Alfonso es dipsómano perdido
Felipe es el dueño
del burdel «La Sirena» (p. 94).

Removed from the Gran Lago and away from their island, the three «humble» epic heroes have become thoroughly degraded. The contrast between life on the Mar Dulce and life in Managua serves to underscore that the lake, despite the intrusion of history, remains in the Cantos—in the poet's memory and imagination, that is—largely untouched as a haven for myth and legend.

Cantos de Cifar y del Mar Dulce is, in short, a poetic cycle of great literary richness. Cuadra has managed to stitch together, with hardly a seam showing, the low and high strains of Hispanic poetic diction. The «songs» preserve a delicate balance of voices. We hear, at times, Cuadra's learned poetic discourse, only to have it disappear, screened by what the poet would have us believe is the voice of a fisherman. But more than not, in the Cantos we have the harmonious coexistence of Pablo Antonio Cuadra, the erudite reader of such obscure poems as Lycophron's Alexandra, and his poetic persona, the unlettered Cifar el navegante. The result of this harmony of voices is the creation of a pre-eminently poetic reality, a world of myth and legend which may have as its point of departure the Gran Lago de Nicaragua, but which is in fact a cycle of poems about a poet's Mar Dulce. Removed from most immediate reality by the filter of memory, the nuances of classical allusions, and a deceptively «popular» language, the Cantos are a sort of hortus conclusus, though not a perfect one, since time and history intrude upon it, making it a less than perfect refuge. Either as a world already lost or as a world on the verge of disappearance, the Mar Dulce endures in Pablo Antonio Cuadra's appropriately elegiac poetry.

University of Wisconsin.

SER/DECIR: TACTICAS DE UN AUTORRETRATO

by

SYLVIA MOLLOY

I

Ya difícil de asir en prosa, la primera persona autobiográfica —el yo que se señala como sujeto «verdadero» de su enunciado— lo es tanto más en poesía, donde lo referencial se supera en nombre de una organización que tiende a lo simbólico. Así, si bien es innegable que el llamado poema autobiográfico tiene por referente la vida histórica, finita, de quien lo escribe (piénsese en el Wordsworth del «Prelude», en el Hugo de *Les Feuilles d'automne*), la intención del texto no es narrar un *continuum* de acontecimientos (escribir una vida), sino presentar salteadamente, icónicamente, facetas de una imagen (revelar una *persona*). El poema enunciado por una primera persona que se expone a sí misma estaría más cerca del autorretrato, tal como lo ve Beaujour, que de la autobiografía: «La fórmula operante del autorretrato es, por tanto: "No os contaré lo que he hecho, sino os diré *quien soy*"»[1]. La fórmula es aplicable al poema liminar de *Cantos de vida y esperanza,* de Darío, siempre que se le dé una vuelta de tuerca adicional: no «os diré *quien soy*» sino, en la inmediatez ilocutoria del texto, «os diré quién *digo* que soy». El poema de Darío vuelve patente esta intención de equiparar, desde el primer verso, el *ser* con el *decir*.

Autorretrato entonces, como bien lo vio Salinas, quien al comentar el poema de Darío encuentra la fórmula memorable: «Se figura [...] su figura»[2]. Sin embargo, a diferencia de la mayoría de los autorretratos cuyo principal propósito es esa figuración en sí, «Yo soy aquel...» aparece en la obra de Darío animado de propósitos adicionales que vale la pena considerar, puesto que determinan la organización interna del poema. Esos propósitos están claramente indicados por el lugar que ocupa el poema —abre *Cantos de vida y esperanza,* a manera de segundo prefacio— y por el lector privilegiado, José Enrique Rodó —tú explícito postulado por el yo textual— a quien está dedicado.

Poema de umbral, poema bifronte, «Yo soy aquel...» presenta a un yo en suspenso, tal como lo veía Valéry: «El Yo se mantiene en el

---

[1] MICHEL BEAUJOUR: *Miroirs d'encre,* Paris: Seuil, 1980, p. 9 (traducción mía).
[2] PEDRO SALINAS: *La poesía de Rubén Darío,* Buenos Aires: Losada, 1968, p. 256.

umbral, entre lo posible y lo cumplido»[3]. Que Darío quería hacer de este poema liminar un texto de juntura, un texto irradiante y no un autorretrato cerrado, queda claro en lo que de él dice en *Historia de mis libros.* Reduce la autonomía del texto y hasta parece menospreciar su calidad poética, valorándolo más bien como continuación del prefacio en prosa, como presentación de un libro más que de un yo: «En unas palabras liminares y en la introducción, en endecasílabos, se explica la índole del nuevo libro»[4]. Propone a continuación un resumen, sin dejar en claro si se refiere al libro entero de *Cantos* o al poema individual «Yo soy aquel...»: «La historia de una juventud llena de tristezas y de desilusión, a pesar de las primaverales sonrisas; la lucha por la existencia desde el comienzo, sin apoyo familiar ni mano amiga», *etcétera.* La larga enumeración de una historia mental y espiritual bien puede referirse al trasfondo personal, autobiográfico, que metaforizará el poema liminar en apretada sucesión de imágenes, pero igualmente puede leerse como trasfondo que metaforizará salteadamente, en unidades aparentemente autónomas —cada poema— el libro entero. De hecho se trata de las dos cosas, como si el poema desbordara literalmente —«y hacia Belén..., ¡la caravana pasa!»[5]— en los textos que lo siguen. Pero a la vez que se abre al porvenir e inaugura una secuencia, el poema aparece resueltamente vuelto a la obra pasada, en actitud de rememoración, de celebración elegíaca y sobre todo —volveré a esto— de rescate textual. El autorretrato dariano elige, como lugar de representación del yo que dice, la tenue línea divisoria entre *Prosas profanas* y *Cantos de vida y esperanza:* el poema es tanto proyección de un ser / decir como recopilación de un ser / decir, lo cual condiciona notablemente la exposición del yo.

La dedicatoria del poema a José Enrique Rodó es otro elemento fuertemente condicionador del texto de Darío. Pocos críticos se han detenido a explorar a fondo sus implicaciones; o la mencionan al pasar[6], o la interpretan de manera decididamente equivocada: «La dedicatoria del poema a José Enrique Rodó señala una intencionada dirección, confiada al intérprete que mejor comprendió la madurez juvenil del poeta, la de *Prosas profanas*»[7]. Es innegable que la dedicatoria del poema al autor de *Rubén Darío. Su personalidad literaria, su última obra* es intencional, pero que Darío viera el gesto como reconocimiento de quien mejor lo había comprendido no lo es. La dedicatoria señala, sí, una intencionada

[3] PAUL VALÉRY: «Tête-à-tête», *Oeuvres,* Paris: Gallimard-Pléiade, 1957, t. 1, p. 340 (traducción mía).

[4] RUBÉN DARÍO: *Historia de mis libros,* en *Obras completas,* Madrid: Afrodisio Aguado, 1950, t. 1, p. 215.

[5] RUBÉN DARÍO: «Yo soy aquel...», *Poesía,* Caracas: Biblioteca Ayacucho, 1977, pp. 244-247.

[6] PEDRO HENRÍQUEZ UREÑA: «Rubén Darío», *Obra crítica,* México: Fondo de Cultura Económica, 1960, p. 101; ENRIQUE ANDERSON IMBERT: *La originalidad de Rubén Darío,* Buenos Aires: Centro Editor de América Latina, 1967, p. 113.

[7] JUAN CARLOS GHIANO: «La versión autobiográfica de Darío», en *Ruben Darío (Estudios reunidos en conmemoración del centenario),* La Plata: Universidad Nacional, Facultad de Humanidades, 1968, p. 31.

dirección: la que tomará el yo hablante dentro del poema para contestar (y corregir) a Rodó, reaccionando contra su lectura de *Prosas profanas* con un complejo autorretrato.

Hagamos un poco de historia, recordemos cómo acusó recibo Darío del ensayo de Rodó. Agradece el tomo enviado con generalidades y con notable sequedad, prometiéndole a Rodó otra carta más larga que nunca escribirá[8]. Tres semanas más tarde, el 21 de abril de 1899, refiriéndose en carta a Unamuno a la falta de americanismo que se le reprocha y que él asume como desafío, habla de Rodó en términos dignos de «El arte de injuriar» borgeano: «Mejor que yo ha desarrollado el asunto el señor Rodó, profesor de la universidad de Montevideo»[9]. Por fin, en 1901, ofende a Rodó al publicar su estudio, sin firma, como prólogo a la segunda edición de *Prosas profanas.* Rodó había autorizado esa publicación; no, desde luego, que se omitiera su nombre. La deliberada omisión de Darío parece obedecer a un doble impulso, característico de su estrategia literaria y profético en lo que respecta el texto mismo de «Yo soy aquel...»: el desafío y la asimilación. En primer lugar, se venga del crítico uruguayo que entre los elogios le opone reparos, reduciéndolo al anonimato, quitándole *autoridad.* En segundo lugar, aprovecha el texto *pro domo sua,* borra o disminuye las reticencias de Rodó asimilándose un estudio sin firma que al figurar como prefacio —*autorizado* por Darío— no puede verse sino como positivo. Bien observa Benedetti:

> El hecho de que Darío haya incluido el estudio de Rodó como prólogo en la segunda edición de sus *Prosas profanas,* no autoriza, sin embargo, a pensar que el poeta no haya advertido las reticencias de su crítico. Estas son tan sutiles y están tan bien incrustadas en el brillo de los elogios, que Darío puede haber hecho cálculo y concluido que, frente al lector corriente, aun las contenciones de Rodó, aun las objeciones implícitas, habrían de parecer variantes del panegírico[10].

Rodó está presente en «Yo soy aquel...» como en negativo, está presente en todo *Cantos de vida y esperanza,* y esto es claro para el propio Darío. Así, en carta a Juan Ramón Jiménez, del 24 de diciembre de 1904, declara de su futuro libro: «Hay de todo. Mas por primera vez se ve lo que Rodó no encontró en Pr[osas] profanas, el hombre que siente»[11]. Nótense bien los términos: no lo que no hay en *Prosas profanas,* sino «lo que Rodó no encontró»; la dependencia, la intención, no podrían ser más obvias. La aseveración errada de Marasso —«Dentro de la amplitud

[8] JOSÉ ENRIQUE RODÓ: *Obras completas,* Madrid: Aguilar, 1967, p. 1366.
[9] ALBERTO GHIRALDO: *El archivo de Rubén Darío,* Buenos Aires: Losada, 1943, p. 47.
[10] MARIO BENEDETTI: *Genio y figura de José Enrique Rodó,* Buenos Aires: Eudeba, 1966, p. 42.
[11] ERNESTO MEJÍA SÁNCHEZ: «Criterio de esta edición», en Rubén Darío, *Poesía,* p. LXIV.

de este prefacio poético, Darío pensó continuamente en Verlaine»[12]— se corrige con el reemplazo de un nombre: en quien sí pensó Darío, continuamente, fue en Rodó. Prueba adicional de que aun años más tarde Darío veía «Yo soy aquel...», y todo *Cantos de vida y esperanza,* a la luz de Rodó es su referencia explícita a los consejos del crítico en la «cabeza» que le dedica:

> Su segundo opúsculo sobre el autor de *Prosas profanas,* o, mejor dicho, sobre este libro de poesías, le afirmó virtuoso de la prosa, de la erudición elegante, *y en la última parte de su trabajo, profeta* (subrayado mío)[13].

La necesidad de Darío de corregir *misreadings* —fuentes fecundas, por otra parte, de su propio quehacer poético— y de reaccionar contra *«celuiqui-ne-comprend-pas»* proveyendo justificaciones, explicaciones, o enmendando las lecturas de sus críticos, es conocida. Sus autodefensas fogosas, a veces desproporcionadas, suelen atribuir excesiva importancia —importancia personal, individual— al emisor de la crítica o del reparo. Magnifica Darío en la introducción a *El canto errante* el «hermoso encarnizamiento» de sus críticos: «Con el montón de piedras que me han arrojado pudiera bien construirme un rompeolas que retardase en lo posible la inevitable creciente del olvido»[14]. Declara haber respondido a sólo tres críticas e indica por qué lo hizo: «por la categoría de sus representantes y porque mi natural orgullo juvenil, ¡entonces!, recibiera también flores de los sagitarios. Por lo demás, ellos se llamaban Max Nordau, Paul Groussac y Leopoldo Alas». No menciona Darío su primera respuesta, algo tosca e ingenua, a Ricardo Contreras, el primer crítico que le hizo reparos; y tampoco menciona al sagitario más sutil de todos, Rodó, cuyas críticas suscitaron su autodefensa más hábil y sinuosa, el autorretrato de «Yo soy aquel...».

Nótese que los críticos a quienes elige responder Darío hacen todos figura de dómines. Darío confirma el hecho al indicar, por un lado, su propia juventud («mi natural orgullo juvenil») y, por el otro, la *categoría* de sus adversarios, representantes de una autoridad que a la vez se reconoce y se resiente. Cuando la crítica del dómine toca directamente la práctica poética de Darío —es el caso de Contreras y de Groussac— la reacción es sensiblemente la misma. Primero, se reconoce la autoridad del dómine: con tono afectadamente modesto y adulón, cuando se responde a Contreras (una suerte de infantil «maestro no lo haré más»)[15]; con tono

---

[12] ARTURO MARASSO: *Rubén Darío y su creación poética,* La Plata: Universidad Nacional, Biblioteca Humanidades, 1934, p. 162.

[13] RUBÉN DARÍO: «José Enrique Rodó», *Cabezas* en *Obras completas,* Madrid: Afrodisio Aguado, 1950, t. II, p. 963.

[14] RUBÉN DARÍO: *Poesía,* p. 302.

[15] Sobre la actitud de Darío frente a sus lectores y críticos, ver SYLVIA MOLLOY: «Conciencia del público y conciencia del yo en el primer Darío», *Revista Iberoamericana,* 108-109 (1979), pp. 443-457, y «'Tú que tienes la luz': hacia el lector esquivo de Darío», *Texto/Contexto en la literatura iberoamericana,* Memoria del XIX Congreso del I.I.L.I., Madrid, 1980, pp. 251-256.

belicoso y desafiante, años más tarde, cuando se responde a Groussac (Groussac [...] fue quien me enseñó a escribir, mal o bien, como hoy escribo» [16]). Segundo, la respuesta pasa a la cuidadosa exposición y defensa de una práctica poética propia, a modo de manifiesto personal, tomando como punto preciso de partida los reparos del crítico.

Pese a sus evidentes peculiaridades, «Yo soy aquel...» se inserta dentro de esa línea de textos autodefensivos. Si los dos movimientos señalados —resentido reconocimiento de la autoridad, enérgica defensa de la práctica poética— no aparecen tan claramente en este poema como en los otros textos de autodefensa, es sin duda en parte porque responder a Rodó no es su único propósito. Pero aun suponiendo que lo fuera, se distingue por otras razones. Primero: el «natural orgullo juvenil» de Darío ha pasado a ser madura seguridad poética; no necesita anunciar que contesta para justificarse, sino simplemente dice que es —o es diciéndose. Segundo: Rodó, por la naturaleza de sus reparos y por el lugar mismo que ocupa en el mundo cultural hispanoamericano, es un crítico muy distinto de los otros dos.

Antes de indagar en la naturaleza exacta de los reparos de Rodó, es preciso recordar la ambigua posición que éste ocupa con respecto a Darío, en la escala que va desde la *juventud* a la *autoridad*. Rodó es cuatro años menor que Darío; cuando escribe su opúsculo sobre *Prosas profanas* todavía no ha escrito *Ariel,* la obra que lo consagraría oficialmente como maestro de la juventud continental. Sin embargo, su posición de mentor, desde la dirección de la *Revista Nacional de Literatura y Ciencias Sociales,* se define y se acepta desde muy temprano. Así lo reconoce Clarín, cuando al prologar *Ariel* trata al autor de «crítico ya ilustre», y así lo reconocería más tarde el propio Darío, en la mencionada «cabeza» de Rodó:

> Desde sus comienzos, la obra de Rodó se concreta en ideas, en ideas decoradas con pulcritud por la gracia dignamente seductora de un estilo de alabastros y mármoles [...] Nació con vocación de belleza y enseñanza. Enseñanza, es decir, conducción de almas. A tal pedagogía es a la que se refiere el Dante en un verso referente a Virgilio. Cuando apareció su primer opúsculo, *Vida nueva,* se vio el surgir de un maestro en su generación, en la generación continental [17].

Un maestro, pero a la vez un semejante, un coetáneo. Es esta una novedad en la galería de interlocutores de Darío, acostumbrado a maestros-padres, a figuras mayores de poder cultural (Groussac, Valera, Mitre, la lista sería larga) [18]), o bien, en el extremo opuesto, a hermanos discípu-

---

[16] RUBÉN DARÍO: «Los colores del estandarte», *Obras completas,* Madrid: Afrodisio Aguado, 1955, t. IV, p. 874.
[17] RUBÉN DARÍO: *Obras completas,* t. II, p. 963.
[18] Para no hablar de poderosos de otro tipo, también presentes en la obra de Darío. Piénsese en «Salutación al águila» y en el lamentable «Mater Admirabilis» dedicado a Estrada Cabrera, dos textos muy posteriores a su encuentro con Rodó.

los, a jóvenes figuras que lo siguen (Pedro Balmaceda, Lugones, Jaimes Freyre, los muchos representantes de «las flamantes letras españolas / ... / que me tocó iniciar») [19]. La compleja postura de Rodó, tal como aparece para Darío —un maestro crítico, por un lado, y, por el otro, un igual dialogante que en parte lo ha leído mejor que nadie— sin duda determina la sinuosa complejidad del poema liminar de *Cantos de vida y esperanza.*

II

El estudio de Rodó sobre Darío, pre-texto dinámico de «Yo soy aquel...», es un admirable ejercicio de estrategia literaria. Su propósito es dar coherencia —y más aún, poder de convicción— al complejo *odi et amo* que parece ser motor del texto. Este aparece, por cierto, como espacio de contienda entre la razón moralizante del Rodó dómine, con su «incorregible inclinación al arte que combate y que piensa» [20], y el impulso hedónico del Rodó lector «dócil a toda poética sugestión» (R, 171) e incluso colaborador activo en «la magia del poeta» *(ib.).* De ahí el curioso vaivén que anima el texto, escindido según las dos líneas que el propio Rodó busca conciliar: significación y sugestión, profundidad y superficie, razón y goce. La singular cautela que domina este estudio ambiguo, lleno de meandros —a partir del ambivalente primer párrafo sobre la no americanidad de Darío, opinión que Rodó atribuye a *otros*—, parecería indicar, por parte de Rodó, un compromiso personal que supera el mero ejercicio crítico: como si la lectura de *Prosas profanas* fuera un placer privado y vergonzante, no sólo capaz «de hacer languidecer a una legión de Esparta» (R, 175), sino amenazadora para el propio Rodó.

Al analizar la poesía de Darío destaca Rodó (¿como reproche?) su carácter solipsista y ritual, su «personalismo nada expansivo» (R, 166), su tendencia a exaltar el «alcázar interior» (R, 165) en desmedro de la realidad circundante. Estamos ante un artificio único, una planta de estufa —«vegetación extraña y mimosa» (R, 166)—, un texto privado. El propio Darío ya había hablado, en las «Palabras liminares» de *Prosas profanas,* de literatura «mía en mí», y Rodó, aparentemente, no hace sino retomar las triunfales y desafiantes palabras del poeta. Pero al continuar con el tema, las observaciones de Rodó —he ahí su magistral ambigüedad— insinúan como de paso, *y sin dejar de valorar,* la falla: «No cabe imaginar una individualidad literaria más ajena que ésta a todo sentimiento de solidaridad social y a todo interés por lo que pasa en torno suyo» (R, 167). La interioridad se vuelve cerrazón, indiferencia. Si se diera una apertura en esta poesía, si el poeta vuelto hacia adentro se diera a los otros, «afirmo que, para hacerle maestro de la verdad,

---

[19] RUBÉN DARÍO: *Poesía,* p. 301.
[20] JOSÉ ENRIQUE RODÓ: *Rubén Darío. Su personalidad literaria. Su última obra,* en *Obras completas,* p. 175. Abreviaré en mi texto: R.

sería necesario prepararle una decoración renovada [...] sin ninguna emanación de vulgaridad» *(ibíd.)*.

A partir de este momento, el ensayo de Rodó se empeñará en señalar (¿como reproche?) el carácter artificial, teatral, de la poesía de Darío, lo que se podría llamar su *impostura*. «Decoración», «apariencia divinizada», «parodia», anota Rodó; se trata del mundo exterior como espectáculo, dotado «de un interés reflejo que adquiere [...] de su paso por la Hermosura» (R, 167). Este proceso de impostura, de mediatización teatral, se observa, según Rodó, no sólo en la circunstancia del poeta, sino en su persona misma, como máscara de comediante:

Nunca el áspero grito de la pasión devoradora e intensa se abre paso a través de los versos de este artista poéticamente calculador, del que se diría que tiene el cerebro macerado en aromas y el corazón vestido de piel de Suecia. También sobre la expresión del sentimiento personal triunfa la preocupación suprema del arte, que subyuga a ese sentimiento y lo limita; y se prefiere —antes que los arrebatados ímpetus de la pasión [...]— todo lo que hace que la túnica del actor pueda caer constantemente, sobre su cuerpo flexible, en pliegues llenos de gracia (R, 168).

En Darío no se da, según Rodó, «el abandono generoso y veraz de un alma que se os entrega toda entera» (R, 168), en cambio se da el amaneramiento, en un proceso que Rodó no vacila en calificar de reductor. Así se desemboca en «una limitación, un *empequeñecimiento* extensivo» (R, 168), que hace «*enfermar de selección*» (R, 170) a una poesía cuya naturaleza literaria está siempre presente. Notablemente —y esto habrá de tenerse en cuenta para la lectura de «Yo soy aquel...»— Rodó señala tan sólo dos ejemplos de la «afortunada visita del Sentimiento a la mansión de este artista, gran señor, que no le tiene entre sus amigos constantes» (R, 182): son «El poeta pregunta por Stella» y «Margarita». Se trata de dos poemas elegíacos cuyo carácter literario, tópico, no escapa al propio Rodó. Pero el hecho de que en los dos se presente un *yo* central, no mediado (y protegido) como en otros poemas por un explícito reino interior, y que lamenta la pérdida específica de una amada, curiosamente garantiza, para Rodó, el valor confesional de los textos: «y la emoción que levanta con ese hálito de verdad que no se simula ni remeda, el melancólico verso en que se la evoca [a la amada], sugiere en nuestro ánimo la sospecha de una historia real» (R, 182).

La división que establece el ensayo para la poesía de Darío (y acaso para toda poesía) es clara: por un lado, ve Rodó «la *honda* realidad personal» (el yo directo, la historia «real», el sentimiento); por el otro, nota el «personalismo nada expansivo» (el amaneramiento superficial, el decorado exterior e interior, la túnica del actor, la pose). Fruto de esa escisión que Rodó no logra suprimir (antes bien la aumenta) es su vibrante *misreading* —«amplifica mi fantasía» (R, 171), anota al pasar— de «Era un aire suave...». Lanzado a una lectura sólo frívola del texto, al que purga de entrada de sentimiento personal, exagera, con sospechoso regodeo por parte de un paladín del «arte que combate y piensa», el amaneramiento del poema. Concluye su comentario sobre una nota inesperadamente luminosa —«la fiesta, en torno, continúa: las Horas danzan festivas, como en la pintura matinal de Guido Reni» (R, 172)— sin advertir el desconcierto final en el poema de Darío, la fiesta, menos matinal que brumosa, que se vuelve «cruel y eterna» pesadilla atemporal.

La visión estrábica que practica Rodó en su lectura de Darío lo lleva a menudo a aligerar ciertos poemas, a enamorarse de esa ligereza —«ese capricho delicioso» (R, 170)— y a la vez a oponerle reparos en nombre de la sinceridad y del sentimiento espontáneo. Así, forzando de nuevo el texto, declara sorprendentemente de «Mía» y «Dice mía» que «el análisis tiene poco que hacer con estas composiciones enteramente *irresponsables* por su índole» (R, 176). «Curiosas *naderías*» (*ibíd.*), «extravagancias loables» (R, 181), dice una y otra vez Rodó, a la vez que se deleita en ellas. Declara que hay quienes encuentran «Año nuevo» un poema trivial, mientras que para él es encantador. Sin embargo, añade, cautelosamente: «La verdad es que renunciaría a justificarlo en las formas habituales de la crítica» (R, 183). La oposición entre artificio deliberado y sentimiento directo culmina, para Rodó, en la tópica comparación que replantea entre Darío y Verlaine. Al contrario de su precursor, cuya falta de artificio exagera Rodó, Darío es el artista calculador, «en cuyo talento —plenamente *civilizado*— no queda, como en el alma de *Lélian,* ninguna tosca reliquia de espontaneidad, ninguna parte primitiva» (R, 184).

El ensayo de Rodó termina con un hábil deslinde entre Darío —a quien se disculpa por gozar del «atributo regio de la irresponsabilidad» (R, 191)— y los verdaderos culpables de frivolidad, los imitadores «que hoy juega[n] infantilmente en América al juego literario de los colores» *(ibíd.).* El texto se cierra con un deseo: que la poesía de Darío sea «producción puesta al servicio de una idea y conscientemente atendida» *(ibíd.);* que sea signo de renovación en el mundo hispánico, que contribuya al «florecer del espíritu en el habla común, que es el arca santa de la raza» *(ibíd.).* En suma: que Darío sea un maestro tal como lo entiende Rodó, que abra un camino con su poesía semejante al que él está por abrir con *Ariel.*

III

Si el estudio de Rodó sobre *Prosas profanas* recalcaba el encierro de Darío, su desafiante *noli me tangere,* el prefacio de *Cantos de vida y esperanza* y el poema liminar se empeñan, de distintas maneras, en dar la impresión contraria. Se corrige la imagen del poeta artífice, ajeno al lector y a las circunstancias, del monje solitario que leía las vidrieras historiadas en las «Palabras laminares» de *Prosas profanas.* «Yo no soy un poeta para las muchedumbres —escribe Darío—, pero sé que indefectiblemente tengo que ir a ellas.» La voz poética que se anuncia en este prefacio y que promete exponer sus preocupaciones, individuales y continentales, parecería reclamar un yo nuevo, acaso cercano del de un Hugo o de un Whitman —generoso, profético, plural— más que el yo confiado en su unicidad que caracteriza *Prosas profanas*. El poema liminar dedicado a Rodó, donde se estrena esa nueva voz, presenta, sin embargo, un yo harto más complejo de lo que las aseveraciones de Darío dejaban prever.

Por primera vez aparece en la obra de Darío una autodefinición directa del yo. ¿Se lo ha acusado de retacear «la *honda* realidad personal»? Responde al reproche de la manera más directa posible, en primera persona y con un autorretrato: «yo soy». Y lo notable de esa declaración inicial es que no desemboca en una representación, ni directamente (como el «Yo soy un hombre sincero», de Martí), ni indirectamente (como el «Je suis un cimetière abhorré de la lune», de Baudelaire). Lejos de vestirlo con «la túnica del actor» que le reprocha Rodó, Darío presenta al yo (aparentemente) desnudo: en su propia enunciación. Ser (ser «personal») = decir (en) primera persona.

Ahora bien, la autodefinición, la equiparación entre ser y decir, notablemente no se basa en la epifanía de la enunciación —no es la igualación del Soy el que Soy con el Soy el que Dice—, sino en un doble desajuste que permite al yo ser (y decir) lo que es a través de lo que ha dicho otro:

> Yo soy aquel que ayer no más decía.

El verso complejo se distingue doblemente de la declaración de identidad, por falta de coincidencia temporal y por falta de coincidencia personal: el yo se proclama como un *aquel* que *decía,* alejado de sí mismo por el pasado y por la alteridad de la tercera persona. Es en esa falla, en esa deliberada no coincidencia, donde se abre, bajo la ilusión de la expresión directa, el espacio de la *figuración* del yo. Por medio de una voz dos veces alienada —«túnica» harto más compleja y sutil que cualquiera de las que señalaba Rodó— se es y se dice en «Yo soy aquel...».

Si es justo señalar, como lo ha hecho Paz[21], el carácter en parte elegíaco del poema, no por ello cabe concluir a la ligera, como han hecho otros, que las primeras estrofas del poema «hablan de una estética ya superada»[22]. *Parece* haberse superado una estética; o más bien (si se tiene en cuenta la dedicatoria) se quiere dar la impresión —mediante el *aquel,* el *ayer,* el empeñoso uso del pretérito y del imperfecto en la primera mitad del poema, el mismo *no más* que parecería ratificar la brusquedad del cambio— de que se ha superado una estética. Pero, en realidad, al asumir al otro que decía en el presente del *yo soy* —al actualizarlo— el yo de «Yo soy aquel...» no clausura, no se desdice, sino

---

[21] OCTAVIO PAZ: «El caracol y la sirena», *Cuadrivio,* México: Joaquín Mortiz, 1965, p. 45.
[22] MARÍA LUISA PUENTE: «El poema prólogo a *Cantos de vida y esperanza*», en *Rubén Darío. Estudios reunidos en conmemoración del centenario,* p. 170.

vuelve a decirse a través de la vieja manera. Se cita. En un ejemplar ejercicio de incorporación textual, la primera mitad del poema imita literalmente la manera previa —no sólo temáticamente; en la entonación misma— para plegarla a nuevos propósitos. Al recuperar a través de la autodefinición los textos anteriores, en abierto trabajo de apropiación y de cita, el yo avala la vigencia inmediata del decir previo *dentro* del poema, no marca su superación. Una vez más el yo dariano no descarta: asimila y *se* asimila.

Dos modalidades del yo se conjugan en las primeras cinco estrofas del poema, las dos vueltas hacia el pasado. Una recuerda y reactiva un ayer literario, otra, en forma aparentemente directa —pero desdeñando la anécdota— evoca un ayer personal, ese «sentimiento» cuya presencia añoraba Rodó. Intentar deslindar esas dos modalidades, o marcar la superioridad de una sobre otra —y más bien, como tienden a hacerlo los críticos «simpáticos», de la segunda sobre la primera [23]—, es tarea inútil. Ambas configuran una sola voz, un único retrato, un solo yo. Si algo cabe insinuar, como significativa ventaja —para coartar las múltiples interpretaciones del yo «humano» por parte de una crítica ávida de identificación— es que la voz que se dice elige autodefinirse *en primer lugar* a través de textos: «el verso azul y la canción profana». Sólo luego, desde ese lugar altamente literalizado, complementa con el recuerdo personal voluntariamente impreciso esa primera autodefinición literariamente minuciosa.

Si el yo de «Yo soy aquel...» se figura, en primer término, en un yo poético pasado —aquel yo objeto del *misreading* de Rodó— es sin duda porque esa modalidad, o más bien esa estructura deseante, tal como la entiende Darío [24], volverá a funcionar dinámicamente, y no como simple añoranza, en el poema liminar de *Cantos*. Si en *Prosas profanas* el yo era manipulador de espacios de sueños y proyectaba en ellos al otro (mujer/página blanca) para poseerlo, el yo de «Yo soy aquel...» también propone, a partir de la falla insinuada por la no coincidencia del primer verso, un simulacro de otredad: «una estatua bella». Sólo que en este caso la estatua, en lugar de remitir a otra presencia como en *Prosas*, remite indudablemente a la primera persona: por la estatua el yo pasa a percibirse no sólo como sujeto de su enunciación, sino de su enunciado. La estatua es emblema del yo, vehículo en que el yo se reconoce poéticamente, y como espejo le devuelve las mitologías que ha elegido (que ha creado) para expresarse. Y donde Rodó había dicho teatro, cálculo, frialdad, el yo corrige esa lectura, completa la visión unilateral propuesta por el crítico. Decía Rodó: «Es, en cierta manera, un parnasia-

---

[23] Así, para citar a un solo crítico, la opinión de MAX HENRÍQUEZ UREÑA: «¡Cuán lejos estamos aquí de la elegancia libresca de *Prosas profanas*! Aquí el poeta traduce en forma a veces desgarradora sus íntimas angustias [...]» (*Breve historia del Modernismo*, México: Fonde de Cultura Económica, 1962, p. 105.

[24] Ver SYLVIA MOLLOY: «Voracidad y solipsismo en la poesía de Darío», *Sin nombre*, vol. XI, 3 (1980), pp. 7-15.

nismo extendido al mundo interior, y en el que las ideas y los sentimientos hacen el papel de lienzos y bronces» (R, 170). Responde Darío:

> En mi jardín se vio una estatua bella,
> se juzgó mármol y era carne viva;
> un alma joven habitaba en ella,
> sentimental, sensible, sensitiva.

A los tres epítetos vendrá a agregarse, estrofas más abajo, otro, capital: *sincera,* como una referencia más a «lo que Rodó no encontró»:

> todo ansia, todo ardor, sensación pura
> y vigor natural; y sin falsía,
> y sin comedia y sin literatura...
> si hay un alma sincera, ésa es la mía.

La sinceridad implica no sólo la falta de pose («sin comedia»), sino la falta de literatura: más abajo el yo recalcará, tajante, haciendo suyo el desdén del «espontáneo» Verlaine en «Art poétique», su «horror de la literatura». Como si las dos declaraciones de desprecio no bastaran, cuida Darío de contrastar en los dos casos, por medio de la rima, la literatura con la pureza (literatura / sensación pura; literatura / alma pura). En un poema tan densamente literario, tan magníficamente mezclado, abarrotado e «impuro» como es este, la declaración parece chocante o meramente huera si se la toma literalmente. No así si se la toma a la luz del ensayo de Rodó, no si se recuerda la desconfianza con que el crítico comentaba la «*naturaleza literaria*» (el subrayado es del autor) de Darío, o la comparación que establecía entre el poeta y el personaje de Gautier que «sólo se siente inclinado a dar limosna cuando la sordidez de los andrajos tienen aspectos de cuadro de Ribera o de Goya» (R, 169). Si naturaleza literaria, para Rodó, es esteticismo empequeñecedor, entonces no es literario ni hace literatura el yo de «Yo soy aquel...», aunque su razón de ser, aunque su textura misma, sea la letra. El yo celebra no el Arte por el Arte (ni en *Prosas profanas* era el caso, nos dice), sino el Arte por la Vida («*Ego sum lux et veritas et vita*»), pero siempre que en la fórmula última no se olvide algo capital: el carácter eminentemente artificial, «literario», del primer elemento (arte) no tiene por qué estar reñido con el segundo (vida), es parte importante de él. Impresionante sistema de vasos comunicantes, el poema insiste en que el arte desemboca en la vida y la vida en el arte.

El texto entero es una práctica gozosa del carácter expansivo e incorporativo que tienen, centrados en el yo que es una de sus muchas formas, vida y literatura, mundo interior y mundo exterior, protagonista y escenario. «El dueño fui de mi jardín de sueño», declara el yo de «Yo soy aquel...», recordando con ese *locus poeticus* los alcázares interiores de *Prosas profanas* que objetaba Rodó. Si ahora abre esa interioridad («tuve hambre de espacio y sed de cielo») lo hace aprovechando los términos mismos en que la había planteado, amplificándola hacia un afuera que es su reflejo. Como observa acertadamente Angel Rama:

> La «selva sagrada» remite, como un espejo, a su constructor: la conciencia poética. Del mismo modo, el «yo» remite a un complemento que lo justifica, la «naturaleza» que ha sido construida como un artificio [25].

Esta selva en la que el yo encuentra la armonía, y se encuentra en armonía, es, para otro crítico, «una mitificación personal, elaborada con elementos conocidos de la Mitología, de la complicación y dualismo de lo humano» [26]. Como todo lugar de Darío —como todo lugar poético— es desde luego fruto de una mitificación privada. Su misterio y su complejidad acaso se aclaren si se tienen en cuenta, en la composición de esa selva, no sólo los elementos que señala Salinas, sino el texto previo de Darío; la mitología personal ya dicha en *Prosas profanas,* base literal de este poema.

Pero si la selva sagrada, por los elementos que la pueblan, recuerda y prolonga el «jardín de sueño», el lugar del yo ante ella, y en ella, es distinto: no es refugio, no es coto privado del que se es dueño, sino un *más allá de sí* extendido, fruto de un personalismo que (para retomar los términos de Rodó) esta vez sí es manifiestamente *expansivo.* Así la peregrinación del yo por la selva sagrada será, *a la vez,* metáfora de la vida humana, «la selva de la experiencia del hombre» [27], y —de manera fundamental— revisitación y remotivación textual. Los elementos del reino interior de Darío ahora, para parafrasear una vez más a su crítico, además de sugerir significan (R, 173).

De manera a primera vista sorprendente, este poema, que se inicia con una voz tan fuertemente autoconstitutiva y con un anuncio tan firme de figuración personal, se despoja, a medida que avanza, de la primera persona. El yo se despersonaliza, se desintegra [28]; si la peregrinación por la selva se presenta individualizada (*mi* intelecto, *mi* corazón), el yo deja de nombrarse directamente; atendiendo acaso a la tarea de guía que le proponía al final de su ensayo Rodó, se generaliza en el puro impersonal de la máxima, del consejo: «ser sincero es ser potente»; «la virtud está en ser tranquilo y fuerte». Si subsiste hacia el final del poema el «yo soy aquel que ayer no más decía», subsiste innominado en Psiquis y en el sátiro, en la boca del fauno y en el pezón, en la caña de Pan: entregado y diseminado a través de su texto previo, que ahora está diciendo y diciéndo*lo* de otra manera.

---

[25] ANGEL RAMA: «Prólogo», en Rubén Darío, *Poesía,* p. XXXIV.
[26] PEDRO SALINAS, *op. cit.,* p. 265.
[27] *Ibid.*
[28] «Junto a la transposición de la intimidad a un conjunto de múltiples objetos culturales, se asiste al comienzo de la desintegración del yo [...]» ANGEL RAMA, *op. cit.,* p. XXXV.

«Todo lo que Rodó no encontró» ha sido encontrado, señalado, ha aparecido como las líneas que del negativo pasan lentamente al positivo (elijo a propósito la imagen) por el trabajo del revelado: en el proceso el autorretrato se ha vaciado, se ha borrado un yo, sólo persisten las letras de su texto.

Princeton University.

CLAUDIO RODRIGUEZ O LA MIRADA SIN DUEÑO

by

PHILIP W. SILVER

L'esprit qui plonge dans le surréalisme revit
avec exaltation la meilleure part de son enfance.
(A. BRETON· *Premier Manifeste du Surréalisme*)

El ensayo que el lector-aficionado comienza ahora a leer sólo pretende auparle a la región de lo indecible-indemostrable y dejarle en la antesala. Claudio Rodríguez (n. 1934), zamorano de nacimiento, trasterrado a Madrid, es ya un poeta tan conocido —a partir del premio Adonais de 1953— que sería ocioso dar aquí otra cosa que una sucinta presentación. Como pertenece, además, con Carlos Barral, José M. Caballero Bonald, Francisco Brines, Eladio Cabañero, Jaime Gil de Biedma, José Agustín Goytisolo, Angel González, Carlos Sahagún y José Angel Valente, a la ya consagrada generación poética de los 50, todos los datos bio-bibliográficos que fueran menester podrán encontrarse en las muchas antologías que se han hecho del grupo. De modo que aquí, más que nada, se va a hablar de la poesía de Claudio Rodríguez y de su peculiar relación con el surraelismo franco-español. Podríamos hacer un análisis retórico de su decir poético, o investigar su deuda para con al tradición mística española, pero hasta que no se desvele su filiación rimbaudiana-surrealista permanecerá inédita la verdadera originalidad de su poesía.

SOBRE EL CONCEPTO DE ORIGINALIDAD EN POESÍA

Por lo general, cuando se dice que un poeta es original, se suele hacer con intención de encasillar o de halagar, si no las dos cosas a la vez. Sin embargo, la palabra misma entraña una aporía que no deja de repercutir en todo discurso crítico que la incluya. En realidad, nos tendría que resultar poco esclarecedora una palabra que, al mismo tiempo que significa «relativo al origen», alude a algo que «no es copia ni imitación». De manera que el lector-aficionado está en su perfecto derecho de protestar cuando la crítica fundamenta ese deleite que supone leer a un gran poeta en una cualidad tan ambigua como es la originalidad. Al señor lector-aficionado que tenga a bien protestar le asiste toda la razón. Y más en un caso como el presente, donde la citada cualidad, no por ser más intensa, se presta menos a examen.

Dejando aparte la larga tradición preceptista, es la segunda acepción de originalidad la que nos atañe aquí. De hecho, en la sabiduría popular crítica, la palabra «original» aplicada a un determinado poeta significa que éste aporta una gran novedad y que su poesía no se parece —que se sepa— a la de nadie. Pero esto es, en resumidas cuentas, lo que la crítica viene reiterando en el caso de la poesía de Claudio Rodríguez. Sin embargo, y aquí nos interpela nuestra aporía etimológica, cuando la crítica emplea la palabra «original», sólo dejaremos de protestar el lector-aficionado y yo si a lo que se estaba refiriendo era a la primera acepción, la de «relativo al origen». Cuando la crítica de turno pronuncia la palabra «original» —en el segundo sentido— no hace más que confesar su incapacidad para descubrir la tradición a que pertenece este poeta. Porque no cejaremos en esto el lector aficionado y yo: no hay poeta sin orígenes, o sea, sin tradición.

Sin embargo, la guerra de los malentendidos críticos no se gana tan fácilmente. Precisamente cuando hayamos logrado convencer a la crítica de que la primera acepción es la más idónea, ella se nos volverá a desmandar e insistirá en ofrecer una interpretación extraliteraria de la originalidad, saliendo nuevamente por los fueros de *su* primera acepción. Es decir, que para la crítica un poeta será original en cuanto conquistador literario de nuevos sectores de la realidad, o de inusitadas experiencias personales. Pero de nuevo el lector-aficionado debería protestar. Todo escritor, ya sea maldito, proletario o burgués, está de vuelta de todo realismo y de toda pretensión autobiográfica. No hay que tomar a la ligera el aforismo de Mallarmé de que el poema se hace con palabras y no con ideas u otra cosa. Al tratar de un gran poeta, es imprescindible reconocer que el poema empieza donde termina el poeta, más allá del proyecto existencial individual. Desde el Romanticismo acá, más de una vez se ha incurrido en el error de querer explicar el poema como si poeta, lenguaje y realidad fuesen vasos comunicantes. Pero no hay tal. Se trata de tres regiones entológicas totalmente distintas y la comunicación entre ellas representa siempre una incógnita que es arriesgado zanjar con ciega precipitación. Aunque Claudio Rodríguez naciera en Zamora, la alta calidad de su poesía es más deudora del hecho mismo de su nacimiento y de las lecturas que pudieron servirle de nutrición que del vino de Toro o del pan de Carvajales. Resulta evidente que si sólo bastasen las circunstancias de una juventud zamorana, una estancia en Madrid y la docencia en Inglaterra, Claudio Rodríguez no se hubiera adentrado en el oscuro bosque de las palabras impresas, donde sólo se entra de rebote y a través de los libros a mano. Por ejemplo, en el «Canto del caminar», la palabra «heñir» del verso «como un heñir de pan sus voces pasan / ...» pudiera parecernos un perfecto indicio del realismo léxico de nuestro poeta, cuando la verdad es otra. Sean cuales fueren sus primeras noticias de la palabra, «heñir» surgió sin duda de este poema, no por haber nacido su autor en Castilla, sino porque dicha palabra se encontraba ya en poemas de Unamuno y de Blas de Otero.

Pero si la verdadera originalidad de un poeta como Claudio Rodríguez no puede explicarse en función de realismos ni biografías, ¿de dónde procede la absoluta convicción con que aplicamos este calificativo a su obra? Procede de nuestra percepción del acierto del poeta al alistarse en una tradición importante. De modo que nuestro poeta sería original por su rara habilidad para enraizarse (buscar las raíces es siempre algo

«relativo al origen») en una determinada tradición literaria que delibera-
damente elige. Elección siempre consciente y difícil que el poeta hace
contra natura, como si una hoja acertase a escoger su ramo o una flor
su tallo. Pues bien, en el caso de Claudio Rodríguez esa originalidad
que la crítica le atribuye unánimemente, le viene del hecho de haber
sabido inscribirse, por afinidades electivas, en la tradición surrealista
que cuajó cuando ciertos surrealistas se descubrieron reflejados en el
automatismo de Arthur Rimbaud.

Ciertos reparos a la generación del 27

Al tratar de la generación del 27, la crítica no cesa de desviar la
atención de la auténtica heterogeneidad del grupo. Tan sólo Luis Cernuda, en un libro escasamente atendido por la erudición, afronta un
hecho esencial que atañe a dos de sus contemporáneos: «En realidad,
tanto Salinas como Guillén, ni por su edad ni por su espíritu, pertenecen
a esta generación...» (Cernuda, 1957, p. 193, n.). Hasta el mismo Dámaso
Alonso, al explicar la trayectoria completa de la generación, reconoce la
existencia —de acuerdo con el aserto cernudiano— de dos períodos entre
los cuales se reparte la producción de este grupo poético, «... el primero,
de ligamiento e integración en vínculos y miembros (respectivamente), y
de relativa homogeneización del concepto de la poesía, período que iría
de 1920 a 1927; y en el segundo, de 1927 a 1936, los vínculos se van
lentamente relajando, y, por lo que toca al concepto mismo de lo poético,
se abre aquí, diríamos, una importante herejía» (Alonso, 1958, p. 185).
Dámaso Alonso y Luis Cernuda, pues, se sitúan ante la misma línea divisoria de la historia literaria, aunque frente a ella adopten dos puntos
de vista distintos y aun opuestos. Dámaso quisiera caracterizar la totalidad de esa lírica sirviéndose de un concepto de la poesía aplicable solamente a su primera época. Por consiguiente, se enfrenta con Cernuda,
que forma parte de la etapa «herética». Hay que hacer hincapié en este
punto de máxima tensión entre dos críticos tan distinguidos. No se ha
recalcado de modo suficiente la existencia de dos períodos dentro de la
supuesta generación. De la misma manera, si en el caso que nos ocupa
no procuramos describir con mayor precisión el segundo de estos dos
períodos —el surrealista—, nunca podremos llegar a descubrir las raíces
hispánicas de la tradición franco-española a la que pertenece Claudio
Rodríguez. Puesto que en su caso también es inaceptable la designación
de original, y dado que le viene muy ancha la de poeta social, no queda
más remedio que ahondar en esta disyuntiva que escinde la generación
del 27.

Varias fórmulas se han propuesto para mantener unidas las dos épocas,
aunque se han prestado todas a cierto confusionismo. Con la erosión del
concepto orteguiano de «deshumanización», la crítica echó mano del de
«poesía pura». Pero semejante táctica ha acarreado el resultado inquietante de evocar la compañera oculta, la «poesía impura», cultivada con
tanto éxito por García Lorca, Neruda, Aleixandre, Hernández y otros,

a despecho de la lírica pura. La crítica, pues, casi a pesar suyo, y debido a la antítesis poesía pura-impura, ha logrado alguna claridad frente a la división interna de la generación. Ahora podemos convocar bajo la bandera de la «poesía pura» a Salinas, a Guillén, a Diego y a Dámaso; y podemos situar en el campo de la «impura» a Lorca, Aleixandre, Cernuda, Alberti y Prados. Enumeraciones que, por imprecisas que sean, tienen la ventaja de no escamotear el fundamental desacuerdo político-literario de los jóvenes surrealistas frente a sus mayores puristas. Ahora, en la nueva perspectiva, la fecha de 1927 ya no señalará un punto de unanimidad, sino la división básica entre los dos períodos de la supuesta generación. O, si queremos precisar más, 1927 representará en adelante no la famosa excursión a Sevilla, sino otros acontecimientos de ese año que apuntan al final del «purismo» y a la irrupción del surrealismo, como la muerte de Juan Gris, inventor del equivalente pictórico del creacionismo, la publicación en Málaga de los primeros poemas surrealistas, ya no creacionistas, de Juan Larrea, y de los primeros poemas de Pablo Neruda publicados en «El Sol» y «Revista de Occidente». Si de una vez para siempre damos carta de ciudadanía al creacionismo-ultraísmo y al surrealismo españoles, entonces podremos partir de estos dos movimientos constitutivos de vanguardia, y emprender una nueva interpretación de la generación del 27 en función de los mismos. Tal revisión de nuestras teorías respecto a la generación brindaría nuevos instrumentos históricos no sólo para estudiar individualmente a los poetas que escribían en la España de los años veinte y treinta, sino a todos los poetas posteriores, como veremos ahora al estudiar el caso concreto de Claudio Rodríguez.

UNA TRADICIÓN INADVERTIDA DEL SURREALISMO ESPAÑOL

En un principio, exactamente como ocurrió en el caso de la resistencia a reconocer la aportación creacionista huidobrina al ultraísmo, se decía que el surrealismo francés, a pesar de su innegable difusión en España, poco o nada tenía que ver con el surealismo español. Sin embargo, y a pesar de los testimonios a su favor de Dámaso Alonso y Vicente Aleixandre, y de hispanistas como Paul Ilie (en *Los poetas surrealistas españoles* [Madrid, Taurus, 1972]) y C. B. Morris (en *Surrealism and Spain* [Cambridge, Cambridge University Press, 1972]), es precisamente la tesis contraria la que va ganando partidarios. Dicha tesis contraria fue lanzada por Vittorino Bodini *(Los poetas surrealistas españoles* [Barcelona, Tusquets, 1971]), y prospera en los libros de Juan Cano Ballesta *(La poesía española entre pureza y revolución* [Madrid, Gredos, 1972]), y de Anthony L. Geist *(La poética de la generación del 27 y las revistas literarias: de la vanguardia al compromiso (1918-1936)* [Barcelona, Labor, 1980]). Ardua ha sido la victoria, pero con la misma se han impuesto preciosas puntualizaciones histórico-literarias. De aquí en adelante se podrá hablar también en España con toda seriedad de la implantación de la más señalada revolución de las letras europeas después del Romanticismo. Y no sólo dispondremos de nuevos criterios históricos, sino también de rigurosos criterios lingüísticos, como los que Francisco García-Sarriá nos brinda, para desvelar esa tradición surrealista española, tantas veces denegada o pasada por alto.

Antes del ensayo clave «¿Lenguaje surrealista?», de García-Sarriá, se había estudiado el surrealismo español a la luz de criterios temáticos o extraliterarios. Además, cierto sector de la crítica impuso la poesía social como norma, de tal manera —y con tanto éxito— que grupos minoritarios como los postistas —Sernesi, de Ory y Chicharro— o el grupo cordobés de «Cántico», y muchos poetas sin clasificar, quedaron relegados a una posición de *offside*.

No es cuestión aquí de desarticular la historia de la poesía de los años del franquismo. Sería, además de impertinente, muy precipitado intentarlo antes de que Víctor García de la Concha termine de historiar el inmenso y rico panorama de la poesía que se trae entre manos. Pero sí me parece imprescindible señalar, mediante algunos ejemplos destacados, la existencia paralela de un rico filón de poetas españoles aún sin clasificar que arranca de los surrealistas del 27. Para mayor sorpresa, el hilo conductor que une a estos poetas y que nos permite hablar de una tradición inadvertida es ese tan debatido automatismo unánimemente denegado por los mismos surrealistas del 27. Sea cual sea el motivo del aparente rechazo del automatismo en España (arraigo de la «poesía pura», catequización creacionista de Huidobro en la Península, o conflicto percibido entre «irracionalismo poético» y compromiso social), el hecho es que la asombrosa brillantez de la poesía surrealista de Lorca, Alberti y Aleixandre no tiene otra explicación. Se trata de ese «automatismo no buscado» de que habla Alberti en sus memorias, según el cual el poeta se dejaba llevar, como apunta García-Sarriá, por la asociación fonética libre hasta el punto de trasgredir los códigos usuales de la lengua. Por lo general, como hace constar García-Sarriá, entre los poetas españoles se trata del empleo de una variante surrealista de la metáfora continuada tradicional; pero también podría denominarse, como ha hecho Gustav Siebenmann al clasificar la poesía de Claudio Rodríguez, técnica de la metáfora metaforizada.

En la perspectiva del automatismo así definido, no es difícil encontrar ejemplos importantes, hasta ahora no reconocidos como tales, en la poesía española de posguerra. Sin ir más lejos, y aparte del caso obvio de los postistas ya mencionados, ahí está *La casa encendida,* de Luis Rosales, uno de los grandes libros de la posguerra, cuya primera edición es de 1949. Pero el caso más sorprendente y ejemplificador de esta tradición inadvertida es un poeta que dista mucho de ser inclasificable: el poeta social por antonomasia, Blas de Otero. Respecto a la obra de este gran poeta, se ha hablado hasta la saciedad de su «originalidad», su «espontaneidad», su incorporación a la poesía de «préstamos literarios, refranes, modismos y canciones populares», como de los «maravillosos rasgos de ingenio verbal» y de los «sorprendentes efectos rítmicos y verbales». Pero como su poesía siempre se estudia en una perspectiva temático-biográfica, situándola en el contexto de la poesía social, ha sido imposible percibir la palabra «surrealismo», escrita en mayúscula a través de toda su poesía desde *Ancia* hasta ese libro tan poco característico —si se le enfoca sólo con criterios políticos— que es *Historias fingidas y verdaderas*. Pero, ¿puede negarse la filiación surrealista de estos dos ejemplos de automatismo, el primero de Alberti y el segundo de Blas de Otero?

> Y si, porque cinco manos
> cayeron sobre tu cuerpo
> cuando inmóvil resbalaba
> sobre los cinco navegables ríos
> que dan almas corrientes, voz al sueño.
>
> *(Sobre los ángeles)*

> así te veo así te encuentro
> mi pequeña paloma desguarnecida
> entre embarcaciones con los párpados entornados
> entre nieve y relámpagos
> con tus brazos de muñeca y tus muslos de maleza
> entre diputaciones y farmacias
> irradiando besos de la frente
> con tu pequeña voz envuelta en un pañuelo.
>
> *(Hojas de Madrid y La galerna)*

A mi parecer, no puede dudarse del parentesco de los dos con el surrealismo. Es más: precisamente lo más «original» de Blas de Otero, desde los «préstamos literarios» hasta las referencias metapoéticas, pasando por la «espontaneidad» paradigmática, son todos recursos poéticos que el surrealismo francés puso de moda de manera tan espectacular allá por los años veinte. Pero tampoco debe extrañarnos que este hecho pasase inadvertido en pleno auge de la poesía social.

CLAUDIO RODRÍGUEZ, POETA SURREALISTA (MA NON TROPPO)

Desde el primer libro de Claudio Rodríguez, *Don de la ebriedad* (1953), es un tópico de la crítica aludir de pasada a la influencia de Rimbaud en su obra. Pero si bien se mira, y cierta exaltación mañanera de la naturaleza aparte, no parece haber en lo temático ninguna convergencia notable. Y en cuanto a la influencia de Rimbaud en cuestiones de métrica, tampoco parece prosperar la comparación. El verso empleado a lo largo de *Don de la ebriedad* es un endecasílabo asonantado bastante tradicional, mientras —como bien se sabe— la gran revolución rimbaudiana se dio en los poemas amétricos en prosa. Pero, entonces, ¿en qué se basa la tan sonada semejanza entre los dos poetas? El parentesco se encuentra en un empleo pródigo por parte de ambos poetas de lo que se llamó a partir de 1924, y en frase de André Breton, el automatismo psíquico.

Ahora bien, si la verdadera originalidad de Rodríguez se debe a un empalme con el surrealismo franco-español, saca ventaja a los demás poetas españoles en haber sido capaz de aprovechar el surrealismo de la generación del 27 y al mismo tiempo tenía delante de los ojos los cercanos ejemplos criptosurrealistas de Luis Rosales y Blas de Otero. Pero si el automatismo de Rosales es de corte surrealista clásico, y el de Blas de Otero se revela sobre todo en exabruptos sintagmáticos que resultan de asociaciones libres estereotipadas (inserción de tópicos, modismos, citas, etc.), el de Rodríguez, además de generar la consabida «arbitrariedad» metafórica, reviste la absoluta novedad en las letras españolas de vertebrar poemas enteros, probablemente por influencia directa de Rimbaud. Por lo menos, en lo que se refiere a la insólita expansión de la metáfora continuada que se da en la poesía de Rodríguez a partir de *Conjuros* (1958), no cabe encontrar precedente más a mano que los poemas en prosa de Rimbaud como «Bárbaro» y «Movimiento».

En un excelente ensayo-prólogo a *Poesías 1953-1966,* de Claudio Rodríguez, Carlos Bousoño no apunta otra cosa cuando destaca la «gran novedad expresiva», la «condensación semántica» y el «irracionalismo metafórico» de nuestro poeta. Pero, a mi modo de ver, todos los aciertos descriptivos de Bousoño al respecto cobran mayor coherencia si se inscriben en la gran aventura del surrealismo franco-español. Bousoño dedica acertadas páginas a la descripción y análisis de lo que él denomina la «alegoría disémica». Sin embargo, este recurso retórico, lejos de ser invención de Rodríguez, o un derivado de la poética novecentista como pretende Bousoño, es en realidad el resultado del empleo semiconsciente del recurso poético-prosaico tradicional de la metáfora continuada, o, si se quiere, es el mismo recurso subvertido por el uso semi-automático.

De hecho, la metáfora continuada tradicional y la versión rimbaudiana-surrealista de la misma tienen en común el estar constituidas por el desarrollo paralelo de dos sistemas asociativos, el uno compuesto de palabras emparentadas a un *tenor primario* (plano real A), el otro de palabras emparentadas a un *vehículo primario* (plano evocado B) (Riffaterre, 1979, p. 220). Además dicho desarrollo está sometido a una «doble necesidad». Por una parte, los dos sistemas, vehículo (V) y tenor (T), deben guardar una relación de verosimilitud con sus respectivos referentes; por otra, deben atenerse a una «ley de selección recíproca». Es decir, «la superposición (metafórica) de un sistema sobre otro, pone de relieve lo que éstos tienen en común y reduce al mínimo sus diferencias...» (Riffaterre, pp. 220-21). Ahora bien, en la metáfora continuada *surrealista* —a diferencia de la tradicional— el «factor que rige el desarrollo de ambos sistemas es la *escritura automática* (elemento dominante, pero que no excluye en absoluto ni la función referencial ni la selección recíproca)» (Riffaterre, p. 221). Lo que sucede en la metáfora continuada surrealista es que una palabra determinada rige la selección de las palabras siguientes, más que por el sentido, por una «semejanza formal» de «paralelismo fonético, juego de palabras», o bien por una «asociación estereotipada (perteneciente a un grupo fonético, a un tópico, a una cita, etcétera), aceptable en el contexto o no» (Riffaterre, p. 221). De manera que, a causa de la influencia de la escritura automática en el desarrollo metafórico, se eslabonan significantes cuyos significados resultan «irracionales» desde la perspectiva de los códigos usuales de la lengua (Riffaterre, p. 222). He aquí por qué la poesía surrealista suele considerarse de difícil lectura: requiere que el lector se deje llevar por la aparente irracionalidad y que acceda a dejarse transformar por el poema.

De la poesía de Rodríguez también se desprende un designio parecido, llamémoslo «surrealista», de arrancar de cuajo al lector de su rutina espiritual y moral, y de embarcarle en una aventura poética destructora de aquella nada infrecuente postura vital que «sólo ve en las cosas / la triste realidad de su apariencia». Puesto que la poesía de Rodríguez no es en el fondo ni descripción ni expresión, no sólo es inoportuno, sino insuficiente enfocarla a la luz de una crítica realista, como viene haciéndose. Al querer analizar la metáfora continuada, característica de esta poesía, con términos como «plano real» y «plano evocado», es inevitable que el crítico tergiverse la misma cosmovisión que quisiera desvelar. Y esto porque, para Rodríguez, en vez de suponer una realidad estable, las apariencias son «sutil añagaza, ruin chanchullo, bien adobado cebo». Aquí, como en el barroco, las apariencias pueden representar un embaucador riesgo para el espíritu, sobre todo por cuanto invitan a adormilarlo en la costumbre y la rutina. Lejos de ser «realista», entonces, la poesía de Rodríguez, al contrario, tiene como único referente, no la realidad, sino un momento ideal, inefable, que antecede a la constitución de la misma. Y es precisamente con el fin de acercar al lector a este momento ideal por lo que Claudio Rodríguez echa mano del automatismo surrealista: mediante el automatismo, poeta y lector se encaminan directamente hacia el origen de las cosas, hacia las fuentes del Ser. Esta búsqueda, motivo de la ebriedad, del transporte, de que habla el poeta, da como resultado, a nivel de la praxis poética, esa escritura automática, cuya máxima expresión es la metáfora continuada surrealista. Enquistado de manera ocasional en los poemas lírico-narrativos de *Don de la ebriedad,* este procedimiento se desplaza en libros posteriores al centro del poema desde donde controla la organización entera del mismo.

Examinemos, de pasada, algunos ejemplos de la metáfora continuada surrealista cuando se da en su situación ocasional de enquiste, y algunos tros en que aparece como estructura vertebrante del poema entero. Es de notar, en los dos primeros ejemplos que damos a continuación, cómo el poeta se apoya sobre todo en la asociación fonética libre para dar con una metáfora en la que, sin embargo, el tenor primario permanece implícito:

(I)   Puertas
con vellones de niebla por dinteles
se abren allí, pasando aquella cima.

(II)   ....
cuando te veo con tal claridad
que siento tu latido que me hiere,
me acosa, me susurra, y casi me domina,
y me cura de ti, de ti, de ti.

(III)   Oh, plumas timoneras. Mordedura
de la celeridad, mal retenida
si el hacha canta al pájaro cercenes
de últimos bosques y la tierra misma
salta como los peces en verano.

(IV)   ....
óyelo bien: no tiemblo. Es la mirada,
es el agua que copera ser bebida.
El agua. Se entristece al contemplarse
desnuda y ya con marzo casi encinta,
De qué manera nos devuelve el eco.

Es asimismo interesante ver cómo en todos los ejemplos aducidos se da un trenzado de los dos sistemas paralelos (T y V), subrayando la ruptura con la realidad y con cualquier apego a ella. Además, en los ejemplos (III) y (IV) puede apreciarse cómo los sistemas V son capaces de desdoblarse en subsistemas. Al contrario de lo que ocurre en la metáfora continuada tradicional, en los ejemplos (I) y (II) se dan metáforas implícitas en las que faltan el tenor primario («puerto») y el vehículo primario («látigo»). En este último ejemplo, bastante sorprendente, la metonimia («latido») genera por asociación fonética libre una metáfora implícita («látigo») como vehículo primario, que encabeza, a su vez, aún con ser invisible, el sistema (V_2, V_3, etc.), constituido por «me hiere», «me acosa», «me susurra», «me domina», «me cura». En contraste el ejemplo (IV) se basa en una asociación estereotipada (un tópico literario: Narciso-Eco).

Ahora bien, lo que hace que este procedimiento sea del todo una novedad en las letras españolas es, como queda dicho, su expansión hasta ocupar el poema entero. De hecho, a partir de *Conjuros,* lo característico de la obra de Rodríguez es la aparición de un tipo de poema enhebrado en una o varias metáforas continuadas de corte rimbaudiano, en las que la «arbitrariedad» del sistema metafórico tiende a trastornar su carácter referencial.

La enorme originalidad de poemas como «A mi ropa tendida», «Caza mayor», «Brujas a mediodía», «Cáscaras», «Dinero» y «Cantata del miedo», se debe precisamente a la expansión de lo que se encuentra ya en los ejemplos (II) y (IV) de *Don de la ebriedad.* Así, en el ejemplo (II), aunque la palabra que aparece a flor de poema sea «latido», el sistema metafórico que en apariencia se desprende de ella no hace otra cosa que estar haciendo alusión a otro sistema que permanece más o menos implícito. Tal es, *mutatis mutandis,* el mismo procedimiento que se descubre en «A mi ropa tendida» o en «Dinero», donde sólo se infiere de una lectura atenta del sistema V lo que pudiera ser el sistema completo T, subyacente y a duras penas perceptible en la superficie del poema. De igual manera, en los poemas de más complicación conceptual, se dan conglomerados de sistemas V varios, regidos por un sistema T maestro (o coordinador) asimismo velado. Igual ocurre, por ejemplo, en «Brujas a mediodía», «Gestos» y «Cáscaras». Lo que pasa en los libros posteriores, a diferencia de *Don de la ebriedad,* es que, *a posteriori,* con el título mismo del poema, el autor está suministrando una contraseña al lector para descifrar el sistema T. Todos ellos pueden considerarse, pues, como poemas elaborados, algunos más, algunos menos, conforme a un determinado automatismo que en nada desmerece el nombre de surrealista.

LOS SILENCIOS DE UN DECIR POÉTICO

Aunque, como hemos visto, la poesía de Claudio Rodríguez se caracteriza fundamentalmente por su automatismo, tampoco cabe despreciar, al estudiarla, otros dos elementos constitutivos de ella: por una parte, la peculiar acogida de «cosas... cotidianas y costumbristas» —como dice muy bien Bousoño—, y por otra, su esencial mudez; esta poesía ofrece en la superficie «un aquelarre de imágenes» que encubre —las más veces— algo poco menos que inefable. He aquí por qué, a mi juicio, está de más hablar de alegoría o simbolismo en el caso de nuestro poeta. No hay «correspondencias» aquí, sino un perfecto acoplamiento entre la urdimbre del «qué» y la trama del «cómo». Lo cual hace que esta poesía, en apariencia meditativa, sea más bien una poesía esencialmente lírica: una forma del decir que, en contraste con la formulación filosófica, no *dice* sino que *es.* Pero tampoco está condicionada esta obra por el afán de «eternizar» las cosas, de arrancarlas del constante fluir hacia la nada. Al contrario, la obra de Rodríguez da fe precisamente del fracaso de tal empresa. Y si queremos servirnos aún de la palabra «alegoría», introducida por Bousoño, sólo cabría hablar de la alegoría de ese mismo fracaso. Como hemos visto, esta empresa poética no es mímesis de ninguna «realidad», sino «alegoría» de la distancia absoluta que media entre palabra y cosa. Poesía, por tanto, esencialmente muda, que no discurre, sino que refleja en su típica estructura básica un trasunto (superficie «realista», fondo informe, inefable) de lo difícil y precario de nuestra residencia en la tierra. Es decir, por una parte, se trata de una poesía que denuncia cualquier conato de cegar o enturbiar las fuentes del Ser, sea la costumbre, la religión, la política, o la mendaz historia. Por otra —y he aquí el primer atisbo de la terrible verdad encubierta por esta obra— la «claridad» cegadora de que se habla en *Don de la ebriedad,* ese don que viene del cielo, es en realidad un *memento mori* y la anulación secreta del progreso de la civilización. Verdad, en fin, tan tremenda que más vale callarla. Cualquier cosa —excepto el *ágape* y el *eros*— de cuantas puedan suministrar una razón de ser, por muy consoladora que sea, es considerada una engañifa.

¿Cómo calificar, entonces, una cosmovisión como la de Rodríguez, donde se codean el júbilo más esperanzador con una verdad tan desesperanzada? No creo que le cuadre mejor calificativo que el de cosmovisión «barroca». Al poeta, en efecto, que ha caído en la cuenta, a cambio de verse condenado a padecer el intransferible secreto de la nulidad de lo ya conseguido, le es dado vivir al acecho de ciertos momentos

privilegiados en los que a través de la «contemplación viva» logra calar
hondo en la constitución misma de las cosas, justo en el instante de su
epifanía. Si a este poeta «barroco» el destino no ha tenido a bien depararle
ninguna visión ultraterrena, por lo menos le permite disfrutar de percep-
ciones originarias.

Al mismo tiempo, si bien es cierto que el poeta es un ser aparte —su
«don» no es, en el fondo, una bendición, sino un castigo—, tampoco se
ve transportado hoy, en razón de su quehacer poético, a aquel alto olimpo
de consideración y prestigio del poeta romántico. Al contrario, al igual
que el labrador ,el albañil o el usurero, el trabajo del poeta no pasa de
ser otro menester más, uno de tantos. Porque cualquier tarea humana,
sea manual o intelectual, carece de valor en sí. Este le afluye sólo si
viene ejercitada como acto de amor y de amorosa solidaridad humana.
De modo que el poeta, o cualquier otro ser mortal, trabajará siempre
en vano si no llega a comprender que la piedra clave de la convivencia
no estriba ni en dar ni en recibir, sino en *saber dar y recibir*, en esa
liberal reciprocidad perpetua, donde no median propiedad ni propietarios.
Así, en el noveno poema de *Don de la ebriedad*:

> Como si nunca hubiera sido mía,
> dad al aire mi voz y que en el aire
> sea de todos y la sepan todos
> igual que una mañana o una tarde.
> Ni a la rama tan sólo abril acude
> ni el agua espera sólo el estiaje.
> ¿Quién podría decir que es suyo el viento,
> suya la luz, el canto de las aves
> en el que esplende la estación, más cuando
> llega la noche y en los chopos arde
> tan peligrosamente retenida?
> ¡Que todo acabe aquí, que todo acabe
> de una vez para siempre! La flor vive
> y, sin embargo, cómo se da, unánime,
> dejando de ser flor y convirtiéndose
> en ímpetu de entrega. Invierno, aunque
> no esté detrás la primavera, saca
> fuera de mí lo mío y hazme parte,
> inútil polen que se pierde en tierra
> pero ha sido de todos y de nadie.
> Sobre el abierto páramo, el relente
> es pinar en el pino, aire en el aire,
> relente sólo para mi sequía.
> Sobre la voz que va excavando un cauce
> qué sacrilegio este del cuerpo, este
> de no poder ser hostia para darse.

Poesía, en suma, de absoluta entrega al momento inefable de la revelación
del Ser, pero también de enorme responsabilidad moral para con los

demás. Una poesía, en fin, que a pesar de su mudez o recato escamoteadores, es siempre alabanza —aún cuando se trate del dolor más desgarrador; profunda poesía ontológica, que nos permite fugaces atisbos de lo que en nombre de la caridad permanece encubierto.

LA MIRADA QUE NO TIENE DUEÑO

Pero, si el ápice del sistema de valores de esta obra está reservado para los cimientos *informes* del Ser, si al poeta, por otra parte, se le escapa cierto desprecio por «ese prieto vendaje / de la costumbre», por la mentira de la historia, e incluso por las palabras de su oficio, ¿no incurre entonces en una flagrante paradoja cuando predica y promueve las tareas humanas de edificar y poetizar? Porque, en resumidas cuentas, toda intervención humana en la materia inerte de este planeta consiste en dar forma a lo informe, alejarlo definitivamente del magma originario del Ser. ¿Es consciente nuestro poeta de tal contradicción?

Como si tuviera muy presente este problema, Claudio Rodríguez trabaja con una gama muy limitada de temas. Lo cual apenas se nota, ya que es la suya una poesía que no se pretende descriptiva; antes bien, se trata de una poesía que alcanza sus mayores logros precisamente cuando aprovecha todas las posibles permutaciones dentro de un mundo imaginario y cerrado; si nos ponemos a examinarlo, veremos cómo van saliendo en hilera todos los elementos de un reducido mundo pastoril moderno —con sus consabidas «condena de la corte» y «alabanza de la aldea»; y cómo dentro de esta caracterización general van apareciendo otra serie de temas característicos. Junto al tema de la naturaleza bravía de la meseta —cielo, llanura, sol— están los del mundo rural, la ciudad amurallada del romancero, y la ancestral labor de las gentes de un campesinado pre-industrial. Otro elemento temático importante es el referente al ámbito familiar: la ciudad natal o adoptiva, la casa-nido, la cama, la puerta, los hermanos, la madre, el hogar, en fin, como *locus amoenus* —a despecho de que el yo poético sea un *flaneur* rural y a veces reniegue de la civilización. En suma, si todo lo relacionado con la familia está aureolado de cierto nimbo mágico, no lo están menos la niñez y la adolescencia ajenas, bañadas en el mismo candor atribuible a todos los orígenes.

Pudiera pensarse, en vista de lo expuesto, que se trata de un poeta sentimental, pero conforme el lector va adentrándose en su obra se va dando cuenta de que la región familiar no significa tanto añoranza —antropológica y no personal— de lo prístino, como modelo presente y futuro de ideal social. El tema familiar sólo cobra todo su verdadero sentido poético cuando se tiene en cuenta que sirve de contrapeso a un mundo natural tan vasto e indiferente que causa pavor. Además, este ideal de solidaridad humana, cuya imagen en miniatura es la familia, es muy riguroso, casi imposible de verse realizado en este mundo. No es otro el *leit motif* de todo el libro, titulado *Alianza y condena* (1965). Y otro magnífico ejemplo de la dureza moral de esta poesía, generosa y cruel, nos lo suministra el último poema de la colección anterior, «Pinar amanecido» *(Conjuros)*. Aquí el autor advierte al que «llegue a la ciudad y sólo vea / la cercanía hermosa del hombre», que las apariencias engañan y que lo que a primera vista pudiera parecer solidaridad, sólo es indicio de que «por estas tierras / ... hay poco amor y mucho miedo siempre». Esta sentencia abrumadora, bastante subversiva, da la justa medida de lo poco que tiene que ver la poesía de Rodríguez con la llamada «social». Y la prueba está en que encarna una visión negativa del mundo que tiene ciertas reminiscencias del mismo tono irremediable, apocalíptico y feroz que se da en el Viejo Testamento. Verse cara a cara con la verdad cegadora de este mundo poético, con la herida ontológica que no se restaña, es enfrentarse con la muerte, no como carantoña a lo Valdés Leal, sino como silencio planetario, absoluta indiferencia cósmica; no es que los dioses, a lo Hölderlin, se hayan retirado a una gran distancia; es que nunca ha habido dioses de ninguna clase. Y si esto es así, huelga decir que la historia, la política, y lo meramente social no pasan de ser, también, «cebo de la apariencia» —ficciones necesarias que hagan medianamente llevadera la existencia sobre la Tierra. En contraste, al «caído en la cuenta», imbuido como nadie del terror primitivo del más absoluto abandono, nunca le es dado olvidar la implacable nulidad de tales ficciones. He aquí por qué dice en el poema que estamos comentando:

> Pobre de aquel que mire
> y vea claro, vea
> entrar a saco en el pinar la inmensa
> justicia de la luz, esté en el sitio
> que a la ciudad ha puesto la audaz horda
> de las estrellas, la implacable hueste
> del espacio.
> Pobre de aquel que vea
> que lo que une es la defensa, el miedo.

Pero volvamos a la paradoja de la productividad humana en el contexto de un mundo poético que valora en sumo grado lo aún no constituido. Veamos, a este fin, cómo tal paradoja llega a ocupar el primer término de un poema como «ante una pared de adobe», también de *Conjuros*. La pared de que se habla en el poema es un resto de redil o choza de pastores, abandonado hace años, donde el «yo poético», vagabundo, pretende cobijarse del tiempo inclemente. Pero dada la duplicidad de la imagen, a caballo entre precaria construcción humana y excrecencia natural de la tierra, la pared ed adobe simboliza, a la vez, transgresión de la naturaleza, y artesanía o logro arquitectónico. De manera que la primera mitad del poema expresa la paradoja de la existencia humana, condenada a la transgresión por la necesidad de sobrevivir. Al mismo tiempo, el acto transgresor queda atenuado, puesto que el poema prevé la inevitable reintegración de la pared «a [su] amo / de siempre, al suelo de Osma», a sus orígenes. Ahora bien, sólo al final del poema se introduce una tercera posibilidad que podría verse como la verdadera resolución de la paradoja. Si la construcción («andamio / de mi esperanza») infringe una ley de esta poesía, no sucede lo mismo con el arar ancestral. Porque éste es una especie de oportuna intervención en beneficio de la tierra, y no sólo del ser humano. Dado que la producción «egoísta» no es del agrado del poeta, y el arar sí, habría que buscar el motivo de su preferencia en ese ideal de reciprocidad antes mencionado. Las casas tienen que construirse para que el hombre pueda guarecerse y no perezca, para que no tenga que enfrentarse, a la intemperie, con la parte indómita de la naturaleza. Pero, en cambio, la intervención del hombre en el arar y el sembrar viene condicionada por la sazón; sólo cuando la tierra está dispuesta a recibir la mano de obra que él aporta será capaz su labor de cundir y dar fruto:

> Tierra de eterno regadío, ahora
> que es tiempo de arar, ¿eres tú campo,
> te abres al grano como entonces, sientes
> aquel tempero? En vano
> cobijarás con humildad al hombre.
> ....
> ¡Mejor la sal, mejor cualquier pedrisca
> que verte así: hecho andamio
> de mi esperanza! Pero venid todos.
> La tarde va a caer. ¡Estaos al raso
> conmigo! ¡Aún no tocadle! Ya algún día,
> surco en pie, palmo a palmo
> abriremos en ti una gran ventana
> para ver las cosechas, como cuando
> sólo eras tierra de labor, y ahora
> rompías hacia el sol bajo el arado.
>
> (Conjuros)

Lo que en un principio parecía paradoja embarazosa para el poeta, a la luz de «Ante una pared de adobe» se convierte en clave de toda su poética. Sólo cuando se emprendan con espíritu altruista y no con una voluntad de posesión tanto la labor de humanar la tierra como el mismo poetizar serán actos que avalen la huella de su labor sobre el mundo. Mediante la intervención amorosa, solidaria del hombre, la «tierra» se hace «mundo». Son distintas maneras de cumplir la tarea humana, de desvelar lo que existe. Pero esta desvelación requiere desvelo y disponibilidad, una actitud atenta para poder reconocer cuándo ha llegado la sazón propicia. Desafortunadamente, por lo que la vida tiene de rutina y costumbre, es poco menos que imposible mantenerse siempre alerta. He aquí por qué las más de las veces, la gracia momentánea —que no es don sino oportunidad— nos coge tan de sorpresa que ni siquiera nos damos cuenta de lo ofrecido y lo perdido. Tal ocurre en el encuentro espiritual incumplido de «Lluvia y gracia», donde un viajero «no comprende el castigo del agua, su sencilla / servidumbre» y «ante la sorpresa / de tal fecundidad, / se atropella y recela». Presa de egoísmo, o desatención, el hombre puede dejarse escapar la oportunidad de toda una vida. Aunque lo normal sea que, por miedo o indiferencia, estemos todos sumergidos en la rutina, el pacto que el poeta tiene firmado con la existencia es de naturaleza distinta. Su vocación y su destino son mantenerse siempre en vilo, su vida toda es un continuo velar las armas de la atención. A través de su mirada, totalmente desprovista de avaricia, la tierra se vuelve «nido» para todos. Poema tras poema, el autor va sondeando los manantiales del vivir cotidiano. Pero en lugar de compenetrarse y fundirse con las cosas, guarda, con un control ejemplar, la distancia de su mirada. O, más bien, cuando de verdad se cumple lo que Claudio Rodríguez denomina «la contemplación viva», el poeta se despersonaliza hasta tal punto que se vuelve mirada pura, incorpórea. Como si la única manera de frenar su natural codicia humana fuera convertirse todo él en mirada sin dueño, la mirada ideal nunca pasa de ser un beso de amorosa despedida:

> Tiembla en el aire
> la última luz. Es la hora
> en que nuestra mirada
> se agracia y se adoncella.
> La hora en que, al fin, con toda
> la vergüenza en la cara, miro y cambio
> mi vida entera por una mirada,
> esa que ahora está lejos,
> la única que me sirve, por la sola
> cosa por la que quiero estos dos ojos:
> esa mirada que no tiene dueño.
>
> *(Alianza y condena)*

Conclusión

Aquí termina una lectura y comienza otra. Mientras el lector se dispone a leer o a releer los poemas ya impresos, Claudio Rodríguez prosigue en la generosa tarea de seguir escribiendo. A pesar de su fama de poeta rural y campechano, si uno atiende a sus preciosas declaraciones sobre la poesía, recogidas por Federico Cambell en *Infame turba*, resulta evidente que a Claudio Rodríguez no le son desconocidas ni la teoría ni la práctica de lo que hemos llamado «automatismo». Pero la entrevista con Campbell no sólo nos facilita esta clave de su originalidad poética, sino que además nos suministra otro dato sumamente revelador: Claudio Rodríguez, de tan difícil clasificación como poeta de la generación poética del 50, siente un enorme aprecio por el galés Dylan Thomas. A estas alturas de nuestro ensayo, ya a nadie puede sorprenderle esta admiración, ni tenerla por un fenómeno casual o incoherente. Dylan

Thomas, junto con David Gascayne, es el más destacado cultivador del surrealismo británico de posguerra.

Columbia University.

BIBLIOGRAFIA

ALONSO, DÁMASO: *Poetas españoles contemporáneos*, Madrid: Gredos, 1952.

BOUSOÑO, CARLOS: Prólogo a CLAUDIO RODRÍGUEZ: *Poesía* (1953-1966), Madrid: Plaza y Janés, 1971.

CERNUDA, LUIS: *Estudios sobre poesía española contemporánea*, Madrid: Guadarrama, 1957.

GARCÍA SARRIÁ, FRANCISCO: «¿Lenguaje surrealista?», *Romanic Review*, May 1981, vol. LXXII, n. 3, pp. 349-356.

RIFFATERRE, MICHAEL: *La production du texte*, Paris: Éditions du Seuil, 1979.

SIEBENMANN, GUSTAV: *Die moderne Lyrik in Spanien. Ein Beitrag su ihrer Stilgesschichte*, Stuttgart: Kohlhammer, 1965.

THE ROAD TO *PLAZA SOLA:* AN INTRODUCTION
TO THE POETRY OF JOSE HIERRO

by

DAVID L. STIXRUDE

The poetry of José Hierro which, according to the poet, should be read as an emerging unity,[1] is very liberally punctuated along the way with poems of position, poems which make significant statements about existential attitude, artistic credo, poetic technique. One thinks, for instance, of poems such as «Para un esteta» *(Quinta del 42)* or «Teoría y alucinación de Dublín» *(Libro de las alucinaciones)* or «Generación» *(Tierra sin nosotros).* «Plaza sola» is, I believe, a much more appropriate poem for summing up essential aspects of Hierro's poetry precisely because it so clearly reflects, rather than states, the poet's most characteristic obsessions. Also, it is not simply a typical poem, but a triumphant resolution of the duality, thought and emotion, that is so central to Hierro's poetry. Finally, our understanding of «Plaza sola» is enhanced by referring to the rest of Hierro's poetry. It seems to me, for example, that «Plaza sola» is a completely triumphant poem, and that the attenuation which the final section might suggest takes on a quite different hue if one allows the poet's accumulated work to haunt one's reading of the poem.

The essential preoccupation of Hierro's poetry prior to *Quinta del 42* is exile from time, frequently expressed as exile from space. The title of his first book, *Tierra sin nosotros,* pinpoints the theme. In retrospect, youth was a time-free dream that evaporated; we woke up to find our bright garden turned into a dust-covered kingdom. What an act of utter desperation it is to try to look twice into the same river. The world is viewed as a sad shore strewn with shipwrecks, even worse, as a space filled with objects from an alien planet «que vive sin nosotros» (p. 70). There is a certain amount of Machadian tonality in the way Hierro sets down his sense of disillusionment, while at the same time his melancholy is accompanied by bitter paradoxes that make us think of Quevedo («Parece que ando por la tierra / asistiendo a mi propio entierro,» p. 57) or the anguished cries of «desarraigado» poets in the Unamuno-Otero tradition («Señor, Señor, Señor: todo lo mismo. / Pero, ¿qué has hecho

---

[1] JOSÉ HIERRO: *Cuanto sé de mí* (Barcelona: Seix Barral, 1974), p. 158. In the prose introduction to *Con las piedras, con el viento,* Hierro states that each book is meant to be an organic whole. All citations of Hierro's poetry are to this edition of his complete poetry.

de mi tiempo?,» p. 79). Beneath often showy coverings of literary reminiscence and idiosyncratic imagery, a very elemental sense of inner struggle begins to assert itself as an insistent feature of Hierro's poetry. The poet returns time and again to the deeply-felt question, who am I: the rational man staking out desperate positions in the face of a well-articulated awareness of time and death, or the youthful dreamer whose unspoken and boundless feelings persist beyond time; the thinking man or the emotional man; the poet who gives expression to feeling or the poet whose feelings inspire the search for expression. Of course, the poet does not generally view himself as sharply split into two halves. There is a great deal of cerebration involved in abstracting the persistent spirit, a great deal of emotion involved in pondering the existential dilemma. It is significant that the first poem of the *Libro de las alucinaciones* is titled «Teoría» and that the joy referred to in the poet's second book, *Alegría,* results in great part from a very deliberate decision to reprogram feelings so that pain will be understood as the pleasure of consciousness. What is clear is that the poet is convinced that his inner life is still dynamic and spontaneous, despite the irrefutable lessons of time.

In *Tierra sin nosotros,* Hierro ties his state of mind to circumstances affecting his entire generation (the poem is called «Generación»). We were taught to be very analytical, very cerebral, he says, but were forced by events to pass through a period of madness which filled us with compassion. We were born «bajo el signo del cerebro,» but then:

> Se desbordó un día la vida.
> Nos tornó locos
> ··
> Aquel que anduvo por los campos
> solitario, pisando odios,
> era un hombre de carne y hueso
> como nosotros (pp. 42-43).

The poem suggests that the change is definitive, and in the sense of profound psychic disturbance brought about by the calamitous Civil War, this must certainly be the case. In another sense, the adamant rejection of a particular aspect of his nature (we were very intellectual, but that all changed one day) becomes part of the dramatic war Hierro wages within himself from this point on. In order not to compound the pain of alienation, the poet decides, in several poems, to accept his situation because it heightens his consciousness of life. Serenity is for the dead (p. 60), it is best now to dream (p. 33), I will not go to sleep (p. 57), I must not go to sleep («Yo quiero vivir en vela. / Alma, ¡cuántos sinsabores!» p. 67). And yet, he cannot waken his body «de sus mentiras y su sueño» (p. 57). Serenity? Just hot air you find in books. Nevertheless, «yo también me hago un poco libro, / me duermo el alma» (p. 57). If I do not watch out, I will be alive and not know it. The poet ends up winning over his other side with his own objection. The last stanza of the book is framed by a characteristic wish: «Sentir... sin saber» (p. 85).

Hierro's second book of poetry, *Alegría,* is an extraordinary book, a wonderfully spontaneous outpouring of exasperated and exuberant perplexity. The universe is enchanted (p. 93), my life is about to burst forth from spring furrows (p. 99), do you not feel the wild, wordless joy that conquers death (p. 100)? But then why are there such dark questions (p. 93) and does the soul not grow weary of unrelieved illusion (p. 136)? Should it «des-soñarse» (p. 136) or should it attempt to banish thought («Es preciso... fingirse / muerto ante al árbol pensativo,» p. 113)? Should thought clothe itself in emotion («Gira, asciende, enloquece pensamiento» p. 102) or should emotion find a new rationale?:

> ... es hermoso
> sentir el alma dolorida,
> porque así sabemos que somos (p. 138).

«Alucinación» and «Razón,» two poem whose titles sum up the thinking-feeling axis, exemplify very well the spiritual instability which *Alegría* conveys. «Alucinación» begins quite literally on the side of feeling: bare feet come into contact with frost during a morning stroll. The immediate reaction is a Guillenesque exultation appropriately decorated with forms of *tanto:* «¡Tanta luz, tanta vida, tan verde cantar de la hierba! / Tan feliz creación elevada a la cima más alta!» (p. 93). But *tanto* not only satisfies swelling emotions, it also jars a dormant intelligence whose painful sense of limitation is awakened once again to the contrast between boundless universe and circumscribed existence. The «cerebro» proclaims its dismal need to understand, thus rendering ironic the poem's title:

> ¡Tanta luz, tan oscura pregunta!
> ¡Tan oscura y difícil palabra!
> ¡Tan confuso y difícil buscar, pretender
> comprender y aceptar! (p. 94)

In «Razón,» on the other hand, the same knowledge is celebrated as feeling, or what the poet so nicely refers to as «las sienes de la alegría» (p. 128). The somber admission, near the beginning of the poem, that the poet now understands many things «desesperadamente vivas» deepens into feeling, «un sentir que algo se aniquila» (p. 129), a feeling so painfully intense that it promotes a joyous reawakening of consciousness, that is, *sentir* becomes *saber:*

> Y así, ¡qué bello, qué grandioso
> andar entre las propias ruinas,
> saber que hay algo que no ha muerto! (p. 129)

The struggle between free impulse and implacable reflection would have a perfect solution in art, if the two sides of the poet's nature could co-exist rather than endlessly replacing each other. The posibility is explored wistfully in the poem «Si soñaras siempre, si amaras.» The *tú* of the poem, the poet's subverbal, dreaming self, the side of him that escapes from time by not remembering, is referred to in the opening lines: «Si soñaras siempre, si amaras / olvidándote, abandonándote» (p. 129). The yo, fashioner of poems, discoverer of «los nombres justos,» proclaims his dependence on his «fresca raíz» whose «hondo canto inexplicable» provides the essential music for his words. Or, at least, he wishes this were the case, for the entire poem is stated in an unpromising conditional tensa which suggests that his «prodigiosa primavera,» his «corazón caliente,» will not likely survive the withering «claridades» of an ever vigilant intelligence:

> Pensaría por ti las cosas
> dejando que me las soñases.
> Con mi velar y tu soñar
> el camino sería fácil (p. 129).

Memory is the constant bar to happiness in Hierro's third book, *Con las piedras, con el viento,* memory the enemy of dream, the companion of thought, the source of destructive questions. It is as if we spent our whole lives throwing rocks at the sky and then waiting for them to rain back down on us (p. 181). The theme is particularly crucial in poems which refer to a lost love, but essentially it is an extension of the confrontation between feeling and thinking. In an early poem, «Los caminos no van,» the harmonious beauty of the visible world so enchants the poet that he loses all sense of time, feels himself to be the «centro vivo» of a benign world (p. 168). It is not long, however, before he is once again beset by thought: «No lo comprenderé nunca» (p. 173), «Necesito saber si se olvida» (p. 173), «Vamos / ciegos. Vivimos sin saber» (p. 181), «Cómo podría olvidarlo» (p. 182). Once again, the indicated solution is a desperate swing away from mental uneasiness toward unconsciousness: «Es mejor no pensar» (p. 189), «Qué apacible dejarse ir / sentir la vida sosegada» (p. 213), «No lucha, no pregunta: mira» (p. 220), «ni la duda, / ni el recuerdo, ni la nostalgia» (p. 221).

Toward the very end of *Con las piedras,* a new kind of perception begins to form which has important consequences in later poetry. In the poem «Reflexiones amargas, no,» after the poet has managed to empty himself of memory, aided by the apparent timelessness of the landscape he is contemplating, he is suddenly swept by the sensation of remembering what he is seeing, without at the same time experiencing any sense of ever having been present in what is recollected. In other words, his heart experiences «recuerdos / que nunca fueron suyos» (p. 222). If what was being remembered were the contents of his own life, there would be only ashes. Reflective activity, implacable enemy of illusion and feeling, has somehow been reduced to sensation and freed from dependence on time. The poem appears to be a turning point, a suddenly discovered solution to all previous dilemmas, as announced in the opening line, «reflexiones amargas, no,» and summed up with startling finality at the end: «me siento alegre. Sé de fijo / que ya se ha acabado la lucha» (p. 222).

Certainly this poem strikes one as a forerunner of the visionary poems *(alucinaciones)* found in later books, especially of the «Teoría y alucinación de Dublín,» where such interesting observations are made on a similar but widened state of mental transport: «Imaginar y recordar... / Hay un momento que no es mío, / no sé si en el pasado, en el futuro» (p. 396). «Reflexiones amargas, no» is not, however, the final poem of *Con las piedras*. The soul's triumphant rise out of self acquires melancholy dimensions in the closing poem, «Mañana.» Is, as the poet now states, it is necessary to withdraw from oneself in order to recapture what endures, what is truly «inolvidable,» then what has been the purpose of one's life in time, and how is present sorrow assuaged by visions of what we never experienced? It is like feeling an acidic twinge without ever having bitten into the apple. It is as if everything occurred behind our backs and our only triumph were the ability to evoke what we were never before aware of:

> Como si todo sucediese,
> misterioso, a nuestras espaldas.
> Cual si evocar fuera tan sólo
> nuestra única avidez lograda (p. 225).

What the poet evokes in this poem is something much more concrete than a primordial morning in the garden of youth. It is the start of a new era in his life, the years spent away from Santander in the «doradas tierras» of Castille, a crucial new beginning quite reminiscent of Machado's second birth «en tierras de Castilla.» Only now, says Hierro, does his time spent there take on its real meaning. When he first arrived, the trenches of war were still uncovered, Castille seemed hostile, «España / no latía su corazón / para el mío» (p. 224). And now, as he looks back, that war-scarred world is gone, replaced in memory by a Machadian landscape of plains, mountains and «álamos» shimmering with the first green of spring. But it is a «mañana / que nunca tuve» (p. 225), evoked «en sueños,» not really in memory.

In what appears to be a stanza on the transformation of ego by love, a mysterious «alguien» suddenly appears, a shadowy figure untouched by time. The figure turns into a kind of spiritual alter ego who dogs the poet's footsteps at first, but soon becomes undistinguishable from him. Finally, awareness of self («pasado propio») is replaced by a sense of otherness. The poet has escaped the painful consciousness of self locked in time, but he has also disturbed his sense of identity: «Pero borra el pasado propio / el ajeno —nuestro— que se alza. / Oh, inolvidable. No recuerdo / qué vi. Se borra todo» (p. 226).

The spiritual background out of which Hierro's famous fourth book, *Quinta del 42,* emerges can be summarized as follows. An intense need to recapture primordial feelings of vital joy is constantly undermined by the melancholy thought that we are creatures of time exiled from time.

There is a strong sense of self divided—of a youthful, emotional side, capable of dream, illusion, self abandonment, at war with a rational, questioning side, beset by memory, bent on destroying illusion and raising self-consciousness. Toward the end of *Con las piedras,* a way is found to function reflectively without having recourse to memory. The emotional transport of recall is preserved, while destructive temporal contents are emptied out. While the sensation of a remembered otherness is satisfying both emotionally and intellectually—emotionally because of the leap over time, intellectually because a recall mechanism is functioning—there still remains the disturbing question of lost self.

The ground work has been laid now for Hierro's highly original «alucinaciones» which seem to rise out of the poetic cauldron into which he so intensely stirs his inner life. The term, as I use it, refers to a small number of poem in which a concrete instance of spatial-temporal dislocation is accompanied by a trance-like state of greatly altered self-awareness.[2] In most of these poems, there is a disturbing confrontation between temporal self visionary self, usually at the end. In «Alucinación en Salamanca,» the poet holds too briefly a vision of himself dwelling in the harmonious serenity of Renaissance Italy. This startling memory of time and place never before experienced is replaced in a sudden devastating rush by a German bomber, vintage 1936. In «Segovia,» on the other hand, the poet's transformation of the Spanish city into a dream of time and space so detaches him from himself («todo era ajeno y extraño,» p. 259) that it is difficult to return. He portrays himself as a slightly distraught third person returning by rail to Madrid: «olvida, Dios mío, recuerda: su nombre, su edad, profesión» (p. 260). In the end, the experience is both disturbing and beneficial, because the dream of Segovia and the dreamer that dreamt it now occupy and greatly extend the emotional space assigned to the past. As a result, the poet's temporal life seems for the moment to have only a present and a future dimension: «Dejó el sueño, inviolado / ... / Y se dijo: yo soy, he de ser» (p. 260).

In «Tarde de invierno,» the loss of self is particularly troubling. It is true that the poet has escaped from the spell of a «tiempo sin mí» with its melancholy memories, but he has also been separated from the very fiber of his life in time—his own actions: «Podría recordar tanto / ... / hazañas propias / que no me pertenecían» (p. 258). What he remembers instead, the well-worked essence of his memory as Machado would put it, the mysterious cloth woven behind his back, as Hierro called it, is a painful feeling of otherness. His inner life has been captured by the alien fields of Castille: «hiriendo / mi realidad... / sueño ajeno, evidencias / ajenas...» (p. 258).

«Plaza sola» is a spiritual and artistic triumph, an exquisite distil-

---

[2] HIERRO, in his prologue to the *Poesías completas* (1944-1962), uses the term in a much broader sense, suggesting that all of his poetry can be divided between «reportajes» (direct, narrative style) and «alucinaciones» (poetry of vague emotion), pp. 16-17.

lation of perceptions and aspirations, a fulfilment of the promise of happiness held by the hallucinatory experience. The poet says that he is embracing a town square with his glances, but we are immediately made aware of a more complex, richly described interaction. He is also «kissing» the square's time-covered mouth, putting his ear to its wooden sides in order to hear the music hidden there. He is «remembering» the square, in other words, evoking its dream. The ensuing vision, clearly indicated by use of italics, issues from a state of rarest spiritual equilibrium. The dust of time is viewed as an enduring accumulation that dries the fearful flow of hours (there is not a single «lágrima de agua» in the fountain). The attributes of thought exist alongside those of emotion. The soul is at rest: «recordar, preguntar, soñar / ahora que nada importa nada» (p. 261).

After the vision, in which the scene bristles with life in a vertigo of movement, color and sound, the poet repeats the description of his initial state of mind, thus indicating that in this instance there is no disturbing return to self. However, he then adds a final couplet, an apparent extension of a long definition of «sosiego,» which ends on a surprisingly desperate sounding line: «Andar sintiendo el alma muerta, / Dios mío, ya sin esperanza» (p. 262). I would strongly suggest that the final lines do not imply a completely negative attitude, a jolting return to an awareness of time,[3] but rather a dramatic way of summing up the state of «sosiego» the poet is still in. Several poems of *Quinta del 42* speak of the temptation of spiritual death. In the «Homenaje a Palestrina,» Hierro indicates simply that «soñar es como morir: / el alma deja la carne» (p. 278). In «Una tarde cualquiera,» the poet surrenders to a sudden «desgana de vivir,» and soon finds himself experiencing a «muerte / llena de vida» (p. 237) which he describes in the most triumphant terms. The reference to lack of hope at the end of «Plaza sola» is consistent with a state of spiritual suspension and has a freer connotation than we usually ascribe to the term: «sin deseos para el futuro.» It would be as much a mistake to attribute an experiential stimulus to «sin esperanza ya» as it would be in the case of the earlier line «ahora que nada importa nada,» the line which immediately precedes the hallucination. The poem celebrates a singular triumph of spirit over time:

> vagar sin fin y sin origen
> sobre tus piedras hechizadas...
> Andar sintiendo el alma muerta,
> Dios mío, ya sin esperanza (p. 262).

University of Delaware.

---

[3] ANDREW P. DEBICKI, in his article «José Hierro a la luz de Antonio Machado», *Sin nombre,* año IX, iii (1978), 41-51, arrives at this conclusion (p. 50).

CARDINAL JUAN MARTINEZ SILICEO
IN AN ALLEGORICAL *ENTREMES* OF 1556

by

RONALD SURTZ

In the year 1556, shortly before Juan Martínez Silíceo, archbishop of Toledo, was made a cardinal, a comet appeared in the sky over the city. Silíceo's enemies interpreted the celestial phenomenon as a sign of his imminent death, but their hopes were dashed when it was the field-marshal Don Pedro de Navarra who died.[1] The prediction indicated, however, the degree of anti-Silíceo sentiments in mid-sixteenth-century Toledo. This tension between the archbishop's supporters and opponents was similarly reflected in the festivities intended to celebrate his elevation to the cardinalate, specifically in an *entremés* that was simultaneously a celebration and an unintended caricature of the new cardinal.

Before analyzing the *entremés* itself, it is necessary to give some idea of the festivities as a whole. Juan Martínez Silíceo had been archbishop of Toledo for ten years when word came that he was to be made a cardinal. Preparations must have begun almost immediately to stage the most elaborate festivities possible, and artisans labored for a month to construct an elaborate triumphal arch in front of the Cathedral. On the bases of the arch were painted Ceres holding a basket of produce («lo qual denotava la grande fertilidad y abundançia de Toledo y su tierra»)[2] and the river Tagus, «en muy bella postura echado sobre un cántaro grande vertiendo agua.» There were also representations of the Cardinal and Theological Virtues. Justice was shown wielding a sword, while Fortitude supported a large column that seemed about to fall. The coat of arms of the new cardinal appeared above them. Temperance and Prudence could also be seen, each with its appropriate symbol. Faith appeared with a chalice in her hand, trampling Mohammed beneath her feet. Hope pinned Judas beneath her feet, while her body turned toward

---

[1] See EL CONDE DE CEDILLO: «Algunas relaciones y noticias toledanas que en el siglo XVI escribía el Licenciado Sebastián de Horozco», *Boletín de la Sociedad Española de Excursiones,* 13 (1905), 182-183.

[2] All quotations regarding the festivities and the *entremés* performed during them are taken from J. LÓPEZ DE AYALA Y ALVAREZ DE TOLEDO, CONDE DE CE-DILLO: *Toledo en el siglo XVI, después del vencimiento de las comunidades* (Madrid: Imprenta de los hijos de M. G. Hernández, 1901), pp. 169-175. The Conde de Cedillo takes his *relación* from Baltasar Porreño's manuscript *Historia episcopal y real de España.* In quoting this and other sixteenth-century Spanish texts, I have added accent marks and punctuation as necessary.

a representation of the Virgin Mary holding the Child Jesus. Charity appeared surrounded by naked children who vied with one another for the grapes she held in her hand, while beneath her feet the impious Sardanapalus was depicted as being beaten by young men. The four doctors of the Church could be seen above all of this. A painting of Mount Parnassus decorated the upper level of the arch, which also contained nine choir-boys dressed as the Nine Muses. Real musicians were hidden beneath the statues of celebrated musicians of Antiquity. The coats of arms of pope Paul IV, Charles V, and Philip II crowned the very top of the arch. Borne on the shoulders of four kinghts, the archbishop was accompanied to the Cathedral by a procession formed by the local nobility, the bishop of Segovia, and the papal nuncio. As the procession neared the Cathedral, the singers and musicians on the arch began a *romance* in Silíceo's honor. All then entered the Cathedral and Mass began.

The Mass was interrupted after the Offertory, and an *entremés* was performed on a *tablado* that had been set up between the two choirs. An old shepherd entered wearing a costume that immediately identified him as representing Silíceo. From his waist hung a steel for striking sparks from a flint, which also appeared in the cardinal's coat of arms. (Born Juan Martínez Guijarro, Silíceo made the emblems on his coat of arms reflect his change of name from the vulgar Guijarro to the more high-sounding Silíceo, derived from the Latin word for flint.) In his hand the shepherd held a red shepherd's crook with a star on it upon which was written the name of Jesus.[3] The old shepherd was accompanied by a boy «que se deçia su hijo adoptivo a manera de simple, el qual se deçia el çelo de la fe, todo vestido de açul, y no deçía otra cosa sino a tiempos donde caía bien padre, papa, papa, padre.»

The shepherd began to recite a series of verses in which he verbally transformed the cathedral into a pastoral *locus amoenus:*

¡O qué hato, y qué rebaño,
qué arboledas, y qué olivas!
¡O qué prado tan estraño!
Nunca vi prado tamaño
plantado de piedras vivas.[4]

The shepherd then blessed the congregation, referring to himself as its *mayoral* and *buen pastor.* He then proceeded to give an account of the new cardinal's life, translating its principal events into their pastoral

---

[3] In 1550 SILÍCEO had published his *De divino nomine Iesus.* The monogram IHS figures prominently in Silíceo's coat of arms.

[4] The expression «piedras vivas» is disconcerting, but could be interpreted as a reference to the congregation, the Christian faithful, as in I Peter 2,5: «et ipsi tanquam lapides vivi». Or, the «piedras vivas» could refer to the flintstone surrounded by sparks or flames appearing on Silíceo's coat of arms, which figured so prominently in the iconography of the festivities.

equivalents. Silíceo began his professional career as professor of Natural Philosophy at the Colegio de San Bartolomé at Salamanca:

> En Salamanca empeçé
> a guardar unos corderos,
> y aunque pocos y terneros,
> muy bien los apaçenté
> en prados y abrevaderos.

Later, Charles V made him the tutor of the future Philip II:

> Viendo mi comienço tal,
> el Çésar nuestro Señor
> me encomendó un reçental;
> criélo con tanto amor
> que él me hiço a mí Pastor
> y él quedó por Mayoral
> en quien tuve gran favor.

and as a reward for his services named him bishop of Cartagena (1541):

> Después de havello criado,
> ya que supo de raçón,
> en pago de lo pasado
> me conçedió este eslavón
> para dar lumbre al ganado.
> Con divisa así tan buena
> me embió a los rebaños
> de Murçia y de Carthagena,
> y fui allí en tal estrena
> que los libré de mil daños.

There he distinguished himself through his efforts to bring certain «lost sheep» into the fold:

> Saqué allí los ençarçados
> y las llagas les curé.
> Y a los que andavan errados
> al repasto los torné
> de los Misterios sagrados.
>   Y a los de largos vellones
> que muy çerreros andavan,
> les di çiertos trasquilones,
> y con la sal se amansavan
> al sabor de mis raçones.
>   Recogílos a corral
> y la roña les unté.
> Con esta ventura tal
> a la Iglesia los llevé
> do fueron libres de mal.

This passage could refer to Silíceo's concern for the religious education of the *moriscos*.[5] Finally, the shepherd speaks of his becoming Archbishop of Toledo (1546):

> Y así por este tenor
> me dieron este rebaño
> con harto creçido amor,
> no porque en él havía daño,
> son porque hato tamaño
> requería tal Pastor.
> Y así yo me he recreado
> en aqueste sancto aprisco.
> Mis ovejas he guardado,
> con ellas me he reholgado,
> todas juntas abarrisco.

Actors impersonating the seven Liberal Arts and Sacred Theology thereupon entered singing a *villancico,* and «le traían al Pastor por joya una piedra pedernal, la qual le dieron encareçiéndosela mucho, y le declararon la virtud y propiedad della, la qual el Pastor tomó, y reconoçió ser qual deçían, y se salieron cantando un villançico.» The Mass then continued and afterwards the ceremony of the conferring of the cardinal's red biretta. Finally, there was a dance executed by choir-boys whose costumes were decorated with the flintstones, steel strikers, and sparks that figured in Silíceo's coat of arms.

One can observe at this point the harmony of inspiration that linked the iconography of the triumphal arch to that of the *entremés* performed in the Cathedral. Silíceo's coat of arms was depicted on the arch and also became part of the costumes of the old shepherd and the dancers. The Nine Muses who sang in Silíceo's honor from the top of the arch adorned with the Seven Virtues changed costumes to become the seven Liberal Arts who honored him in the *entremés.* To the representation of the four doctors of the Church on the arch corresponded the allegorical figure of Sacred Theology who took part in the playlet. Just as Faith, Hope, and Charity presided over the defeat of Mohammed, Judas, and Sardanapalus on the arch, so in the *entremés* Silíceo was portrayed as extirpating heresy and impiety.

---

[5] In 1542 Silíceo participated in a *junta* of theologians convoked by Charles V to consider the problem of the *moriscos.* See VENANCIO D. CARRO, OP: *El Maestro Fr. Pedro de Soto, O. P. y las controversias político-teológicas en el siglo XVI,* I (Salamanca: Convento de San Esteban, 1931), pp. 106-107. The index of MS 9393 of the Biblioteca Nacional (Madrid) lists a letter by Silíceo «sobre la instrucción católico-política que se había de dar a los moriscos de España». Unfortunately, the corresponding folios are missing from the manuscript. It was safe to refer to Silíceo's dealings with Spain's *morisco* population, for members of that minority were unlikely to seek benefices in the Cathedral of Toledo and thus posed no threat. There is no reference in the *entremés,* of course, to Silíceo's role in the establishment of the *estatuto de limpieza* in Spain's primatial see. That was simply too touchy a subject.

The entire *entremés* is, of course, meant to be a panegyric to the new cardinal, involving as it does the pastoral transposition of his life and its symbolic consecration by the Liberal Arts through the presentation of their gift. But certain facets of the entertainment are unintentionally ambiguous and could be interpreted either positively by Silíceo's friends or negatively by his enemies.

To be sure, Silíceo was not without enemies. He had been personally responsible for the adoption by the Cathedral of Toledo of an *estatuto de limpieza* (1547), which prevented persons of Moorish or Jewish ancestry from holding offices in the archbishopric of Toledo. The *estatuto* was met with praise and dismay on the part of those it affected.[6] Prince Philip was reluctant to support his former tutor in this matter and ordered the suspension of the *estatuto*. Charles V submitted the matter to his Royal Council, which voted to uphold Philip's injunction. Meanwhile, Silíceo's supporters had obtained a secret brief from pope Paul III that approved the *estatuto,* and Silíceo began to scrutinize the *limpieza* of candidates for benefices in Toledo. This practice was officially confirmed by pope Paul IV in 1555 and by Philip II in August of 1556. Thus, the elevation of Silíceo to the cardinalate in March of 1556 fell between the papal and royal ratifications of the *estatuto,* and the corresponding festivities took place in a Toledo still divided into supporters and opponents of the statute.

Meanwhile, the question of *limpieza* had brought Silíceo into conflict with the ever-expanding Jesuit order.[7] Silíceo objected to the presence of large numbers of New Christians in the new order, and when, in 1551, the Jesuits founded a school at Alcalá without first seeking Silíceo's permission, the archbishop issued a decree that forbade any member of the order to exercise his priestly functions without first submitting to an examination administered by Silíceo himself. A compromise was worked out in 1552 by which Silíceo would revoke his interdict and Jesuits of New Christian origin would be excluded from Silíceo's archdiocese, but as Albert Sicroff has noted, «on ne peut dire que l'Archevêque se soit jamais vraiment réconcilié avec la Compagnie de Jésus» (p. 275).

Silíceo's stand on the question of *limpieza de sangre* had thus won him many enemies. His position on the subject can be partially explained by reference to his own life. Sicroff, noting the extremely humble birth of the new cardinal, comments: «Il est à présumer qu'il souffrait amèrement de son origine plébéienne. La latinisation du vulgaire Guijarro en Silíceo en est le symbole» (p. 96). The implantation of the *estatuto* would thus be a kind of revenge upon those more well-born than Silíceo, but of New Christian origin. As Sicroff has noted: «La préoccupation de pureté de sang était d'origine plébéienne et elle allait prendre le carac-

---

[6] I base my overview of the implantation of the Toledo statute on ALBERT A. SICROFF: *Les controverses des statuts de «pureté de sang» en Espagne du XVe au XVIIe siècle* (Paris: Didier, 1960), pp. 102-139.

[7] SICROFF, pp. 270-275.

tère d'une révolution sociale, dans laquelle, sous prétexte de "pureté de sang", on contesterait les positions et les privilèges dont les nobles jouissaient au nom de leur noblesse» (p. 95). According to Ruiz de Vergara y Alava, when Charles V asked Silíceo for a résumé of his life, the new archbishop could not vaunt his nobility, only the purity of his blood: «La ascendencia, que pone para ilustrarse en aquella memoria, es sólo de que sus padres fueron Christianos viejos, y que su madre le parió sin comadre.» [8] Such a notion of pride in low birth is very clearly reflected in one of the strophes recited by the old shepherd in the *entremés*:

Aquesto sólo heredé
de los mis antepasados:
no blasones escusados
sino estar firme en la fe,
que son los premios doblados.

Here the cardinal-shepherd seems to be saying that although his surname betrays his lack of noble blood, he has received a far better inheritance from his ancestors—«estar firme en la fe»—which, I believe, can be interpreted as a defense of his plebeian origins based on the presumed purity of blood (and hence, purity of faith) of the peasant.

Moreover, the figure of the shepherd in the playlet is at once a consecrated religious symbol, denoting both humility and the notion of the «good shepherd», and the pastoral equivalent of the Old Christian peasant.[9] The possibility of interpreting the entertainment as a defense of the Archbishop's origins further suggests itself because one of the arguments used by the opponents of his *estatuto de limpieza* was precisely that persons of low birth would do more harm to the prestige of the Church of Toledo than the higher-born *conversos*. Diego del Castillo stated:

... mi voto es que en caso que el estado desta Sancta Yglesia cerca de las personas que adelante han de ser en ella admitidas por beneficiados se aya de mudar, limitar, o restringir de como haora se platica, diría que sólo en ella de aquí adelante se admitan cavalleros ylustres, o nobles hijosdalgo, o letrados graduados por rigor de examen conforme a las pregmáticas destos Reynos, y no otra persona alguna porque admitir otra gente baxa y popular sin tener otras qualidades que les aiuden so color de ser los tales christianos

[8] See his *Historia del Colegio Viejo de San Bartholomé,* I (Madrid: 1766), p. 282.

[9] An example of the identification of the shepherd with the Old Christian can be found in the defense («Contra algunos zizañadores de la nación de los conuertidos del pueblo de Israel») of the New Christians that Fray Lope de Barrientos wrote after the Toledo uprising of 1449. Fray Lope refers to the Bachiller Marcos García de Mora, the leader of the Old Christian faction, as a «preuaricador e público dañador, de baja sangre pastoril». See Fray Luis G. A. Getino: *Vida y obras de Fr. Lope de Barrientos* (Salamanca: Establecimiento Tipográfico de Calatrava, 1927), p. 184.

viexos es destruir la grandeza y authoridad desta Sancta Yglesia, y la orden della...[10]

On the other hand, in a dossier addressed to Charles V, Silíceo countered this view with the argument that the loyalty to the Church of the learned *conversos* was dubious and that their very erudition could cause problems. The peasant, however, would sooner suffer martyrdom than deny his faith. Moreover, was it not the uncultivated Peter who became the first pope, and not the learned Paul?[11] Thus, proponents of the Toledan statute could rejoice in seeing one of such lowly birth raised to the highest ecclesiastical dignity in Spain, while Silíceo's enemies could view the new cardinal's portrayal as a shepherd as simply the iconographic equivalent of a person of the lowest birth.

Such ambiguities of interpretation are further reflected in other aspects of the symbolism of the *entremés*. The central set of symbols is taken from Silíceo's coat of arms, whose significance he explained as follows:

> Dize que como él no recibió de sus antepasados ningunas armas o insignias de nobleza deste mundo, luego que vino a la silla Arçobispal acordó escoger las que el padre celestial dio a su hijo Iesu Christo, que son más excelentes que todas las de la tierra, conuiene a saber, el nombre de Iesus. Este puso en cifra, fixo en piedra blanca, que es el pedernal: el qual tocado con las oraciones de los Christianos que le inuocan (que son los eslauones) saca lumbre y fuego, esto es, la virtud del Espíritu santo, que es comparado a fuego... De suerte que sus armas son el santo nombre de Iesus, de que él era singularmente deuoto, con el fuego de pedernal, aludiendo a su sobrenombre Siliceo.[12]

In the *entremés* the steel strikers were worn as ornaments by the shepherd-cardinal, and the flintstone was presented to him by the Liberal Arts. As Francisco de Pisa suggests, these symbols probably originated in the archbishop's name, the *piedra pedernal* being the Castilian equivalent of the cardinal's adopted Latin surname, Siliceus. The *relación* of the festivities refers to the *piedra pedernal* as a *joya* (literally, a precious stone; figuratively, a prize), but this is an overestimation. The symbolism of the entertainment is thus ambiguous and could also be interpreted in a relatively unflattering manner. The shepherd-cardinal is indeed rewarded, but his prize is a piece of flint, which could be viewed by Silíceo's enemies as a suitably vulgar reminder of his vulgar origins.

The *entremés,* with its emphasis on the simple faith of the Old Christian, is an accurate reflection of Silíceo's own ideas. The ambiguities of the text are unintentional and arise on the level of its reception in mid-

---

[10] Quoted in SICROFF: *Controverses*, p. 103.

[11] Paraphrased by SICROFF: *Controverses*, p. 134. In the *entremés*, the boy who represents «el çelo de la fe» is described as a *simple*.

[12] FRANCISCO DE PISA: *Descripción de la imperial ciudad de Toledo* (Toledo, 1605), fol. 261r.

sixteenth-century Toledo. Although the *entremés* is intended to glorify the deeds of the new cardinal, some might view it as a defense of his low birth and a celebration of his pure blood, while others might see the vulgar *piedra pedernal* and the humble shepherd merely as symbols of the vulgarity of Silíceo's origins. In any case, the *entremés* became the polyvalent reflection of contemporary social and religious tensions into which its Toledan spectators read affirmative or negative evaluations. As such, the playlet mirrors one of the growing paradoxes of sixteenth-century Spanish society. The exclusion of the intellectual, higher-born New Christians and the promotion of the often ignorant, low-born Old Christians was a form of discrimination that ignored both noble birth and merit to focus upon the religious faith of one's ancestors. The interplay of pride and shame in humble birth so strikingly represented in the *entremés* thus reflects the paradox of a society in which being born to a family of peasants had become the ultimate qualification for holding office in the nation's primatial see.

Princeton University.

AMOR DE DON PERLIMPLIN CON BELISA EN SU JARDIN, DE FEDERICO GARCIA LORCA

NOTAS PARA LA HISTORIA DE LA OBRA: TEXTOS, EDICIONES, FRAGMENTOS INEDITOS

by

MARGARITA UCELAY

Si tenemos en cuenta que la publicación de *Amor de Don Perlimplín con Belisa en su jardín,* de Federico García Lorca, fue póstuma[1] y hecha en circunstancias poco favorables para la comunicación, justificaremos el hecho de que una obra que data apenas de hace cincuenta años, cuya génesis, en mayor o menor grado, podemos seguir con cierta detención —incluso recordar—, presente todavía múltiples variantes y su texto no esté aún fijado con exactitud. De aquí el proyecto de edición crítica en que trabajo estos días y el esquema de la historia de la obra que trazaré a continuación lo más someramente posible.

Quiero, en primer lugar, agradecer a Isabel García Lorca el conocimiento de los inéditos que con toda paciencia y generosidad me permitió recoger del archivo familiar y fotocopiar. No considero necesario a estas alturas tratar de justificar la publicación de inéditos, ya sean primeros bocetos o meros fragmentos, como el que incluimos, dejados como tal por la voluntad de su autor. Federico García Lorca es ya un clásico y el *Perlimplín* una de las joyas de nuestra literatura dramática. De extraordinario interés es para el estudioso el poder seguir en todo lo posible la génesis de su creación.

Comenzaremos con una breve cronología de las noticias y vicisitudes por las que pasó esta obra hasta la fecha de su estreno:

1924, otoño: la primera mención aparece en carta a Melchor Fernández Almagro: «Y hago ahora una obra de teatro grotesca:

"Amor de Don Perlimplín
con Belisa en su jardín".

Son las aleluyas que te expliqué en Savoia, ¿recuerdas? Disfruto como un idiota»[2].

1926, Granada: en carta a Melchor Fernández Almagro incluye «este trozo de mi *aleluya erótica Amor de Don Perlimplín con Belisa en su jardín*»[3].

---

[1] *Amor de Don Perlimplín con Belisa en su jardín* (Buenos Aires: Losada, 1938).
[2] FEDERICO GARCÍA LORCA: *Obras completas* (Madrid: Aguilar, 1974), 19.ª edición, vol. II, p. 1078. Todas las referencias sucesivas serán a esta edición.
[3] *Obras completas,* vol. II, pp. 1095-1098.

1928, Entrevista con Ernesto Giménez Caballero. Declara que *Amor de Don Perlimplín con Belisa en su jardín* está «en preparación» [4].

1928, ¿diciembre?: En esta fecha debió entregar el manuscrito a Cipriano Rivas Cherif para que fuese estrenado por El Caracol, grupo dramático del que éste era director. El Caracol se había inaugurado a fines de noviembre de 1928. Las tres copias que se hicieron mecanografiadas profesionalmente, encuadernadas en cartulina amarilla y selladas en cada página «Sala Rex, Mayor 8» —domicilio de El Caracol—, deben datar de estos días.

1929, 6 de febrero: la censura gubernativa se incauta de las tres copias de El Caracol, que quedan depositadas en la Dirección General de Seguridad. La fecha 6/2/29 puede leerse estampada en lápiz rojo en la copia que se conserva.

1929, julio: Estados Unidos. Angel del Río nos dice que Lorca está «retocando» el *Perlimplín* [5].

1929, agosto-septiembre: Estados Unidos. Angel del Río menciona que Lorca le ha leído el *Perlimplín* ya terminado [6].

1929, 24 de diciembre: Nueva York. Lorca lee el *Perlimplín* en casa de los Brickell y lo entrega a Mildred Adams para que lo traduzca [7].

1931, Madrid: Mildred Adams, a petición de Federico, le devuelve el *Perlimplín*. Lo necesita, dice éste, porque la obra va a ser estrenada [8].

1932, otoño: Lorca promete a Pura Ucelay dirigir *La zapatera prodigiosa* para su grupo teatral del Club de Cultura Femenina, a condición de que consiga rescatar de la censura lo que él llama «su única copia» del *Perlimplín,* obra que declara ser complemento de *La zapatera.*

1933, ¿febrero?: Pura Ucelay consigue una de las tres copias del *Perlimplín* hechas por El Caracol, que la censura había retenido desde febrero de 1929. El subtítulo «Aleluya erótica» justificaba su claficación entre «obras pornográficas». Las otras dos copias —Pura Ucelay da testimonio de su existencia— quedaron en la Dirección General de Seguridad y suponemos desaparecieron en el incendio que consumió el edificio, situado en la calle de la Reina, durante la Guerra Civil.

1933, 5 de abril: Estreno de *Amor de Don Perlimplín con Belisa en su jardín,* bajo la dirección de Federico García Lorca, por el grupo

---

[4] Idem, p. 889.
[5] Introducción a Federico García Lorca, *Poet in New York,* traducción de Ben Bellit (New York: Grove Press, 1940), pp. XV-XVI.
[6] Ibid.
[7] MILDRED ADAMS: *Federico García Lorca* (New York: Braziller, 1977), p. 146.
[8] Ibid.

teatral del Club de Cultura Femenina, que rebautizado por Lorca
pasa a llamarse «Anfistora».

Textos y ediciones

A juzgar por los datos más arriba apuntados, es indudable que Lorca
volvió a escribir el *Perlimplín* durante su estancia en América, en el verano do 1929. Esta segunda versión de la obra, que llamaríamos «el
Pelimplín americano», continúa, que sepamos, dasaparecida, aunque sus
huellas pueden seguirse en las correcciones y añadidos de mano del propio
Federico hechas sobre la copia de El Caracol rescatada por Pura Ucelay
de la censura y utilizada para los ensayos de la obra por Anfistora
en 1933.

Existe, además, la traducción que Mildred Adams hizo de la versión
americana que conserva la Hispanic Society of America en Nueva York,
muy interesante precisamente porque el escaso conocimiento del español
de la autora la lleva a traducir literalmente. Quizá se originan también
en «el *Perlimplín* americano» las extrañas variantes que se registran en
la traducción inglesa de James Graham-Lujan y Richard L. O'Connell [9].

Pura Ucelay conservó la copia mecanografiada en 1928 por El Caracol y corregida en 1933 por Lorca, a la que me referiré como «texto A»,
pero hizo además ella misma otra copia a máquina incluyendo los cambios
requeridos por la puesta en escena, a la que llamaré «texto B». Estos
dos son los textos de Anfistora que conservo y en los cuales se puede
trazar la diferencia entre la obra de Lorca poeta y dramaturgo del
texto A y Lorca director de escena del texto B, que impone al primero
sus correcciones y cambia, añade o corta sin piedad, según las exigencias
del montaje. A estos dos textos pueden trazarse las ediciones posteriores [10].

La primera edición, dirigida por Guillermo de Torre (Buenos Aires:
Losada, 1938), sigue la copia B mecanografiada por Pura Ucelay con todos
sus errores, atribuibles no sólo a una copista no profesional, sino a una
máquina de escribir defectuosa.

La fecha de 1931 que Margarita Xirgu pone al frente del texto entregado por ella a Guillermo de Torre y que se reproduce en esta edición,
carece de sentido. Es posible que la urgencia con que Federico requirió
de Milderd Adams en 1931 la copia americana obedeciese a la posibilidad
de que la obra fuese estrenada por la Xirgu, pero el texto que aparece
en Losada, en 1938, sigue punto por punto la copia B de Anfistora, incluyendo la tachadura de la censura, que había dejado totalmente ilegible
la línea referente a los cuernos dorados del protagonista y que Federico,
como es natural, no hubiese conservado al reescribir la obra en América.

---

[9] Federico García Lorca: *Five Plays* (New York: Scribner, 1941).
[10] La familia García Lorca conserva otra copia mecanografiada que no he tenido
todavía oportunidad de cotejar detenidamente. A primera vista he creído que se
trataba de copia del texto A, pero no puedo asegurarlo con certeza por el momento.

Arturo del Hoyo, a cargo de la edición de *Obras completas,* de Aguilar[11], mantiene que su texto tiene por base el de la edición Losada, corregido «con arreglo al manuscrito autógrafo que custodia la familia». Cuando al cabo de muchos años he sabido que no existe manuscrito autógrafo del *Perlimplín,* he llegado a la conclusión de que del Hoyo se está refiriendo al manuscrito A de Anfistora, que presenta correcciones hechas en tinta por Federico y que Pura Ucelay facilitó a la familia García Lorca en el momento en que se estaba preparando la edición de Aguilar. En otras palabras, del Hoyo corrige el texto B de Anfistora a base del texto A.

Por lo que respecta a las dos ediciones hechas en Nueva York por Ernesto G. Da Cal y por mí misma[12], también desgraciadamente se prestan a confusión, ya que, igual que la de del Hoyo, se basan en la edición Losada con correcciones del texto A. Y lo que es aún peor, en la primera de estas dos ediciones, la de 1955 (que estuvo a cargo de la editorial Dryden Press, asimilada más tarde por Holt), tuvimos que sujetarnos a la censura de los editores, censura americana de signo económico, no político, ya que en los años cincuenta se temía que el *Perlimplín* fuese obra demasiado atrevida, que escandalizase a los maestros o, lo que podía ser peor, a los familiares de los estudiantes.

Todas las ediciones posteriores[13] siguen a Losada o a Aguilar en distintas proporciones. El resultado ha sido una serie de textos híbridos que hacen necesaria la edición crítica que fije el texto definitivo.

No es mi intención culpar a nadie (tendría que culparme a mí misma por los errores de mi propia edición). La causa de que durante muchos años no le diese la importancia debida al texto A de Anfistora, que heredé de Pura Ucelay, fue la afirmación de del Hoyo de la existencia del manuscrito autógrafo en el archivo de la familia García Lorca. En cuanto a la existencia del texto B, ha sido para mí un verdadero descubrimiento: sólo muy recientemente he logrado identificarlo entre los papeles de mi madre.

BOCETOS Y FRAGMENTOS INÉDITOS

Los bocetos y fragmentos inéditos del *Perlimplín* que se conservan en el archivo familiar de los García Lorca son de un enorme interés para seguir el proceso de gestación de la obra. Son cinco, que yo ordeno aquí en lo que creo ser su secuencia cronológica.

Fragmento A: dos cuartillas dobladas por la mitad, escritas por las cuatro caras, en lápiz, sin numeración, sin título. El encabezamiento dice «Casa de Don Perlimplín». Considero éste el primer boceto. Se trata de

[11] *Obras completas,* vol. II, p. 1415.
[12] ERNESTO G. DA CAL y MARGARITA UCELAY: *Literatura del siglo XX* (New York: Holt Rinehart and Winston, 1955 y 1968).
[13] RICARDO DOMENECH (Madrid: Editorial Magisterio Español, 1975); EUGENIO F. GRANELL (Madrid: Taurus, 1976); MIGUEL GARCÍA POSADA (Madrid: Akal, 1980).

un diálogo rimado entre Don Perlimplín y la Criada, que no tiene nombre aún. Interviene la Voz de la Muerte que anuncia el fallecimiento de la madre del protagonista y su recomendación en el testamento de que Don Perlimplín se case. Se interrumpe bruscamente la escena en la discusión del matrimonio entre amo y criada. El carácter entre infantil y grotesco de la aleluya queda muy acentuado.

Fragmento B: cuatro hojas arrancadas de un cuaderno, escritas por un solo lado, en lápiz. Llevan por título *Teatro de aleluyas* y contienen una interesantísima y lúcida teorización de lo que el poeta intenta que sea este teatro. En la segunda página incluye el título de la obra que proyecta: «Historia de [Don] Perlimplín y Belisa en su jardín.» Vemos que titubea en el «Don» de Perlimplín, que ha sido puesto y borrado, pero que después de todo le viene dado al personaje por la aleluya tradicional. Se llama «Historia», pero el dístico de la aleluya está ya presente, al igual que el nombre de Belisa y el jardín de Perlimplín.

Fragmento C: seis cuartillas en tinta, numeradas y escritas por una sola cara. Desarrolla la misma escena del fragmento A: diálogo entre Don Perlimplín y la Criada, que interrumpe la Voz de la Muerte. La escena se corta abruptamente en el mismo punto que en el primer fragmento, es decir, en medio de la discusión entre amo y criada sobre el matrimonio que la madre de éste ha aconsejado antes de morir. Se alterna el diálogo entrecortado, en prosa, con el verso de aleluya o cantinela infantil.

Ambos fragmentos, A y C, son bocetos del «Prólogo» que da comienzo a la obra, pero este segundo —el C— está mucho más trabajado: Perlimplín lleva su «Don», la criada tiene ya su nombre de Marcolfa y la obra ha adquirido su título definitivo:

«Amor de Don Perlimplín
con Belisa en su jardín»

Podría ser éste el punto —otoño de 1924— en que comunica a Melchor Fernández Almagro que trabaja en una «obra de teatro grotesco» y después de dar el título añade: «son las aleluyas que te expliqué [...]. Disfruto como un idiota» escribiendo. Y, en efecto, podemos comprender esta afirmación porque la escena es verdaderamente graciosa, con una serie de entradas y salidas rápidas y paralelas de los dos personajes, que nos recuerdan los teatros de juguete, donde el movimiento, puramente lineal, queda impuesto por las tiras de papel con que se dirigen los actores desde los lados del escenario. El tono marcadamente festivo, realmente grotesco de este fragmento está lejos de la lírica musicalidad de ópera italiana del «Prólogo» de la redacción definitiva, y, sin embargo, presentimos que se trata de algo «tremendamente serio», como nos anunció en su definición de «El teatro de aleluyas» del fragmento B, donde nos da a entender que su eco infantil es engañoso, porque son historias contadas por niños, pero «niños de hace siglos». De aquí que el simple dístico de aleluya del título encierre en sí todo un significado complejo.

La palabra *Amor* encabeza desde este momento la obra, aunque tácitamente podríamos haberla ya intuido en la palabra *jardín* del fragmento anterior, ese «jardín del amor» de la canción infantil que más de una vez reconocemos en los primeros poemas, escenario ritual del sacrificio amor-muerte en que desemboca la obra. El fragmento se interrumpe abruptamente con una última línea de Perlimplín, presagio de tragedia: «Pero, ¿y la mujer?».

Fragmento D: son tres cuartillas en tinta, escritas por una sola cara. Se trata de material mucho más trabajado. Podrían corresponder a la escena que envía en 1926 a Melchor Fernández Almagro y que identifica como *Escena Segunda, Cuadro Tercero* y, aunque con variantes, corresponde a la misma escena de la redacción final. En dicha carta se incluye por primera vez el subtítulo: «Aleluya erótica», que subraya el carácter amoroso, entre infantil y sagrado, ingenuo y perverso, grotesco y lírico.

Las tres páginas de este fragmento están numeradas 2, 3 y 5. Falta, pues, la primera página. La 2 y la 3 son un boceto del Cuadro Segundo, Escena Primera, en que Perlimplín rechaza las noticias que Marcolfa le da de la conducta de Belisa. Marcolfa se marcha llorando y sigue un curioso monólogo de Perlimplín, que queda suprimido en los textos que conocemos. Falta la página que llevaría el número 4. La página 5, en que entra Belisa de su paseo, corresponde, con variantes, a la Escena Segunda del Cuadro Segundo de la obra.

Fragmento F: lo forman dos cuartillas en tinta escritas por una sola cara. Es el que incluimos a continuación y consiste, como podemos ver, en una escena que corresponde a la noche de bodas del Cuadro Primero. A mi parecer, estas dos cuartillas podrían pertenecer al mismo manuscrito que el fagmento D y que la Escena Segunda, Cuadro Tercero, que envía Lorca a Fernández Almagro en 1926. Podemos, pues, pensar para esta fecha en un manuscrito muy completo.

Este fragmento F no es exactamente un boceto que el poeta estilizará más o menos en su redacción final, sino una escena completa muy elaborada, relativamente con pocas correcciones, que se omite, al modo de dos hojas que se sacan del texto, en un proceso de depuración: Los siete u ocho personajes (cuatro mujeres, tres mozos, una bailarina) desaparecen, reanudándose así el carácter de dúo que se mantiene a través de todos los bocetos de la obra. La vivacidad estrepitosa del baile, acompañado de la canción, con las guitarras y castañuelas, se aminora en el alejamiento y se reduce a una «música suave de guitarras», que subraya el erotismo de Belisa, o a unas «flautas» lejanas que anuncian la aparición y desaparición de los dos duendes. Estos dos quedan como los únicos encargados de reflejar el comentario social de la noche de bodas, sustituyendo con su delicadeza y melancolía las bromas gruesas e insinuaciones de los mozos y mujeres del pueblo.

En otras palabras, la omisión de este fragmento supone la supresión —a mi modo de ver, muy acertada— del elemento popular tan presente en *La zapatera* o en los *Títeres de cachiporra* e incluso en *La comedianta*. El mismo poema (inédito hasta ahora) con que termina la escena, tiene

—no obstante su belleza— un marcado aire marinero un tanto extraño a la ocasión. Estamos, pues, ante un ejercicio de decantación, de limpieza, que denota una clara visión de propósito en el artista, que sabe dominar su natural exuberancia. Al mismo tiempo, vemos volver, como un eco, líneas, nombres, ideas ya presentes en sus intentos de juventud o, como en este caso, en los primeros borradores que se conservan. Valga de ejemplo el nombre de «Perlimplina» que, en el primer fragmento, el que llamamos A, es el nombre que se da a la madre del protagonista; o esa graciosa invocación a Cádiz, que reaparecerá en otro sitio más apropiado —el *Canto nocturno a los marineros andaluces*—:

> Cádiz, que te cubre el mar,
> no avances por ese sitio [14].

Barnard College.

---

[14] *Obras completas*, vol. II, p. 1394.

c) 1

~~Cuadro 2º~~

~~Sala principal de la casa de Don Perlimplín~~

Moro.
Cuando salgas al belun
No te llamarás Belisa
Tu marido te habrá puesto
El nombre de Perlimplina.

~~Erat~~ Moro 2º
~~Niña~~
El Mora se estará quitando
Las diambres de sedalina

Moro 1º
y le arrastrará el caballo
~~Drojeto~~
~~pei...~~ sin peinas y sin horquillas

~~Suenen las guitarras~~. Sale la luna.

No 1
No 2
Mo 2º
Arboló de las ramas verdes
arboló de las blancas niñas
los mercaderes de naranjas
Vienen cantando de la China

Mujer 1º   Se dice---
M   2º   (poniéndola la mano en la boca) Pero silencio (¡eh!)
murmullo   se nos dice---

[La]

[Cuadro 2.º]

[Sala principal de la casa de Don Perlimplin.]

Mozo.   Cuando salgas al balcon

No te llamarás Belisa

Tu marido te habra puesto

El nombre de Perlimplina.

[le]
Mozo 2.º   Ahora se estará quitando

[Niña]   las chambras de sedalina

Mozo 1.º   y le arrastrará el cabello

[sujeto] [pendi] sin peinas y sin horquillas

[Suenan las guitarras. Sale la luna.]

Mozo 1.º   arbolé de las ramas verdes

Mozo 2.º   arbolé de las [blancas] blanca niña[s]

Mozo 3.º   Los mercaderes de naranjas

Vienen cantando de la China

Mujer 1.ª Se dice – – –

Mujer 2.ª (queriendole tapar la boca) Pero silencio (rien)

Mujer 1.ª Se nos dice...

241

C) 2

Mujer 4ª (interviniendo)   — ——— Que Belisa...

~~A mujer 2ª~~   ~~No es extraña~~

Moro 1º   ~~A qué~~
        He visto un cierre mucho.

Mujer 1ª viene A y niñas...

Mujer 2ª   Aquel fábulan
        Su cara encendida. (ríen)
        ~~Z cara~~ Ca (un)
        Compro una copian de
        con las colchas amarillas

Mujer 3ª

Mujer 3ª   ¿de que le sirvió?   ¿Se dijo?

Mujer 4ª

Mujer 1ª

~~A to 6ª~~   ~~Todo lo sabe~~

Mo 1º   ¡Viva el baile de Sevilla!
        (empiezan unas guitarras
        y castañuelas)

— Bailalina —   Los peces miran   La barca
        Lívele van los marineros
        Allá la luna empañada
        y la barca mira al viento

        ¡Cádiz que te cubre el mar
        ¡No te vayas   tan adentro!

        Vestidos de plata y oro
        pasean los marineros
        los peces suben las alas
        y las bajan para verlos.

Mujer 4.ª   (interviniendo) ... Que Belisa...

[Mujer 2.ª No me extraña]

Mozo 1.º   [Ayer]

           Hoy he visto un ciervo mocho.

Mujer 1.ª   (riendo) ¡Ay niñas!...

Mujer 2.ª   Aquel balcon

Mujer 1.ª   Tiene la luz encendida. (rien)

Mujer 2.ª   Dentro está Don Perlimplin

           ¿Estará también Belisa?

Mujer 3.ª   Compró una cama de [plata] niquel

           con las colchas amarillas

Mujer 4.ª   ¿De que le sirvió?

Mujer 1.ª   ¿Se dijo?...

[Mujer 4.ª Usted lo sabe]

Mozo 2.º   ¡Viva el baile de Sevilla!

  (empiezan a sonar guitarras y castañuelas)

bailalina   Los peces miran [la mar] la barca

           donde van los marineros

           Ellos la luna empañada

           y la barca mira al viento

           —

           ¡Cadiz que te cubre el mar

           No te vayas tan adentro!

           Vestidos de plata y oro

           pasean los marineros

           Los peces suben las olas

           y las bajan para verlos.

AN ARCHPRIEST AND AN ABBESS?

by

RAYMOND S. WILLIS

The *Libro de Buen Amor (LBA)* is spangled with lexical riddles that must have first teased, then amused, the auditors who solved them. One good example is the word play in st. 337*d,* telling of a she-wolf who lived in a place that the audience listening to a recital undoubtedly would have heard as «Bilforado,» the name of a town between Nájera and Burgos on the road to Compostela, now Belorado: «Doña Loba que mora en Bilforado.» [1] An ingenious listener would have realized, however, that wolves do not live in cities, but a wolf might live in a burrow, a *forado* in Old Spanish, and it might be a poor place, *vil,* hence a *vil forado,* which sounded exactly the same as the town. [2] But this did not set an irrevocable precedent, because some 4,000 lines later, and again in the fantasy land of fable, some animals did live in Spanish towns and were identified with them: the city mouse of the familiar fable lived in Guadalajara and his country friend in Monfernando. In this amazing book, anything may turn out to be its own opposite.

Scholars have by no means solved all the verbal puzzles in *LBA.* For instance, no wholly convincing explanation has yet been offered of what impelled Juan Ruiz to choose the common noun *endrina,* signifying the bluishblack fruit of the blackthorn shrub, as the Spanish name for a personage called *Galatea* in the Latin source of the long passage on her seduction. And one wonders by what convolutions of logic could the term *buen amor* (itself controversial) become the name of both a panderess, old Trotaconventos, and the Book of the Archpriest: «Por amor de la vieja e por dezir razón / "buen amor" dixe al libro e a ella toda sazón» (933*ab*).

On top of this, the disturbing thought cannot be evaded that some riddles may still be lurking, undetected as such, under apparently candid surfaces. This is not idle conjecture, because the Archpriest himself alerts us to the possibility when he says of his text: «Do cuidares que

---

[1] Unless it is otherwise indicated, citations are from R. S. Willis, ed., *Juan Ruiz, Libro de Buen Amor* (Princeton: Princeton University Press, 1972).
[2] The reading *bilforado* (not capitalized) occurs in one of the three extant MSS of the poem, MS *S* (for Salamanca). The form *vil forado* is in MS *G* (for Gayoso). The third MS *T* (for Toledo), lacks the passage. Diplomatic transcriptions of these MSS can be consulted in M. CRIADO DE VAL and E. W. NAYLOR: *Arcipreste de Hita, Libro de Buen Amor,* 2nd ed. (Madrid: Clásicos Hispánicos, 1972).

miente, dize mayor verdad» (69a) and by inference the converse might well be true: «Where you suppose the poem is telling the truth, it is actually deceiving you.»

With this in mind, I shall scrutinize the first love affair in *LBA* to test whether two innocent-seeming words may actually be carrying— undetected as yet— a message that could scandalize prudish ears while tickling the hearing of more liberal listeners.

This superficially simple story reveals itself on inspection to be a nest of puzzles within puzzles. Even the text poses serious problems, because the MS testimony is incomplete yet suggests that, whether by accident or design, there existed at least two versions. The longer is apparently represented by MS *S,* where it occupies the stanzas numbered 77-104 in composite editions. In *T* the entire episode is missing, along with the first 25 folios. In *G* the story breaks off at 99a, after which there is a rupture in the MS. Along the way, *G* skips sts. 90-92, as it had also skipped 75, just ahead of the episode. Portions of the passage are also preserved on the two surviving folios of a Portuguese version, MS *P* (for Porto).[3] MSS *G* and *P* testify to a shorter version than that in *S,* lacking the stanzas with composite numbers 90-92 and 104.[4] The scholarly consensus, though not the unanimous view, is that these four quatrains were interpolated into the *S*-family of MSS, but the reason for this is by no means clear.[5]

In both versions, the anecdote is disconcertingly inconclusive. The motives for the actions of the two protagonists are either left unstated or receive conflicting explanations. The tale, from which essential elements are inexplicably missing, has two endings. And, finally, since the little misadventure is neither piquant nor edifying, one may well wonder why Juan Ruiz made it the start of a fictional autobiography whose express purpose was stated as «que los cuerpos alegre e a las almas preste» (13d).

To summarize the episode, the poet-protagonist was captivated at the start by a *dueña* (not otherwise identified), who granted him only the

---

[3] The text can conveniently be consulted in CRIADO DE VAL-NAYLOR. The orthography of *P* (which I have inspected) is meticulously executed, placing exactly 18 stanzas on each folio. On fol. I [my numbering] the two opening stanzas of the episode (77-78) stand last on the verso side, on which, higher up. st. 75 is skipped, as in *G.* Fol. II begins with st. 100 and ends the episode at 103, thus omitting 104, which it at the end of the *S* version. MS *G* cannot be compared here, because, as mentioned, it breaks off after 99a.

[4] Since in both *G* and *P,* folios that carried parts of the episode are missing, some conjecture cannot be avoided. Both MSS agree in skipping st. 75, just ahead of the episode. Then *G* skips 90-92 and, presumably, so did *P* on the lost sheet that once stood between the two extant folios. From the end of fol. I to the start of fol. II there is a gap of 21 numbers, but since *P* carries exactly 18 stanzas per folio, it follows that three of stanzas 79-99 of *S* must have skipped, and by analogy with *G,* presumably 90-92. Again by analogy, it can be presumed that *G* lacked 104, as *P* does.

[5] For a thorough discussion of this, see DIEGO CATALÁN: «Aunque omne non goste la pera del peral... (sobre la 'sentencia' de Juan Ruiz y la de su *buen amor*), *HR,* 38, No. 5 (1970), 56-96.

favors of pleasant conversation and merriment. She spurned a lyric (contents not revealed) that he sent her by a messenger-woman (unnamed), whom the lady castigated with a fable teaching that a wise person (presumably herself) learns from the error of someone else, as did the vixen that learned how to serve a satisfactory portion of roast ox to the king of beasts, after he had punished the wolf for stinting him. (The relevance of the fable is elusive.) Next, in S only (90-92), we are told that the suitor's *poridad* (his secret, unspecified) became publicity known and the *dueña* was parted from him (by agents not identified). This account is absent from the shorter version, and it is wholly inconsistent with the next two stanzas (93-94), common to both versions, where a separation is also mentioned, but here it is explained that ill-intentioned rumor-mongers succeeded in bringing it about by trickery, falsely alleging that her suitor was publicly impugning her virtue. (One wonders why the quatrains were retained in the *S*-version after 90-92 were interpolated.) The lady's reaction is swift, she declares that not all friends are loyal and that lovers do not give as much as they promise, here presumably vows of eternal loyalty (although there is a disturbing implication of monetary gifts.) She then illustrates the discrepancy between promise and fulfillment by telling the messenger-woman the fable of how the Earth, when in labor, terrified all people by her frighful roars of pain, only to give birth to a tiny mole. On concluding, she informs the go-between that she no longer care for her suitor. Then comes the finale of the shorter version (103). The rejected narrator-suitor says that the *dueña* became incensed over a mere trifle (not identified): «Tomó por chica cosa aborrencia e grand saña» (103*a*). And a subsequent line reads: «aquél es engañado quien cuida que engaña.» So the biter got bitten: does this signify that the suitor had been playing a cynical game all along? Or was the *dueña*'s withdrawal a practical joke on him? On whose part: hers or the rumor-mongers? We shall never know, for the shorter version ends with the next line (103*d*), where we are told that the suitor converted the affair into a melancholy song (text not in the MSS). The longer version adds that the suitor sent the lady versified apologies (for what misdeed?), and that these lyrics were rejected by her. The necessity for this addition is not evident.

We already have a sufficiency of puzzles, but one more must be added. Is there a hidden message in the story that, when perceived by an attentive auditor, rendered the bland little anecdote spicy and entertaining? In search of an answer, it may prove instructive to explore the two opening quatrains for possible double meanings, as with *Bilforado*, but perhaps more subtle.

> 77. Assí fue que un tiempo una dueña me priso;
> del su amor non fui en esse tiempo repiso;
> siempre avía d'ella buena fabla e buen riso;
> nunca ál por mí fizo, nin creo que fazer quiso.
> 78. Era dueña en todo e de dueñas señora;
> non podía ser solo con ella un ora;

mucho de omne se guardan allá do ella mora,
más mucho que non guardan los judíos el Atora.

In these lines are two words that may repay close examination:
dueña and *señora,* which has an archaic feminine doublet *señor.* In *LBA*
dueña and *señora/señor* both serve as forms of address and as common
nouns.

As salutations they may be dismissed briefly, because in that function
they are not relevant to the passage under examination. Of the two,
dueña has the more restricted role, since Juan Ruiz used it, always in the
plural, only for addressing the women in his audience: «*Dueñas,* abrid
orejas, oíd buena lición» (892*a*).[6] Obviously the minstrel-poet spoke with
more flattery than exactness, since his audiences, especially on holidays,
certainly contained more plebs than aristocratic ladies to whom the
traditional signification of *dueña* (deriving, as it does, form Latin *dominam*) would apply.

In direct address, *señora/señor* is in effect a title that can be used
at every level of the medieval hierarchy that is depicted in *LBA*. At the
top it carries the full force of its connotation of seignory in feudal
parlance, which then dwindles as we descend the social ladder until, at
the bottom, we can detect irony in its usage, on the part of the poet, if
not on that of the fictional speaker. High above all others is the Blessed
Virgin, Queen of Heaven and Earth, to whom the poet prays: «Señora,
dame tu graçia e dame consolaçión, / gáname del tu Fijo graçia e ben-
diçión, / dame graçia, Señora de todos los señores...» (9*c*-10*a*).[7] Compet-
ing for the lowest rung are found a procuress and a mare-herder: the
besotted suitor of Endrina calls Trotaconventos *madre señora* (701*b*) and,
in the Guadarrama Mountains, the philandering poet-protagonist calls a
yeguariza trefuda, metamorphosed into Alda of the lovely coloring, *serra-
na señora* (1039*a*), though here parody of the pastoral genre may be
suspected. Between the extremes, we find the Goddess of Love import-
uned by Endrina's lover as *señora doña Venus* (585*a*); Endrina herself
is addressed by her suitor as *señora* (657*a*) and by Trotaconventos as
señora fija (724*a*). The procuress also uses the salutation with an unnamed
dueña fermosa (1325*b*) and repeatedly when addressing the nun Garoça
(1344*d* et passim).

Turning now to *dueña* as a noun, there can be little doubt that a contemporary of Juan Ruiz would have taken it to mean, in the context of
its first appearance (77*a*), as a scion of an *ome de buen linaje,* as the

[6] Normally only one occurrence is cited here of words used more than once
in *LBA*.

[7] This passage is found only in *S*, whose orthography is reproduced here as in
Criado de Val-Naylor. The reading *los señores* was convincingly emended to the
archaic feminine *las señores* by M. R. Lida [de Malkiel]: «Notas para la interpretación, influencia, fuentes y texto del *Libro de buen amor*», *RFH*, 2 (1940),
137-39. J. Corominas: *Juan Ruiz, 'Libro de buen amor'* (Madrid: Gredos, 1967),
in his note to st. 10*a* accepted the emendation and extended it to change *señora*
to *señor* in the first hemistich of the verse, but he did not do so with *señora* in
the first line quoted here, nor, to my present chagrin, did I in my edition.

Siete Partidas puts it (II, 21, 2). And the listener would find subsequently, with one major exception that will be discussed below, that Juan Ruiz regularly associated *dueña* with the gentry or nobility. Right after the fiasco with Cruz, the *panadera* (112-22), the poet says: «Tomé amiga nueva, una dueña encerrada, / dueña de buen linaje e de mucha nobleza» (167*d*-168*a*). Doña Venus makes it clear that a *dueña* is not a common woman: «si quieres amar dueña o otra qualquier muger...» (430*a*). The lover says of Endrina: «busqué e fallé dueña de qual só deseoso... fija de algo en todo e de alto linaje» (580*d* and 583*a*), and she is further described as a *dueña de buen solar* (598*b*).

In the praise of little women (1606-17), which states its theme as the *dueña pequeña* (1606*c*), 4 instances of *muger* alternate with 8 of *dueña*, which clearly is used here generically to signify «woman.» This may also be true in the fable of the two sluggards (457-67) who competed for the hand of a *dueña* (457*c*). (She is addressed by the suitors as *Señora*.) Here there is no indication of her social status, which is of no consequence in the mythical ambiance of fable.

At a considerable semantic remove from the meaning of Latin *dominam*, we find *dueña* in *LBA* as a synonym for *monja*.[8] This meaning is made explicit in the description of the triumphal procession of Don Amor: «Todas dueñas de orden, las blancas e las prietas, / Cistel, pedricaderas e muchas menoretas» (1241*ab*). In alternation with *monja*, *dueña* occurs repeatedly in the Garoça episode (1338*c* et passim). This was standard usage in Old Spanish, and in evidence it will suffice to cite Berceo, whose authority in monastic matters is unimpeachable. The anchoress Oria is a *dueña reclusa* (*Vida de Santa Oria*, 41*b*). In the miracle of the pregnant abbess, the nuns are *dueñas* (*Milagros*, 505*c*, 561*b*, 563*a*, etcetera) and the abbess also (513*c*, 529*a*, 530*a*, etc.).[9]

As for *señora/señor*, when it is used as a common noun and not as a form of address, its meaning clearly has at its core, on every occurrence, the signification of one who, whether by birth, marriage, or preferment, has the privilege of exercising governance over others of inferior status. This seignory is shown to be exercised on several levels of the medieval hierarchy, but never below that of an owner of property.

Again at the pinnacle stands the Virgin Mary, identified in song (1684) as *señor* (verse *c* below) with the archaic form authenticated by the meter:

> En ti es mi esperança,
> Virgen Santa María,
> En señor de tal valía
> Es razón aver fiança.

[8] The noun *monja* occurs at intervals (441*b* et passim) and is used repeatedly in the Garoça episode (1332*b* et passim).

[9] *Vida de Santa Oria*, ed. Janer in *BAE*, 57 (n.d.), 137-44. *Milagros de nuestra señora*, ed. Brian Dutton (London: Tamesis, 1971), 159-76.

By the conventions of courtly love, the object of adoration was the liege lady and the lover her vassal who does her bidding; and so it is in st. 92*a* of the passage under examination: «Por cumplir su mandado de aquesta mi señor...» The feminine form is attested to here by rhyme with *amor, dolor,* and *trobador.*

In the Endrina story, the suitor pronounces himself the servitor of his beloved, but here the archaic form is not used, and instead we find *mi señora* (687*a*), possibly because Juan Ruiz wished to signal that this episode did not have a courtly provenance, nor tone, for that matter.[10]

On two occasions, the mistress of a household is its *señora.* The first (1376*c*) is the lady of the opulent town house to which Mur de Guadalajara brought his new friend, the country mouse. The other, in the fable of the ass and the lap-dog (1401-06), enjoys leisure to play with her pet, owns property that provides wood and grain, and commands servants who do her bidding. In neither case is there indication of noble birth, but both women enjoy wealth and position, and they clearly rule their households. Below this station, the designation *señora/señor* does not drop in *LBA.*

The findings of this survey can now be applied to sts. 77-104. It is immediately noticeable that *dueña* occurs three times in four lines, and also that the normal prose order of words is inverted in *de dueñas señora.* As for the repetition, although in various forms it was a commonplace rhetorical embellishment, this insistent iteration in a context of plain narrative could not fail to elicit attention. Furthermore in the brief interval of seven stanzas, a listener could hardly have forgotten that previously, in lines 69*c*-70*d*, the noun *punto* with the verb *puntar,* when repeated five times, produced a gamut of possible meanings so varied that modern scholars have not come to an agreement on them. The word play centers on music (the Book had just declared itself akin to all musical instruments) and there are allusions to fingering (or strumming) instruments and to playing (or singing) musical notes; but other meanings may enter in, such as intervals, coming to a halt (as with a period at the close of a sentence), and even to point-by-point analysis as done by medieval scholastic logicians.

In any event, once the repetition of *dueña* had alerted the listener to the possibility of more than one meaning (as just previously with *punto*), the dual signification, «lady» and «nun,» could hardly be overlooked. Then, with the hint of dual meanings now in the forefront of his mind, what might the auditor make of the phrase *de dueñas señora,* conspicuous for the hyperbaton? If rephrased as *señora de dueñas,* one possibility certainly was a person who exercised authority over nuns, in other words a mother superior, a prioress, or an abbess, depending on the category of the nunnery; I choose abbess arbitrarily.

Once again the testimony of Berceo is instructive. In the miracle of the pregnant abbess, when the examining bishop is shown berating the

---

[10] Neither meter nor rhyme suggest that *señora* here, or in 794*c*, may be a scribal substitution for feminine *señor.*

nuns for slandering their abbess. Berceo does not use the term *abbadesa,* although he had used it repeatedly from the very start (506*a,* 531*a,* 548*c,* etc.).[11] Instead he stressed the obligatory subserviance of nuns to their superior by using *señora:* «Duennas—disso [el obispo]—fiziestes grant traïción: / pusiestes a la señora en tan mala razón / que es muy despreciada vuestra religïón» (561*bcd*).[12] Berceo, as we all know, chose to write in the speech used by plain people conversing with their neighbors, so we can safely accept that *señora,* in association with *dueñas,* is a standard colloquial term for «abbess.» We can also find the term in a work of aristocratic pretensions, the *Libro de Apolonio,*[13] whose Spanish versifier transformed the priestesses of the temple of Diana at Ephesus into *duenyas* who wear woolen habits (579*c*) and the high priestess into both *senyora* (580*c*) and *abadessa* (581*a*).

An abbess, let it be said in passing, would not have been considered, even by the most literal-minded auditor, as being too lofty in status to be visited by the poet-suitor in *LBA,* for Juan Ruiz had announced himself just previously as an archpriest, an ecclesiastical dignity second only to that of bishop.

To continue, it is, I believe, a virtual certainty that our hypothetical auditor would have made the association of *de dueñas señora* and «abbess» only after having first, and indeed immediately, taken the phrase as a figurative statement of the lady's superiority over other women. This metaphorical interpretation has been, with one exception,[14] the consensus of editors and translators, who can be represented here by two illustrations: Corominas explicates the phrase as *señoril entre señoras, señora por excelencia;*[15] and it is anglicized as «a lady of ladies» by R. Mignani and M. A. Di Cesare.[16]

I, too, believe that the figurative meaning is the «manifest» signification of the phrase,[17] but I am suggesting that there may also be a latent meaning, as there was with *punto* and *Bilforado.*

To return to the hypothetical auditor, once he was alerted to the possibility of a conventual, as well as a wordly, meaning to the phrase *de dueñas señora* (and in the circuits of the mind, thoughts travel, with the speed of lightning), he might well have been on the qui vive for further double meanings in the verses that followed. And in the very

---

[11] Berceo also used the from *abbatissa* in 505*a.*

[12] Quoted from the Dutton edition.

[13] Ed. Manuel Alvar (Madrid: Castalia-Fundación Juan March, 1976).

[14] The exception is G. Chiarini, ed., *Libro de buen amor* (Milan-Naples: Riccardo Ricciardi, 1969) who states in a note to 78*a:* «Si notino le diverse accezioni del termine *dueña,* 'dama' nel primo caso e 'doncella' nel secondo.» Nowhere else in *LBA* does *dueña* signify «housemaid», and, furthermore, it would have been pointless for Juan Ruiz to tell a medieval audience that the adult daughter of an *ome de buen linaje* was waited upon by domestics. I do not know on what evidence Chiarini based his translation.

[15] In a note to 78*a* of his edition.

[16] *The Book of Good Love: Juan Ruiz* (Albany: State University of New York Press, 1970), p. 54.

[17] In the English translation of 78*a* in my edition, I render the expression as «the very queen of ladies».

next line he would have heard, «I never could be alone with her,» which could be true of a closely chaperoned home, but also of a locutory, which is hardly a private place. The quatrain continues, «They are very vigilant against men where she dwells,» and again this could apply to a strictly run private house or to a nunnery. And as for the fourth verse, what might be as sacrosanct for Christians as the Torah was for the Jews? Among other things, the priceless jewel of the chastity of the brides of Christ, guarded securely behind convent walls.

The next stanza (79) introduces the motifs of wealth and the lady's good breeding. The *dueña,* we are told, «sabe toda nobleza de seda e de oro,» her carriage is stately, she is beyond the temptation of glittering gold. All this would apply to any well-born heiress, but it was furthermore true in those times that the competent authorities were wont to appoint precisely such persons to important posts in religious foundations. An example is the sister of Gómez Manrique, who was vicaress of the convent for whose nuns the poet composed his *Representación del nacimiento de Nuestro Señor.*

In 80*ab* a riddle of a different sort, but perhaps associated in a subtle way with the religious meaning of *dueña,* comes to the surface: «Enbiel' [a la dueña] esta cantiga, que es deyuso puesta, / con la mi mensajera que yo tenía empuesta.» To judge from the lady's angry reaction, the words were offensive, but why did the suitor employ a courier, when he already had access to the *dueña* for conversation and merriment? Even though someone was always present, surely he could have slipped her a message at some opportune moment. But perhaps the explanation for sending a runner to the residence of the lady is not to be sought in terms of verisimilitude, for it may be that the poet (as distinct from the persona of the poet-protagonist) was already starting to lay the long verbal fuse that would lead eventually to the explosion of the actual name *Trotaconventos* in st. 738*a.* Certainly in 80*b,* both trotting and a convent might be inferred by a listener.

After st. 80, the narrative is interrupted by the fable of the lion's share of the feast (81-89). Then come the three stanzas found in *S* alone, 90-92, that were mentioned in the summary. And here we again find the possibility of a latent meaning in 90*d*: «la dueña muy guardada fue luego de mí partida.» The guardian could have been either the traditional over-age governess or a *tornera,* so once again the hearer is titillated by the fun of veiled scandal, if only in imagination.

The next five quatrains (93-97) would seem on first encounter to halt definitively the progression of dual images. In these lines, as was said in the summary, the lady is tricked into believing ill of her suitor and she chides him, through his messenger-woman, with an *enxiemplo* that begins: «Quando quiere casar omne con dueña muy onrrada...» (97*a*). The application of these words seems unmistakeable: this must surely be a fable about a layman who wishes to marry a respectable lady in civil life. But right in *LBA* there is solid evidence that these words can mean something entirely different from their «manifest» signification. Corominas points out that on at least four occasions in the poem the verb *casar* does not mean to wed, but to cohabit without benefit of clergy.[18] In 795*b* Don Melón, mistakenly believing that Endrina is still married, laments that «fasta que su marido pueble el cementerio / non casará [Endrina] conmigo, que sería adulterio.» What *casar* means here is unmistakeable. In 1508*b* the protagonist says, after the death of his beloved Garoça: «Rogué a la mi vieja [i.e. Trotaconventos] que me quisiesse casar…» and the panderess immediately propositions a Moorish girl, who recognizes her intentions as readily as we do. In 1576*c* Trotaconventos, speaking from the tomb, tells us «con buena razón muchos casé,» and all the world knows her profession. The fourth instance, in 1316*a*, might be questioned, because the unions are mentioned in association with churches and altars.

As for the «honorable lady,» if the auditor would wait till st. 1385 (perhaps another case of a long fuse), he would hear the nun Garoça say to Trotaconventos, who is trying to entice her to form a liaison with the poet:

> Más valen en convento las sardinas saladas,
> fazer a Dios servicio con las *dueñas onrradas* [my italics]
> que perder la mi alma con perdizes assadas
> e ficar escarnida como otras deserradas.

There can be no doubt here about the meaning of *dueñas onrradas,* nor that on occasion ill-advised nuns suffered the consequences of letting themselves be led astray.

Finally, near the close of the section under examination, the auditor hears that «era la dueña mucho letrada» (96*a*) and he gathers that she could read Latin, for she recites a *fabla…de Isopete sacada* (96*d*).[19] To the modern reader perhaps, there is no special implication here, but the Archpriest's contemporaries all knew that, for women, proficiency in Latin was limited to occasional daughters of wealthy nobles (or even royalty), and once again the poet supplies a trait that could apply with verisimilitude to an abbess, selected in all probability from the aristocracy.

Consequently, all through sts. 93-97 the possibility of a dual image persists, despite first appearance to the contrary. After 97 a fable again intervenes, the one about how the Earth gave birth to a tiny mole (98-100). The narrative resumes briefly (101-102) when the *dueña* applies

---

[18] Note to 891*a* in his edition of *LBA.*

[19] *Isopete* (or *Isopet*) was a widely current name for some of the medieval Latin collections of Aesop's fables. These collections, not all of them designated *Isopet,* stemmed not from Aesop but from the Roman Phaedrus. The text used by the *dueña,* which is to say Juan Ruiz himself, was in Latin verse, as was demonstrated by Félix Lecoy. He lists the important collections that circulated, all in Latin save a few in Romance language translations. FÉLIX LECOY: *Recherches sur le «Libro de buen amor» de Juan Ruiz,* with a New Prologue, Supplementary Bibliography and Index by A. D. Deyermond (Westmead, England: D. C. Heath, Ltd., 1973).

the moral to her suitor, then she parts from him, leaving no clue to her identity.

Finally comes the ending, or rather the two endings (103 and 104) described in the summary. Neither insinuates anything relative to the person of the *dueña,* who is present as the unexpressed subject of verbs. In effect, these quatrains simply seal off the episode.

The close leaves us with the discovery that in a scant 18 quatrains (the digressive fables can be discounted), there is a wholly disproportionate number of words, phrases, even entire verses, occurring over and over, whose latent meanings suggest «abbess,» while their manifest signification is clearly «lady.» This is a textual fact that is supported by lexical evidence elsewhere in the poem and from without, as well.

So the story ends with things still in suspension. Was the *dueña* a fictional secular personage, or was she possibly, and for the reader, at the same time, a *dueña* who was a *señora de dueñas*? I submit that by the very nature of *LBA* there cannot be an unequivocal answer, and furthermore that this ambiguity was by design of the poet. Ambivalence is present everywhere in *LBA,* sometimes in the form of word play, sometimes as irony, or even as broad farce. Consequently the possibility of a dual image in the first love misadventure cannot be dismissed summarily. Neither can it be substantiated objectively. And the enchantment of this situation is that it has the added spice of remaining conjectural. It is not a dilemma. It does not confront us with the choice of «lady» or «abbess,» but with the question «an archpriest and an abbess?»

Princeton University.

GEORGE BORROW: EL SORPRENDENTE EXITO
DE *LA BIBLIA EN ESPAÑA*

by

CARMEN DE ZULUETA

El 10 de diciembre de 1842, el editor londinense John Murray, de Albermarle Street, publicó un libro, *La Biblia en España,* escrito por George Borrow. El éxito instantáneo de la obra sorprendió tanto al autor como al editor. En siete meses, antes de terminar el año 1843, se habían publicado seis ediciones. Al año siguiente se había traducido al francés y al alemán y una versión abreviada había aparecido en Rusia. No se tradujo en España. Las autoridades españolas no hubieran permitido la publicación de una obra que contaba las peripecias de un agente de la Sociedad Bíblica Británica y Extranjera que había recorrido la Península tratando de distribuir Evangelios y Biblias en castellano, caló, vascuence, sin las notas exigidas por la jerarquía católica. Habría de pasar casi un siglo para que apareciera, en 1921, la traducción hecha por un intelectual ateneísta, poco conocido entonces, Manuel Azaña. El libro se reeditó durante los años del franquismo, en la misma traducción, y ha adquirido hoy una cierta fama dentro de un grupo de intelectuales de izquierda que lo consideran como uno de los relatos históricos más importantes para conocer la España de la primera mitad del siglo XIX [1]. Poco después de su publicación, *La Biblia en España* se reseñó en las revistas literarias de Inglaterra y del continente y el nombre de George Borrow se incorporó a todos los nuevos diccionarios biográficos de Europa y de América [2].

¿Quién era este autor que tan inesperadamente conseguía una fama instantánea? No era un autor nuevo que hacía una entrada espectacular en las letras mundiales; al contrario, había publicado ya, a lo largo de varios años, artículos literarios y traducciones de poesía de muchas lenguas más o menos exóticas. Un libro suyo, *The Zincali or an Account of the Gypsies in Spain,* acababa de aparecer, publicado también por Murray, en abril de 1841. Había sido reseñado favorablemente, pero, a

[1] JUAN GOYTISOLO, en su «Presentación crítica de J. M. Blanco White», en *Obra inglesa de D. José María Blanco White* (Barcelona: Seix Barral, 1972), dice: «un día habrá que examinar con detenimiento las razones en virtud de las cuales los testimonios más significativos y válidos sobre la primera mitad del pasado siglo fueron obra de un expatriado (Blanco White) y dos forasteros (Borrow y Ford)», p. 24.

[2] Ver WILLIAM IRELAND KNAPP: *Life, Writings and Correspondence of George Borrow,* 2 vols. (London: John Murray; New York: J. P. Putnam's Sons, 1899), vol. I, pp. 396-401.

pesar de ello, las ventas no fueron muy grandes. Se vendió relativamente poco y su popularidad aumentó sólo al publicarse *La Biblia en España.* Los lectores, entusiasmados con esta obra, querían leer algo más del autor y compraron *The Zincali.*

Es interesante señalar también que, a pesar de la fama adquirida por Borrow con su *Biblia en España,* su carrera literaria no se desarrolló en el *crescendo* que hubiera sido de esperar.

Establecido Borrow en Inglaterra a su vuelta de España, en 1840, escribe, después de *La Bibilia en España,* otros libros: *Lavengro, The Romany Rye (El caballero gitano), Wild Wales (El Gales salvaje), The Sleeping Bard (El bardo durmiente), Romano Lavo-Lil (El lenguaje de los gitanos de Inglaterra),* libros que no aumentaron su prestigio ya adquirido y que no tuvieron tampoco el éxito de venta anticipado.

Es posible, pues, pensar que en *La Biblia en España* se da una combinación especial de factores —el carácter del autor y sus aptitudes literarias, el tema de España y el interés por ese país en aquel momento histórico, la propaganda bíblica— que hacen que el libro se vuelva un *best seller* en la Inglaterra victoriana, en el resto de Europa y en los Estados Unidos.

Entre estos factores hay uno, la personalidad del autor, que es una constante en todas sus obras. Los demás, limitados a *La Biblia en España* y en combinación con el carácter y condiciones literarias del autor, determinan el éxito instantáneo a que me he referido. En primer lugar, se debe señalar el «factor España» por el interés que este país suscita entre los románticos europeos. Sin embargo, España no es solamente el país idealizado del *Romancero,* de toreros, gitanos y árabes que atrae a los escritores románticos; es también, para los ingleses, una realidad del mundo en que viven: es la Guerra de la Independencia *(The Peninsular War)* en un pasado cercano, y la Guerra Carlista en los años en que Borrow viaja por la península.

La labor de agente de la Sociedad Bíblica a que Borrow se dedica añade una dimensión especial a su obra. *La Biblia en España* es un libro de viajes, pero no es la mera descripción pintoresca. Hay un propósito que va más allá de la simple diversión del autor viajero y de la del lector y que es la obra misionera de aquél a través de uno de los países más papistas y más supersticiosos del mundo.

Analizaré a continuación estos diferentes factores para tratar de explicar el porqué del éxito del libro.

EL AUTOR

La imagen de George Borrow que ha llegado hasta nosotros es una combinación de los relatos de los que lo conocieron y de su figura como persnaje de sus propias obras, tal vez su mejor creación literaria. Borrow se esfuerza desde su adolescencia en presentar a sus contemporáneos una imagen de aventurero misterioso y romántico. Su infancia no fue la infancia del niño inglés de su época. Fue una infancia errante, siguiendo los destinos del padre, oficial del ejército inglés durante las guerras napoleónicas. Borrow no recibió la educación normal de un muchacho de su clase, limitada por lo general a una escuela privada en una ciudad inglesa; por el contrario, fue de una escuela a otra, en Irlanda, en Escocia, para acabar en Norwich (Norfolk), su tierra. En estos años desarrolló su interés por las lenguas, para las que tenía extraordinaria aptitud. Desarrolló también su interés por los gitanos, de los que se hizo amigo y cuya vida describe en sus obras autobiográficas *Lavengro* y *Romany Rye*. Como su familia no era rica ni aristocrática, el joven Borrow trató de destacarse entre sus compañeros de colegio aludiendo vagamente a orígenes gitanos (Romany Rye quiere decir caballero gitano), tiñéndose la cara de color oscuro y distinguiéndose como gran nadador, jinete, luchador y andarín. En diciembre de 1832, ya adulto, fue a una entrevista a la Sociedad Bíblica de Londres, a pie desde Norwich, una distancia de 112 millas que recorrió en veintisiete horas y media. El viaje le costó tan solo cinco peniques y medio, con los que compró una pinta de cerveza, media de leche, un panecillo y dos manzanas[3]. Llegó a la sede de la Sociedad muy temprano, antes de que entrara nadie, y sorprendió a uno de los secretarios por su extraña apariencia. Su constitución física no era la que se podría esperar de un literato con aspiraciones de misionero. Era muy alto, de un metro ochenta y cinco de estatura, fornido, con el pelo prematuramente blanco y las cejas muy negras. Todo ello creaba una extraña imagen que sorprendía a los que lo conocían por primera vez. El mismo confiesa que la naturaleza no lo había formado para ser «a pallid indoor student»[4]. La sorpresa del secretario de la Sociedad Bíblica aumentó cuando al preguntarle al extraño desconocido si había dormido bien, Borrow le respondió que no tenía conciencia de haberse dormido mientras caminaba de Norwich a Londres. Si se añade a estas características, poco usuales en un literato y menos aún en un misionero, el hecho de una personalidad retraída, poco comunicativa, sometida a extrañas depresiones que él llamaba *the horrors,* tendremos una imagen completa de este extravagante joven.

Uno de sus biógrafos, Martin Armstrong[5], ha tratado de explicar el carácter de Borrow por medio de un estudio psicoanalítico. Para Armstrong, Borrow es el hijo rechazado por el padre, quien favorecía al hermano mayor, John, y protegido por la madre, a la que adoró toda la vida. Esta situación familiar explicaría que Borrow rechazase siempre toda autoridad, primero en la escuela, más tarde en su vida profesional. Explicaría también un deseo de compensar un sentimiento de inferioridad ganando la popularidad entre gentes de clase inferior: campesinos españoles, gitanos, gentes humildes de todo tipo. Armstrong, basándose en la relación de Borrow con su madre, explica su matrimonio con la viuda

---

[3] Ibid., vol. I, p. 152.
[4] HERBERT JENKINS: *The Life of George Borrow* (New York: G. P. Putnam's Sons; London: John Murray, 1912), p. 60.
[5] *George Borrow* (London: Arthur Baker Ltd., 1950).

Mary Skeppers Clarke, mayor que él, con alguna fortuna personal, y lo atribuye a la necesidad de una imagen maternal y protectora.

Es cierto que Borrow no era un hombre común ni en su apariencia física ni en sus gustos y costumbres. Es cierto también que él cultivaba el halo de misterio que lo rodeaba representándose en sus obras con todas las características del héroe romántico. Imagino que Borrow quedaría sumamente satisfecho de la presentación que de él hace el teniente coronel inglés E. Napier [6]. «El desconocido» (the unknown), esbozado con la técnica pictórica de un apunte del natural, llena todos los requisitos del héroe romántico: escenario artístico —el alcázar de Sevilla; misterio—, no se sabe de dónde es ni qué edad tiene. Nadie puede informar al oficial inglés sobre el desconocido, ni decirle quién es ni por qué viaja. Para completar la escena, o más bien cuadrito romántico, aparece una bella gitanilla a pedirles limosna. «El desconocido» le habla en una lengua hindú que la muchacha entiende, pero no habla bien. Lleva al caballero, seguido del oficial inglés, a una cueva llena de gitanos. Allí el «desconocido» pronuncia una palabra y la vieja gitana, a quien se ha dirigido, se postra a sus pies. Los demás miembros de la tribu le saludan llenos de respeto. Napier nunca da el nombre del misterioso caballero, ni indica su nacionalidad. Nos dice que habla todas las lenguas. Alude a que es probablemente un espía ruso. El libro de Napier apareció en 1842, muy poco después de La Biblia en España. Es muy posible que los lectores supiesen que el «desconocido» era George Borrow.

El aura de misterio, de magia, acompaña a Borrow. En 1839 el marqués de Santa Coloma lo busca por Sevilla. Sabe en qué calle vive, pero no conoce la casa. Después de mucho preguntar por él y de describir su apariencia física, uno de los vecinos le dijo: «Oh, usted quiere decir el Brujo» [7].

En La Biblia en España, Borrow se presenta a sí mismo con los atributos con que ha impresionado o tratado de impresionar a la gente en torno. Manuel Azaña, en el prólogo a su traducción al español del libro, analiza muy bien la técnica usada por Borrow: «No emplea en esta obra las confidencias; no se confiesa con el lector; su procedimiento consiste en dejar hablar a los que le tratan para pintar el efecto que su persona y sus hechos causan en el ánimo del prójimo; asomándonos a ese espejo vemos la imagen de un Don Jorge muy aventajado: subyugaba y domaba a los animales fieros; los gitanos le adoraban; era la admiración de los manolos; temíanle los pícaros; confundía al posadero ruin y a los alcaldillos despóticos; encendía en sus admiradores devoción sin límites...» [8].

[6] Lt. Col. E. Napier: Excursions along the Shores of the Mediterranean (London: Henry Colburn, 1842), 2 vols., vol. II, pp. 81 y ss.

[7] Rev. Wentworth Webster, en The Journal of the Gypsy Society, citado por Jenkins, obra cit., p. 316.

[8] «Jorge Borrow y La Biblia en España», en Obras completas, ed. de Juan Marichal, 4 vols. (México: Oasis, 1966-68), vol. I, pp. 1073-1090.

ESPAÑA

Este autor-personaje, que tan hábilmente manipula Borrow y que se ajusta tan bien al gusto de la época, es el primer factor que atrae al lector de *La Biblia en España*. El segundo, importante también, es la tierra española por la que el héroe deambula. España, país romántico por excelencia, es un clisé aceptado por el romanticismo europeo. No hay más que recordar el interés de los primeros románticos alemanes por la literatura española, o los nombres de Víctor Hugo, Théophile Gautier y Prosper Mérimée en Francia. Borrow, sin embargo, no se deja llevar por la moda literaria ni por el estereotipo de la España convencional de pandereta. Como Azaña ha observado con mucho acierto, aunque Borrow conocía la lengua y la literatura españolas antes de su viaje a España, esta preparación no le extravía «poniéndole delante de una España fingida, libresca, falsamente poética... Lector de romances y novelas españolas, acomete la aventura de España... "tierra de antiguo renombre, tierra de maravillas y de misterios" que siempre había ocupado lugar considerable en sus ensueños infantiles. Este prestgio español no le alucina al poner la planta en nuestro suelo. Deja en paz los mitos. Va en derechura al pueblo genuino, vivo y parlante» [9]. En efecto, los personajes de *La Biblia en España,* desde los posaderos, los arrieros y los gitanos, hasta los libreros y ministros del gobierno, son seres reales, nunca son estereotipos. Sus diálogos, aun trasladados a la lengua inglesa, reflejan el habla del pueblo español. Los lectores del libro de Borrow debemos estar agradecidos a Richard Ford, el autor inglés que preparaba su famosa guía de España [10], por los consejos que le dio al autor de *La Biblia en España*. Ford había leído el original de *The Zincali,* a petición del editor Murray, y había descubierto en él indudables aciertos, junto con defectos que podrían subsanarse en obras futuras. Después de conocer personalmente a Borrow a través de John Murray y de hacerse su amigo, le escribió estas palabras en una carta:

> My advice again and again is to avoid all fine writing, all descriptions of mere scenery and trivial events. What the world wants is racy, real, genuine scenes, and the more out of the way the better. Poetry is utterly to be avoided... Stick to yourself, to what you have seen, and the people you have mixed with. The more you give us of odd Jewish people, the better...
>
> Avoid *words,* stick to *deeds...* Give us adventure, wild adventure, journals, thirty language book, sorcery, Jews, Gentiles, rambles, and the interior of Spanish prisons. The way you got in, and the way you got out [11].

[9] Ibid., p. 1084.
[10] *A Hand-Book for Travellers in Spain and Readers at Home* (Carbondale: Southern Illinois Univresity Press, 1966), 3 vols.
[11] En KNAPP, obra cit., vol. I, p. 387.

Después de leer *La Biblia en España* queda muy claro que Borrow siguió al pie de la letra el consejo de su amigo Ford, como lo confirma en una carta a John Murray, de agosto de 1841: «A queer book will be this same "Bible in Spain", containing all my queer adventures in that queer country whilst engaged in destributing the Gospel, *but neither learning, nor disquisition, fine writing, or poetry*» [12].

Ford, en carta a John Murray, después de la publicación del libro, demuestra su admiración: «Perhaps my understanding the *full force* of his "gratia" makes me over partial to this wild missionary; but I have ridden over the same tracks without tracts, seen the same people, and know that *he* is true, and I believe that he believes all that he writes to be true» [13].

Lo que para el contemporáneo Ford es verdadero se convierte, años después, para Menéndez Pelayo, en desorbitada fantasía. El libro, obra de «un cuáquero, personaje estrafalario y de pocas letras, tan sencillo, crédulo y candoroso como los que salen con la escala a recibir a los Santos Reyes», es «disparatado y graciosísimo», «capaz de producir inextinguible risa en el más hipocondríaco leyente» [14].

Vemos, sin embargo, en relatos de viajeros ingleses contemporáneos de Borrow, descripciones de una realidad española bastante cercana a la descrita por este autor. El teniente coronel E. Napier describe las actividades de los ladrones en Vélez [15]. Ford, en una de sus cartas a Henry Unwin Addington, ministro de Inglaterra en Madrid, le da consejos para un posible viaje a Andalucía: «You will fin a *coche* at Andújar, and sufficient number of *Miquelites* [sic]. They have lately taken so many robbers, executed some, banished others that the road is quite safe» [16]. Samuel Edward Cook, conocido como S. E. Widdrington, en un folleto de crítica a la política del tercer Earl of Carnarvon, describe las luchas de fanáticos en la guerra carlista: «a set of monks... sallied out with the crucifix at their head, and proclaimed Don Carlos in the streets [of Bilbao]». Y más adelante califica a los dos bandos: «a fanatic set of Atheists and Deists, and an equally fanatic set of "cristianos viejos", as they style themselves, or people who profess to have no other object in murdering or even torturing defenceless men, than the promoting of the glory of God, and the forwarding true, true religion!» [17].

Si a la inseguridad de los caminos infestados de partidas carlistas y de bandidos (muchas veces los mismos), se añaden las violentas epide-

---

[12] SAMUEL SMILES: *A Publisher and his Friends* (London: John Murray; New York: Chas. Scribner's Sons, 1891), 2 vols., vol. II, p. 485. El subrayado es mío.

[13] Ibid., p. 492.

[14] *Historia de los heterodoxos españoles* (Madrid: Librería Católica de San José, 1881), 3 vols., vol. III, p. 661.

[15] Obra cit., vol. I, p. 149.

[16] *The Letters of Richard Ford*, edited by Rowland E. Prothero (New York: E. P. Dutton, 1905).

[17] «Observations on the present state of the war in Spain; being an answer to certain parts of 'Policy of England, etc.'. With some hints for the pacification of that country. By the author of 'Sketches in Spain'.» (London: T. & W. Boone, 1838), p. 3 y p. 8.

mias de cólera que diezman la población de ciudades y aldeas, tendremos una idea aproximada de lo que significaba viajar por España en los años en que Borrow la recorrió. Sus aventuras fueron probablemente reales, y el público lector, influido por la literatura romántica entonces en boga, las leyó con extraordinario interés. La realidad española —bandidos, posadas, cárceles, gitanos— alcanzaba niveles no soñados ni por la más fantástica ficción.

España, para el lector inglés de la primera mitad del siglo XIX, es algo más que el país romántico de Europa; es también parte de su realidad cotidiana. Durante la Guerra de la Independencia, tropas británicas ocupan parte de la Península para luchar contra Napoleón, al lado del pueblo español en armas. Para ellos y para sus familiares, España deja de ser el país exótico y lejano de las leyendas románticas y se convierte en la dura realidad de sierras y llanuras, batallas y campamentos.

Finalizada la guerra, muchos súbditos británicos se radican en la Península. Andalucía, con su clima suave, atrae a oficiales del ejército inglés. Algunos compran propiedades en aquella región para huir de los húmedos y grises inviernos de su país. Tal vez no sea disparatado afirmar que la costumbre inglesa de invernar en Andalucía tiene su origen en este momento. Otros oficiales, irlandeses en su mayoría, se quedan al servicio del estado español para ayudar en la lucha contra los carlistas. Un ejemplo es el dramático caso de George Dawson Flinter, relatado por Borrow en su *Biblia en España*. Flinter, al servicio de la Reina como Capitán General de Toledo, se suicida degollándose con una navaja barbera al ser criticado por las Cortes [18].

Las cartas de Richard Ford a su amigo Addington dan testimonio de la cantidad de súbditos británicos que viven o viajan por España en los años de 1830. El propio Ford ha alquilado la casa en que vive en Sevilla de un irlandés, el general O'Neil. Ha venido a Andalucía con una carta de presentación para el general Joseph O'Lawlor, administrador del Soto de Roma, finca en la vega de Granada donada al duque de Wellington por el gobierno español, en gratitud a su ayuda durante la Guerra de la Independencia. A lo largo de sus cartas, Ford menciona al Capitán Cook, «not *the* Captain Cook», sino al capitán de la Marina inglesa que bajo el nombre de Widdrington publicó varias obras sobre España [19]. Menciona también a Mr. Watherell «encouraged by the Spanish Government to set a tannery at Seville» [20]; alude a Mr. Ste. Barbe, el inglés afrancesado, quien acompañado del marqués Astolphe de Custine «being duly dressed as *majos* by Pindar of Seville, departed for Tariffa» [21]; y al comandante Charles Downie, «the d...st bore in Jaén, Spain, or anywhere, [who] will call upon you and plague your heart out with bad English» [22].

Basten estos ejemplos concretos para demostrar que numerosos ingle-

---

[18] *The Bible in Spain* (New York: G. P. Putnam's Sons, 1923), pp. 500-502.
[19] Ver nota 17. Escribió también: *Spain and the Spaniards in 1843*.
[20] *Letters*, p. 1.
[21] Ibid., p. 43.
[22] Ibid, p. 50.

ses vivían y viajaban por España en esa época y que conocían de primera mano la turbulenta realidad española de ese período, sacudido por golpes de estado, pronunciamientos, cambios constantes de gobierno, que tiene como transfondo las guerras carlistas.

La importancia de Inglaterra en la política española se deja sentir en *La Biblia en España*. Mendizábal, presidente del Consejo de Ministros, en su entrevista con Borrow, responde irritado a la petición que éste le hace para que se le permita publicar la Biblia sin notas: «My dear sir, it is not Bibles we want, but rather guns and gunpowder to put the rebels down with, and, above all, money, that we may pay the troops» [23]. Inglaterra, en la mente de los españoles, representa la ayuda militar y económica en aquellos momentos de crisis. El ministro británico en Madrid, Sir George Villiers, es naturalmente una figura clave en las negociaciones entre España y su país, y su apoyo salvó a Borrow de numerosas persecuciones e inclusive de la cárcel.

Es la situación caótica de España, sin embargo, el mejor aliado de Borrow en sus campañas misioneras por aquel país. La falta de comunicaciones, la desorganización producida por la guerra, hacen que Borrow pueda abrir impunemente su despacho de Biblias en la calle del Príncipe en Madrid. Le permiten también circular libremente por la Península, distribuir sus libros y tratados en ciudades diferentes y hasta pegar carteles por las calles de varias poblaciones anunciando en venta de Biblias y Evangelios.

Es lógico que el público inglés, que oía hablar de España en su Parlamento, que tal vez conocía soldados u oficiales que habían luchado allá contra Napoleón, o que servían aún en el ejército de la Reina contra los carlistas, leyera con avidez las gráficas descripciones de Borrow de sus viajes por aquel país.

EL MISIONERO

Las misiones protestantes inglesas y norteamericanas son un fenómeno del siglo XIX. Aunque ya existieron algunas en el siglo XVIII, el movimiento misionero adquiere su fuerza en los años de 1800. *The American Board* se establece en 1809 [24]. *The British and Foreign Bible Society* [25], unos años antes, en 1804. Se funda con el propósito de hacer circular por el mundo entero las Sagradas Escrituras, sin notas ni comentarios, y reúne en su junta directiva una serie de denominaciones cristianas que se habían mantenido separadas hasta entonces debido a diferencias más o menos externas en sus ritos. El momento histórico en que se funda la Sociedad Bíblica no parece muy propicio: Napoleón planea la invasión de las Islas Británicas. Sin embargo, la Sociedad prospera y en pocos

[23] *Bible*, pp. 166-67.
[24] Ver FRED F. GOODSELL: *Thou shall be my Witness. An interpretation of the History of the American Board*. 1810-1960 (Boston: ABCFM, 1959?).
[25] Ver WILLIAM CANTON: *The Story of the Bible Society* (New York: E. P. Dutton, 1904).

años tiene sucursales en Europa, en el Medio Oriente y en Asia. La organización necesita agentes y prefiere aquéllos que combinan el espíritu cristiano y misionero con el conocimiento de lenguas extranjeras.

El joven Borrow nunca había pensado en la labor de misionero como una posible carrera. La literatura era lo que le atraía. En una carta a su amigo Roger Kerrison, en enero de 1824, le dice: «I intend to live in London, write plays, poetry, etc., *abuse religion* and get myself prosecuted» [26]. La carrera literaria, sin embargo, no le dio ni el éxito ni el dinero que esperaba y, más adelante, en 1830, escribe a Sir John Bowring: «As at present no doubt seems to be entertained of Prince Leopold's accepting the sovereignty of Greece, would you have any objection to write to him concerning me? I should be very happy to go to Greece in his service ...I am uneasy to find myself at four and twenty drifting on the sea of the world, and likely to continue so» [27]. Otros proyectos, comentados también en cartas a Dr. Bowring, son: solicitar un puesto en el Museo Británico; servir en el ejército francés en la próxima campaña beduina; enlistarse en el ejército belga; servir en el ejército británico: «I might be an acquisition to a corps in one of the Eastern colonies» [28].

¿Qué ocurrió para que Borrow se decidiese a correr el mundo como agente de la Sociedad Bíblica? La razón primordial fue económica. Al morir su padre, la pensión que éste recibía se interrumpió y George Borrow sintió la urgente necesidad de ganarse la vida. Una amiga y vecina suya, Mrs. Mary S. Clarke, que habría de ser su mujer al pasar los años, lo recomendó al vicario de Lowestoft, el reverendo Francis Cunningham, miembro activo de la Sociedad Bíblica. Cunningham, a su vez, lo recomendó al reverendo Andrew Brandram, secretario de dicha sociedad. En la carta de recomendación (27 de diciembre de 1832), escribe al candidato: «he is a person without University education, but who has read the Bible in thirteen languages. He is independent in circumstances, of no very defined denomination of Christians, but I think of a certain Christian principle... He is of the middle order of Society, and a very produceable person» [29]. Brandram decidió entrevistar a Borrow y, después de la entrevista con los secretarios de la Sociedad Bíblica que ya he mencionado, Borrow recibió la oferta de ir a Rusia, enviado por la Sociedad, para colaborar con un señor Lipovzoff en la edición de los Evangelios en manchú, destinados a la China. Como condición para ese trabajo, tenía que aprender la lengua manchú y presentarse a un examen de dicha lengua en un plazo de seis meses. Borrow aceptó la oferta y seis meses después pasaba el examen, al que se presentó también otro candidato, y recibía la comisión de ir a San Petersburgo en 1833, como empleado de la Sociedad Bíblica. Terminada la edición en manchú, Borrow, deseoso de prolongar su empleo, propuso distribuirla personalmente en la China,

[26] Citado por JENKINS, obra cit., p. 41. El subrayado es mío.
[27] Ibid., pp. 81-82.
[28] Ibid., p. 85.
[29] Ibid., p. 93.

viajando a ese país por tierra, a través de Rusia. El Zar le negó el permiso de viaje y Borrow volvió a Inglaterra, a su nativo Norfolk, en 1835, siempre con la esperanza de que la Sociedad Bíblica lo contratase para otro trabajo.

Al ver a Borrow convertido en misionero, sus conocidos y vecinos no pudieron menos de sorprenderse. Uno de ellos, Miss Harriet Martineau, comentó en su *Autobiografía:* «When this polyglot gentleman appeared before the public as a devout agent of the Bible Society in foreign parts, there was a burst of laughter from all who remembered the old Norwich days» [30]. Más de cien años después, la escritora inglesa Rose Macaulay escribe: «He needed a job, he enjoyed roving about foreign parts, he liked using and displaying his gift for foreign tongues, and he dearly liked to annoy Roman Catholics. Neither of the two motives which have often moved missionaries, the love of God and of humanity, came his way» [31].

En algunas de sus cartas a la Sociedad Bíblica el propio Borrow deja ver que no está hecho de madera de misionero. La reacción de los secretarios de la Sociedad es inmediata ante la aseveración de Borrow de que es muy supersticioso, o su descripción de la profetisa de la Mancha, o su mención de «su buena suerte». El reverendo Brandram, en mayo de 1839, le contesta entre otras cosas: «bear with me now in my criticisms of your second letter [2nd of May]. You narrate your perilous journey to Seville, and say in the beginning of the description: "My usual wonderful good fortune accompanying us". This is a mode of speaking to which we are not well accustomed; it savours, some of our friends would say, a little of the profane... We are odd people, it may be, in England; we are not fond of prophets or "prophetesses"» [32]. Borrow se excusa y trata, en el futuro, de expresarse de acuerdo con el *cant* de los misioneros. A lo largo de sus relatos, intercala frases que evocan inmediatamente ese tipo de lenguaje. Se podrían encontrar muchos ejemplos en *La Biblia en España.* Basten simplemente dos. El primero, al principio del libro, después de describir la terrible tempestad que casi hace naufragar el barco en que viaja: «The oldest sailors on board acknowledged that they had never witnessed so providential an escape. I said, from the bottom of my heart, Our Father, hallowed be Thy name» [33]. Y, más adelante, cuando le advierten que el carlista Gómez anda por Andalucía y que él, Borrow, puede sucumbir a sus manos: «I had, however, no fears, and the full confidence that the Lord would open the path before me to Madrid» [34].

Después de su vuelta de Rusia, Borrow consiguió que la Sociedad Bíblica lo enviase a Portugal y a España, países cuyas lenguas ya conocía. El resultado de este viaje como agente de la Sociedad fue *La Biblia en España.* El hecho de que Borrow fuese representante de tan prestigiosa organización favoreció la venta de la obra en Inglaterra y le proporcionó

30 Citado por KNAPP, obra cit., vol. I, p. 72.
31 *They Went to Portugal* (London: Jonathan Cape, 1946), p. 174.
32 JENKINS, obra cit., p. 291.
33 *Bible,* ed. cit., p. 211.
34 Ibid., p. 261.

un sector de lectores pacatos y religiosos que nunca hubieran comprado un simple libro de aventuras. En las palabras de Jenkins: «*The Bible in Spain* was the book that was to electrify the religious reading public» [35]. El que Borrow no fuera el misionero tradicional, sino más bien un aventurero romántico convertido en misionero por las circunstancias, fue un incentivo más para la popularidad del libro. Los lectores de literatura religiosa no habían leído nunca un libro tan ameno que llevara el *imprimatur* de una organización tan respetable como la Sociedad Bíblica.

En las páginas precedentes he tratado de explicar el éxito sorprendente de *La Biblia en España*. A la extravante personalidad del autor se une su talento descriptivo, mejorado en este caso por los consejos de Richard Ford. Se añaden a estos factores la importancia de España en la literatura de la época y la conexión de ese país con la política inglesa del momento. Finalmente, el elemento de propaganda bíblica, que motiva el viaje de Borrow, es un factor más que asegura el interés de un gran sector del público británico.

Pasados los años, casi a un siglo y medio de distancia, ¿cómo explicar la fascinación especial que el libro ejerce aún sobre el lector contemporáneo? La clave, para mí, está en que el libro tiene una inapreciable cualidad: es verdadero. Lo que Ford sintió al leerlo, lo sentimos los lectores de hoy: *La Biblia en España* encierra en sus páginas una imagen viva y real de una España que no es la de los libros de historia, ni tampoco la de la ltieratura romántica, pero que es más valiosa por ser menos conocida. Es la España de gitanos y de bandidos, de arrieros y de ventas, de cárceles y de alcaldes de barrio. Es la España que Borrow recorrió y de la que supo dejar viva constancia en su extraordinario libro.

Herbert H. Lehman College.

---

[35] Obra cit., p. 342.

TABULA GRATULATORIA

William and Esther Abrams
Jorge Aguilar Mora and Rosario Ferré
José Amor y Vázquez
Efraín Barradas
María Luisa Bastos
Theodore S. Beardsley Jr.
Frank Paul Bowman
Kenneth Brodney
Victor H. Brombert
Clarence F. Brown
Jack de Benedictis
Matilda Bruckner
Rodolfo Cardona
María de la Soledad Carrasco
Carmen Castro
Deborah Compte
Stephanie Davis-Lett
Demetrio Delgado de Torres
Department of Comparative Literature, Princeton University
Department of Romance Languages and Literatures, Princeton University
Rosita Díaz
Arcadio Díaz Quiñones
Alfred Foulet
Robert Fagles
Jorgina Gil-Delgado de Satrústegui
Angela Giral
Peter Goldman
Lucien and Marguerite Goldschmidt

Joaquín González Muela
Richard Greenebaum
Gordon K. Greenfield
Ricardo Gullón
George Haley
Aden Hayes
Léon-François Hoffmann
Robert B. Hollander Jr.
Paul Ilie
Peter T. Johnson
Harold G. Jones
Thomas A. Kelley
Ruth Lee Kennedy
John R. Kirk
Gwen Kirkpatrick
David and Ruth Kossoff
Denah Lida
Amalia and Josefina Lloréns
John and Jan Logan
Emilio Luengo Miró
Olympia Luengo de Pallarés
André Maman
Juan and Solita Marichal
Dorothy Marshall
Ramón Martínez López
John R. McElfresh
Gordon McNeer
Jeremy T. Medina
Ronald Méndez-Clark
Hermann and Gerda Miessner
Oscar Montero
Frederick Morgan and Paula Deitz
Monika München
Suzanne Nash
Juan Negrín
Manuel de la Nuez
Eleanor K. Paucker
Marta Peixoto
Alice M. Pollin
Willis Pratt

Richard L. Predmore
Geoffrey W. Ribbans
Francisco Rico
François and Carol Rigolot
Elias Rivers
Dalia Rodríguez Aponte
Ronald Rosbottom
David Rosonbloom
Karl-Ludwig Selig
A. Donald Sellstrom
William M. Sherzer
Gonzalo Sobejano
Julian Street Jr.
Juan Carlos Temprano
Alan S. Trueblood
Karl D. Uitti
Pierre Ullman
Joan C. Ullman
Philip Van Slyck
Nancy Palmer Wardropper
Jonathan Weiss
Peter White
Ann and Mitsuru Yasuhara
Xavier Zubiri